GW01607268

Illustrators
Mike Atkinson, Jim Dugdale, Ron Jobson, Janos Marffy,
John Marshall, Roger Payne, Mike Saunders

CLB 2266
This edition published 1989 by Colour Library Books Ltd.,
Godalming, Surrey, England.

ISBN 0 86283 734 0

Printed in Singapore.

THE ILLUSTRATED JUNIOR ENCYCLOPEDIA

Compiled by
Michael W. Dempsey and Ian James

Colour Library Books

Contents

THE CHILDREN'S FIRST
NATURE ENCYCLOPEDIA

With full table of contents, glossary and index

THE CHILDREN'S FIRST SCIENCE ENCYCLOPEDIA

With full table of contents, glossary and index

THE CHILDREN'S FIRST GEOGRAPHY ENCYCLOPEDIA

With full table of contents, glossary and index

THE CHILDREN'S FIRST NATURE ENCYCLOPEDIA

The CHILDREN'S FIRST NATURE ENCYCLOPEDIA

Contents

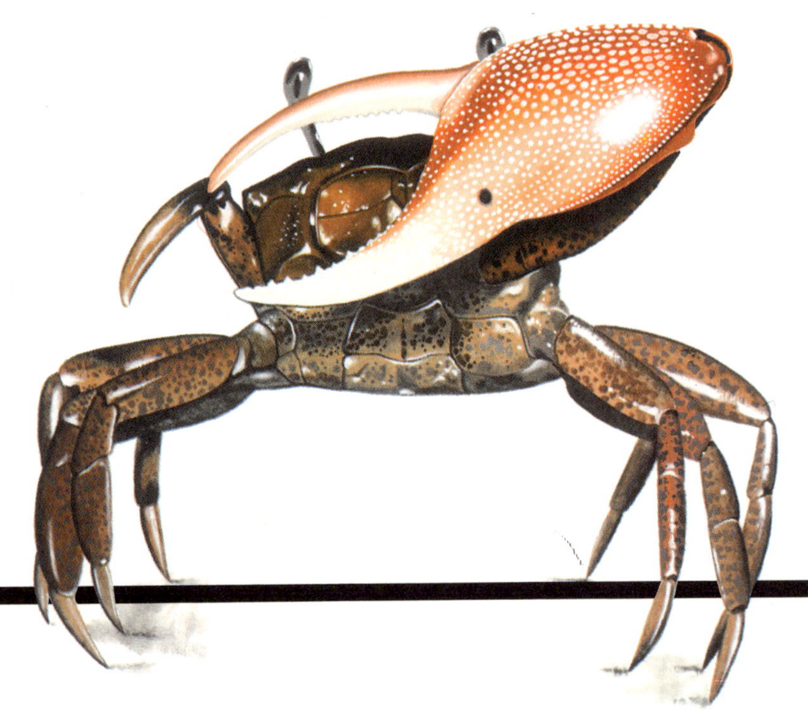

Above: Freshwater insects are eaten by small fishes such as minnows. They in turn are eaten by larger fishes such as trout, as well as by birds like the kingfisher. This is a simple food chain.

The Balance of Nature

In the wild, plants and animals depend on each other for survival. Most plants make their own food with the help of energy from the sun. Animals, on the other hand, must eat plants or other animals to obtain the energy they need. The process by which energy is passed from one creature to another is called a food chain. Thus plants use the sun's energy to produce food from simple materials. Animals called herbivores eat the plants, and they themselves are eaten by carnivorous animals. If the numbers in any part of the chain rise or fall dramatically, this affects other links in the chain. Thus if a crop fails, the herbivores starve and fewer predators will survive. This is part of the process called the balance of nature.

Food chains are not always as simple as this. The carnivore may eat many types of prey and may itself be eaten by several other types of predator. When several food chains become interconnected in this way they form a food web.

CARBON CYCLE

All living things contain carbon. As much as 18 per cent of all living material is carbon, so it is a very important chemical. Carbon is never lost but is always recycled.

All living things breathe out carbon dioxide, and plants use the gas to make food when they photosynthesize. When the plant is eaten by an animal, the carbon is taken into its body. Later on, the animal returns some of the carbon to the atmosphere when it breathes out carbon dioxide. When an animal or plant dies, the carbon in its body is again returned to the atmosphere, this time through the action of bacteria. In this way the carbon is recycled through the environment and very little is lost.

Below: When rabbits eat plants they take in carbon but, like all living things, they release it as carbon dioxide when they breathe out. Plants take carbon dioxide in again when they photosynthesize, and in this way the carbon is recycled.

Animal Populations

The numbers of animals and plants remain fairly constant from year to year. There are several factors which keep their populations in check. First the amount of food available is often limited, so the more animals there are, the less food there is to go round. If the numbers of an animal suddenly increase for some reason then the numbers of its predators soon increase as well. This gradually brings the numbers down again.

Sometimes the controls fail and numbers of a species increase unchecked. If they affect man they are called pests. In many cases man has upset the balance of nature and brought about the population explosion without realizing it.

Many insects feed on plants, but will often feed on only a few species. In the wild, the plants are generally spaced out. This spacing out helps to keep the insect population at a steady level.

But if the insect finds an area where its foodplant is abundant its numbers will soon rise. Man often grows vast areas of crops for food. As a result those insects that can eat the crop benefit and soon become pests.

Above: The Colorado beetle can become a serious pest of man's crops. It is particularly fond of potatoes and if not controlled can devastate a whole harvest.

Man often controls pests by spraying them with chemicals. But sometimes he can use natural agents as a form of biological control. Rabbits have been controlled by the introduction of a disease called myxomatosis which is transmitted by fleas. In recent years, however, many rabbits have become immune to myxomatosis.

Ichneumon wasps also make good agents of control since they lay their eggs in other insects and eventually kill them.

Right: The mongoose is skilled at catching wary prey such as the black rat. It helps keep down the numbers of rats and acts as a natural 'control' agent.

Above: Charles Darwin was born in 1809, the son of a Shrewsbury doctor. Having abandoned careers in medicine and the church, he joined HMS *Beagle* as ship's naturalist. His voyages took him all round the world and helped inspire his theories of evolution.

Evolution in Action

Above: During his visit to the Galapagos, Darwin observed remarkable variation in the finches. On the widely separated islands there were separate races. Darwin suggested that all the races had evolved from the same original stock, a species from South America, and that each had adapted to the particular conditions on each island.

Nowadays, evolution is an accepted fact, but it has not always been so. Once, people thought that life arose spontaneously from things like mud, water and air. The Biblical idea of creation was also widely accepted until scientists like Charles Darwin began to introduce new ideas.

Darwin's studies led him to believe that the present-day variety of life on earth had developed from much simpler creatures which lived long ago but had gradually died out, being replaced by more complex ones which were better suited to their environment. Only the most successful animals and plants survived and passed their characters on to their offspring. His ideas were criticized and ridiculed at the time, especially by the church, but he is now known to have been correct about many of his ideas concerning evolution.

Below: Although no-one would confuse the adult forms of man, chicken and dogfish, it would take an expert to identify their embryos. Darwin suggested that the reason for their similarities was that they are all descended from a common ancestor and, during their development, they go through all the stages of evolution. All vertebrate embryos share many similar features as they develop, looking very much alike at some stages. At an early stage all embryos have gill pouches on their heads, a feature only retained in the adult form by fishes.

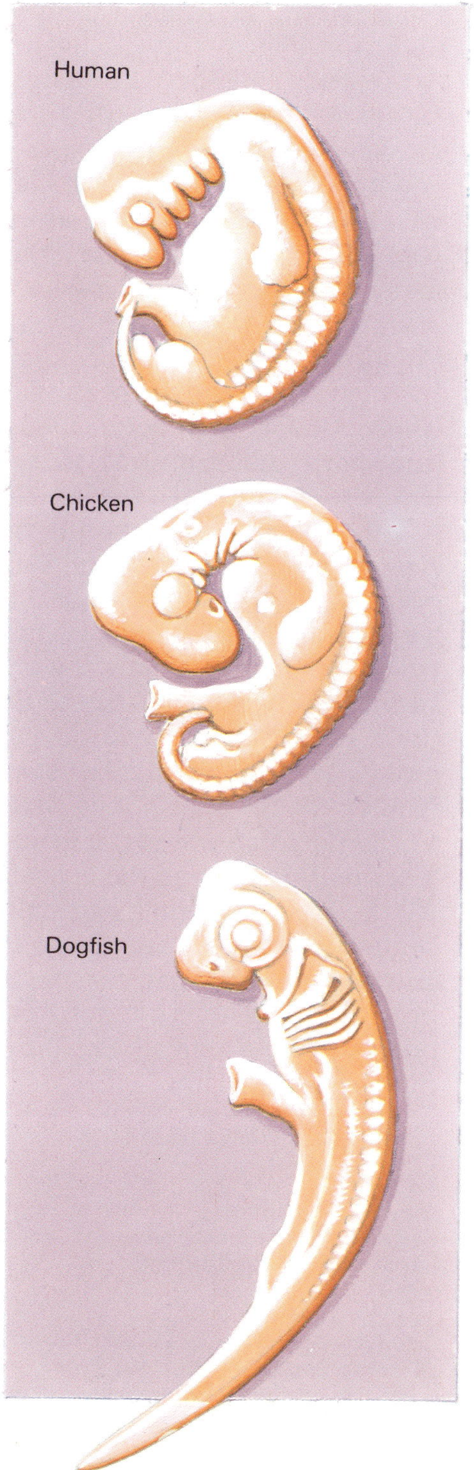

Studying Evolution

Of the countless millions of animals and plants which have lived and died on this earth before us, a small number died in places where their remains could be preserved as fossils until the present day. Some animals and plants lend themselves to fossilization because of their tough bodies. This is why there is an abundance of fossil pollen, and numerous species of shellfish. By examining changes in the fossil species and relating these to the geological time scale, we can begin to piece together the story of evolution – a process which still goes on today.

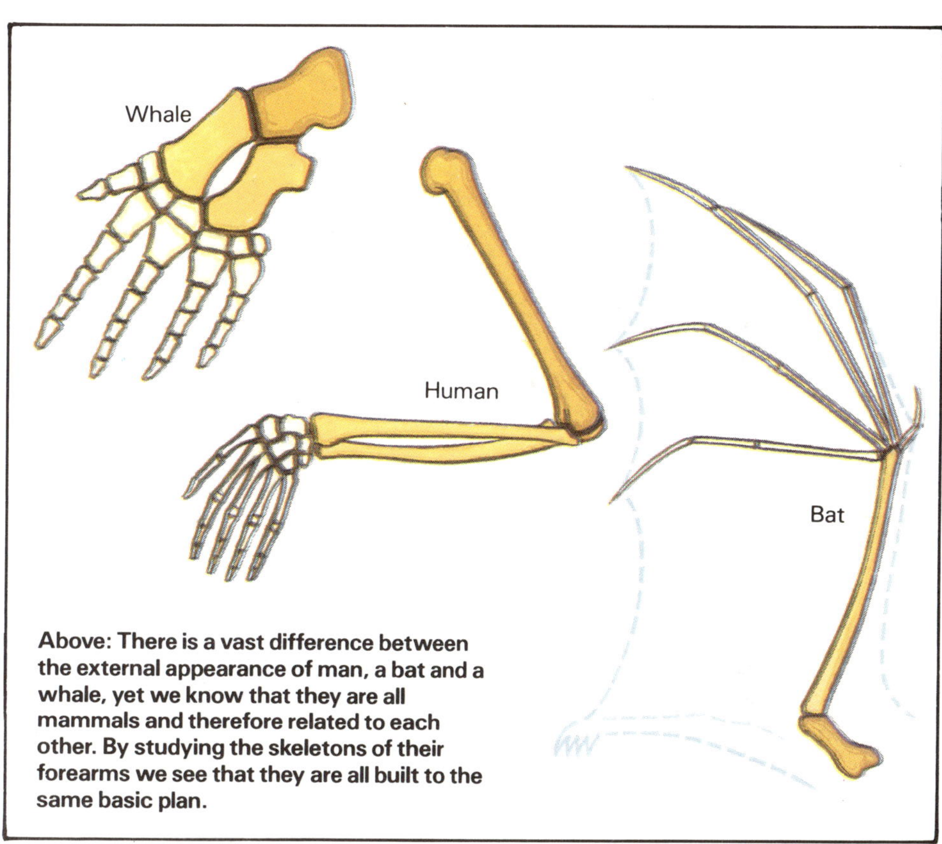

Above: There is a vast difference between the external appearance of man, a bat and a whale, yet we know that they are all mammals and therefore related to each other. By studying the skeletons of their forearms we see that they are all built to the same basic plan.

After travelling widely throughout the world and making detailed observations abroad and at home on domesticated animals, Darwin proposed that all life on earth had evolved gradually from the simplest forms over a vast period of geological time. As evidence for his theories he used fossil records, the 'artificial selection' of breeders of domestic pigeons, and his observations on adaptations of species on isolated islands.

In his book 'The Origin of Species', published in 1859, he explained his ideas about natural selection. Animals and plants produce a vast number of offspring in each generation, far more than are needed to maintain a stable population of the species. Most of the young die before they reach adulthood. Darwin proposed that only those most able to survive would do so, the rest would be 'selected out' by nature.

The Animal Kingdom

The Animal Kingdom can be divided simply into two large groups: animals without backbones (also known as invertebrates) and animals with backbones (also known as vertebrates).

Some of the more familiar invertebrate animals we see around us include insects, crabs, worms and spiders. Animals like cats and dogs, snakes, frogs, birds and fishes belong to the other group, the vertebrates.

Vertebrate animals are generally much bigger than invertebrate animals. They also *seem* to be more common. However, there are many more invertebrate animals in the world than there are vertebrate animals. About 95 per cent of the whole Animal Kingdom is composed of invertebrate animals. Many of them spend much of their lives hidden from view, however — in the soil, in the sea or concealed among the bark of trees.

Animal Classification

Animals (and plants) are grouped together according to particular features that they have in common. We have already seen how animals can be grouped into vertebrates and invertebrates. The next major division within the Animal Kingdom is the phylum. Animals within a phylum also share many features in common. For instance, the animals grouped together in the Phylum Arthropoda all have a tough, external skeleton called an exoskeleton, and jointed legs.

Within each phylum the animals are arranged in separate classes. Animals within each class share many common features of body structure. Thus, within the Phylum Arthropoda, the Class Insecta includes all those animals whose bodies are divided into three parts and bear three pairs of legs — in other words, the insects.

The next division, within the classes, is the order. Within each order are usually a number of families. Families contain animals which are similar in many ways. In the world of birds, all the tits (blue tit, coal tit and so on) are grouped together in the same family.

The next division is the genus. The final division is the species. All the species within a particular genus are basically alike. It is only animals of the same species breeding together which can produce young animals capable of themselves breeding.

Right: This family tree of the Animal Kingdom shows the main groups of animals which have appeared on earth.

Left: Although they all look quite different, all these animals are mammals. Their bodies bear fur and they suckle their young.

Crustaceans
Segmented worms
Flatworms
Echinoderms
Fishes
Birds
Molluscs
Roundworms
Reptiles
Insects
Mammals
Amphibians
Arachnids
Protochordates
Sponges
Bryozoans
Protozoa
Comb jellies
Jellyfishes

World Wildlife

About 200 million years ago, when dinosaurs roamed the Earth, the continents were joined together in a vast supercontinent called Pangaea. But slowly the continents drifted apart and animals living on one land mass became separated from those living on another. Each group of animals continued to change – to *evolve* – but, isolated from each other, they evolved in different ways. This is why, today, certain animals are found only on certain continents; why, for example, kangaroos are found only in Australia and llamas only in South America. The map shows animals typical of each area.

NORTH AMERICA

Only a narrow stretch of water separates North America from Asia. Often in the past the two land masses have been joined by a land bridge, and animals have been able to pass from one to the other. For this reason, many of the animals found in North America are closely related to those found in Asia and Europe.

SOUTH AMERICA

South America has many animals found nowhere else in the world. Some are quite strange in both appearance and behaviour, such as the sloth, spending its days hanging upside-down in the trees, or the toothless anteater, rummaging through ant hills with its long nose. There is also a wealth of beautiful birds such as the scarlet macaw in the tropical rain forests.

EUROPE AND ASIA

Many people live in Europe and Asia, and much of the land is farmed, so the larger wild animals are mostly confined to nature parks. But some animals, such as the fox, have adapted to living among people. Others, such as the giant panda, live only in the deepest parts of the forest.

AFRICA

The grasslands of Africa have the most varied collection of large grazing animals in the world – including the giraffe, elephant, rhinoceros, antelopes and many others. These animals and the carnivores which prey on them roam free in vast national parks.

AUSTRALASIA

Australia was the first continent to break away from Pangaea. It did so at a time when most of the world's mammals reared their young in pouches. These animals, called marsupials, flourished in Australia, but soon became extinct in other parts of the world. The koala and kangaroo are both marsupials, and are found only in Australia. The tuatara, a reptile found in New Zealand, is the nearest living relative of the great dinosaurs.

Animals of Long Ago

Right: *Pteranodon* was a huge flying reptile that lived during the Cretaceous Period, some 130 million years ago. It had a wingspan of about 7 metres. *Pteranodon* probably clambered up on to cliffs and launched itself into the air to soar and glide over the sea. *Pteranodon* had a long bony crest at the back of its head to help counter-balance the huge beak.

Far right: *Alamosaurus* lived in parts of Europe and North America during the Cretaceous Period. It was a large plant-eating dinosaur. *Tyrannosaurus* (the name means 'tyrant lizard') is shown here attacking *Alamosaurus*. *Tyrannosaurus* was the biggest carnivorous reptile ever to have lived. It stood over 6 metres tall.

The first animals appeared on earth many millions of years ago. Their remains sometimes become preserved in rocks. When this happens the remains are known as fossils. By studying fossils, scientists have discovered almost everything they know about the animal life of long ago.

Life began in the oceans. The first forms of life were small, primitive creatures rather like the sponges and jellyfishes of today. In time, larger creatures such as crabs evolved. Then fishes appeared in the seas. Some of these fishes were huge, armour-plated monsters which preyed on other sea creatures.

Eventually fishes evolved which could breathe air. From them developed animals which were able to live both on land or in the water. These were the amphibians, the ancestors of the salamanders, frogs and toads. They first appeared about 350 million years ago.

Once the land had been conquered by animals, other creatures evolved. Next to arrive were the reptiles. For many millions of years, conditions on earth were exactly right for the reptiles, and they flourished in many parts of the world.

Left: About one and a half million years ago, great ice sheets from the North Pole crept over many parts of the northern hemisphere. To keep warm, animals such as the woolly mammoth shown here grew long coats. Other shaggy coated animals included the woolly rhinoceros and the cave bear. The sabre-toothed tiger was one of several meat-eating animals which preyed on creatures at this time.

Pteranodon Alamosaurus Tyrannosaurus

The biggest reptiles were the dinosaurs. Dinosaurs ruled the earth for about 130 million years. Giant plant-eating reptiles wallowed in the swamplands, browsing on vegetation. On dry land herds of horned dinosaurs roamed about. Many of these plant-eating dinosaurs fell prey to ferocious carnivores like *Tyrannosaurus*.

Some reptiles took to the air, gliding about on leathery wings. Others returned to the sea to feed on fishes and other marine creatures. About 65 million years ago, however, most of the reptiles suddenly died out.

Below: Some animals have become extinct in more recent times. The dodo, a bird about the size of a turkey, was once found on Mauritius island in the Indian Ocean. When sailors from visiting ships landed on the island they stole its eggs and killed the birds for food. The last dodo was killed little more than 200 years ago.

The Age of Mammals

By the time most of the reptiles had died out, the mammals and birds had already evolved. The mammals quickly filled all the habitats occupied by the reptiles. The first mammals were small, mouse-like animals. In time many other kinds of mammal also appeared. Some of these were plant-eaters and others became carnivorous, feeding on the plant-eaters. Today, the mammals are the dominant animals on earth.

Scientists have found fossil bones from many of these early mammals. We know that some were gigantic. There were ground sloths bigger than elephants, and a giant rhinoceros called *Baluchitherium* that was nearly as tall as a house.

Nature Trails

The best way to find out about animals and plants is to take a walk in the country, or even take a look in a town garden.

Many national parks and country parks have nature trails marked out to lead naturalists to the places where they can see the most interesting plants and animals. They often provide identification plates similar to those opposite, to help people to put a name to what they see.

Most naturalists following nature trails find that it is a good plan to take a notebook and pencil, to make a record of anything they see, and even a sketch to help identification later. Binoculars are a great help for studying birds, and a pocket magnifying glass is essential to find out the details of plants which may look alike to the casual eye.

There is another form of nature trail, too – that left by the feet of animals as they go about their daily lives. Such footprints show up best in snow, but they can also be detected in soft ground, and even in dewy grass. There are other marks, too, that betray the presence of animals, such as the claw marks which badgers leave on the trees and logs they use as scratching posts, or holes in a bank which are home to some small creatures.

The best time to see and identify tracks left by animals is when snow is on the ground. Remember animals leave slightly different marks according to the way they are moving, and this shows up clearly in snow.

Fox, trotting

Badger, bounding

Roe deer

Rabbit

Shrew

Mouse, bounding

Rabbit, hopping slowly

Squirrel, jumping

Stoat, bounding

Nature in the Garden

It is not always necessary to go on a nature trip to the countryside, or to the seashore, in order to find plenty of wildlife. For many of our own back gardens provide a wonderful haven for plants and animals.

Some gardens are better than others for attracting wildlife. The best ones are those with plenty of trees growing in them, and where a part of the garden is allowed to grow 'wild'. This can easily be done by sowing some wild flower seeds in a small corner, or allowing a little of the lawn to grow longer than usual.

A pond will also prove to be a welcome feature for wild animals, many of which will come to drink, feed or lay their eggs. A small pile of rocks of even just a few bricks will make a home for spiders, slow worms and other small creatures.

However, even if your garden is a neat, tidy place without any trees, there will always be some wildlife present. All gardens have soil, of course, and this is where many of the smaller creatures of the garden live. Earthworms are the gardener's friend, for they help mix the earth together, and create air passages for the roots of plants. Other animals of the soil include beetles and their larvae, centipedes and millipedes, and ants. If you carefully lift a large stone in the garden you will often see ants scuttling about, for they often build their nests under stones.

Sometimes gardeners find large heaps of soil on their carefully tended lawns. These are caused by moles, which burrow through the earth and push the soil they have excavated up on to the grass.

Hidden among the fallen leaves or creeping between the stems of the flowers in the flower beds are other animals such as slugs and snails.

Many of the creatures of the garden are very secretive. They remain hidden from view and only emerge from the safety of their hiding places to feed at night. Birds, however, are among the easiest of garden animals to see. We can encourage them by planting trees, or by growing bushes with berries which they can eat in the autumn. In winter, a bird feeding table will also attract hungry flocks, eager for something to eat.

Wild plants, too, will find their way into the garden. The plants we call weeds are really just wild flowers growing uninvited. In autumn, mushrooms and toadstools will appear mysteriously from the ground, and lichens, mosses and other lowly plants will soon colonize rocks.

Above: You can easily make a wormery yourself. The one shown here is made from two sheets of glass with soil sandwiched between them, but a jam jar containing some moist soil and a few leaves is just as good. Watch the earthworms mix the soil as they burrow through it.

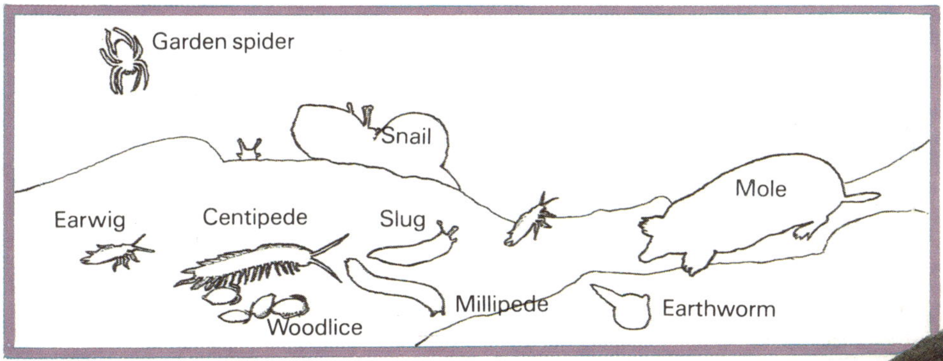

Garden spider
Snail
Mole
Earwig
Centipede
Slug
Millipede
Earthworm
Woodlice

Below: Some common garden animals. Many of the smaller creatures spend the day hidden under stones or leaves, but at night they are much more active and can easily be seen with the aid of a torch.

The World of Insects

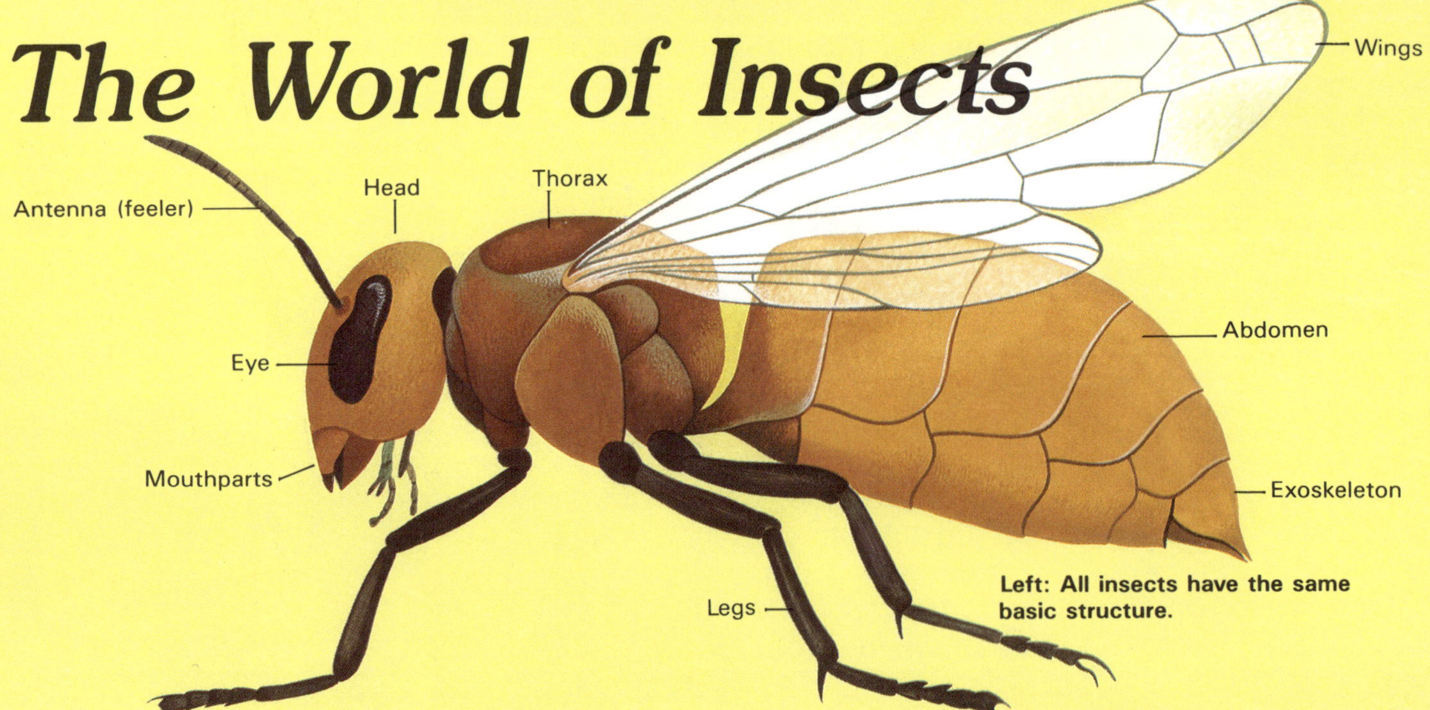

Left: All insects have the same basic structure.

Insects are the most numerous and widespread group of animals on earth. There are more species of insect than all the rest of the species in the Animal Kingdom put together. Over a million different kinds have been discovered. Insects are found in almost every sort of habitat, from deserts to lakes, and from the soil to the air. The only place which insects have been unable to colonize successfully is the oceans, but they make up for this by their abundance elsewhere. Insects vary enormously in their general shape as well as in their size. They range from the microscopic to beetles the size of a large mouse.

Despite the enormous variety of insect life, they all have certain features in common. Like many of their invertebrate relatives, insects have an external skeleton called an exoskeleton which provides support and protection. The bodies of adult insects are divided into three parts: the head, the thorax and the abdomen, and on the middle part are found three pairs of jointed legs.

Insect Lives

Perhaps the most striking feature of insects is their ability to fly. It is the conquest of the air which has helped insects to become so successful. Some insects, such as beetles, are relatively cumbersome in flight and can cover only short distances. Others, however, such as dragonflies, spend virtually all the hours of daylight on the wing. Their mastery of the air, and their excellent vision, allow them to catch even the speediest of airborne prey.

The wings of many butterflies are extremely colourful and are used for a variety of purposes such as display, defence and camouflage, in addition to their use in flight.

Insects eat many different types of food. Many, like the antlion larva above, are carnivores while others eat only plant material. Some insects even eat plants at one stage in their life and animals in another. Others are scavengers, or attack man's clothes, books and carpets. Even more extraordinarily some insects, such as certain moths, do not feed at all as adults.

Above: The antlion is a curious insect which is found in dry, sandy soils. The larva is a fierce carnivore with a liking for ants, but it is so slow and cumbersome that it has to use cunning means to catch its food. Instead of chasing its prey, the antlion larva buries itself in the sand and digs a pit. Any unfortunate ant which falls over the edge of the pit slowly but surely slides down into the jaws of the waiting larva.

Insects have well-developed senses that tell them everything they need to know about their surroundings. Unlike our own eyes, the 'compound' eyes of insects are composed of up to 25,000 separate chambers each with a small lens. Although giving

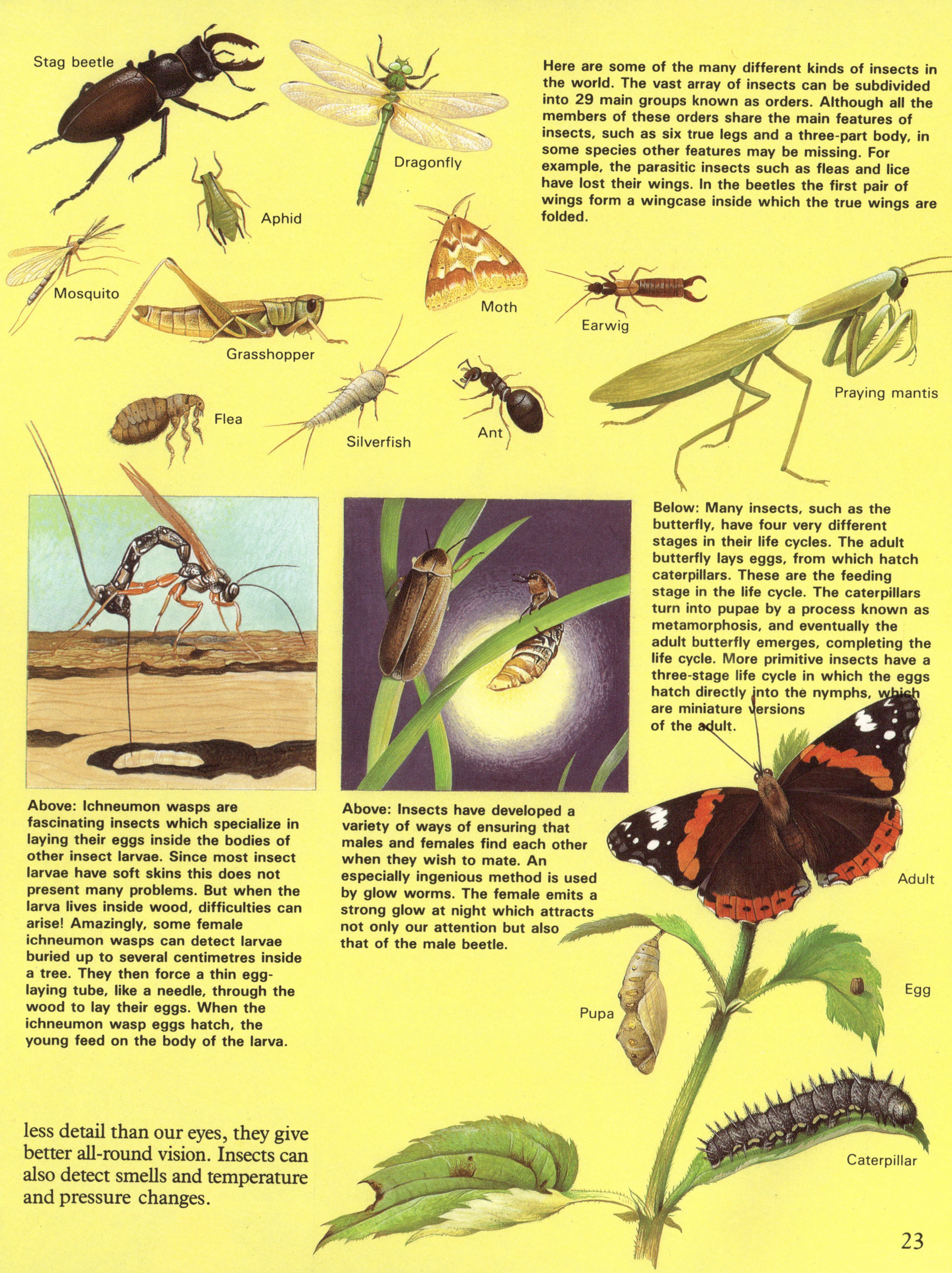

Here are some of the many different kinds of insects in the world. The vast array of insects can be subdivided into 29 main groups known as orders. Although all the members of these orders share the main features of insects, such as six true legs and a three-part body, in some species other features may be missing. For example, the parasitic insects such as fleas and lice have lost their wings. In the beetles the first pair of wings form a wingcase inside which the true wings are folded.

Below: Many insects, such as the butterfly, have four very different stages in their life cycles. The adult butterfly lays eggs, from which hatch caterpillars. These are the feeding stage in the life cycle. The caterpillars turn into pupae by a process known as metamorphosis, and eventually the adult butterfly emerges, completing the life cycle. More primitive insects have a three-stage life cycle in which the eggs hatch directly into the nymphs, which are miniature versions of the adult.

Above: Ichneumon wasps are fascinating insects which specialize in laying their eggs inside the bodies of other insect larvae. Since most insect larvae have soft skins this does not present many problems. But when the larva lives inside wood, difficulties can arise! Amazingly, some female ichneumon wasps can detect larvae buried up to several centimetres inside a tree. They then force a thin egg-laying tube, like a needle, through the wood to lay their eggs. When the ichneumon wasp eggs hatch, the young feed on the body of the larva.

Above: Insects have developed a variety of ways of ensuring that males and females find each other when they wish to mate. An especially ingenious method is used by glow worms. The female emits a strong glow at night which attracts not only our attention but also that of the male beetle.

less detail than our eyes, they give better all-round vision. Insects can also detect smells and temperature and pressure changes.

Social Insects

Above: Bees chew bark to make papery nests. These are sometimes built in crevices or suspended from branches. Workers collect pollen to make wax chambers for their young, and nectar to make honey.

Below: Some ants build large mounds of twigs and other plant material. These contain runs and galleries in which the ants live. Many species of ants have a special relationship with aphids. They collect honeydew from the aphids and in return protect them from predators.

Most insects lead independent lives, coming together with others of their kind only for mating. However, some insects can only survive in complex societies. On their own they would soon die.

In insect societies the whole colony is often based on one breeding female, called a queen. In most cases, all the other members of the society are her offspring. There is usually a well-defined division of labour, with different types of colony members produced for different tasks. This is called a caste system. For example, some members of the colony will defend it, and they have large, aggressive mouthparts. Others may be concerned with collection of food and repairing the nest or hive, and may have chewing mouthparts.

In the ants and termites, the solitary queen is often little more than an egg-laying machine. She devotes all her life to laying eggs but cannot defend or feed herself.

Ants

Ants are interesting social insects which live in large colonies either underground or in loose mounds. Their homes contain a complex system of tunnels and galleries. Ant societies contain three castes: the males, fertile females which become queens, and workers. In the summer, many ants produce wings and fly about looking for mates. These flights are called swarming flights. After mating the fertilized female sheds her wings and searches for a site to start a new colony.

Honey Bees

Honey bees are social insects which man uses to his advantage. In the wild, honey bees nest in cavities, but they take readily to artificial hives. Here their honey can be collected without harming the bees.

There are three castes in a honey bee society. At the centre of the colony is the large queen. She is fertile and lays eggs throughout her life, although she only mates once. The next caste is the drones. These are male bees. Their function is to mate with the queen, and they take no part in the running of the hive. The third caste is the workers, which make up most of the bees in the hive. Like the queen, they are female, but they are sterile. As their name suggests, they do most of the work, gathering pollen, making honey and defending the hive with their stings.

Honey bees show many interesting types of behaviour. In hot weather, they fan the entrance to the hive with their wings to produce a draught. The workers also perform elaborate 'dances' which tell other hive members the directions to the best food.

Termites

Termite mounds, like the ones shown at the bottom of this page, are a conspicuous feature of the African Plains, and are common throughout the tropics. These impressive structures may be up to 6 metres tall. Many are made of cemented soil and so they are virtually impregnable.

Termite society is rather different from those of ants, bees and wasps. There are four castes rather than three. A colony is started after winged males and females swarm. When a pair have settled, they shed their wings and the female becomes the queen of the new colony. She becomes grotesquely enlarged and lays more than 10,000 eggs a day when she is mature. The male is also important because he has to fertilize the queen several times throughout her life.

The soldiers are armed with a huge set of jaws with which to defend the mound from attackers. The fourth caste is the workers, who gather the wood which is the main food for termites. They have special bacteria in their intestines which help them digest it.

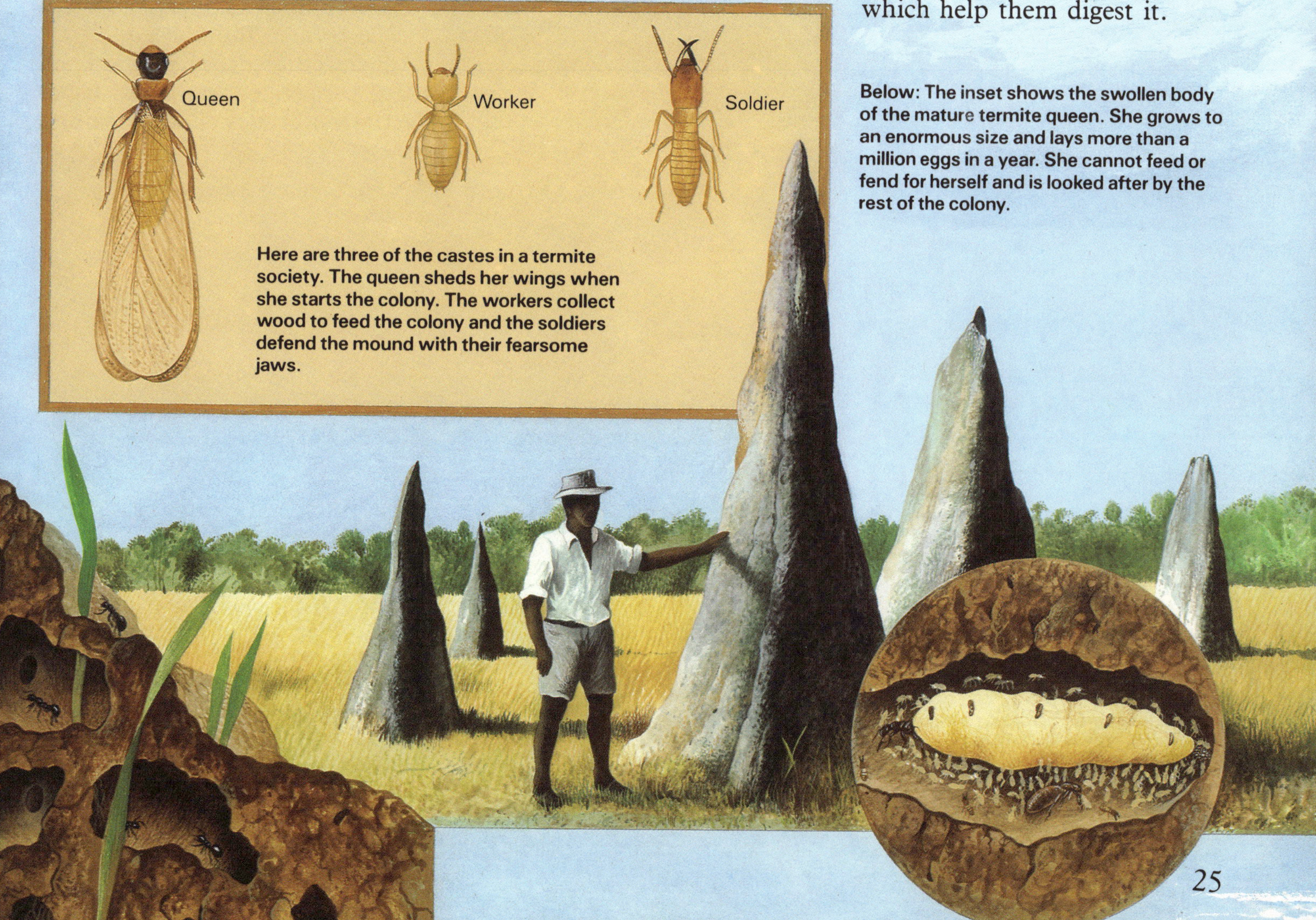

Here are three of the castes in a termite society. The queen sheds her wings when she starts the colony. The workers collect wood to feed the colony and the soldiers defend the mound with their fearsome jaws.

Below: The inset shows the swollen body of the mature termite queen. She grows to an enormous size and lays more than a million eggs in a year. She cannot feed or fend for herself and is looked after by the rest of the colony.

Pondlife

Freshwater ponds often teem with life. Colourful displays of flowers grow around their edges, and a wealth of animal life lives below the surface. The animals which dwell there must cope with very different problems from those of their relatives on land. They must be able to move about in the water and find a way of obtaining oxygen for breathing. The pond dwellers also have to cope with extremes of temperature; sunny days can heat the water up, while in winter the water's surface may freeze.

Some of the pond's inhabitants, such as fishes, can only live in water, but others, such as frogs and dragonflies, spend the early part of their lives in water and their adult stages on land, returning to the pond to breed in the spring.

Life in Ponds

The pond is not a simple environment, but is really a mixture of several separate habitats. The aquatic plants and animals have all evolved to live in very precise zones of the pond. Some plants will grow only in the drying mud on the margin of the pond while others, which cannot survive drying out, must be constantly immersed in water. Duckweed likes to drift in the open water while other species, such as water lilies, remain rooted in the mud at the bottom.

It is, however, the animal inhabitants which are most specially adapted to life in the pond. The surface of the water is very important. It is here that oxygen enters the pond from the air. It is the place where some animals move from air to water, and also where light penetrates the waters below. However, it can also be a prison to many land animals which get trapped in its surface film. Not surprisingly, a variety of scavengers live on the surface and pick off the unfortunate animals caught there. Still more scavengers live underneath this surface film, often trapping air on their bodies to keep them buoyant.

Below the surface is the open water, inhabited by newts, fishes and water beetles. These creatures

Right: This panorama of a pond illustrates some of the creatures which live there. In the water itself, great crested newts and sticklebacks feed on the wealth of insect life present. These in turn sometimes fall victim to the carnivorous great diving beetle. Beneath the surface of the water, many plants grow, rooted in the muddy bottom. When they flower, they either produce floating flowers, such as those of the water lily, or tall flowering spikes like those of reeds and bulrushes. Many birds are associated with fresh water. Herons patiently stalk fishes in the shallows while coots dive for plant and animal food.

feed on others which hide among the tangled pond weeds, and seldom visit either the surface or the bottom.

On the bottom, where the silt collects and where the remains of dead plants and animals fall, many species such as bloodworms and crustaceans tolerate its inhospitable conditions and find it a safe sanctuary away from the eyes of hungry predators.

In order to obtain the oxygen they require for breathing, many freshwater insects come to the surface to breathe, although some, such as damselfly nymphs, have developed simple gills to help them extract oxygen from the water. Many diving beetles have an ingenious way of breathing. They trap a bubble of air under their wingcases and this acts as a kind of 'aqualung'. But, like its human equivalent, it must be topped up from time to time, so the beetle makes regular visits to the surface.

Above: The development of tadpoles into frogs is a remarkable process. In early spring, frogs gather in large numbers in ponds to reproduce. The eggs are laid in great masses, and are surrounded by protective jelly which swells in the water producing the familiar 'frogspawn'. At first the little embryo is just a black dot, but it soon grows to form a tadpole and hatches after a couple of weeks. At this stage the tadpole breathes using feathery gills and rasps algae from the surface of pondweeds. Over the next few weeks it loses its external gills, develops legs and finally loses its tail. At this stage its metamorphosis is complete and the young froglet leaves the pond.

Water plants produce oxygen when they photosynthesize. One little animal named Hydra has found an ingenious way of making use of this. It incorporates small, single-celled green algae between its cells and then 'breathes' the oxygen they produce.

HALFWAY ANIMALS

Frogs, toads and newts belong to a group of animals known as amphibians. They are thought to have evolved from fish ancestors and to have given rise to reptiles. Fishes are almost exclusively aquatic animals, whereas reptiles are almost entirely land dwellers. Amphibians are usually just as much at home in water as they are on land.

When adults, frogs, toads and newts can breathe by taking in oxygen through their skins, but they can also gulp air through their mouths. This enables them to leave the water when they wish. Although some amphibians may spend most of their adult lives away from water, they must all return to the water to breed.

The Seashore

A great variety of interesting and unusual wildlife is to be found on the seashore. In fact, some of the plants and animals of the seashore — such as seaweeds and sea urchins — are found nowhere else.

All the animals and plants of the seashore are extremely hardy, for as well as having to cope with the pounding of the waves they must be able to survive when the tide goes out, leaving them exposed to the drying sun and wind. At this time they are also easy prey for predators, and so must find ways of protecting themselves.

The most common plants of the seashore are seaweeds. Seaweeds belong to a group of plants called algae. The seaweeds grow on the beach according to their ability to withstand exposure when the tide is out.

The most curious seashore plants are the lichens. Some resemble patches of tar stuck to the rocks. Others look like little orange crusty patches.

Types of Seashore

There are several different kinds of seashore. Rocky shores are usually richest in wildlife. The rocks provide good anchorage for the seaweeds, and the crevices offer a safe haven for snails, worms, crabs and other creatures. Many of the snails' relatives, such as limpets and mussels, clamp themselves to the rocks. Countless barnacles, related to crabs and prawns, also cover many of the rocks.

In the rockpools starfishes, anemones and fishes lurk, safe from the wind and sun.

Sandy shores are more difficult places for wildlife to survive. There is little shelter for animals, and so they must burrow beneath the sand to find a moist, secure place to live. Lugworms, fanworms and a great variety of bivalves such as cockles, razorshells and tellins are to be found living in the sand.

Even more harsh environments are shingle beaches. The relentless, grinding action of the pebbles would crush most animals. Therefore the only living things here are specially adapted flowering plants like sea kale.

Above: You will often find shells such as these on beaches. These shells once belonged to animals called molluscs, one of the commonest groups of creatures on the seashore. Other common molluscs include periwinkles and limpets.

Below: Seashores, particularly sheltered rocky shores, teem with animal and plant life. Some creatures live attached to the rocks themselves, while others seek refuge in rockpools or under the sand. Birds such as gulls and waders patrol the shore, looking for food.

ADAPTING TO LIFE ON THE SEASHORE

Some of the seashore animals have strong shells into which they can retreat at low tide, remaining moist and secure until the tide returns. Others are masters of camouflage; certain crabs and worms look like the seaweed in which they hide. The fronds of the seaweed also help to keep the creatures moist.

The seaweeds attach themselves to rocks by means of a root-like structure called a holdfast. They also have soft, slippery stems and fronds which enable them to sway in the currents and avoid becoming damaged. Some species, like bladderwrack, have special air bubbles in their fronds, which help them to float.

Life in the Seas

The seas and oceans cover nearly three-quarters of the world's surface, and are extremely rich and varied habitats. From the shallowest coastal waters to the huge expanses of the open ocean, and from the icy polar waters to the tropical seas, they literally teem with life.

Shallow Seas

In the shallow coastal waters we often find plants and animals similar to those found on the seashore, such as seaweeds, crabs, snails, bivalves (molluscs with hinged shells), starfishes and many other familiar creatures such as seals and sea lions.

In the warmer parts of the world the shallow waters are often the home of corals. These tiny creatures, related to anemones, build chalky homes around themselves. Eventually these may extend for many kilometres. Coral reefs are fascinating places in which fishes, starfishes, sea urchins and anemones and other creatures all live together in a bewildering array of colours and shapes.

Above: These dazzling clown fish are among the many colourful species which inhabit coral reefs. The world's biggest coral reef is the Great Barrier Reef, extending for 2012 kilometres along the north-eastern coast of Australia.

Below: Most sharks are fearsome predators of the sea, although a few species eat only plankton. Dolphins and porpoises are kinds of whale. Whales are mammals which spend all their lives in the sea. Many seabirds feed on fishes which they catch near the surface.

Open Oceans

The smallest forms of life in the open sea are the plankton. These are tiny, microscopic plants and animals which float near the surface. They provide food for many of the other species of animal living in the sea. Even some of the huge whales and sharks live just on a diet of plankton. Most of the sharks, however, are fierce predators of other animals, particularly the huge shoals of fishes which roam the oceans. Species such as the hammerhead and the great white shark are even feared by man, for attacks on humans are not uncommon in waters in which they are found.

Turtles and sea snakes are reptiles frequently encountered in the open sea. Turtles are generally found in warmer waters. They spend most of their lives at sea, only hauling themselves on to beaches at night to lay their eggs in the sand. As soon as they hatch, the baby turtles must scuttle back down the beach to return to the safety of the sea.

Sea snakes are highly venomous, and about 50 species are known to inhabit the sea, mainly in the waters of the Indo-Pacific region. They feed on small fishes.

Portuguese man o'war

Jellyfish

Above: Jellyfishes and the Portuguese man o'war drift in the open oceans. They catch fishes and other small creatures, using their trailing tentacles which are armed with powerful stinging cells.

Deep Sea

In the gloom of the deep sea, where light never reaches, some of the most bizarre creatures are to be found. These include giant squids, prawns and angler fishes.

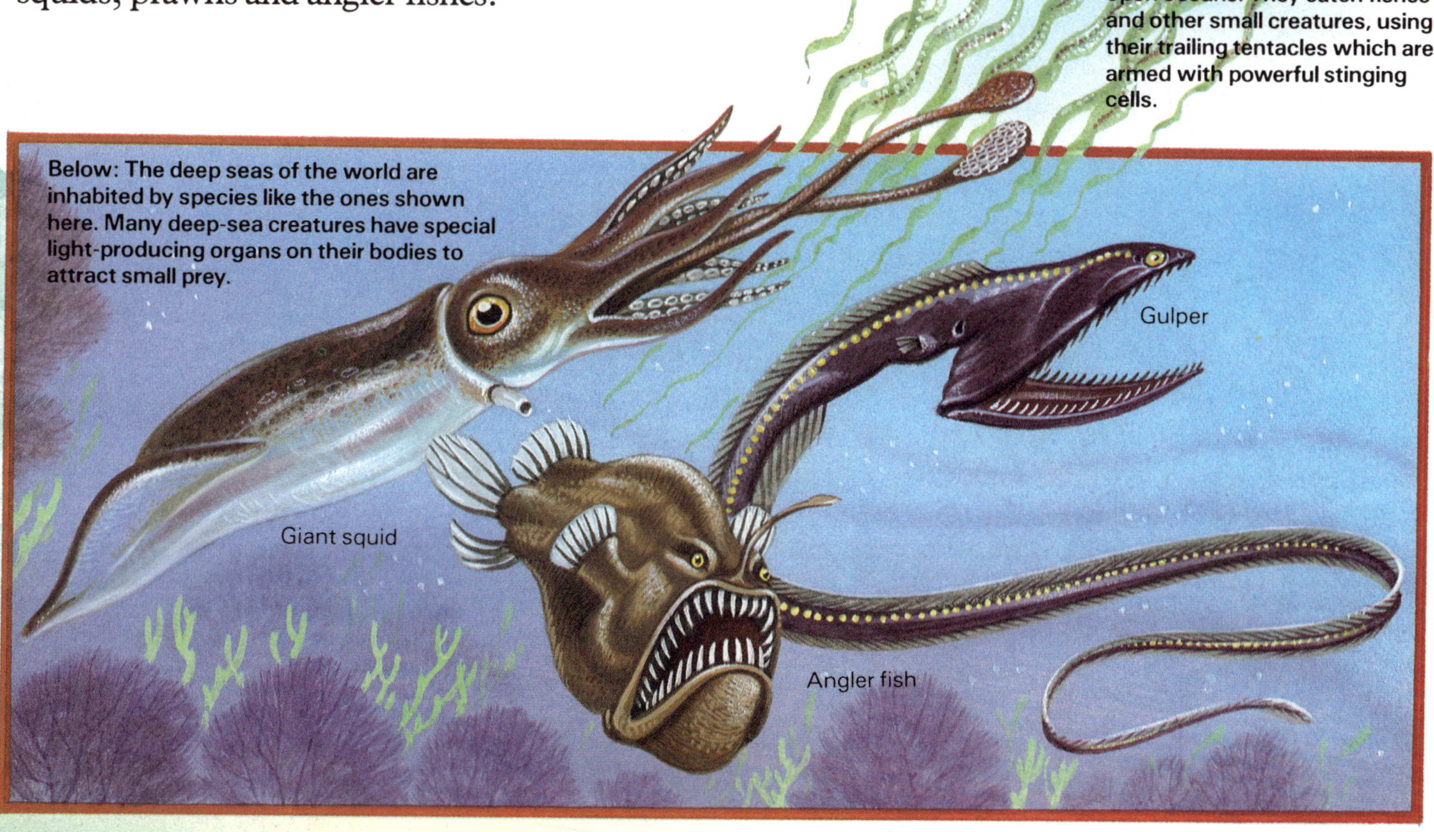

Below: The deep seas of the world are inhabited by species like the ones shown here. Many deep-sea creatures have special light-producing organs on their bodies to attract small prey.

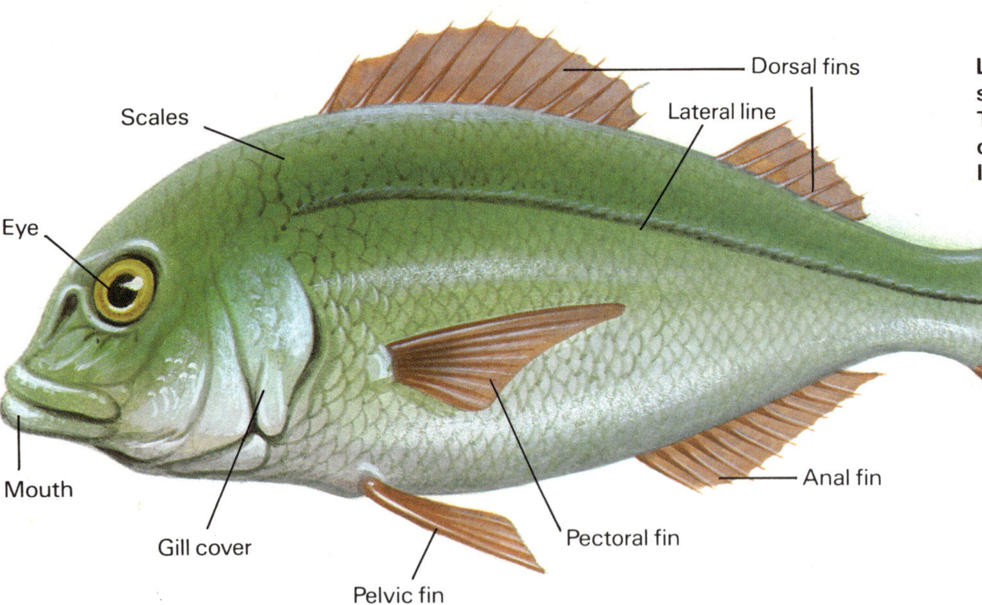

Left: Despite tremendous variations in body shape, all fishes conform to a basic plan. The tail fin is used in movement and the other fins give control and balance. The lateral line is an important sense organ.

Water enters mouth

Water leaves via gill openings

All Kinds of Fishes

The fishes are a very varied and successful group of vertebrate animals which have colonized the world's oceans, lakes and rivers. Fishes are cold-blooded creatures whose bodies are covered with scales. They are specially adapted to live and breathe in water, although some can spend limited amounts of time on dry land.

Among the most primitive of fishes are the lampreys and hagfishes. These eel-like creatures do not possess proper bones nor a proper set of jaws. Nevertheless, they are a successful group and have, instead of jaws, a rasping sucker. They feed by attaching themselves to the sides of other fishes and rasping away at their flesh.

Sharks, rays and skates lack proper bones as well, but they have a strong cartilage skeleton to support their bodies. Most sharks have a fearsome array of teeth in their powerful jaws. They are mainly predatory creatures which hunt other fishes as well as squid and various invertebrates. In tropical waters there are species of shark which reach huge sizes. Both the feared tiger shark and the man-eating great white shark often exceed 6 metres in length. The massive whale shark, on the other hand, is harmless to man, feeding on microscopic plankton. Skates and rays are relatives of sharks. Their bodies are flattened, for they spend much of their life on the seabed.

The most numerous group of fishes are the bony fishes. Most of those which we eat, or keep as pets, are in this group. The extraordinary lungfishes are found in tropical lakes. They survive the dry season by curling up in a mud chamber. Their 'lung' allows them to breathe air through a small opening in the chamber.

Above: Fishes breathe by extracting dissolved oxygen from the water, using a series of internal gills over which water is continually passed. The process can easily be observed in aquarium fishes and first involves the fish taking in water through the mouth. With the mouth closed, a swallowing movement forces the water over the gills and out through the gill openings.

Right: The pike is often called the freshwater shark, because of its voracious appetite and its fearsome array of teeth. It takes its prey by surprise and its body is well adapted for this purpose. The markings on its flanks provide camouflage as it lurks in the weeds, and its large tail fin gives it excellent acceleration. With its huge gape it can easily grab prey and the teeth prevent its escape.

Other Bony Fishes

The cod family are large, bony marine fishes which provide food for man as well as many other fishes and birds. They usually have large eyes and mouths, and powerful bodies which enable them to swim well. Some of them can live in very deep water. The herring family are also important for food, and are found in vast shoals in some seas where many birds and other creatures depend on them for food. The salmon family are streamlined and powerful swimmers, and many of them live in the sea, but make long migrations up rivers to spawn.

In fresh water, members of the carp family are very common, ranging in size from tiny minnows to the large carp themselves, and they include the familiar goldfish.

Tropical lakes and rivers support large numbers of fishes from the cichlid family which are often brightly coloured and very active swimmers.

The perch family are armed with spines and strong scales and hunt other fishes for their food.

Adult plaice

Above: When the young plaice hatches from its egg it is much like any other bony fish. After a few days, however, changes begin to take place and one eye moves across the top of its head. Eventually it ends up alongside the other and the young fish begins to swim on one side with its eyes uppermost. It is now perfectly adapted to life on the sea bottom.

Far left: In the spring the male stickleback builds a little nest into which he lures a female. If satisfied with the arrangements, she lays her eggs in the nest and departs. For a couple of weeks, the male guards the eggs and looks after the young when they hatch, herding them back into the nest at the first sign of danger.

Above left: The mouthbrooder protects its eggs in a most unusual way. After they have been fertilized, the female collects the eggs in her mouth and carries them around until they hatch.

The Reptilian World

Reptiles are scaly, cold-blooded vertebrate animals which lay eggs with hard, protective shells. The reptiles descended from amphibians 300 million years ago. Today, reptiles are found mainly in the warmer parts of the world.

Many millions of years ago, there were many more kinds of reptiles on the earth than there are today. During the period in the earth's history known as the Mesozoic Era, huge reptiles roamed over many continents. Other reptiles conquered the sea and air. About 70 million years ago many reptiles died out, however.

Above: The anaconda is a large snake from South America which kills its prey by constriction or squeezing, before swallowing it whole. The anaconda is also found in rivers.

Left: A cobra rears up in this position before striking at its prey.

Below: Snakes can open their mouths extremely wide. This is how they are able to swallow big prey.

Living Reptiles

The biggest group of living reptiles is the Squamata. These include the snakes and lizards. Snakes are reptiles which have lost the use of their legs over the course of evolution. They move along by means of special movements of their muscular bodies, and they also use their scales to help obtain a grip as they move. A few species swim in the sea.

All snakes are predators, feeding on many different kinds of animal food from eggs to creatures as big as pigs. Some snakes kill their prey before eating it by first squeezing it to death. To do this they quickly surprise their victim and wrap their coils tightly around it. Smaller prey is often swallowed alive. Snakes such as adders, cobras and rattlesnakes first inject their prey with a venom before swallowing it.

Lizards have adapted to many different ways of life. They are also predators but, unlike the snakes, only two species are venomous. The biggest lizard is the Komodo dragon of Borneo. This huge creature measures 3 metres in length. It eats large prey. Most lizards, however, feed on small mammals and birds, as well as on insects and other invertebrates.

The Crocodilia forms the second group of living reptiles. This group includes the crocodiles, caimans, alligators and the gharial. Members of the Crocodilia look very much like their ancestors which existed when reptiles ruled the earth.

Right: The chameleon is a curious lizard which creeps about branches looking for insects to eat. It can swivel both its eyes in different directions. It catches its food on the end of a long, sticky tongue.

Below: The heads of three different crocodilians.

Below: The giant tortoise of the Galapagos Islands is big enough for a man to ride. A common tortoise is shown by its side.

Crocodilians look like huge, armour-plated lizards. They are all adapted to a life spent in water, where they lurk partly submerged beneath the surface waiting for prey. Sometimes they will snatch animals that come to the water's edge to drink. At night they may leave the water to sleep on a sandbank.

The tails of crocodilians are specially flattened for swimming, and the nostrils are placed high on the snout, enabling them to breathe even when lying partly submerged in water.

Crocodilians are found in many parts of the world. They live in the fresh waters of tropical Asia, Africa, Australia and America. One species, the estuarine crocodile, is found in the estuaries of rivers in parts of Asia and Australia. It also swims out to sea.

The most unusual-looking crocodilian is the gharial of India. It has long, thin jaws armed with sharp teeth. Despite its fearsome appearance, however, it catches nothing bigger than fishes.

The Chelonia comprise the tortoises, terrapins and turtles. The chelonians carry on their back a bony shield, and their underbodies are protected by a large, flat, bony plate. When danger threatens these animals can pull their heads and limbs inside their protective armour. Unlike other reptiles, chelonians do not possess teeth, but they have sharp, bony beaks. Also, unlike other reptiles, some chelonians are herbivorous.

Although there are exceptions, most tortoises are land-living creatures, most terrapins live in fresh water, and turtles live in the sea.

The last group of living reptiles is the Rhynchocephalia. Only one living member of this group exists. This animal is called the tuatara. It lives on remote islands near New Zealand, and looks rather like a lizard with spines on its back. It often shares a burrow with a bird, the Manx shearwater.

Birdlife

It would be impossible to mistake a bird for any other animal, for only birds possess feathers. It is feathers which have given birds mastery of the air.

There are nearly 9,000 species of birds throughout the world today, living in every sort of habitat from the seashore to the jungle. The smallest birds are the brilliantly coloured hummingbirds, whose nests are no bigger than a thimble. At the other end of the scale is the ostrich, a flightless bird standing 2.5 metres high.

Birds have adapted to feed on all manner of food. There are some species, the birds of prey, which hunt other animals. Others eat seeds and fruit. A few feed on nothing but insects. Hummingbirds hover over flowers and suck up nectar.

Above: The eagle has a sharp, flesh-tearing beak.

Above: Ducks have wide, flat beaks for sifting mud.

The Development Inside a Bird's Egg

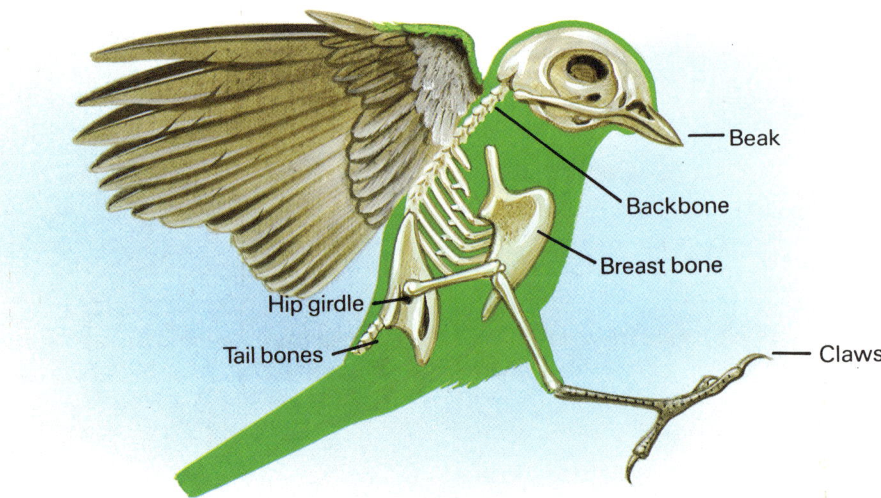

Left: This is how the skeleton is arranged inside a typical bird such as a crow.

Bird Flight

The ability to fly is the key to the great success of birds. Flight has enabled birds to travel huge distances in search of new territories; to travel from continent to continent during migration; and it has allowed them to escape from their enemies when danger threatens.

For successful flight birds must have lightweight, streamlined bodies. Bird bones are hollow, but specially strengthened, and the feathers help to give them a smooth shape in the air. Lift and motion through the air is provided by the feathers on the wings. The tail is used for steering. Birds which spend hours soaring over oceans have long, narrow wings. Birds which fly fast have sickle-shaped wings. Birds which must fly between the trees have shorter, powerful wings.

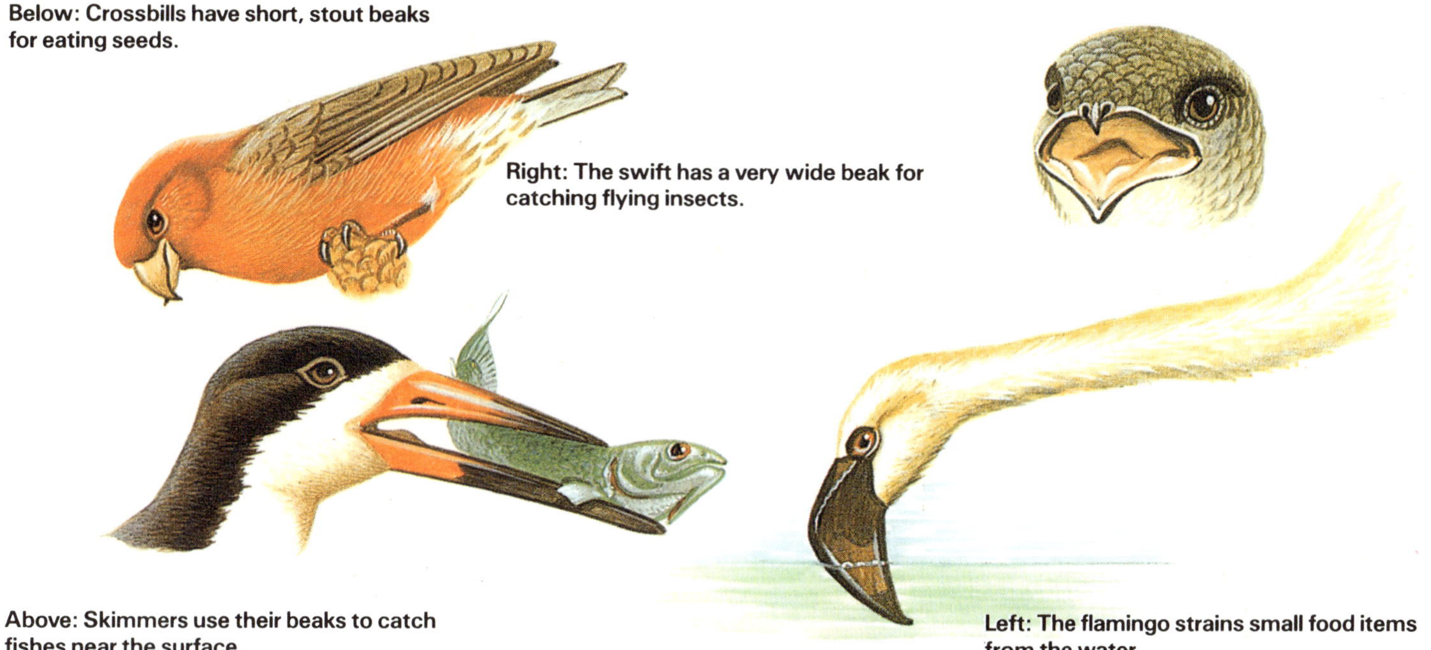

Below: Crossbills have short, stout beaks for eating seeds.

Right: The swift has a very wide beak for catching flying insects.

Above: Skimmers use their beaks to catch fishes near the surface.

Left: The flamingo strains small food items from the water.

Birds and their Young

Many animals build a nest in which to rear their young in safety, but the most familiar of these are birds' nests. Not all birds build nests, however. Some species simply lay their eggs on the ground. The cuckoo is an unusual bird which lays its eggs in the nest of another species.

Before nesting begins, most birds choose a territory and defend it against rivals. The number of eggs laid by the female depends on the species. It may be just one, or as many as 20. Once hatched, the young chicks are fed by their parents until they are big enough to fend for themselves. Most chicks are blind and helpless at birth, but the chicks of waterbirds are born fully feathered and can swim straight away.

Great crested grebes have an elaborate courtship display known as a mating dance.

Right: Many birds, like this whip-poor-will, use their plumage for concealment.

Birds Around the World

Birds are found all around the world, from the hottest deserts to the icy polar caps. Some are specialized and have restricted distributions. Thus, secretary birds are found only on the African Plains, and hummingbirds are found only in the Americas. Other species have wider distributions. The golden eagle, for instance, is found all over the northern hemisphere.

Birds are grouped into families which share recognizable features. Some families have representatives in all parts of the world. For example, ducks, geese and swans can be found in almost every habitat, and all share a similar appearance with webbed feet and a flattened bill. Puffins, and their relatives the auks, on the other hand, are only found in the northern hemisphere.

Nectar Eaters

Hummingbirds are a very specialized group of birds which can hover while collecting nectar from flowers. They are usually very colourful birds with iridescent plumage. Hummingbirds are only found in the Americas, with most species occurring in Central and South America.

Bird Movements

Despite their powers of flight, some birds move very little during their lives. Ptarmigan, for example, are arctic gamebirds which remain in the same habitat even under the harshest of winter conditions, and seldom fly unless disturbed. In complete contrast, albatrosses and shearwaters spend the major part of their lives at sea on the wing, ranging across the oceans of the southern hemisphere. They spend only a few short weeks ashore each year during the breeding season.

In Africa, the sunbirds have also evolved to collect nectar. They cannot hover and are not related to hummingbirds, but look remarkably similar at first glance.

Birds of Prey

Birds of prey are found all over the world. They have sharp talons which they use to grip their prey, and a hooked beak to tear the flesh. They range in size from the tiny pygmy falcon, no bigger than a sparrow, to immense eagles which can soar effortlessly for hours on end.

Some birds of prey are specialized to feed on carrion. These are the vultures and the condors. They are not very closely related, although they look similar. Condors are found only in the Americas whereas vultures only occur in Europe, Africa and Asia.

Birds of the Antarctic

The most characteristic birds of the antarctic are the penguins. These rather comical birds feed on the abundant marine life in the polar seas.

There are many different species but they all share the same characteristics. They have lost the ability to fly. Instead, they use their wings as flippers to swim, almost like flying, under water. Their feathers form a dense, insulating layer against the freezing waters and biting wind. They are an extremely successful family, and colonies often number over a million birds.

Below: Birds are found on all continents of the world.

Apes and Monkeys

Apes and monkeys, together with the tree shrews, lemurs, lorises and bush-babies, make up the group of animals known as the primates. In many ways primates are extremely interesting creatures, because man is also a primate. Many monkeys and apes spend their lives in the safety of the treetops. A few, however, have returned to live a life on the ground. Ground-dwelling species include the baboon, the gorilla and, of course, man himself.

Apes and monkeys are intelligent creatures. They have relatively large brains, and forward-facing eyes which help them to judge distances well. Their hands and feet are designed to help them grip branches as they leap from tree to tree. They often live together in well-organized family groups.

These three animals are primitive primates related to the monkeys and apes.

Below: Baboons are large, African, dog-like monkeys which live mainly on the ground. They live in family groups and eat all kinds of food. They defend themselves fiercely if attacked.

Above: Gibbons are apes with very long arms. They swing through the trees with great ease, but can also run along branches. They live in Asian forests and feed mainly on fruit.

Chimpanzee

Orang-utan

Above: Chimpanzees are highly intelligent apes which spend part of their lives in the treetops of African forests and part on the ground. They can use their hands in a way very similar to us.

Right: Spider monkeys are extremely agile climbers which can also use their tails to hang on to branches.

Below left: Mandrills are forest-dwelling baboons which live in Africa.

Above: The orang-utan is an ape which lives in Borneo and Sumatra.

Left: Despite their huge size and fierce appearance, gorillas are shy, plant-eating apes.

Spider monkey

Mandrill

Monkeys

Monkeys are divided into two groups: those that live in places like South America, and those that live in Africa, India and Asia. Some monkeys are active during the day, where they search for fruit, leaves, insects or other small animals to eat. Others come out only at night, when their strange calls fill the warm night air.

Apes

There are ten species of apes, all of which live in the tropical forests of Africa and Asia. One group, which includes the gorilla, orang-utan and chimpanzee, is known as the 'great apes'. Apes are the group of primates most closely related to man.

Cold Lands

The polar regions are the coldest and bleakest places on Earth. Antarctica, around the South Pole, is mostly covered by thick ice, and fierce blizzards blow loose snow over the surface. Temperatures rarely rise above freezing point during the day and a world record −88.3°C has been recorded near the South Pole. No people live permanently in Antarctica, but some scientists work there in heated homes under the ice. Penguins live around the shores of Antarctica and the seas are rich in fish and whales.

Polar bears live on the ice floes of the Arctic Ocean, hunting seals and young walruses. And around the Arctic Ocean are parts of North America, Europe and Asia, called the *tundra*. Here the snow melts during the short summers, when temperatures may rise to 10°C. Flowering plants then carpet the ground, but it is too cold for trees. Migrating animals such as reindeer graze in the tundra. Arctic people include the Eskimos. They once lived by hunting. They built winter homes of ice called igloos, but most Eskimos now have modern homes.

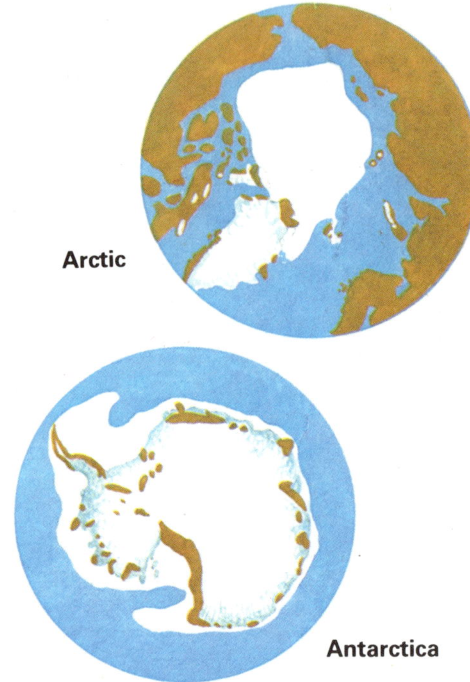

Above: One map shows the ice-covered continent of Antarctica around the South Pole. The other map shows the region around the North Pole, which contains the icy Arctic Ocean. The northern parts of North America, Europe and Asia surround this ocean. These lands have long, cold winters, but plants grow in the short summers.

Below: Penguins gather in large colonies on the icy coasts of Antarctica. The emperor penguin hatches its egg on its feet and the young birds huddle together for warmth.

Most people in the great Sahara Desert live around oases. These fertile places have wells or springs which tap water in rocks below the surface. Some nomads cross hot deserts in camel caravans. Camels are called the 'ships of the desert'. This is because they can go long distances without drinking. But when they reach an oasis, they often drink up to 100 litres of water in only 10 minutes. The camel is suited to the desert in another way. A web of strong skin connects its two widely spaced toes and prevents its feet from sinking into the sand.

Many animals live in the desert despite the heat and the dryness. The smaller animals hide away during the day to escape the fierce sun and venture out at night. Many of them get the water they need from the seeds they eat.

Hot Deserts

Hot deserts cover about one-fifth of the world's land areas. They have mostly clear skies and high temperatures. The average rainfall is under 250 millimetres a year. Several years may pass with hardly any rain, then a thunderstorm may drench the land. Seeds which have been dormant for years rapidly germinate and many plants flower. When this happens in the Australian desert, people flock to the area to see this superb spectacle.

The world's largest desert is the Sahara in North Africa. It contains sand dunes, plains of loose gravel and bare, rocky uplands. Most plants in hot deserts, such as thorn bushes and cacti, are drought-resistant. The most useful desert animal is the camel. It can go for long periods without water. It loses weight, but regains it when it drinks. Deserts become fertile when they are irrigated (watered). Some deserts, like those of the Middle East, are rich in oil and natural gas. These fuels lie hidden far below the surface.

Penguins are awkward creatures on land, waddling around on their webbed feet. To move faster they slide on their bellies over the ice, pushing themselves along with their stubby wings. In the water penguins are fast and agile as they chase fish under water.

Grasslands

Tropical grasslands, called savanna, campos or llanos, occur north and south of the equator in Africa, South America, southern Asia and northern Australia. They are in warm regions with high rainfall. But, because they have a marked dry season, forests do not develop except in such areas as river valleys. Tropical grasslands are used for cattle rearing and some crop farming. But there is a danger that the winds will blow away the exposed soil in the dry season. Such soil erosion can make a region infertile in a few years. In Africa, the savanna supports many animals.

Temperate or mid-latitude grasslands have less rain and much colder winters than tropical grasslands. Trees are also rare on the dry, windswept plains. Huge areas of temperate grasslands, which are also called prairies, steppes or pampas, have become cattle ranches or vast wheat farms. The wildlife has been much reduced. In Australia, sheep have replaced most of the kangaroos and wallabies of the grasslands.

Above: Cattle ranching is a major activity in such savanna regions as East Africa.

Below: Temperate grasslands in North America have become leading wheat-growing regions. The land is flat and easy to farm.

Woods and Meadows

Above: Forests once covered the moist temperate regions in the middle latitudes. In England, these forests have been replaced by a complicated patchwork of fields.

Below: Moist temperate regions in New Zealand support great numbers of sheep.

Moist temperate regions have some rain all the year round, with warm summers and fairly cold winters. Such regions once had huge forests of deciduous trees, such as ash, beech, chestnut, hickory, maple and oak. These trees shed their leaves in winter in order to protect themselves against the cold. Such forests once grew over most of western Europe, northern China and the eastern USA, areas which now contain some of the world's most densely populated regions. Most of these forests have been cut down. Their wood was used for building and as a fuel. In the USA, the forests largely vanished in about 300 years and the land was used for farming. The wildlife dwindled and soil erosion became a serious problem. This also happened on the lower slopes of the mountains of South Island, New Zealand. Britain's forests were replaced by a pleasant landscape of ploughed fields, river meadows, hedgerows and occasional clumps of woodland. But the destruction of forests led to a great decline in wildlife.

Northern Forests

Cold snowy climates are warmer than polar regions, but colder than temperate regions. Vast coniferous forests, called taiga, grow in cold snowy climates. Coniferous trees include birch, fir, pine and spruce. These cold forests are found only in the Northern Hemisphere. No large land masses in a similar latitude exist in the Southern Hemisphere.

Many furred animals, such as ermine, mink, otter and wolverine live in the forests. They have attracted hunters, who have greatly reduced the numbers of these animals. Larger animals include bears, bull moose, caribou, reindeer and wolves. Many trees in these cold forests are valuable softwoods. They are cut down and floated along rivers to sawmills. Sawn timber is used to make furniture and many other things. Many logs are made into wood pulp and paper. The northern forests do not contain many people, because of the cold weather and their generally infertile soils.

Above: The map shows the vast belt of cold coniferous forest that sprawls over North America, northern Europe and northern Asia. It lies south of the tundra and north of the deciduous forests and grassland.

River Valleys

Rivers carry worn pieces of rock from their upper courses to the sea. As the rocks move along, they break down into smaller and smaller pieces. Finally, they become fine alluvium. This alluvium is spread over river valleys when rivers flood. It sometimes piles up in deltas, areas of new fertile land at the river mouths.

Fertile river valleys and deltas are the most densely populated regions on Earth. Farmers can produce large crops because of the rich soil and plentiful water. Some valleys have been centres of early civilizations. These include the valleys of the Tigris-Euphrates in Iraq, the Nile in Egypt, the Indus in Pakistan, the Ganges in India, and the various river valleys of eastern China.

Above: Rivers flow swiftly down their steep upper courses but they become slow-moving when they near the sea. The lower valleys and deltas of many rivers are thickly populated. In parts of China, including Hong Kong, people live on river boats called sampans, right.

Below: Buffalo plough the flooded 'paddy' fields in which rice is grown. Rice from the great river valleys is the staple diet of Asia.

Animals of Australia

Australia is a huge continent in the South Pacific. Together with other islands such as New Zealand and New Guinea, it forms an area called Australasia. Naturalists have always been fascinated by the wildlife of Australia, for many of the animals there are found nowhere else in the world today.

Many millions of years ago the land masses of the Australasian region were connected to the rest of the world. All the animals roamed freely across the continents because at that time they were not separated by great oceans.

Then, the continents began to drift apart. Australia and the other countries of Australasia slowly moved towards the South Pole. Now, all the kinds of animals which were living there became separated, or isolated, from all the other countries of the world by thousands of kilometres of ocean.

Before the drift began most of the mammals were of the kind called marsupials. They had pouches in which the young developed. There were also some other, even stranger, mammals called monotremes. They laid eggs. Cut off from the rest of the world, Australia's mammals developed into many species quite different from the mammals which later arose in other parts of the world.

Above: Some of Australia's birdlife is also very unusual. The kookaburra is related to the kingfishers. It has a very distinctive call and because of this is also known as the 'laughing jackass'. Some Australian birds, such as the bee-eater, birds of Paradise, parrots and cockatoos, are beautiful birds with extremely colourful plumage. Birds of Paradise and parrots live in dense forests, but bee-eaters prefer sandy banks and kookaburras live near water.

INTRODUCED MAMMALS

The arrival of the first men in Australia several thousand years ago caused some important changes. The earliest men brought with them domestic dogs. Some of these returned to the wild and began to prey on the marsupial mammals, which were unable to defend themselves. The later settlers brought sheep and cattle. The farmers who tended these animals drove many of the native animals off their grazing land. Other introduced mammals such as rats and rabbits also competed with the marsupials for food and territory. Today, many marsupials are in danger of extinction, and special measures have been taken to protect them.

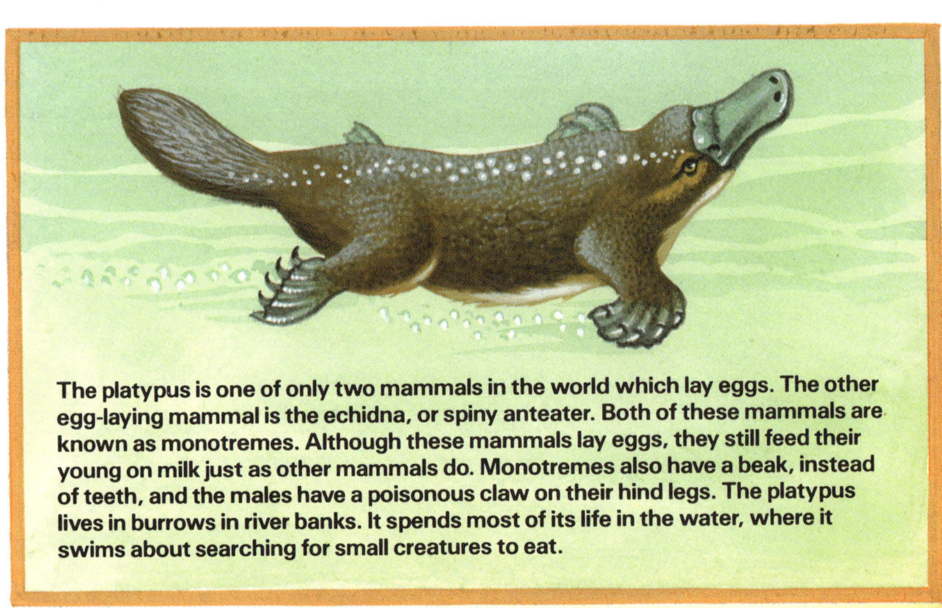

The platypus is one of only two mammals in the world which lay eggs. The other egg-laying mammal is the echidna, or spiny anteater. Both of these mammals are known as monotremes. Although these mammals lay eggs, they still feed their young on milk just as other mammals do. Monotremes also have a beak, instead of teeth, and the males have a poisonous claw on their hind legs. The platypus lives in burrows in river banks. It spends most of its life in the water, where it swims about searching for small creatures to eat.

Right: This scene shows some more Australian animals. Many of Australia's animals live in the hot dry interior of the country known as the outback. The frilled lizard raises the frill around its neck in order to frighten would-be predators, although the animal is in fact harmless. Note the young kangaroos, known as joeys, which are carried in their mothers' pouches. Flocks of budgerigars roam across Australia, feeding on seeds. In some places they are considered pests, as they feed on crops. In the forests of eastern Australia the koala is to be found. This mammal looks like a small bear with tufted ears. It feeds on eucalyptus leaves and is only active at night. The emu is a large, flightless bird. Although it cannot fly, it can run extremely fast to escape from its enemies.

Life on the African Plains

Below: A cheetah chases after a group of impala, scattering giraffes and ostriches as it does so. Although very young elephants might fall victim to predatory cats, the cheetah would not dare attack with a protective adult elephant close by.

The African Plains are vast belts of grassland stretching across the continent. Some of the African Plains occur in the temperate regions of southern Africa, but most are found in the tropics. Rainfall occurs for only a short period in tropical grasslands. When it rains the grass grows high and lush. Between the rains the land looks rather barren, with few trees.

The grasses provide food for a variety of large animals such as elephants, giraffes, deer and zebra. Smaller animals like insects and snakes find shelter and food among the grasses, too.

Life on the African Plains can be harsh. The grazing animals must constantly be on the lookout for predators, and they may struggle to survive in years when droughts occur. During droughts, the grasses shrivel and die, fires are common, and even waterholes may dry up. Then, the great herds of grazing animals must often roam far in search of water and food.

Animals of the African Plains

One of the most astonishing sights in nature is to see the huge herds of animals such as wildebeest, many thousands of individuals strong, as they move slowly across the plains. Sometimes herds of different animals such as zebras and antelopes will join together for mutual protection, the whole herd alert to danger.

Few of the grazing animals compete with each other for food, for each type specializes in eating different vegetation. The tall acacia trees can only be reached by giraffes, smaller bushes are eaten by other grazers like eland, and the grasses are eaten by rhinoceroses, zebras and gazelles.

The birdlife of the African Plains includes the huge, flightless ostrich as well as birds of prey like the secretary bird, which attacks and eats snakes. Hidden among the vegetation are hordes of insects, spiders and other small creatures. These provide food for small rodents and reptiles, which themselves may fall prey to other predators.

Predators

The many herds of grazing animals provide food for the carnivorous animals of the African

Plains. The best known of these are the cats—the lions, cheetahs and leopards. Antelopes and zebras form the main food for the cats. Each of the cats has its own special way of catching food. Lions normally hunt in groups. They may lie in wait at a waterhole or surprise a herd on the open plain. Often some of the lions in the group will chase prey to where other lions are waiting.

Cheetahs rely on their great speed to catch prey. They will wait silently, crouched among the grass, until they single out a victim from the herd. Then they bound after their prey at great speed. Cheetahs can run at over 100 kilometres per hour for short distances, but they soon become exhausted and give up the chase if they have not caught their prey within about 40 metres. Leopards eat small antelopes and birds.

Once the prey is brought down and killed with a bite to the neck, it is dragged to safety and eaten. Members of a pride of lions will often feed on the prey together, the strongest individuals taking the best pieces. When the cats have had their fill, it is time for other creatures of the plains to join the feast. First to arrive will often be the hyaenas, which scrap noisily between each other over the left-overs. Then come the vultures, and finally the scavenging insects.

In the Amazon Jungle

The Amazon Jungle is part of a huge rain forest covering much of tropical South America. Rain forests are special kinds of forest. Here, the temperature is high all year round and heavy rainfall occurs frequently. These conditions are just right for rich plant growth, and within rain forests we find many kinds of luxuriant trees and other plants such as orchids, ferns and bromeliads.

LIFE IN THE JUNGLE CANOPY

Although some animals are to be found living on the floor of the rain forest, many more creatures live among the canopy. Brightly coloured birds like toucans and parrots fly among the treetops, and groups of monkeys live in noisy family groups. Here we also find the predatory animals such as snakes, and harpy eagles which swoop down to snatch birds and small monkeys in their sharp talons. Sometimes predatory cats such as jaguars also climb the trees in search of prey.

Right: The world's tropical rain forests are found in equatorial regions where the temperature is always above 65°F and where at least 200 centimetres of rain falls each year.

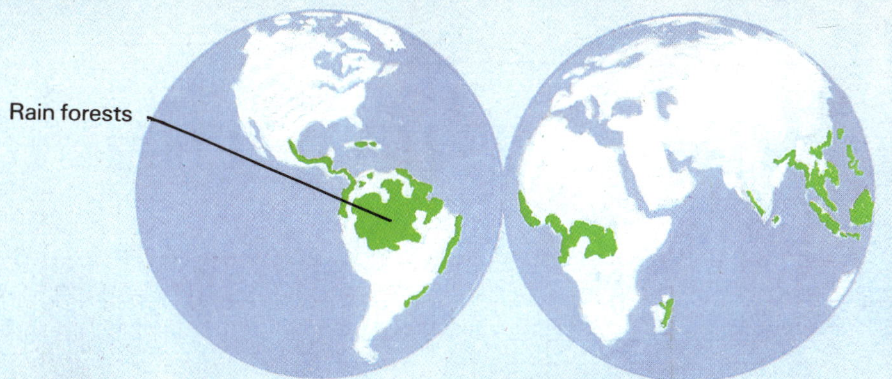

The trees in rain forests consist of species like ebony, teak and mahogany. They grow close together, with their upper branches thrusting towards the sky. The top-most parts of the trees form a layer known as the canopy. The leaves of the canopy layer shade most of the sunlight due to their density, and so the forest floor is gloomy, with little plant growth. Most of the other plants of the rain forest grow on the trunks and stems of the trees, about 15 metres off the ground where some sunlight still penetrates. Plants which grow on other plants are called epiphytes.

Below: Seen from the air, the Amazon rain forest appears as a dense canopy of leaves. These upper branches are the home of many animals, such as monkeys, birds and snakes. On the floor, where little light penetrates, live creatures such as huge beetles and centipedes, as well as deer and the pig-like tapir. Jaguars move stealthily among the tree roots, waiting to pounce on their prey.

Life in the Mojave Desert

Deserts are found in parts of the world where there is very little rainfall. Most deserts are hot, dry places but some are very cold. On average, less than 25 centimetres of rain falls each year in deserts. Sometimes it may not rain in the desert at all for several years. Then torrential rain will fall, bringing floods which sweep through the desert.

Deserts are usually rocky or sandy, with little vegetation. The plants and animals which live in deserts have to find special ways of living in the harsh, dry conditions.

The Mojave Desert is in southern California, in the U.S.A. It covers an area of about 38,850 square kilometres.

Animals of the Mojave Desert

As in other hot deserts, animals of the Mojave Desert have developed special methods to help them keep cool and conserve water. Many animals burrow underground by day. In the Mojave Desert the temperature may be 35°C lower underground than on the surface by day. At night, when the temperature has dropped, the animals leave their burrows to hunt for food.

Animals such as desert rats have large eyes which help them to see at night. Hunters such as snakes rely on sensing the warm bodies of their prey in order to track them down.

When desert animals must travel about during the daytime, they move very fast so that they do not remain too long in contact with the hot ground. The roadrunner uses its great speed to catch lizards and small snakes.

Plants of the Mojave Desert

The largest and most spectacular plants of the Mojave Desert are the cacti. Saguaro cacti can grow to over 16 metres in height. Cacti absorb water very quickly when it rains and then store it in their thick leaves and stems. Plants which can do this are called succulents. The creosote bush is another strange desert plant which can actually survive being dried up by the sun's rays.

When the rains come, all the desert plants quickly bloom, and seeds which had lain dormant in the ground suddenly germinate. For a short while the barren desert becomes a flower-filled landscape.

Animals such as the scorpion and the kangaroo rat build underground burrows.

Above: The desert is full of animal life, although most species spend the day hiding away in the shade. The map at the top shows the main deserts of the world.

Ends of the Earth

The polar regions cover the most northern and most southern areas of the globe. In the northern hemisphere the polar region is called the arctic, and in the southern hemisphere it is called the antarctic. Animals that live in the polar regions have to endure some of the harshest conditions on earth. There are permanent snow and ice fields over much of the areas, and there is always the chance of a sudden icy blizzard, even in summer.

Rich Life in the Seas

Most of the land in the polar regions is either covered with snow, or is frozen just below the surface. As a result, few animals can find food here.

However, the polar seas are extremely rich in food, and provide food for birds such as penguins, and mammals such as bears, whales and seals.

Long Days and Nights

In the polar regions, the sun never climbs very high in the sky, even at the height of summer. As a result, its warming effect is never properly felt. However, throughout the summer it never sets, giving the polar inhabitants perpetual daylight.

In the winter, however, the sun only rises above the horizon each day for a few hours at most. At the poles themselves it does not rise at all for several weeks. Many of the animals move away from the poles in winter to find milder climates and more daylight.

Top left: Some animals stay and endure the arctic winter. A few, like the ptarmigan, turn white to camouflage them against the snow.

Left: In the summer, the arctic tundra is visited by many migrant birds such as waders and geese. The ptarmigan and arctic fox lose their white coloration.

Below: The dramatic antarctic is home to millions of penguins.

How Animals Communicate

Animals communicate with each other for several reasons. Between members of the same species they may communicate in order to find a mate in the breeding season, or to warn other rivals that they have chosen a particular place as their territory. Watch a bird such as a robin. In the breeding season it will fly from tree to tree, or perhaps perch on a fence, and each time it lands it will sing. In fact, what it is really doing is flying around the boundaries of its territory, telling other robins to keep out.

The fiddler crab communicates by means of 'hand signals'. When the male wishes to attract a female, it sits on the sand and beckons the female with a wave of one of its pincers, which is specially enlarged.

Above: Songbirds, like the American robin shown here, sing to warn other birds that they have chosen a territory, and to attract a mate.

Left: Male moths can pick up the scent given off by females using their feathery antennae.

Below: The male fiddler crab tries to attract females to mate with him by waving one of his pincers, which is specially enlarged.

Whales swimming through the vast oceans of the world communicate by sound. Scientists have often recorded the mournful calls of the humpback whale, which can carry over hundreds of kilometres.

Animals often tell each other about the presence of food, or warn each other of possible danger. Sometimes one bird in a feeding flock will alert the others to a source of food and the rest of the flock will quickly gather to feed. In order to survive, different species of animals have learned to heed each other's warnings. The frantic clap of wings made by a pigeon alarmed in a wood is also a signal to other animals such as squirrels and deer that danger is present. And when lions come to feed at an African waterhole the first grazing animal to spot the danger quickly alerts the others, as zebra, wildebeest, gazelles and even elephants all run to safety.

Many animals are poisonous, and this prevents them being eaten

Right: Timber wolves live in forests and snow-covered wastes. They communicate to other members of the pack by means of special calls. This helps to keep the pack together, even at night.

by predators. Animals which are poisonous, or which are highly venomous, advertise this fact by having brightly coloured bodies. Coral snakes, arrow-poison frogs, ladybirds, kingfishers and wasps are just a few of the many animals which tell other animals that they are poisonous. Sometimes other harmless animals mimic these poisonous species in the hope that they, too, will be left alone by predators.

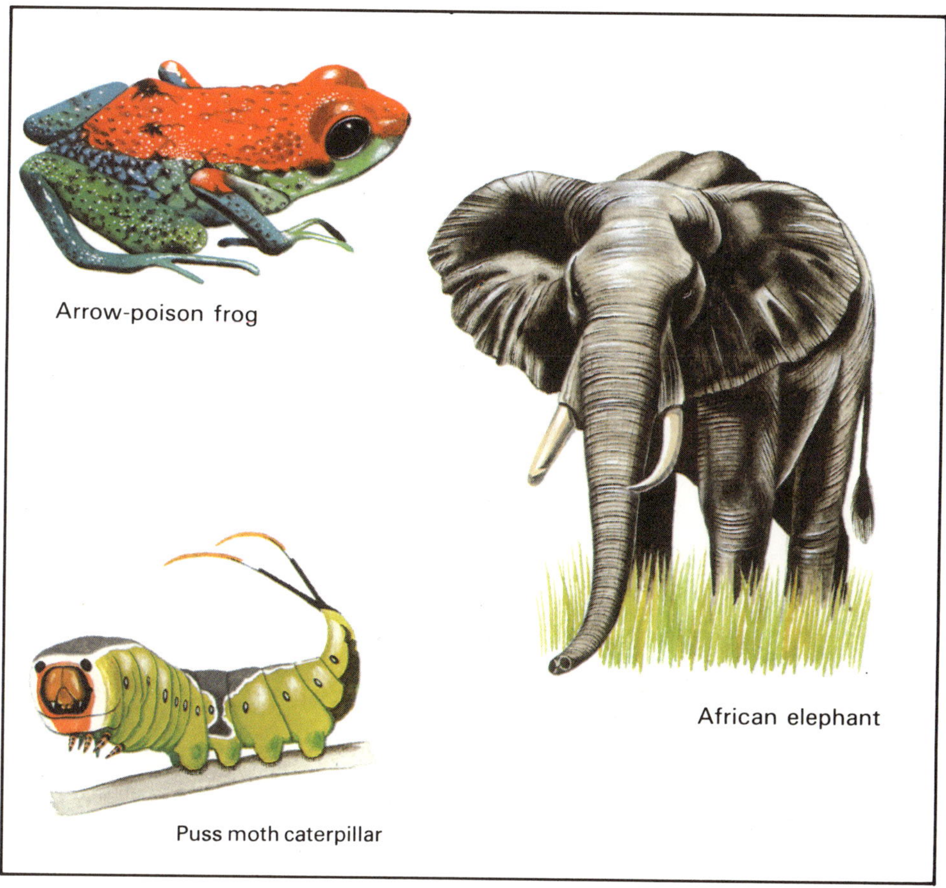

Right: The skins of arrow-poison frogs contain a very powerful poison, and their brightly coloured bodies warn predators that they are poisonous. The African elephant gives warning to its enemies by drawing its ears forward in a threat display. The caterpillar of the Puss moth is harmless, but tries to alarm would-be predators by rearing up and showing its eye spots.

THE BEE DANCE

One of the most fascinating examples of communication is to be found among honey bees. Hive members returning from a foray tell other bees about the location of good sources of food, by performing a kind of dance. The speed and direction of the dance indicate the position of the food very accurately. If the food is within 100 metres or so the bee performs a round dance — quick circular motions made first in one direction and then the other. If the food is further away she performs a waggle dance — a figure-of-eight performed while waggling her abdomen. The angle at which she performs the dance tells other bees about the direction of the food.

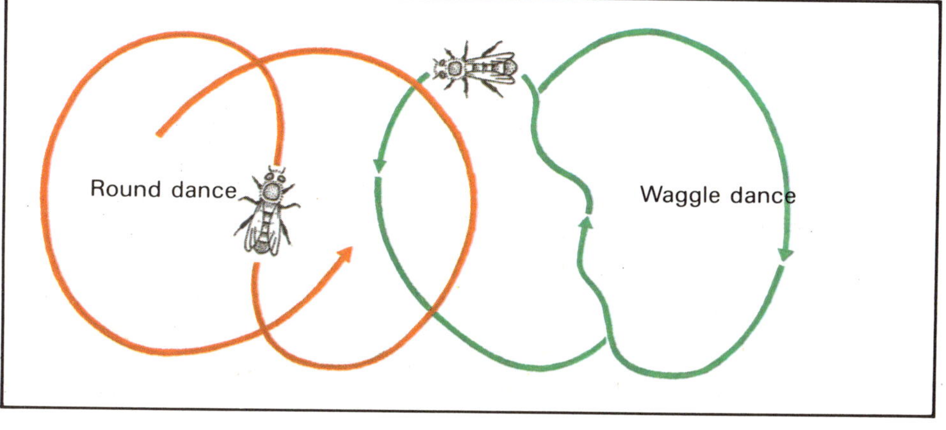

Right: Honey bees returning to their hive after a food foray inform other hive members about the location of food, by performing a sort of dance.

Attack and Defence

For many animals, life in the wild is harsh. Most grazing (plant-eating) animals are preyed upon by meat eaters. Even animals which eat other creatures may themselves become a meal for a bigger predator.

Animals which attack others in order to eat them use many different methods to catch their prey, and an array of weapons with which to overpower them. For example, large predatory mammals such as lions, tigers and cheetahs have powerful limbs, and jaws armed with sharp teeth. Most big cats chase their prey before knocking it to the ground with a blow from their paws. Then they bite the victim in the neck, quickly killing it.

Sometimes animals attack each other for reasons other than to catch food. During the mating season particularly, animals will fight, occasionally to the death, over a mate or a territory.

Above: The trapdoor spider lies cunningly concealed in a trap, waiting for prey. As soon as a likely meal passes, the spider rushes out and overpowers its victim by injecting it with a deadly venom.

Above: The peregrine (left) dives from the air on to its victim. It can fly at such great speed that few birds can escape it. The polar bear (right) catches seals which emerge from ice holes to obtain air.

Left: Dragonfly larvae have special jaws called a mask with which they grab their prey.

Left: Lions hunt their prey together. Some of the lions chase the prey to where other lions are lying in wait for them.

There are many ways in which animals try to avoid being eaten. Some animals are poisonous or distasteful to eat, and warn would-be predators of this fact by wearing bright 'warning colours'. Others are just too big to be eaten; no predator could attack and kill a fully grown rhinoceros or elephant.

Some creatures are quite able to look after themselves. Many types of antelope have sharp horns which can cause severe wounds to unwary predators. Others live in a herd, and are able to run fast. Quite often the predator will single out the weak or old members of the herd and leave the stronger members to escape.

Many creatures, particularly insects, rely on camouflage or a secretive way of life to avoid being spotted by predators.

Left and above: Animals like the eland have sharp horns which can inflict a severe wound on predators. The porcupine is armed with a great number of spiny quills. These sharp spines give a painful lesson to any animal attempting to eat the porcupine.

Above: The mountain hare has protective colouration. In winter its coat turns white to match the snow. The stick insect relies on being mistaken for a twig. The pangolin curls into an armour-plated ball, while the hawkmoth uses the 'eyes' on its wings to alarm would-be predators.

Friends and Foes

Above: The speedy cheetah makes a dash to catch an antelope. But if the antelope can keep running the cheetah soon tires and gives up the chase.

Above: The pangolin, or scaly anteater, rolls itself into a ball when danger threatens.

Below: The Australian frilled lizard tries to frighten away its attackers by hissing and spreading out a fold of skin.

Animals in the wild have few friends, and many enemies. On land, the grazing animals, such as deer, antelopes, elephants and bison form large herds. A herd itself is a protection against danger, but often the stronger animals deliberately guard the weaker; for example, when musk oxen form their protective circle they place the younger animals in the centre.

In the sea, fish often stay together in huge shoals, and so do many species of whales. Whales and dolphins have been seen supporting and escorting an injured companion.

Animal Partners

Some of the most remarkable 'friendships' are those between animals of different species. They live together for mutual support, a state known as *symbiosis*. The hermit crab lives in a discarded shell, and has a sea anemone on the outside of the shell. The stinging cells of the sea anemone protect the crab, and the anemone benefits from food particles discarded by the crab. When the crab grows and moves to a bigger shell, it takes its sea anemone with it.

Little fishes known as wrasses living in the Indian and Pacific oceans act as cleaners for bigger fish. They eat parasites, such as fish-lice, on the bodies of the larger fish, which queue up to be cleaned.

Above: Some examples of insect camouflage on a tree trunk. At the top a katydid nestles among leaves of a similar colour. The stick insect poses to look just like a twig on the side of the tree, while the treble bar moth has colouring like the trunk itself. The leaf-insect 'hides' by sitting openly on a leaf. Even bright colours can be a camouflage, as can be seen in the yellow crab spider crouched on a buttercup awaiting its prey.

When Danger Threatens

Danger in the wild comes from the *carnivores*, the flesh-eaters, who prey on the *herbivores*, the plant-eaters. The term 'carnivore' includes not only such large animals as tigers and hyenas, but also many birds which prey on small creatures such as insects.

Some animals, such as the springbok, rely on their speed to escape from danger. The hedgehog curls up, presenting a predator with an unappetising ball of prickles. Many animals have *protective coloration*: their colouring matches that of their background. For example, a white Arctic hare is hard to see against snow. Small creatures often look like something else: there are moths which resemble bird droppings, insects which look like leaves or twigs, and plaice which match the sea bed on which they lie. Many creatures, such as wasps, are harmful to eat, and have *warning coloration*, generally red or yellow and black. Other animals mimic this coloration, even though they are not unpleasant to eat; for example, hoverflies look very like wasps.

Right: Oxpeckers are African starlings which spend their lives living on large animals, such as the Cape buffalo shown here. They feed on ticks and other parasites which they pull out of the animals' skin. They warn their hosts when danger is about by uttering loud cries and flying about in the air. The large animals take no notice of their companions except when they give the alarm. The birds make their nests in holes in trees, or in rocks.

Animals and their Young

Above: Many species of snakes coil themselves around their eggs. This helps to protect the eggs from predators, but also keeps the eggs warm during incubation.

Animals must reproduce in order that each species can continue. The simplest animals, like the amoeba, reproduce by simply splitting into two. Most animals, however, reproduce by means of a male and female mating together.

For many animals, the first task in reproduction is to find a safe place to lay their eggs or give birth to their young. In the insect world, many species lay their eggs in holes or crevices, or glued safely to the underside of leaves away from the eyes of predators. Some insects, for example some kinds of wasps, even put in a supply of food ready for the young to eat when they hatch.

Other species of animals may have to fend for themselves as soon as they are born.

Below: Mammals, like the opossum shown here, feed their young with milk, produced in the mammary glands of the female.

Above: Many insects undergo a four-stage life cycle. The adult lays eggs which hatch into larvae. The larvae feed and grow, and turn into pupae. From the pupae emerge new adults.

Right: A reed bunting feeding its chicks at the nest.

Many kinds of birds build nests in which to lay their eggs and rear their young. During spring, both parents will often work ceaselessly hour after hour, building an elaborate nest of twigs, grass, leaves and down so that their chicks will hatch safe from enemies such as snakes or other birds.

Some animals display a remarkable degree of parental care towards their young. We often think of crocodiles as ferocious animals but, as soon as the young hatch from their eggs, the mother crocodile carries her babies gently in her mouth to a safe place.

Once born, the job of finding food begins. Although many creatures must find food for themselves when they are born, most of the more advanced animals, such as birds and mammals, rely on their parents to provide nourishment for them until they have grown big enough to feed themselves.

Above: Scorpions show a remarkable form of parental care. When the young have hatched, they climb on to their parents' back and are carried about, safe from danger.

Below: Many animals, like these brown bear cubs, are taught how to hunt by their parents. Play fighting also helps them to fend for themselves in the wild. The mother watches over the cubs while they play.

Animals on the Move

Each year many animals make long journeys in search of food, shelter from harsh weather or a place to breed. These journeys are called migrations. Among the best-known migrations are the annual journeys from Europe to Africa made by cuckoos, swallows, warblers and many other birds.

Many animals live in parts of the world where the climate changes throughout the year. In the temperate zones these changes are regular and are called seasons, although in the tropics there is little change from one month to the next. As the seasons change the conditions can become less suitable for feeding or breeding; some animals can cope with these changes,perhaps by hibernating, but others overcome the threat of harsh conditions by moving to more favourable areas.

Insect Migration

We normally think of migration as being undertaken only by larger animals, but many insects, especially some butterflies, undergo migrations as lengthy as those carried out by birds and mammals.

The red admiral is a colourful butterfly which is found in north Africa and the Mediterranean. Each spring, however, some of them move northwards into Europe and breed as far north as England and Scandinavia. The following autumn, a few of the new generation fly south to escape the onset of the cold weather. Although many perish on the way, some survive the return journey — an impressive feat for an insect.

Above: The herds of wildebeest on the African plains follow the rains. In this way they can eat the new growth of grass. The animals are constantly on the move, covering hundreds of kilometres a year.

Left: European eels are spawned in the Sargasso Sea. The Gulf Stream carries the young eels to our shores and they move into fresh water. After about ten years they return to the sea to breed.

Above: In some years lemming numbers reach plague proportions. To escape the overcrowding many go on mass migration. At this time predators such as snowy owls and foxes benefit from their abundance.

Below: Bird migrations often involve vast distances and require spectacular navigational skills. Many migrate from northern regions to more temperate areas. Some, like arctic terns, cross to the southern hemisphere for the winter.

Migration of Larger Animals

Both marine mammals as well as land-living species undergo migrations. Seals leave their breeding grounds in spring, and return to warmer seas to spend the winter. When feeding becomes poor many mammals just keep moving until they find better conditions. Herds of animals in Africa follow the rains, grazing the fresh growth of grass that follows. Some reptiles also migrate. Marine turtles haul themselves on to the same beach every year to lay their eggs.

The movements of birds have evolved to become extremely predictable, and they often follow distinct routes over long distances. The arctic tern is famous for its travels from its breeding grounds in the arctic to its wintering area in the antarctic. In its travels it covers over 32,000 kilometres a year, and probably over 160,000 kilometres in its lifetime. As well as travelling further in its life than most other living creatures it also sees more daylight than species which remain in one area.

Nocturnal Life

When darkness falls over the town and countryside, another world comes to life — the world of nocturnal plants and animals. The animals which had been active during the day seek safe places to shelter for the night, and other creatures take their place.

When the sun goes down the temperature drops, and moisture forms on the ground and in the air. These are ideal conditions for the small creatures which thrive in a damp environment. Earthworms, insects, spiders, centipedes and other small invertebrates creep from their hiding places to find food or to mate.

In the darkness other, larger creatures feel safe, too, and leave their burrows to hunt. Mice and voles search for insects, seeds and other food items. They in turn fall prey to the hunters of the night — the predatory animals such as foxes, stoats and owls. Larger creatures such as deer leave the safety of the woodland to graze in the clearings.

Most nocturnal animals are specially adapted for their night-time existence. Badgers and deer have a well-developed sense of smell, for instance. Deer also have acute hearing. Moths can detect the scent given off by females from great distances. Owls swoop down on their prey without warning, for their wings make scarcely a sound as they beat.

Animal Architects

Above: The Great Barrier Reef is the only structure built by animals which can be seen from space. It was constructed by tiny marine organisms called coral polyps, like the ones seen here, which encase themselves in a tough chalky shell.

When we visit a cathedral we marvel at the skill of the men who constructed it. But if we consider the building feats achieved by some animals, often working entirely alone, some of these are equally amazing.

Animals build for similar reasons to people; to make a shelter from the elements, protection for themselves or their young, or in order to catch food. Animal shelters and homes range from the little tubes of caddis larvae, to the often complex nests which birds build for their eggs and young.

Some animal constructions are quite small, and are designed to accommodate only their makers. Others, such as termite mounds, are enormous, and provide a home for thousands of individuals. Building material also varies. Some animals use materials they gather from their surroundings, and others produce the building material themselves. Spiders, for instance, make their webs from the silk which they spin inside their own bodies.

Nests

Birds are among the most familiar of animal architects. At the start of each breeding season, many species of birds build a nest in which to lay their eggs and rear their young. Many nests are quite simple structures consisting of interwoven twigs or grass stems. Sometimes these are neatly arranged, and in other species they are a jumbled mass of material. Often these nests are placed in the fork of a tree or in a crevice, giving the nest support.

Nests are usually built from material which the birds gather close by. This makes the nest quick to build, as well as helping it blend into the surroundings. The long-tailed tit's nest is particularly difficult to spot, since the birds use a mixture of lichens, spider's silk and dry grass.

Below: Many spiders produce sticky silk which they spin into beautiful but deadly webs. These trap flying insects which the spider quickly bites and paralyses. The victim is then wrapped in silk, ready for eating later.

Other Homes

The larvae of the caddis fly are also skilled architects. These soft-bodied freshwater insects protect themselves by building tough tubes in which to live. Each species has its own favourite building material; some use plant leaves, others use sand or snail shells. The tube is open at one end, and the larvae drag themselves around using their front legs.

Termites are tropical insects which live in large colonies. Their mounds, which are usually made from soil, are very strong. They can also become very large, often exceeding 6 metres in height. This feat is all the more remarkable when you consider that the animals which built them were less than 1 centimetre long.

Above: Weavers are birds which build nests together in thorn bushes. The nests are very carefully woven from grass, and often have long entrances designed to prevent predators getting in.

Above: Many wasps are social insects which build papery nests in which to rear their young. They construct layers of hexagonal-shaped chambers in which the eggs are laid and the young wasp larvae grow.

Below: The beaver lodge is a remarkable structure of twigs and logs with its own underwater entrance. Built on a river, the beaver constructs a dam to raise the water level around the lodge.

Living Together

Below: Grazing animals, like these herds of buffalo on the American plains, join together in great herds for protection. The herd guards the youngest members which might fall victim to predators, and each animal is always on the lookout for any signs of danger.

We have already seen how the world of plants and the world of animals are closely interwoven together. Without plants, no animals could survive. Many animals would have no source of food or shelter, and this would mean no food for the other animals which prey upon them. Likewise, many plants rely on animals for their survival. Without insects and other animals, many flowers would not be pollinated nor would their seeds be dispersed. Insectivorous plants such as the sundew and the Venus fly trap must also catch and digest insects and other small creatures in order to obtain the nitrogen which is essential for their healthy growth.

Many animals also need the help of other animals to help them avoid predators or to help them find food. For this reason some species join together in great herds. Sometimes, however, animals which are quite unrelated join together to improve their chances of survival.

PLANT AND ANIMAL PARTNERSHIPS

Although most of the partnerships in nature are between different species of animals, or between different species of plants, there are some partnerships in which a plant and an animal live together. Many aquatic animals, such as corals or the freshwater creatures known as Hydra, contain green algae within their bodies. The algae have a safe place in which to live, and in return they provide oxygen and absorb the various waste materials produced by the animals. Within the bodies of many animals live bacteria. These help to break down the cellulose found in plants and so enable the animals to digest grass.

Above: The hermit crab often carries an anemone around on its shell. The anemone protects the crab, and in return shares some of the crab's food.

Above: Clown fishes are brightly coloured inhabitants of coral reefs. They feel quite safe swimming among the deadly stinging tentacles of anemones which also inhabit the reef. The anemones let the clown fishes swim among their tentacles to escape predators, in return for ridding them of parasites.

Animal Partnerships

In the Animal Kingdom there are many examples of animals living together for the benefit of one, or both, partners. The simplest form of this behaviour is when one animal spends its life living close to another animal for its own benefit. Birds such as cattle egrets ride on the backs of grazing animals as they walk slowly through the long grass. As they walk, they disturb insects and other creatures which the egrets then swoop down to feed on. Although the grass-eating animals do not themselves benefit from the association, they do not suffer either.

Sharks are often attended by fishes known as remoras. The remoras attach themselves to the sharks by means of suckers on their heads. They eat the scraps left over by the shark when it feeds, which in return uses the remoras as a 'vacuum cleaner' service, for they remove parasites from the shark's skin.

Sometimes two different species of animals rely so much on each other for food or protection that they are unable to live so successfully on their own. This condition is know as symbiosis. There are many examples of symbiosis in the Animal Kingdom. The partnerships shown on this page between the hermit crab and the anemone, and between the clown fishes and the anemone are two.

Top left: Oxpeckers are African birds which are allowed to feed on the skin parasites of rhinoceroses. In return, the oxpeckers alert the rhinoceros of danger.

Left: Spur-wing plovers and dikkops help keep crocodiles free of parasites.

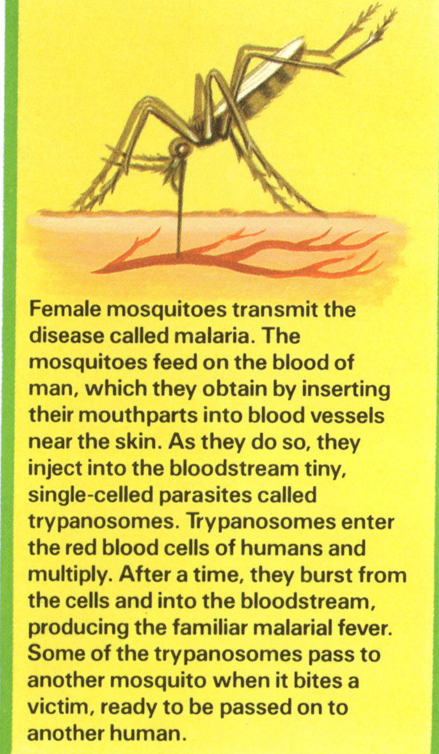

Female mosquitoes transmit the disease called malaria. The mosquitoes feed on the blood of man, which they obtain by inserting their mouthparts into blood vessels near the skin. As they do so, they inject into the bloodstream tiny, single-celled parasites called trypanosomes. Trypanosomes enter the red blood cells of humans and multiply. After a time, they burst from the cells and into the bloodstream, producing the familiar malarial fever. Some of the trypanosomes pass to another mosquito when it bites a victim, ready to be passed on to another human.

Animal Curiosities

Throughout the Animal Kingdom there is an incredible array of sizes, shapes, colours and behaviour. At first glance some of these animals may seem particularly strange, but in nature there is always a good reason for any peculiarity. What, to our eyes, may seem strange, is in fact essential for an animal's survival in its chosen environment. The more we study nature the more we realize that there is no 'ordinary' animal. Each species has evolved its own shape, colour and behaviour to ensure its survival.

Nevertheless, there are some animals whose appearance and life styles almost defy the imagination. There are fishes that fly and others that walk on dry land, mammals that can fly in complete darkness, spiders that spin webs under water and many more extraordinary creatures.

Below: Many animals hide from predators, but not so the colourful sea slug which actually advertises its presence. The bright colours warn predators of its unpleasant taste.

Unusual Spiders

Many spiders spin silk webs to catch their prey. As if this extraordinary feat were not enough, some use their silk in even more unusual ways. For example, the spitting spider does as its name suggests; it spits silk over its prey until it is so entangled that it cannot escape.

The purse web spider does not spin an ordinary web at all. Instead, it lives under ground in a silken tube strengthened with plant fibres. Part of the tube lies on the ground, however, and when a passing insect crawls over its surface, the spider rushes up the tube and grabs the victim through the tube. Needless to say, the tube needs considerable repair after this!

Below left: The water spider spends its life under water, constructing air-bells in which to live and lay its eggs.

Below right: The crab spider pretends to be the inside of a flower. When an insect lands, it is grabbed by the waiting spider.

Odd-shaped Eggs

Bird's eggs are sometimes brightly coloured and sometimes camouflaged to escape the attention of predators, but nearly all eggs are the same shape. The egg of the guillemot is different, however. Its egg is pear-shaped, being blunt at one end and pointed at the other. Guillemots breed on sea cliffs and lay their eggs on steep ledges. The peculiar shape of the egg prevents it rolling off the edge. If it becomes dislodged it just rolls round in a circle.

Above: Flying fish can glide for over 100 metres, using their specially developed fins. This ability helps them escape when being pursued by predators under the water.

Below: Until 1938 the coelacanth was thought to have been extinct for 60 million years. This 'living fossil' is now known to live in deep water in the Indian Ocean.

Below: The goliath beetle of Africa is the heaviest insect on earth. Weighing over 100 grams it is heavier than many small mammals and birds.

Below: Most species of bat are able to fly in complete darkness, easily avoiding obstacles and catching insects on the wing. They use echolocation to find their way around, although they are not in fact blind.

Above: The axolotl is a remarkable amphibian related to salamanders. It lives its life as a permanent larva, and uses feathery gills with which to breathe. Even more remarkably, it can even breed while still a larva.

Cactus wren

Above: The cactus wren is a rare example of an animal which uses a tool. By holding a stick in its beak, it prises insects out of crevices in bark.

The Plant Kingdom

There are nearly half a million species of plants on the earth. With the exception of some primitive types, they all need three basic ingredients to survive: air, light and water. Plants are found in almost every type of habitat, including most of the surface waters of the world's rivers, lakes and oceans. Most species live in temperate and tropical regions but plants are extremely adaptable, and have even conquered such inhospitable environments as hot mineral springs and dry deserts with little rainfall.

How Plants Live

Although there is a great variety in the shape, size and appearance of plants, all of them, apart from fungi and bacteria, make their own food using simple raw materials and energy from the sun. They trap the sun's rays using the green pigment chlorophyll, and combine water and carbon dioxide (a gas present in the air) to make simple sugars. They also release oxygen into the air — which all living things need for respiration. This process, known as photosynthesis, is vital to the survival of all life on earth.

Plants include some of the smallest things as well as the largest. The surface waters of ponds and lakes teem with microscopic algae, many of which exist as just a single cell. By contrast, the giant redwood trees of California may grow over 90 metres tall.

Some plants reproduce so rapidly that new individuals are produced within minutes by simple division, whereas the bristlecone pine trees live to be more than 3,500 years old. Each year they still produce a new crop of seedlings.

Almost all types of plants are eaten by one species of animal or another. Animals that eat plants are called herbivores, and they include such creatures as cows and locusts. Other animals eat only meat and these are called carnivores. However, the animals that they prey upon will have eaten plants. If it were not for plants, animal life could not exist on earth.

Right: This evolutionary 'tree' shows how the different groups of plants have evolved throughout the geological ages.

Dicotyledons
Ginkgo
Conifers
Tertiary/Quaternary Period
Monocotyledons
Cretaceous Period
Cycads
Jurassic Period
Ferns
Angiosperms
Gymnosperms
Horsetails
Triassic Period
Permian Period
Mosses
Liverworts
Club mosses
Carboniferous Period
Brown Algae
Fungi
Lichens
Devonian Period
Bryophytes
Fungi
Green Algae
Silurian Period
Red Algae
Fungi
Ordovician Period
Golden Algae
Slime moulds
Blue-green Algae
Bacteria
Cambrian Period

Lowly Plants

The lowly plants have existed on earth for much longer than the flowering plants we grow in our gardens. Many have remained almost unchanged for millions of years. They generally have a simple structure and, with the exception of ferns, do not have supporting fibres. This means that they cannot grow to any great size.

Most of the lowly plants contain the green pigment chlorophyll. This helps them to trap sunlight energy and make their own food. The exceptions are the bacteria and fungi which have to use other sources of food such as the dead bodies of plants or animals, and are responsible for decay.

Advanced plants mostly have flowers and produce seeds in order to reproduce. Lowly plants, however, often reproduce by means of spores. The bacteria and many of the algae reproduce by simple division, and like the rest of the lowly plants they need damp conditions.

Left: Mushrooms and toadstools are the reproductive parts of fungi. Most of the fungus lives underground forming a complex web of thread-like strands called a mycelium.

The spores of fungi are always present in the air. They grow and thrive when food, such as bread, is left in damp conditions, forming patches of mould.

Algae

Algae are the simplest forms of true plant life. They possess chlorophyll, but many contain other pigments, giving them many colours. They range from simple, single-celled plants which make ponds appear green, to immense seaweeds, several metres long.

Fungi

Unlike algae, fungi cannot make their own food and depend on a ready-made source. Many feed on dead matter and cause decay.

Lichens are strange plants which are the result of a partnership between algae and fungi. The relationship is called 'symbiotic', and both partners benefit from it. Their growth is very slow.

Mosses and Liverworts

Mosses and liverworts are simple plants which lack true roots and stems. They are restricted to damp habitats and reproduce by spores produced in capsules.

Ferns

Ferns are generally long-lived plants. They have a rootstock and a strong, supporting stem which can conduct water and dissolved food substances. This means that they can often reach a large size. They still produce spores during reproduction and depend on water for part of their life cycle.

Below: Fern spores are spread by the wind

Above: Ferns come in a variety of forms. Some are rooted in the soil and grow to large sizes. Others colonize walls or even grow on other plants, but all need damp conditions.

Right: Seaweeds are algae which grow on rocky shores. Mosses are common on walls and in damp places.

Flowers

Flowers contain the male and female cells of a plant. For successful fertilization to take place, the pollen (male cells) from one plant has to reach the ovum (female cell) of another. However, plants have one basic problem—they are rooted to the ground. To overcome this, plants have evolved all sorts of ways of transferring the pollen.

Despite their unlikely appearance, grasses are true flowering plants which produce countless thousands of minute pollen grains that are carried by the wind. Not surprisingly, most end up in the wrong place but enough reach another grass flower to ensure their survival. More typical flowers have colourful petals and often a strong smell to attract insects. In return for a meal of nectar, the insects transfer the pollen to the next flowers which they visit.

Flower Plan

Although some species of flowers sometimes contain only the male or the female cells, most contain both but go to great lengths to prevent self-fertilization.

Despite a great variety of appearances most flowers conform to a basic plan with sepals, colourful petals, stamens which produce the male cells called pollen, and a central stigma containing the female cell or ovule.

The parts of a flower

How a plant disperses its seeds

Above: Coconut seeds float in the sea.

Above: Willowherb seeds are carried by the wind.

Above: Burdock seeds have hooks which catch in the fur of animals.

Above: Poppy seeds are shaken from the pod.

Above: Flowers occur in a whole variety of shapes, sizes and colours. They range from the inconspicuous flowers of grasses to the large and showy flowers of the sunflower. Some plants, such as the cactus, flower only briefly and irregularly, whereas others are in bloom for a full season—or even continuously.

Trees

Trees, woods and forests cover nearly one quarter of the earth's surface. They are a very important part of our environment, for they provide food, homes and shelter for a great variety of other living creatures. The key feature of all trees is their central woody stem or trunk. This grows as the tree grows, and provides support and protection.

Trees can broadly be split into those which drop their leaves each year (called deciduous trees) and those which do not (called evergreens). Many evergreens bear their seeds in cones and have needle-like leaves; these trees are called conifers. There are also some broadleaved trees, such as holly, which do not shed their leaves each autumn.

Palms are a special group of trees. Although they are deciduous, they are placed in a group of plants called monocotyledons, the group which also includes the grasses.

Above: The hazel is a deciduous tree. It has tiny female flowers, and male catkins which produce pollen. The seeds are encased in a tough shell, or nut.

Right: By counting the rings on a cross-section through a trunk you can estimate the age of a tree. Each ring roughly corresponds to a year's growth.

Below: There are many different types of tree throughout the world. Here are some typical species.

How Trees Grow

As well as providing support for the tree, the trunk carries the water supply for the leaves of the tree. Although the centre of the trunk is usually tough and woody, the outer tissues consist of tubes through which water is transported from the roots to the leaves. Some of this tissue also transports food from the leaves down to the roots and other parts of the tree. The trunk tissues are protected by the bark. If this is damaged, the tree may die.

Leaves are the vital life-supply for all plants. They produce food by photosynthesis, using the energy of sunlight to combine water and carbon dioxide. There are many different shapes of leaves, but all are designed to make best use of the available light.

In some parts of the world, the climate does not change during the year and the tree grows continuously. But elsewhere the climate varies, with either cold and hot seasons or dry and wet periods. The tree grows best in favourable conditions and, as a result, we can see growth rings in the trunk, each dark ring corresponding to a year's growth. In a good year the ring is thicker than in a poor year. By counting the number of rings, the age of the tree can be worked out.

In order that trees may reproduce, the female part of the flower must first be pollinated. In some trees, male and female parts are in the same flower. In others, they are in separate flowers or, sometimes, on separate male and female trees, such as holly.

Above: The spruce is a conifer with tiny flowers. The fertilized seeds grow and ripen in cones.

Right: An oak tree supports a whole community of plants and animals. Some animals feed on its leaves or acorns while others in turn prey upon them. Many beetles and fungi feed on the decaying wood and leaves.

Records in Nature

HIGHEST MOUNTAINS (metres)

Above: During the Earth's long history, many mountain ranges have been created by movements in the rocks, and then gradually worn away by water, wind and ice. The highest peaks today are in the youngest mountain ranges – the Himalayas, Andes, Rockies and Alps. There may well have been higher mountain peaks millions of years ago.

There is a great range in the size of living things. At one end of the scale there are viruses – organisms on the very borders of life – which are too small to be seen without the aid of powerful electron microscopes. At the other extreme there is the blue whale which can weigh over 120 tonnes, and the Californian redwood tree which grows as high as a 35-storey building.

The life-span of living things also varies greatly. Small insects, such as the mayfly, have an adult life-span which can be measured in days or even hours, while the tortoise may live for 150 years or more. Some plants, especially trees, live far longer. There are giant sequoia trees in California which began life almost 4,000 years ago, and bristlecone pines which are as old as the pyramids.

LONGEST RIVERS (approx. kilometres)

Nile, Africa, 6,700
Mississippi-Missouri, N. America, 6,300
Amazon, S. America, 6,250
Yangtze, Asia, 5,200
Congo, Africa, 4,600
Amur, Asia, 4,600
Lena, Asia, 4,400

The table shows the average maximum life-spans of various animals. It is based upon records of animals in captivity. Animals in the wild have shorter life-spans.

The speed at which animals move is often difficult to measure accurately, but there is no doubt about the record holder. The spine-tailed swift can fly at more than 180 km/h. The fastest land animal is the cheetah, which can exceed 100 km/h over short distances. The proverbial tortoise does well to reach 1 km/h.

Wonders of the Plant World

In its own way, the Plant Kingdom is just as unusual and fascinating as the Animal Kingdom. Also, like the Animal Kingdom, the Plant Kingdom has its share of curious-shaped species, and plenty of species with strange and bizarre ways of life.

We have only to think of fungi, those peculiar plants which can grow without the aid of sunlight and seem to pop out of the ground overnight, to realize that some plants are very odd. However, as we shall see, there are others which can confuse scientists even more!

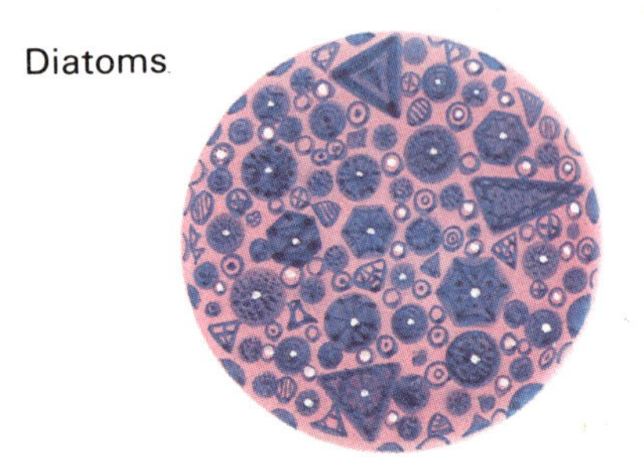

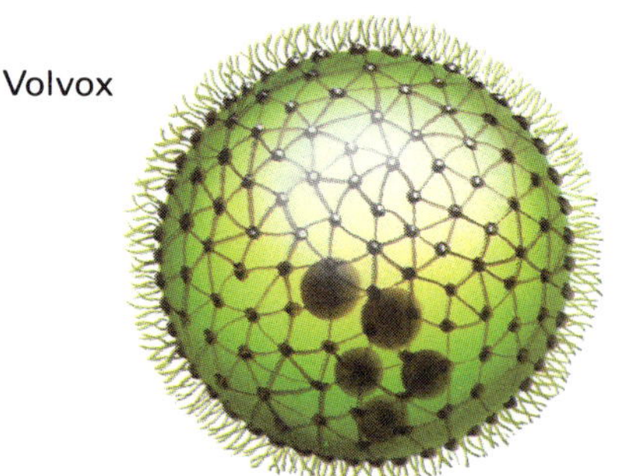

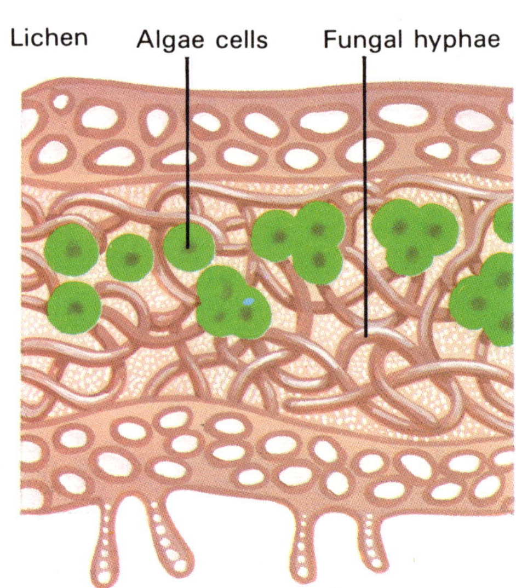

Left: Diatoms and colonies of single-celled algae like Volvox can move freely about in the water.

Right: This cross section through a plant stem shows how its water and minerals are absorbed by the suckers of mistletoe. Mistletoe grows on trees such as poplars.

Bottom left: Lichens are unusual plants made up of single-celled algae sandwiched between a fungus.

Lowly Plants

One of the ways that we normally use to tell animals from plants is by the fact that animals can move about, while plants stay fixed in one place. But among the group of primitive plants called the algae there are several species that can actually move about on their own.

Diatoms are tiny algae living within a silica shell, which can glide about in the water. Volvox is a plant which consists of a group of single-celled algae each of which has tiny hairs. By beating these Volvox can also move about in the water.

Flowering Plants

Among the flowering plants there are also many unusual species. Although most flowering plants

make their own food by using the energy of sunlight trapped in their leaves, there are some kinds which 'steal' the minerals and food substances from other plants.

Dodder is a twining, parasitic plant whose stem sends suckers into the host plant.

Mistletoe is known as a partial parasite. It can make its own food using sunlight, but first it must rob a host plant of some vital minerals.

The most unusual flowering plants are the carnivorous species. They live in places, such as bogs, which lack the nitrogen they need for healthy growth. Therefore they catch insects and other small creatures in special traps (which are really special leaves) and absorb the nitrogen from their bodies.

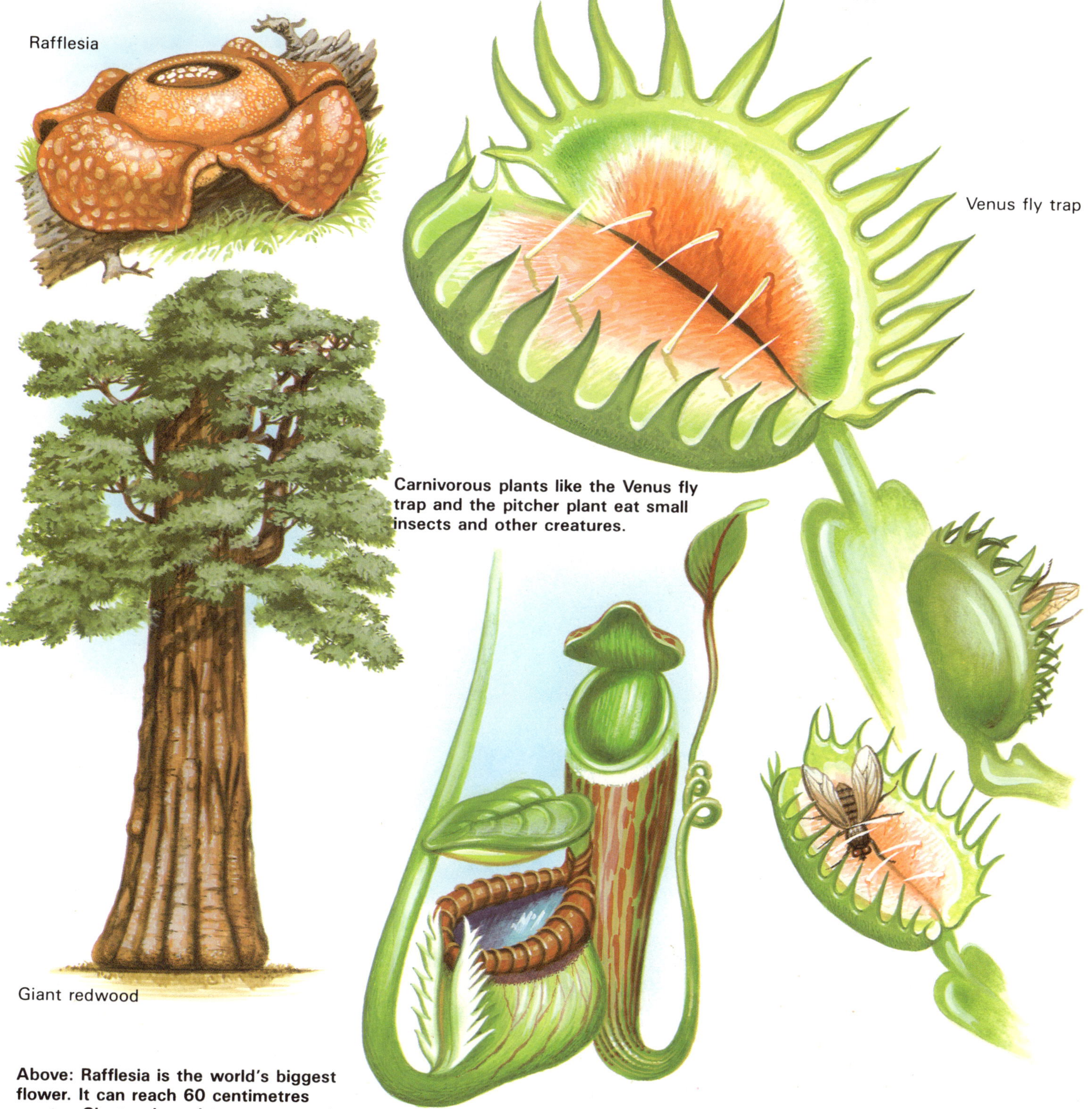

Carnivorous plants like the Venus fly trap and the pitcher plant eat small insects and other creatures.

Above: Rafflesia is the world's biggest flower. It can reach 60 centimetres across. Giant redwood trees can reach heights of 110 metres.

Glossary

Abdomen One of the main parts of the body of an arthropod such as an insect. The abdomen is made up of the end segments of the body. In vertebrates, it is the part of the body containing the intestines.

Algae A large group of non-flowering plants. The biggest and most important algae are the seaweeds, but many single-celled species of algae also exist.

Amphibian A cold-blooded vertebrate animal descended from fishes. Most amphibians must return to water to lay their eggs. Common amphibians include frogs, toads, newts and salamanders.

Antenna One of the projections found on the head of insects and crustaceans used for sensing the environment. Some crustaceans also use their antennae for swimming.

Bird A warm-blooded vertebrate animal whose body is covered with feathers. Birds descended from reptiles and lay shelled eggs.

Bivalve A kind of mollusc whose shell is made of two parts. Common bivalves include mussels, cockles and scallops.

Breeding season The times of the year when certain animals come together for the purpose of mating and producing young.

Burrow The underground home of an animal.

Camouflage The ability of a living creature to disguise itself to avoid being seen by its enemies.

Carnivore A meat-eating animal, such as a lion or tiger.

Caste One of the different kinds of individuals in a social insect colony, such as a worker or a guard.

Caterpillar The larva of a moth or butterfly. The job of the caterpillar is to eat and grow, in readiness for turning into an adult.

Catkin A group of tiny flowers, usually hanging down from a main branch or stem.

Chlorophyll The green pigment found in all groups of plants except for the fungi. Chlorophyll is contained within cell structures called chloroplasts. It is used to trap the energy from sunlight to enable plants to make their own food.

Cone The reproductive structure of a conifer, bearing either female parts (ovules) or male parts (pollen). In dry weather the cones open to shed their pollen and enter the female ovules.

Conifer A cone-bearing tree, such as a pine, spruce or larch.

Coral A small, marine animal related to the anemones which builds around itself a chalky skeleton. Some corals live by themselves, but many form huge colonies.

Deciduous tree A tree which sheds all its leaves at a certain time of the year.

Dinosaur A member of a group of prehistoric reptiles which lived during the Mesozoic Era. Most dinosaurs were extremely large.

Dormant In a resting state. Many plants undergo a dormant period when conditions are unsuitable for further growth.

Embryo A stage in the development of an animal or plant following fertilization of an egg or ovum.

Exoskeleton The hard, protective outer covering of the arthropods. The exoskeleton is composed of a material called chitin.

Fang A long front tooth of a snake, or of a carnivore such as a lion.

Feather The special structures covering the bodies of birds. Feathers are mainly used for flight, insulation, camouflage and display.

Fish A cold-blooded, aquatic vertebrate animal whose body is covered with scales.

Flower The reproductive structure of flowering plants. Some species have flowers which contain both the male parts (pollen) and female parts (ovules), and others have the male and female parts on separate flowers.

Fossil The preserved remains of a dead animal or plant.

Frond The leaf of a fern, or the strap-like parts of a seaweed or lichen.

Germination The process by which a seed produces a root and shoot, eventually forming a new baby plant.

Gill A structure found in aquatic animals used for extracting oxygen from the water when breathing.

Habitat The particular place where plants or animals live, such as a seashore or a woodland.

Herbivore A plant-eating animal, such as a cow or zebra.

Holdfast The root-like structure by which seaweeds attach themselves to rocks.

Incubation The process of maintaining eggs at the correct temperature whilst they undergo development prior to hatching.

Invertebrate One of the large group of mainly small animals which do not possess backbones.

Larva The stage in the life cycle of some animals before they turn into adults. Larvae are usually capable of fending for themselves, but look different from the adult form.

Lichen A slow-growing, non-flowering plant consisting partly of an alga and partly of a fungus.

Mammal A warm-blooded vertebrate animal which suckles its young. Common mammals include elephants, dogs, cats, monkeys and tigers.

Mammary gland Gland found in female mammals which produces milk for feeding the developing young.

Mesozoic Era A time in the earth's history comprising the Triassic, Jurassic and Cretaceous Periods. The Mesozoic Era lasted from about 225 to 60 million years ago.

Metamorphosis The change, in an animal, from the larval form to the adult.

Migration The seasonal movement of certain animals from one place to another, in search of better food or breeding conditions.

Mushroom The spore-producing body of certain fungi.

Monotreme A primitive, egg-laying mammal found in Australasia. Two living species are known; the platypus and the spiny anteater or echidna.

Moss A lowly, spore-bearing green plant. Mosses occur on the bark of trees, on walls, in ditches and other damp places.

Nectar A sugary fluid produced by many flowering plants, which is attractive to insects.

Nocturnal Active at night.

Nut A hard, woody structure containing a plant seed. For example a hazel nut.

Nymph A stage in the life cycle of certain insects. Nymphs resemble the adults except that their wings are not usually developed.

Ovule The egg-containing structure of a seed-bearing plant.

Parasite A plant or animal which lives in, or on, another organism and from which it gets its food.

Petal One of the parts of a flower. Petals are usually brightly coloured to attract insects to visit the flower.

Plankton Microscopic animals and plants which float in the upper layers of the world's oceans and lakes.

Pollination The transfer of pollen from the anthers to the stigma.

Pupa The stage between the larva and the adult in certain insects such as butterflies and moths. Also known as a chrysalis.

Predator An animal which hunts other animals for food.

Reptile A cold-blooded, scaly vertebrate animal descended from amphibians. Most reptiles lay shelled eggs. Common reptiles include snakes, lizards, crocodiles and tortoises.

Rodent One of a group of gnawing mammals. Rodents are the most widespread of all mammals and include squirrels, rats, mice and beavers.

Scale One of the flat, horny plates covering the bodies of certain animals such as reptiles and fishes.

Spore Reproductive structure produced by certain lowly animals and by many groups of plants. Spores are released from the parent and eventually give rise to new individuals.

Stigma The region of the female flower parts on which pollen must land during fertilization.

Succulent A plant which stores water within its tissues, for instance a cactus.

Temperate zone The regions of the world lying between the tropical zones and the polar regions.

Territory The part of a habitat which an animal defends against others of its species, usually for the purpose of breeding.

Thorax One of the parts of the body of an insect. The thorax is composed of three segments and bears the legs and wings.

Toadstool The spore-producing body of certain fungi.

Tropical zone The regions of the world lying to the immediate north and south of the equator.

Venom The poisonous liquid produced by certain animals such as some species of snakes and spiders. Venom is injected into the victim by biting or stinging, sometimes as a means of protection and sometimes to render the prey harmless before being eaten.

Vertebrate One of the group of mainly large animals which possess a backbone. Vertebrates include fishes, amphibians, reptiles, birds and mammals.

Nature Index

Numbers in italics refer to illustrations.

R

S

T

V

W

X

Z

THE CHILDREN'S FIRST SCIENCE ENCYCLOPEDIA

370 004

The CHILDREN'S FIRST SCIENCE ENCYCLOPEDIA

Contents

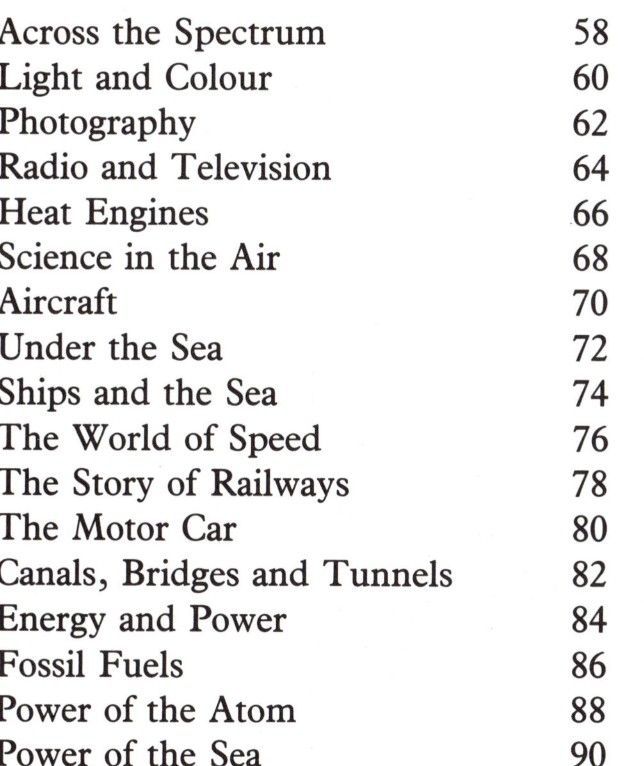

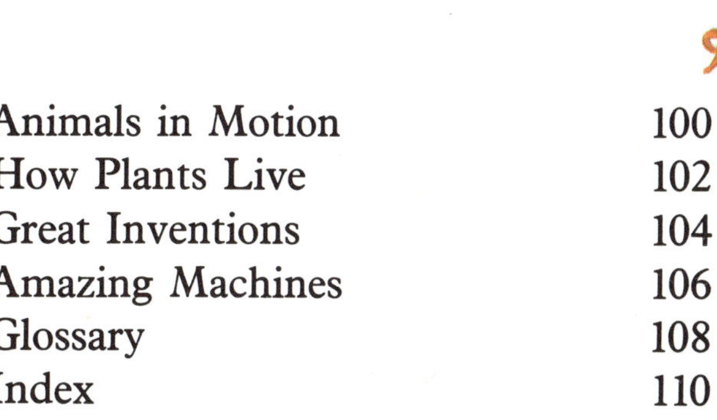

Stars and Galaxies

If you look up at the sky on a clear night you will see thousands of stars – each a small twinkling point of light. Yet many of these stars are ten thousand times more powerful than our Sun. Most of the stars we see belong to our galaxy – the Milky Way. The Milky Way is a huge flat disc of stars – million upon million of them – all going round and round like a giant bicycle wheel. Our Sun is a quite ordinary star lying about two-thirds of the way out from the centre. The Sun travels around the hub of the galaxy at a speed of 250 km per second. But the Milky Way is so vast that it takes the Sun 225 million years to make just one trip all the way round.

Other galaxies of stars exist far out beyond our own Milky Way. As far into space as astronomers can look with their biggest telescopes, more and more galaxies come into view. And each of these galaxies contains thousands of millions of stars. These great galaxies are so far away they appear

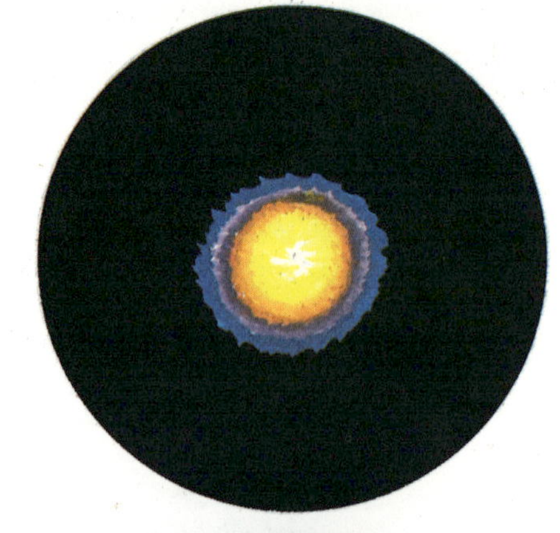

1 2 3 4

A big telescope such as the one in the picture sees far into space. It is aimed by computers and moved by electric motors. Among the objects it can pick out are great clouds of gas and dust that hide the stars behind them, such as the Horseshoe nebula (1), the Ring nebula, about 1400 light years away (2), the Crab nebula (3), the Orion nebula, in which new stars are forming (4), and the Dumbell nebula (5), a huge cloud over 20 million million kilometres across.

Left: It is possible that all the matter in the Universe was once contained in a 'primeval atom' which exploded some 20,000 million years ago. This is known as the Big Bang theory.

A star such as the Sun is born when a cloud of gas and dust contracts and starts to glow. There are several stages in the life of a star. Gravity first of all pulls the cloud material together and makes it heat up. This may take 20 million years. Nuclear fusion reactions begin inside the star and keep its temperature steady for thousands of millions of years. Then many stars begin to swell up, the surface cools and they become *red giants* or supergiants. Our Sun will not reach its red giant stage for thousands of millions of years. After millions more years it will shrink once more to become a small very dense *dwarf star* about the size of the Earth. It will be so dense that a tablespoonful of its matter will weigh several tonnes.

dimmer than single stars in our own galaxy. The light we see from some of them has taken 8,000 million years to reach us, and light travels at a speed of 300,000 km every second!

And the astronomers have discovered a strange thing. The distant galaxies are all flying away from us and from each other. The further away they are, the faster they appear to be flying apart. Back-tracking the flight of the galaxies, astronomers have worked out that they must all have been close together or all joined up about 20,000 million years ago. This may have been the time of the Big Bang when all the universe began.

Astronomers are puzzled by strange objects called *quasars*. These bodies on the edge of space throw out very powerful radio and light waves – so powerful that their light is greater than a hundred galaxies, even though their size is quite small. Perhaps the quasars will help us to find out how our universe came into being.

There are many different sizes and colours of stars in the night sky. They represent different stages in the life of a star.

Stars and Galaxies

Our Sun is one of 100,000 million stars in the Milky Way galaxy. Galaxies of stars are held together by gravity. Most galaxies are spiral in shape, like the Milky Way galaxy shown on the next page. The Milky Way galaxy measures 100,000 light years across, but it is only one of millions of galaxies in the Universe.

Scientists believe that stars form from clouds of hydrogen, other gases and dust. Gradually, gases are drawn towards the centre, which becomes hot and glows. Nuclear reactions, caused when hydrogen is changed into another gas, helium, create enormous energy. Soon a new star is born, with a surface temperature of 6,000°C. Our Sun is a medium-sized star. Its diameter is 1.4 million km, 109 times the size of Earth.

Death of a Star

Stars last many millions of years, but eventually the hydrogen supply runs down, and the core of helium starts to collapse. This causes great heating and the outer parts of the star swell up like a balloon, creating a red giant star. When our Sun becomes a red giant, it will swallow up Mercury and Venus, and possibly Earth too. But this will not happen for 5,000 million years. At last, the red giant shrinks to become an Earth-sized, cold, white dwarf star.

CONSTELLATIONS: KEY

Northern Hemisphere
1 Pegasus, Flying Horse
2 Cygnus, Swan
3 Hercules, Kneeling Giant
4 Boötes, Herdsman
5 Ursa Major, Great Bear
6 Leo, Lion
7 Gemini, Twins
8 Orion, Hunter
9 Perseus, Champion
10 Polaris, Pole Star
11 Ursa Minor, Little Bear

Southern Hemisphere
12 Cetus, Sea Monster
13 Orion, Hunter
14 Lepus, Hare
15 Vela, Sails
16 Crater, Cup
17 Crux, Southern Cross
18 Lupus, Wolf
19 Scorpio, Scorpion
20 Sagittarius, Archer
21 Capricornus, Sea Goat
22 Phoenix, Phoenix

Below: Star charts of the northern hemisphere, left, and the southern hemisphere, right, show star constellations. There are 88 constellations in all. They are named after people, animals and objects and each has a Latin and an English name. (See key, right.)

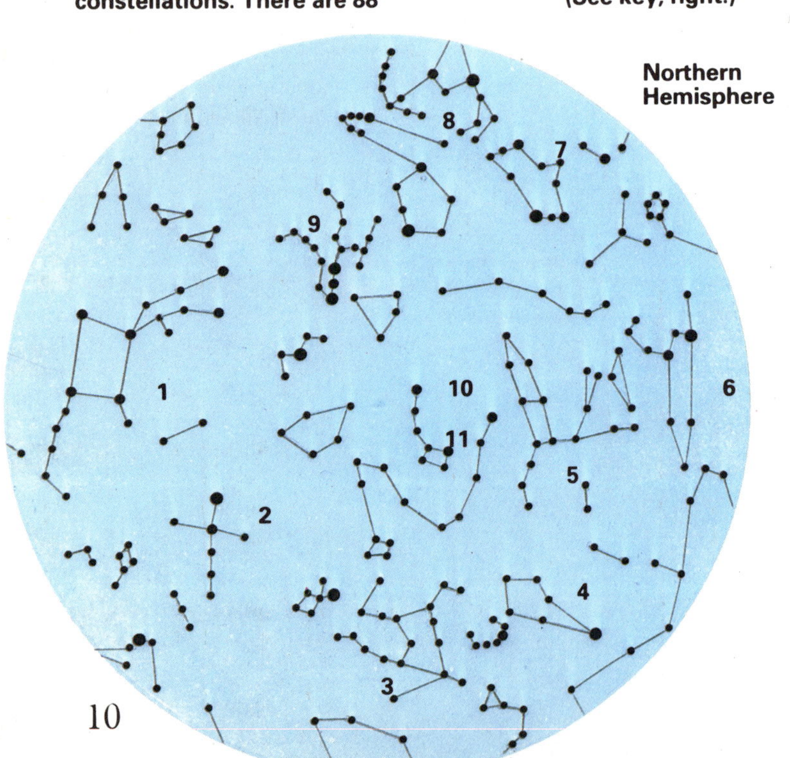

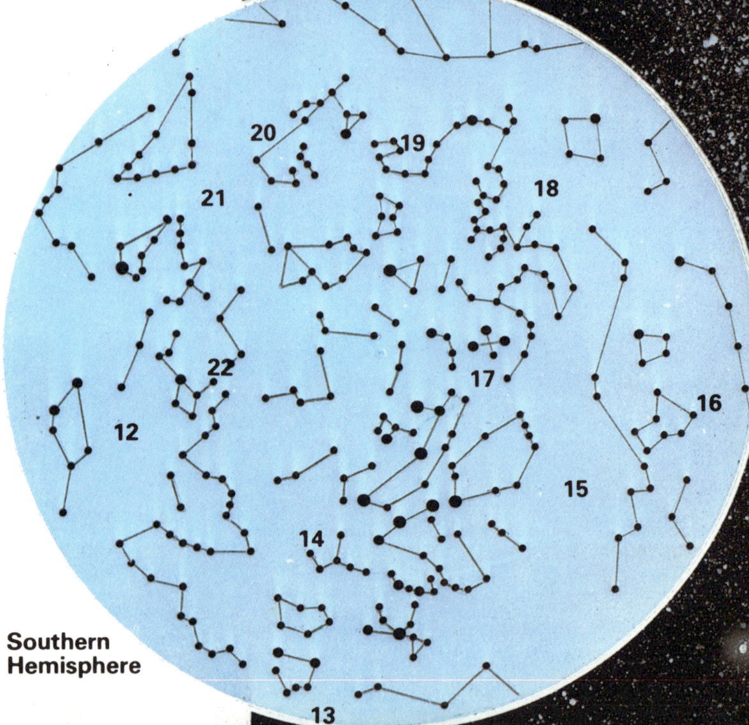

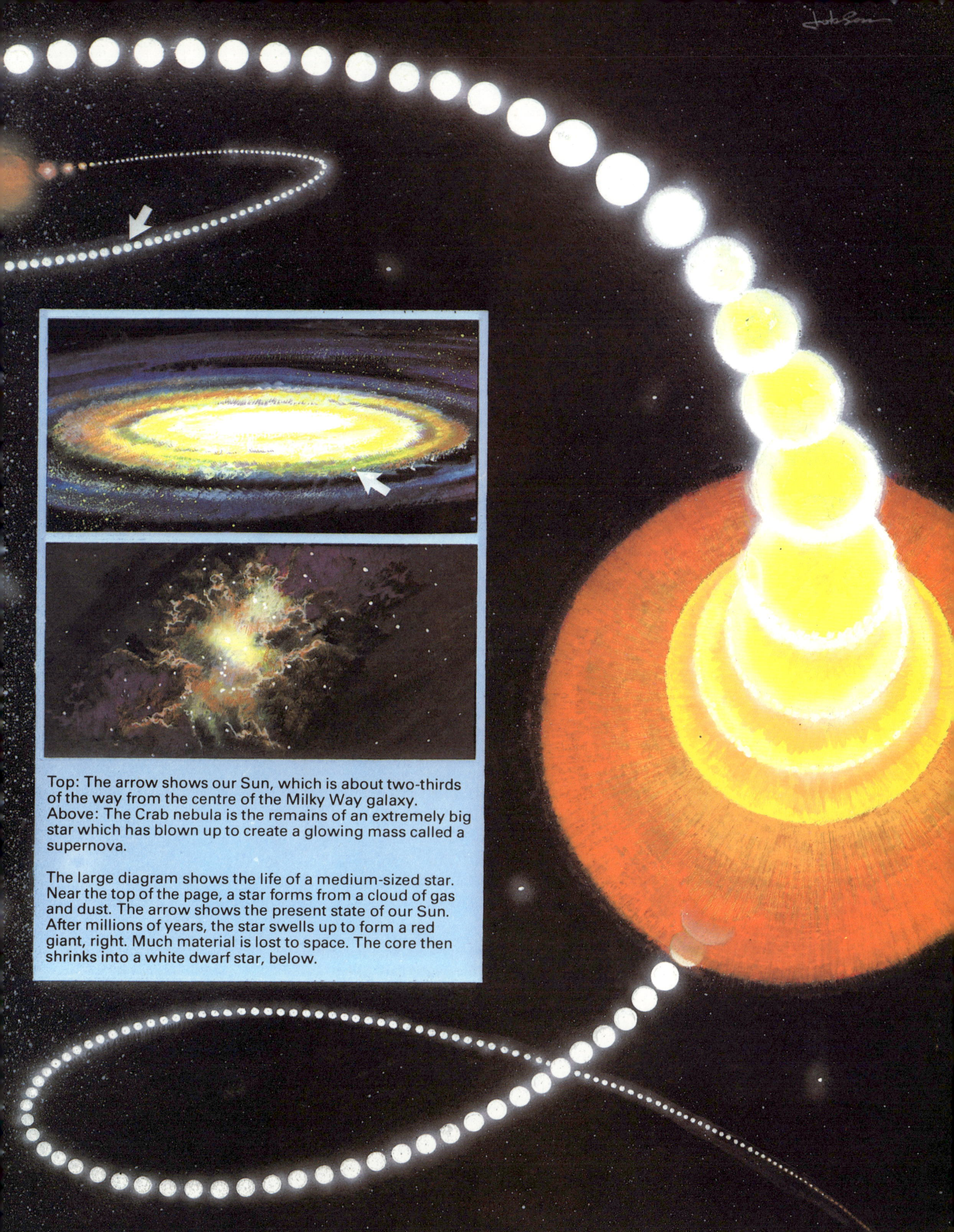

Top: The arrow shows our Sun, which is about two-thirds of the way from the centre of the Milky Way galaxy.
Above: The Crab nebula is the remains of an extremely big star which has blown up to create a glowing mass called a supernova.

The large diagram shows the life of a medium-sized star. Near the top of the page, a star forms from a cloud of gas and dust. The arrow shows the present state of our Sun. After millions of years, the star swells up to form a red giant, right. Much material is lost to space. The core then shrinks into a white dwarf star, below.

Family of the Sun

The Sun is a huge ball of very hot gas, about 1,380,000 kilometres across. But it is only one of millions of stars in the universe. It looks big to us because it is so close. The next nearest star to us is about 250,000 times as far away as the Sun. Dark spots can often be seen on the Sun's surface. These sunspots come and go and their number varies from year to year. They look dark because they are cooler than the surrounding hot gas. The Sun also shoots out huge flames from its surface. These *prominences* can stretch out for a million kilometres into space before falling back into the Sun.

Never look at the Sun, either with the naked eye or through the lens of a telescope or binoculars.

Our planet Earth speeds through space on its yearly journey around the Sun. Eight other planets, their moons and smaller lumps of rock and ice are also travelling endlessly around the big, hot Sun. All these put together we call the Solar System – 'solar' means 'of the Sun'.

The Sun is a huge ball of very hot gas, so big that more than a million Earths could be fitted inside it. It is the Sun's *gravitation* – its pull through space – that keeps all the planets and other bodies in the Solar System travelling around it.

Our home planet, Earth, takes just over 365 days to go once round the Sun. We call this a year. The Earth is also spinning like a top. It takes 24 hours to go round once. This is a day. It is the Earth's daily spin that makes the Sun and the stars appear to rise and set. All the other planets go round the Sun and spin, just as Earth does. But they all spin at different speeds and orbit the Sun in different lengths of time. The far-away planet Pluto takes about 250 years to go once around the Sun. Little Mercury, the closest planet to the Sun, goes around it in only 88 days.

6 7 8 9

The more scientists find out about the other planets in the solar system, the more we realize what a wonderful place Earth is (3). Everything about Earth is just right for us. It is the right distance from the Sun. If it were as close as Venus, the heat and the choking carbon dioxide gas would have built up a thick, boiling hot atmosphere. Mars is our closest neighbour, but if the Earth was as distant from the Sun and as small as Mars water vapour would turn to ice and most of the atmosphere would vanish into space. If Earth were as far away from the Sun as Neptune, the whole planet would be nothing but frozen hydrogen surrounding a core of rock and ice. The picture above shows what it might be like on Neptune.

PLANET FACTS

Mercury, the smallest planet, is not much larger than our Moon. It is 4850 km across, the Moon is 3476 km (1).
Venus, the second planet, is the brightest object in the sky after the Sun and Moon. Scientists think Venus is so bright because it is surrounded by an unbroken layer of white clouds (2).
Mars is called the Red Planet because its surface rocks are reddish. Viking space probes landed on Mars but could find no sign of life on the planet (4).
Jupiter (5) is the biggest planet. Its surface is made up of swirling clouds with one big red spot always there.
Saturn is well known for the rings that encircle it. The rings are made of tiny ice fragments (6).
Uranus (7) and *Neptune* (8) are distant icy planets. They look like small greenish discs when seen through even the largest telescope.
Pluto (9) is usually the planet furthest from the Sun. Some astronomers think it may be even smaller than Mercury. Its orbit is so strange that at the moment it is closer to the Sun than Neptune.

The Earth in Space

The Earth spins around on its axis once every 24 hours. Its axis is an imaginary line that goes through the North and South Poles. But because the Earth's axis is tilted, we have seasons. If the axis were straight up and down in relation to the Sun, we would get the same amount of sunlight every day. There would be no spring, summer, autumn and winter.

Towards the end of June, the northern part of the Earth tilts most towards the Sun. Around the North Pole it is sunlight for 24 hours a day. The southern parts of the Earth get less sunlight at this time because the Sun's rays strike the southern lands at a slant. At the South Pole it is dark all the time. Six months later, the Earth's axis tilts the other way. At the end of December, the seasons are reversed. Southern lands get most sunshine, northern lands get very little. It is summer in Australia and winter in Britain.

Twice a year, at the end of March and September, the Sun shines directly over the equator. All parts of the world have equal night and day.

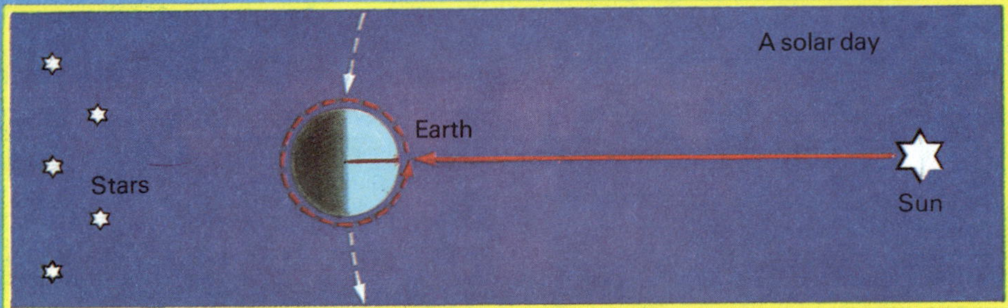

The movements of the Sun, planets, their moons and the stars are very complicated. The Moon moves round the Earth; the Earth moves round the Sun, the Sun moves round our galaxy. And they all spin on their own axes. We set our clocks according to the time it takes the Earth to spin around once on its axis *relative to the Sun* – 24 hours. But during those 24 hours the Earth also moves on its journey round the Sun. And it also moves relative to the stars.

The Earth revolves once, relative to the stars, in 23 hours 56 minutes – four minutes less than the solar day. This means that the stars appear to rise and set four minutes earlier each day. This adds up to 24 hours a year. The stars rise and set at a given hour only once a year, on or near the same date. This is when the Earth has returned to the same point in its trip around the Sun. To make their jobs easier, astronomers often use something called *siderial time* – star time. In this siderial time scale, the stars rise and set at the same time every day.

How the Planets Began

Astronomers have wondered for many years how the planets came into being. Most of them now believe that the planets formed from the vast cloud of gas and dust that produced the central Sun. The cloud consisted mostly of hydrogen, the commonest element in the universe. Over millions of years the gas condensed in clumps. Heavy elements like iron and nickel formed at the core of each planet. Above this central core floated lighter elements that became the rocks of the Earth's crust. Thus our Earth was born about 4,600 million years ago. First it was an inferno of molten red-hot rock surrounded by burning gases. Gradually it cooled down, rain filled the oceans and Earth became the planet that we know.

The four pictures show the same places at different seasons as the Earth circles the Sun. On the left, it is summer in northern lands and winter in the south. On the opposite page, it is autumn in northern lands and spring in the south. At the bottom of this page, it is winter in the north and summer in the south. The picture below shows spring in northern lands and autumn in the south.

It is summer in the northern hemisphere when the northern part of the Earth tilts towards the Sun (1). In March and September, the Sun shines right down on the equator. All parts of the world have equal day and night (2). In December it is winter in the north and summer in the south (3).

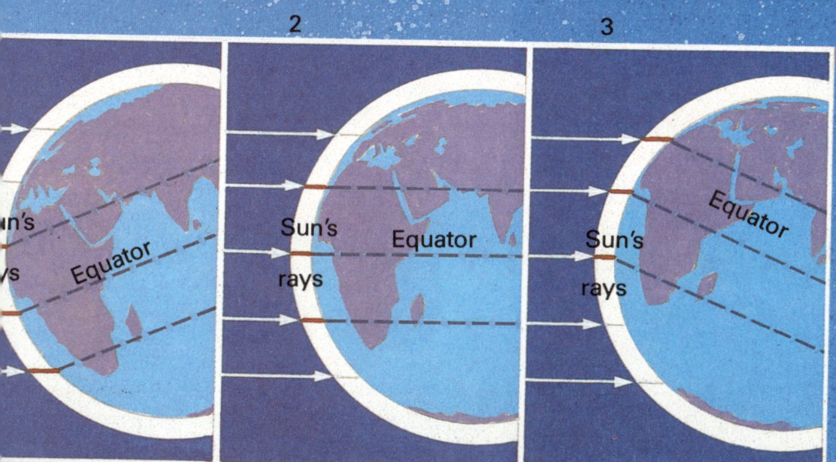

The Moon

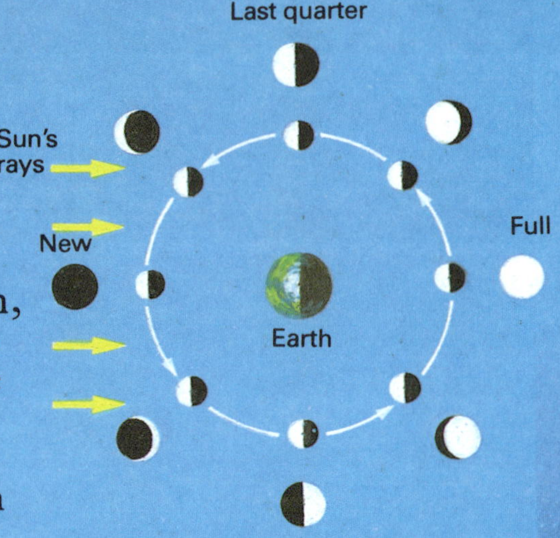

The Moon goes through a 29½-day cycle of 'phases' as it circles the Earth. These phases happen because we see only the half of the Moon that is illuminated by the Sun. At New Moon, the Moon cannot be seen because its dark face is turned towards the Earth. After two or three days, it has moved far enough to be seen as a thin crescent in the sky. After seven days it is a perfect half circle called the First Quarter. A week later it is full. We see the full sunlit circle as it lies opposite the Sun in the sky. After this, the phases go into reverse – the Moon wanes until it disappears once more.

The Moon is our nearest neighbour in space. It travels around the Earth at a speed of about 3,664 kilometres per hour. It orbits the Earth once every month or so. The Moon, like the Earth, is constantly spinning. It takes it a month to complete one spin. This means that we always see the same face of the Moon from Earth.

When the night sky is clear, we are often surprised how brightly the Moon shines. But the Moon doesn't shine with its own light. It is merely reflecting light from the Sun. Astronauts on the Moon see Earth as a big ball of light. Again, the light from Earth is only reflected sunlight.

Seen from Earth, the Moon looks about the same size as the Sun. But this is only because the Moon is so close to us. In fact, the Moon is quite small – about the same size as Australia. It is so small that it does not have enough gravity to hold an atmosphere around it. There is no air on the Moon, so spacemen have to take their own air with them. And the Moon has no weather – no wind. During the day, the Sun beats down with an intense heat of about 120°C – hotter than boiling water. During the lunar night, the temperature falls to a freezing −160°C.

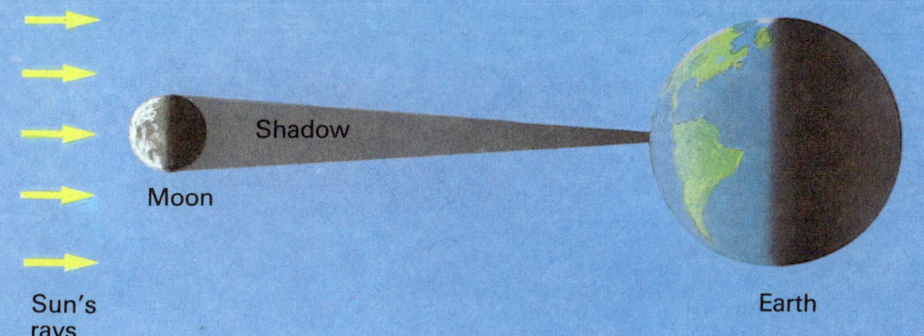

It is strange that the Sun and Moon appear in the sky to be the same size although the Moon is really 400 times smaller. It is just much closer to us. The Moon sometimes passes in front of the Sun, blotting out the Sun's light. This is a *solar eclipse.* The Moon's shadow is a cone, as you can see in the picture. To see a total eclipse we must be inside that cone. When the tip of the shadow cone reaches Earth it is only about 240 kilometres across. It is only in this 240 km-wide circle that people see a total eclipse of the Sun.

The Moon has many of the valuable minerals that are becoming scarcer and scarcer on Earth. Perhaps in years to come the Moon's minerals will be mined and transported as in the picture below. Lunar gravity is only one-sixth of Earth's, so it is much easier to shoot things off its surface into space. The minerals could be put in huge buckets and fired off a track by magnetic waves. This mechanism is called a mass driver. Out in space, the minerals could be 'caught' by a space tug (right) and taken to wherever they are needed.

Journeys into Space

On March 16, 1926, an American scientist, Dr Robert Goddard, fired the first liquid-fuelled rocket into space. Goddard's rocket rose only 60 metres into the air, but this was the first tiny step towards bigger and more powerful rockets that took people to the Moon and probes right out of our Solar System.

A mere 31 years after Goddard's rocket, the Russians launched Sputnik 1, the first man-made satellite to orbit the Earth. This happened on October 4, 1957, and it was on that day that the Space Age began. Since then, hundreds of satellites have been fired into space and the Shuttle blasts off into space and lands back on Earth with an ease we are now beginning to take for granted.

Probes to the Planets

Some of the most exciting space projects have been the unmanned probes sent up to find out more about other planets in our Solar System. In 1976, two *Viking* spacecraft landed on Mars. They carried out tests to find out whether any form of life existed on the Red Planet; but they could find none.

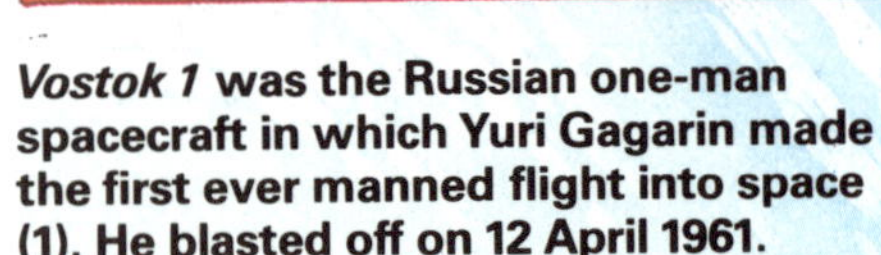

Vostok 1 **was the Russian one-man spacecraft in which Yuri Gagarin made the first ever manned flight into space (1). He blasted off on 12 April 1961.**

The Americans who landed on the Moon travelled in *Apollo* craft (2). The Command Module for the men was in the nose of the spacecraft.

Venera 4 **(3) was one of several Russian craft that reached Venus and released a capsule by parachute (right). The *Veneras* radioed back to Earth several important discoveries.**

American *Pioneer* probes (4) flew close to Jupiter in 1973 and 1974. They took some remarkable close-up pictures of the giant planet.

A *Viking* Mars craft is seen at (5).

Left: A *Voyager* space probe flying past Saturn's rings. In 1977, two *Voyagers* were sent on their way to Jupiter. From Jupiter they went on to take exciting pictures of Saturn. Now *Voyager 2* is speeding on its way towards Uranus and Neptune. It should reach Neptune in 1989. The radio information it will send back from the distant planet will take nearly half an hour to reach us!

The picture below shows the Space Shuttle with Spacelab in its cargo bay. Scientists will be able to work in Spacelab for up to a month.

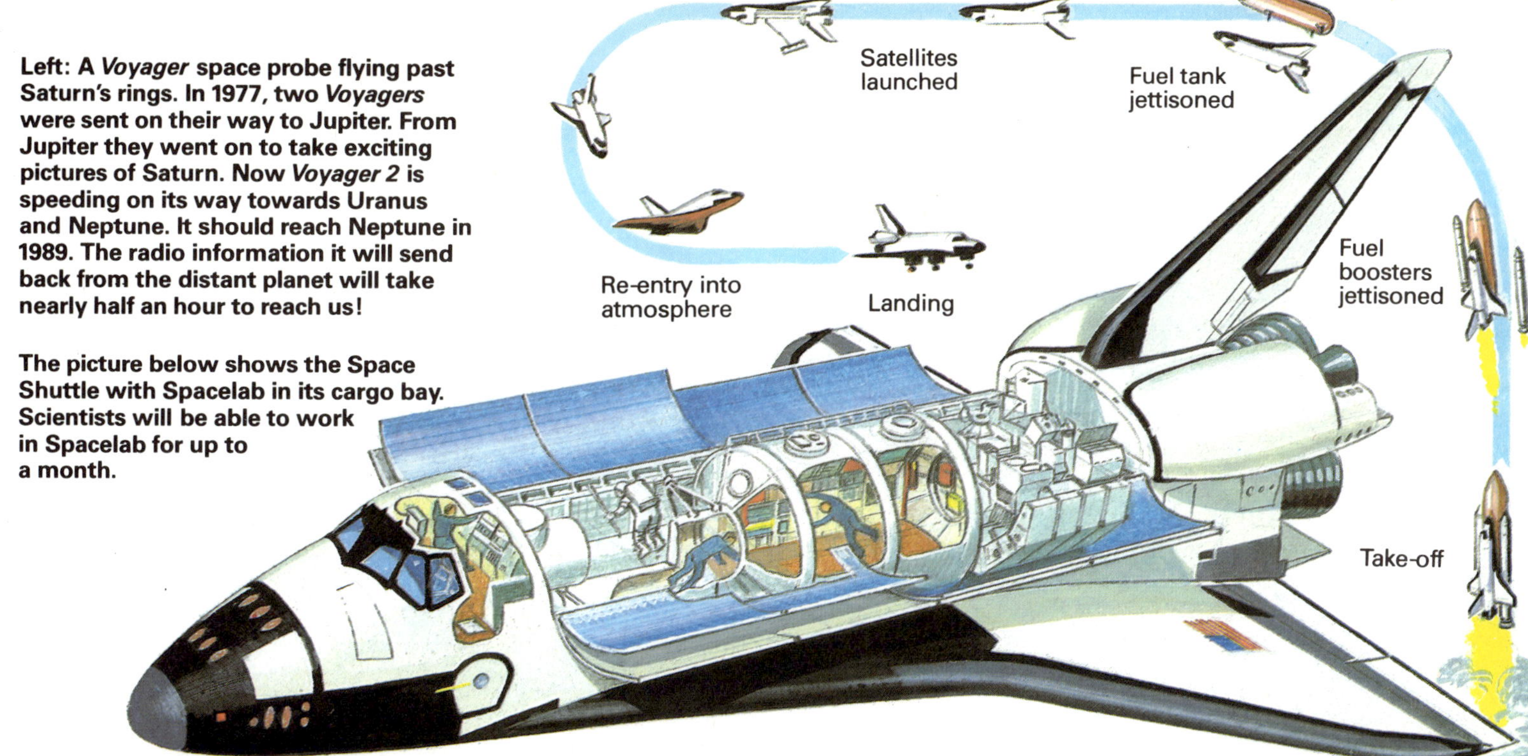

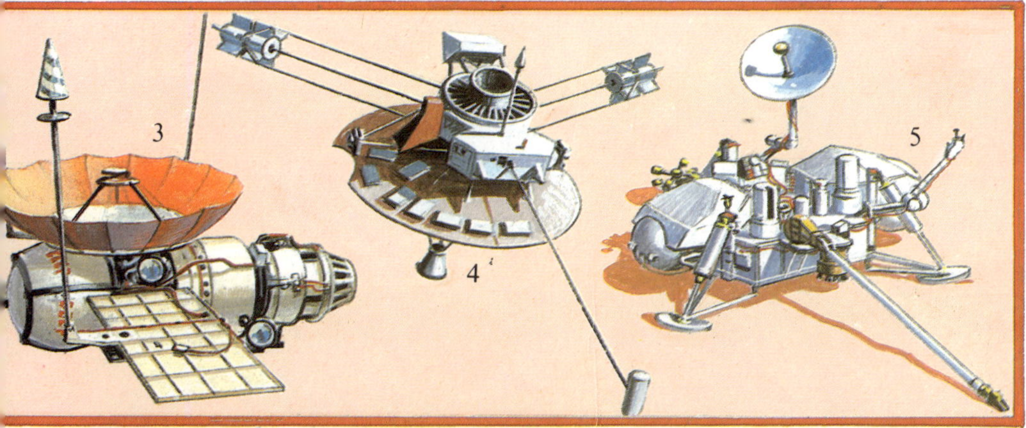

The Space Shuttle

When the Space Shuttle *Columbia* blasted off in 1981 a new kind of space travel began. After a flight of 54½ hours in space, it glided back to a perfect landing on a desert airstrip.

Before the Shuttle, all rockets and manned spacecraft were used only once. This made space flight very expensive. The Space Shuttle is a combined launch rocket and spacecraft that can be used many times.

The Shuttle is launched by rocket like other spacecraft, but it glides back to land on a runway like an aircraft. It has three main rocket engines which are fed with fuel from a big tank. This tank is dumped when all its fuel is gone. Two extra rockets are attached to the sides of the Shuttle to help it into space. These rockets fall away as the ship climbs, and drop by parachute into the ocean. There they are recovered and can be used again. As the Shuttle glides back through the atmosphere, special tiles protect it from the fierce heat.

Cities in Space

The biggest problem to face the world within the next few decades may be how to feed and house all its people. The world's population is growing fast, especially in Third World countries. Before the year 2080 the population of our Earth may be three times its present size. Unless we can halt the population explosion and find new sources of food and raw materials, people may have to move out into space.

There have been many designs for giant space colonies with room for thousands of people. These colonies would be vast cylinders or spheres, going round and round to give Earth-like gravity for the people who live there.

Artificial Gravity

To make life possible for people who go to live in space, there must be gravity. Gravity is the force that pulls us all towards the centre of the Earth – that gives us weight. Out in space there is no gravity. People and things just float around.

Island Three

One idea for a space colony is called *Island Three*. It would be made up of two or more huge cylinders positioned at a fixed distance from the Earth and Moon. The cylinders are 30 kilometres long and about 6 kilometres around. Giant mirrors reflect sunlight through three long windows in the sides of the cylinders. The angle of the mirrors can be altered to make artificial day and night and temperature changes. Even changing seasons can be created. Inside the cylinders will be three long land areas where people live and grow crops, just as they would on Earth.

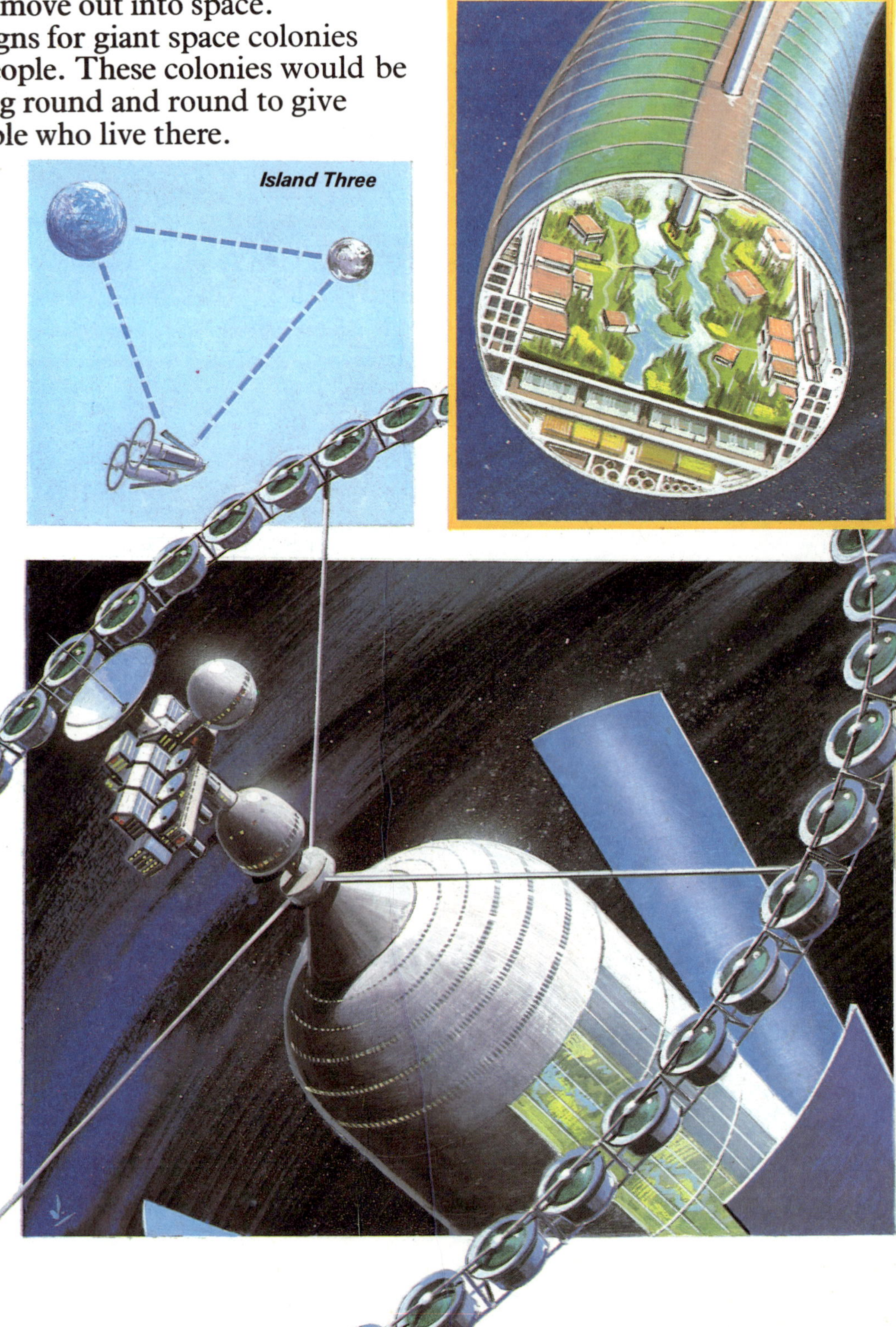

Island Three **will have a solar power station at one end and a ring of factory units at the other. There will also be vast docking facilities for spaceships.**

Artificial gravity can be made by spinning a whole space colony at just the right speed. The force of the spin pushes everything towards the outside. To anyone in a space colony, 'up' will be towards the inside. Two people on opposite sides of the craft will be upside down in relation to each other.

A Torus Colony

Another idea for a space colony is the building of a huge torus or wheel, like the one shown here. The wheel is rotated around the central hub once every minute. This creates an artificial gravity that holds all the land, water and people in place inside the vast tube. The tube itself is 2000 metres across. On the central hub is a solar power station that provides energy to run the whole colony. Also in the hub are factories where many of the colonists work, perhaps using materials mined on the Moon. Life in the tube would be made as much like life on Earth as possible for the colonists.

A space colony on the Moon

Will we go to other Stars?

In the future, people may be able to go to other star systems outside our Solar System. But at present we do not know how it will be possible. The nearest star to us, other than our Sun, is Alpha Centauri, and it would take a present-day rocket ship about 100,000 years to get there! So we will have to develop much faster rocket engines than those we have at present.

But we will almost certainly begin by putting people on other planets and moons in our Solar System. The picture above shows a colony on the Moon. Life will not be too easy for the first settlers. It will take them some time to get used to the very small gravity and the need to carry their own air around with them. Water will either have to be imported from Earth or manufactured on the Moon. Food will be grown in large greenhouses.

THE ATMOSPHERE IS A THIN SKIN
Although the atmosphere stretches upwards from Earth for a few hundred kilometres, it is really a very thin shell compared to the size of the Earth. If the Earth were the size of an orange, the atmosphere would be no thicker than the skin. You can see this in the picture on the left.

Nothing can burn without oxygen. We can prove this by a simple experiment. Light a candle and stand it in a bowl of water. Place a jar over it. As the candle burns, the oxygen in the jar is used up and the water slowly rises inside the jar to take its place. Then the candle goes out. The oxygen has been used up.

The Air We Breathe

Our planet is surrounded by a blanket of air we call the *atmosphere*. It stretches upwards for several hundred kilometres and it contains gases that all living things must have. We are all in contact with air every second that we live, but we are seldom aware of it. It is quite invisible and has no taste or smell. You can feel the air when the wind blows. You can see clouds being pushed along by the air. Air can turn windmills. And if there were no air we would live in a silent world. Sound needs air to travel through. It cannot travel in a vacuum.

Although the atmosphere is hundreds of kilometres thick, over three-quarters of all our air is in the few kilometres nearest to Earth. As we go higher, the air grows thinner and thinner. At the top of a high mountain, there is so little air that we have difficulty breathing. There is not enough life-giving oxygen in each breath we take. That is why people who climb Mount Everest take their own oxygen supply with them. Inside airliners, the air pressure has to be kept as it is on Earth so that people can breathe normally.

Although we cannot see air, it is a substance just as rocks are. It is pulled down towards the Earth by the force of gravity – it has weight. When we talk about air pressure, we are talking about the weight of air pressing down on us, and air has quite a lot of weight. It presses on every square centimetre of our bodies with a force of over 1,000 grams.

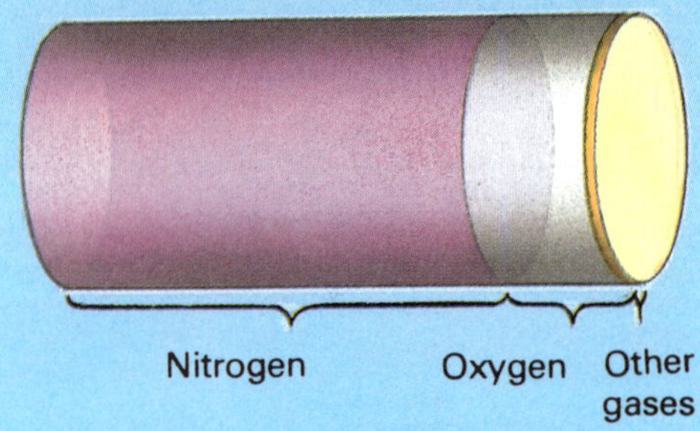

In the experiment with the candle and the jar, it was found that extra water sucked into the jar was about one-fifth of the jar's volume. This shows that about one-fifth of the air is oxygen. Air is made up of a mixture of gases that we cannot see. Over three-quarters of it is nitrogen (78 per cent). As oxygen makes up about one-fifth (21 per cent), this leaves only 1 per cent, which is made up of small quantities of other gases such as *argon, helium, carbon dioxide, hydrogen, ozone,* etc. Air also contains some water vapour – separated particles of water too fine to see. When we talk about *humidity* we are talking about the amount of water vapour in the air. When the air holds as much water vapour as it can hold without mist appearing, we say the humidity is 100 per cent.

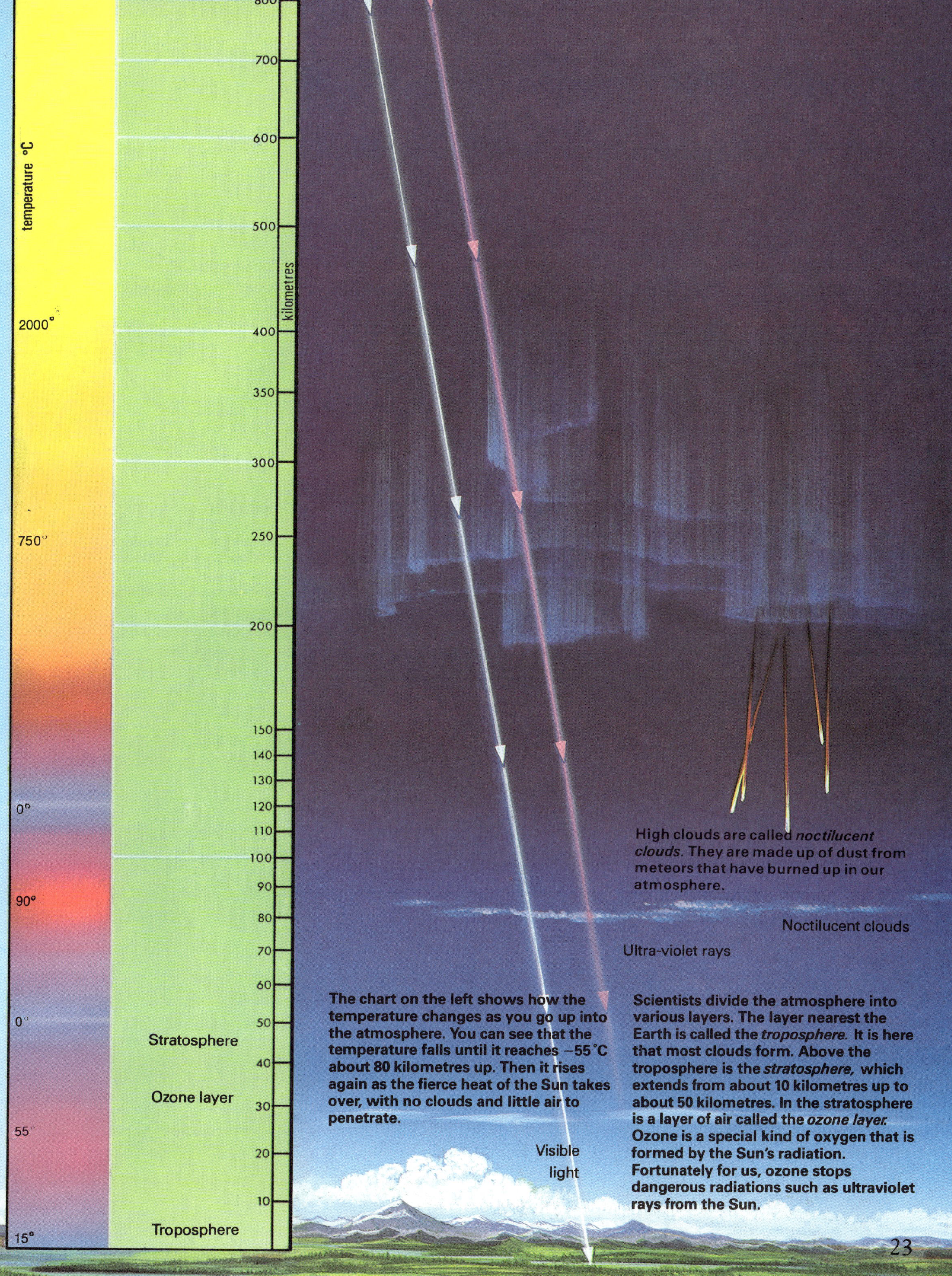

High clouds are called *noctilucent clouds*. They are made up of dust from meteors that have burned up in our atmosphere.

The chart on the left shows how the temperature changes as you go up into the atmosphere. You can see that the temperature falls until it reaches −55°C about 80 kilometres up. Then it rises again as the fierce heat of the Sun takes over, with no clouds and little air to penetrate.

Scientists divide the atmosphere into various layers. The layer nearest the Earth is called the *troposphere*. It is here that most clouds form. Above the troposphere is the *stratosphere,* which extends from about 10 kilometres up to about 50 kilometres. In the stratosphere is a layer of air called the *ozone layer.* Ozone is a special kind of oxygen that is formed by the Sun's radiation. Fortunately for us, ozone stops dangerous radiations such as ultraviolet rays from the Sun.

Weather in the Making

Life is only possible because of the layer of air wrapped around our Earth – the layer we call the atmosphere. The atmosphere protects us from the Sun's fierce rays and gives us air to breathe. It also gives us our ever-changing weather.

Weather depends on the movement of air we call winds. Movement of air is caused by differences in the temperature of the air. When air is heated or cooled, it moves.

Several things cause temperature differences in the air. Some parts of the Earth get more heat from the Sun than others. Because the Earth is curved, the Sun's rays are

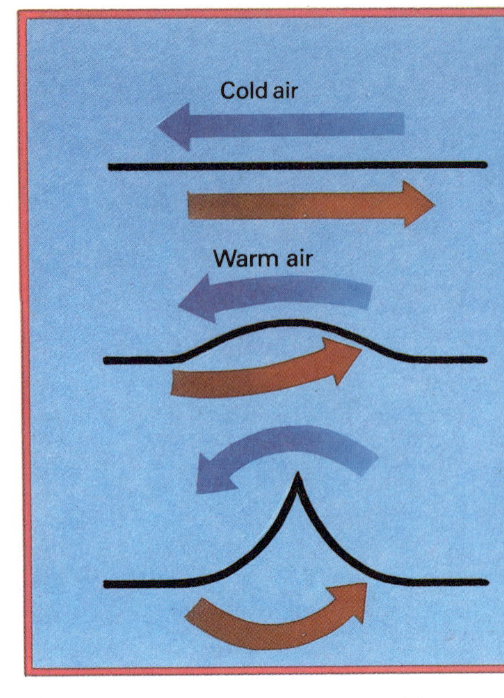

The diagram on the right shows why the Sun's rays do not heat the Earth evenly all over. Because the Earth is a ball, the rays come straight down on the equator. At the poles they arrive at a slant, so the heat is spread over a larger area.

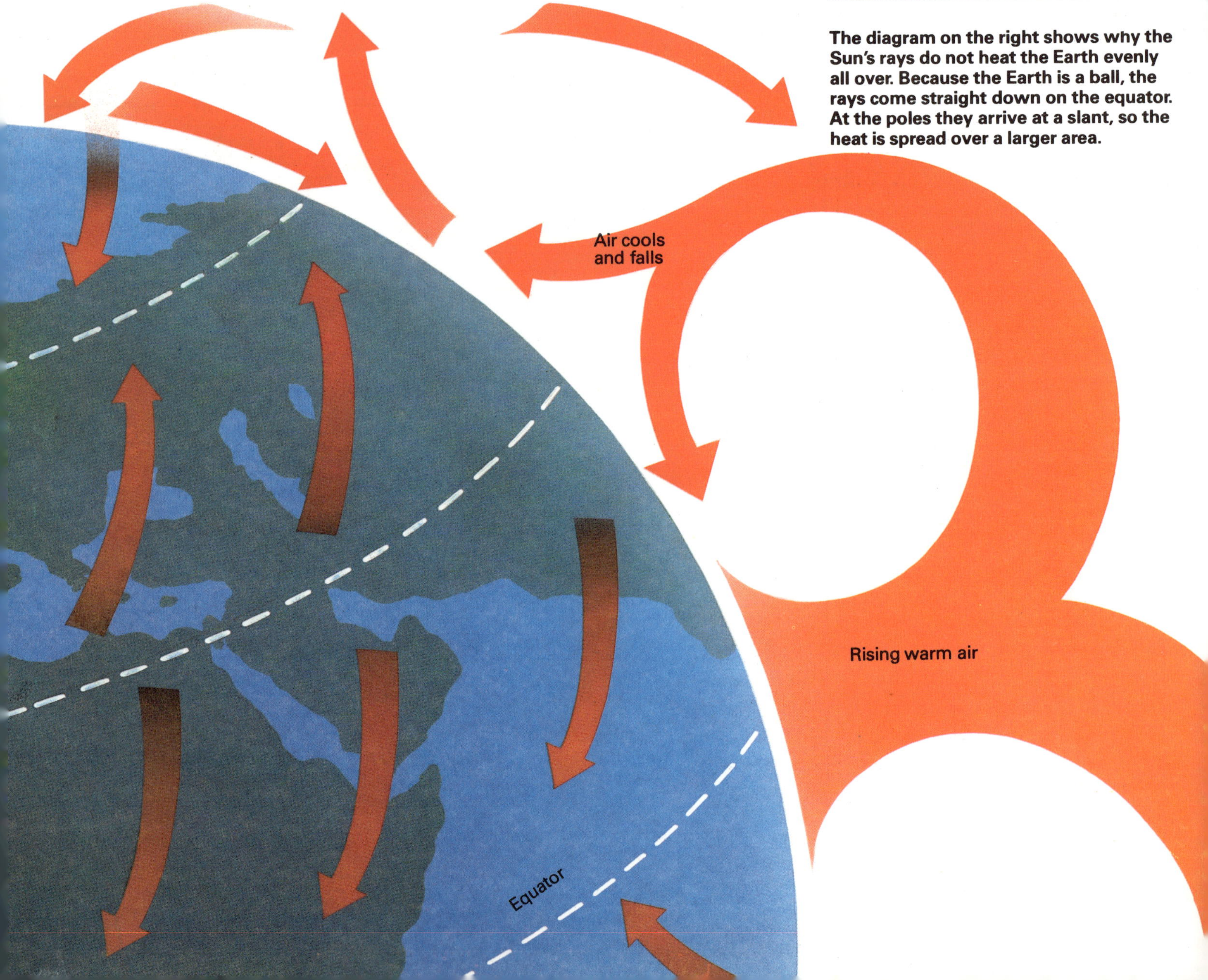

Air cools and falls

Rising warm air

Equator

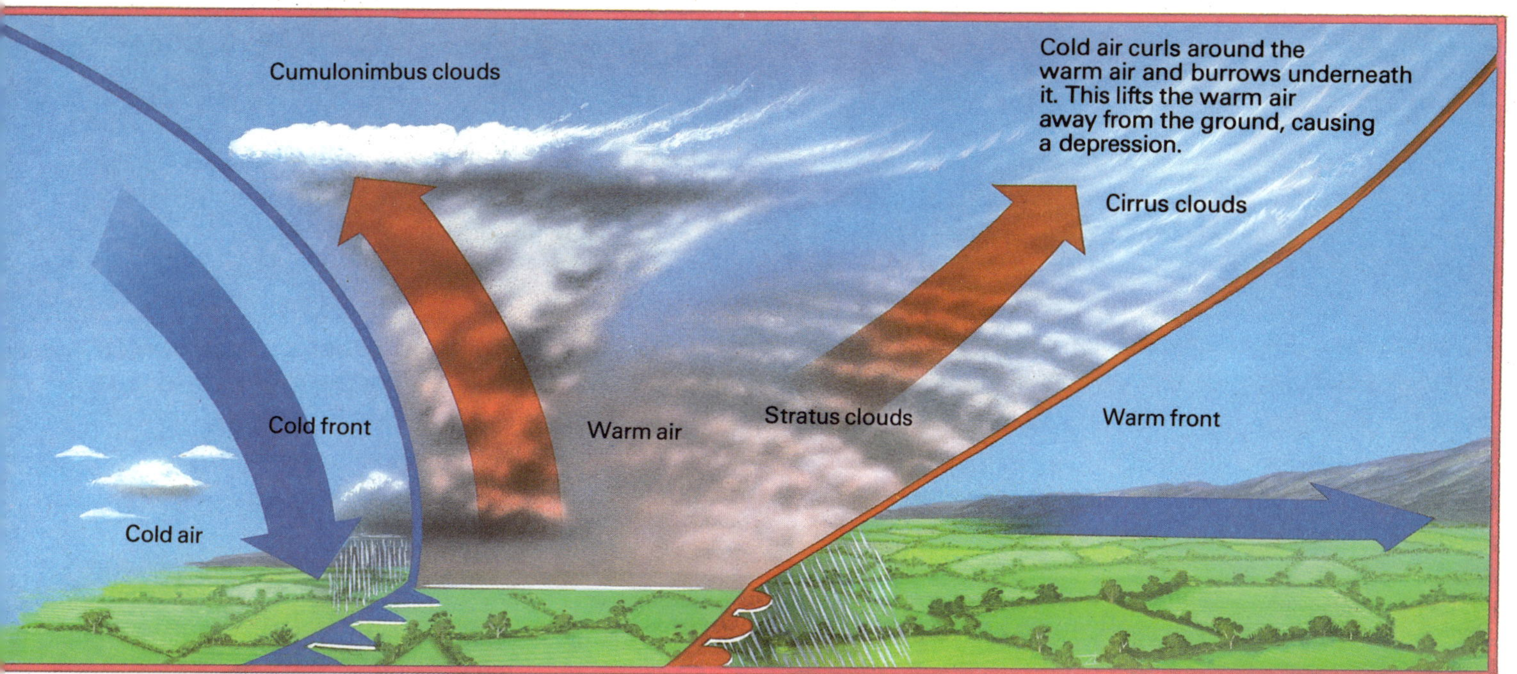

Periods of unsettled weather, with rain, gales and sometimes snowstorms are caused by centres of low air pressure called *depressions.* Depressions happen when cold air from the poles meets warm air from the tropics. The cold air curls around the back of the warm air and a depression is made.

The diagram on the left shows some of the main air movements round the Earth that give us our weather. Rising warm air at the equator moves off towards the North and South Poles. As the air cools in the colder atmosphere high up, it falls again and is sucked back towards the equator. There it takes the place of the rising warm air. Other air from the equator goes on towards the poles and forms other circular movements of air masses. In addition, the rotation of the Earth drags the winds to the west. Other air movements are caused by differences between land and water and how well they hold heat. The changing seasons also have an important effect on the great air masses.

strongest at the equator. At the cold poles, the same amount of Sun heat is spread over a bigger area. So the air around the equator is warmer than the air around the poles. Warm air rises. The rising air at the equator moves off towards the North Pole and the South Pole. It also becomes cooler as it goes up, so part of the way to the poles some of the air sinks and returns to the equator. This makes a circular movement of air.

There are other air movements between the poles and the equator. In addition, the Earth's rotation pushes the winds to the west. But this wind pattern is made more complicated because the Earth's surface is made up of land and sea. Land heats up more quickly than water; it also loses its heat more quickly. This causes differences in the air temperature over various parts of the world and therefore air movements. The changing seasons further complicate the weather pattern.

All these things cause great masses of air to wander about the Earth's surface. It is these wandering air masses that give us our changing weather. They meet up with each other, they rise and fall and, of course, they carry rain. People who study weather and make forecasts take measurements of temperature, pressure, wind force and direction and humidity (the amount of water in the air). They draw weather charts and make predictions with the help of big computers.

Continents Adrift

Only about a quarter of the surface of our planet is dry land. The rest is sea. Most of the Earth's land lies north of the equator and is broken up into the masses we call 'continents'. But it was not always so. Over 200 million years ago, when the first dinosaurs were beginning to roam the world, all the Earth's land was joined together in one huge mass. This great land mass has been called Pangaea. Over millions of years, Pangaea moved and broke up to form the continents as we know them. This movement is still going on at a rate that varies between a centimetre and 12 centimetres a year. It is called the 'continental drift'.

If we compare the shapes of the coasts of western Africa and eastern South America we can see that they fit together quite well. And if these continents are matched, not on the shore lines but at their under-sea *continental shelves,* the jigsaw fit is better still. (All the continents have under-sea shelves sloping out from them.) America and Africa were once joined together.

Lava

Magma

The picture on the left shows what happens inside a volcano. The deeper you go under the Earth's surface, the hotter it gets. At a depth of about 30 kilometres it begins to get so hot that some rocks simply melt. This molten rock is called *magma.* Some of this magma is pushed up through cracks and holes. These are volcanoes. There are different kinds of volcanoes. Some erupt quietly, oozing out molten rock called *lava.* The lava may spread out for kilometres before it cools and hardens. Lava of this kind builds gradually sloping mountains. Explosive volcanoes throw out rocks mixed with gas and steam that has been trapped underground.

Earthquake zone

Volcano

One plate pushed under another

The Earth's crust beneath our feet is made up of two main kinds of rock. Great blocks of granite-type rock, which we call the continents, are embedded in a heavier kind of hot, half-liquid rock. The continents are great plates 'floating' on the hot rock underneath. They move very slowly, but the huge mass of the plates means that they move with tremendous force. When two plates come towards each other, the great force of the meeting pushes one plate under the other. In plate collisions such as this, mountain ranges are slowly pushed up and there may be earthquakes.

In the course of time, the continents have travelled enormous distances. By examining fossils in the rocks, and by other means, scientists are able to plot the history of a place's climate. They know, for instance, that frozen Antarctica was at one time in the tropics. And it is possible to tell the likely future movements of the continents. Africa, for example, will drift north, slowly closing the Mediterranean Sea. Australia will continue its slow journey northward. And by measuring magnetic field directions fixed in rocks of different ages, experts have been able to plot the drift of Britain's North Sea oil rocks from the time when they were south of the equator 400 million years ago.

The theory of the drifting continents has also helped to explain how closely related animals are found in lands now separated by thousands of miles of sea.

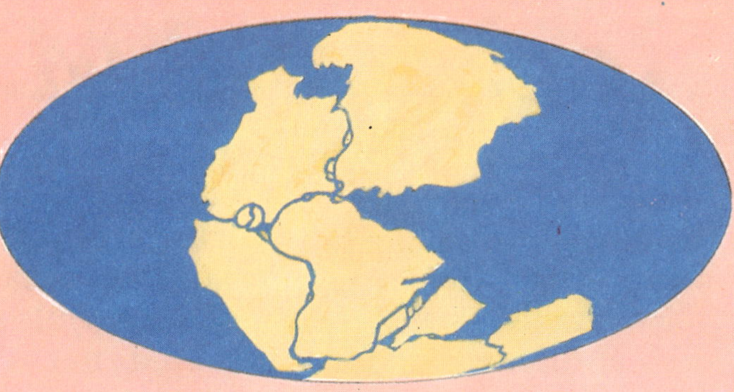

200 million years ago

60 million years ago

Today

Rocks and Minerals

Much of the Earth is rock. Mountains and hills are made of rock. The soil is mostly fine rock particles. Stones and pebbles are small pieces of rock. And all the rocks in the Earth's crust are made up of substances called minerals. There are thousands of different minerals and, like all substances, minerals are built up from chemical elements. There are only about a hundred elements – substances such as oxygen, iron and carbon. Most minerals are made up of mixtures of several elements. But a few have formed from only one element. Diamond, for example, is a pure form of carbon.

The most common elements in the Earth's crust are oxygen and silicon. Quartz, the most common mineral, is a mixture of these two elements.

The Three Types of Rock

There are three main types of rock in the Earth's crust. They are called *igneous, sedimentary* and *metamorphic* rocks. Igneous rocks formed from hot molten material from inside the Earth. Sedimentary rocks are made up of tiny particles including the remains of fossils of microscopic creatures that lived in the sea millions of years ago. As these creatures died, their shells dropped to the sea floor and piled up and were squeezed until they became rock. Limestone, sandstone and chalk are sedimentary rocks. Metamorphic rock has been made by the changing of existing rock by heat or pressure. Marble is a metamorphic rock.

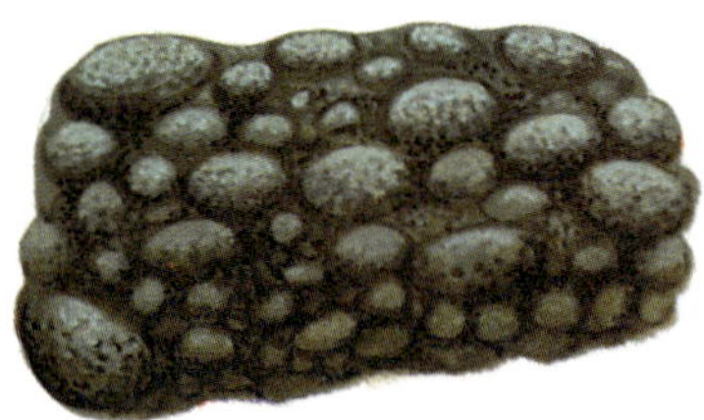

Chalk is a soft, white limestone. It was formed as mud on the bottom of an ancient sea. Chalk consists mainly of tiny shells and calcite crystals.

Conglomerate is a mixture of rock fragments cemented together by finer particles. The pebbles in conglomerate are any hard rock such as flint or quartz.

Sandstone is a common sedimentary rock. The wearing away of sandstone makes up a large part of our beaches. The main ingredient in sand is quartz.

Minerals

The panels on the left show some of the many minerals that are found in the crust of the Earth. The minerals in the far left panel contain metals. Minerals that contain sufficient metal for it to be extracted are called ores. The minerals in the near left panel include semi-precious stones and gems. Most of them do not contain metals.

The minerals pictured are: (1) Malachite, an important and beautiful ore of copper; (2) Galena, the chief ore of lead; (3) Wulfenite, a strikingly coloured ore of the valuable metal molybdenum; (4) Zincite, an ore of zinc; (5) Iron pyrites, also known as Fools' gold because its colour has led prospectors in the past to believe they have struck gold; (6) Agate, an attractive form of quartz; (7) Quartz crystals; (8) Amethyst, another form of quartz, widely used in jewellery; (9) Diamond, an extremely pure form of carbon; (10) Emerald, an extremely complex mineral containing beryl and aluminium. The last three minerals are shown cut and polished as they are normally seen in jewellery.

Fossil prints left in ancient rocks tell the scientists much about the past. This is a fossil of a fern plant that lived about 250 million years ago.

Granite is the most common igneous rock. It is made up mainly of quartz crystals.

Slate is a common metamorphic rock. Look at a piece of slate and you will see signs of the great pressure that formed it.

Basalt is crystallized lava that once poured red hot from a volcano.

Volcano

Landscapes

Some of the strangest effects of erosion can be seen in deserts, where sharp grains of sand are blown by the wind. The sand is blasted against fixed rocks, smoothing them into fantastic shapes.

The surface of the Earth and the landscapes we see around us are slowly changing all the time. Rain, sun, wind and frost constantly break down rocks. Great mountain ranges are worn down to rolling plains in millions of years. Solid rock is ground into mud. We call this breaking up and wearing away *erosion*.

Running water is the most important force in changing the land. Rain washes soil down hillsides and sinks into the ground, to appear elsewhere as streams and rivers. The rivers cut into their banks and beds and carry stones and mud down to the sea. Sometimes streams travel underground and hollow out caves.

Erosion is at work in deserts, too. There the wind piles up loose sand in huge, shifting dunes. Wind-blown sand blasts exposed rocks, polishing and carving them into strange shapes.

But erosion does more than just alter the landscape. It makes soil. Soil is just surface rock that has been broken down and mixed with decayed plants.

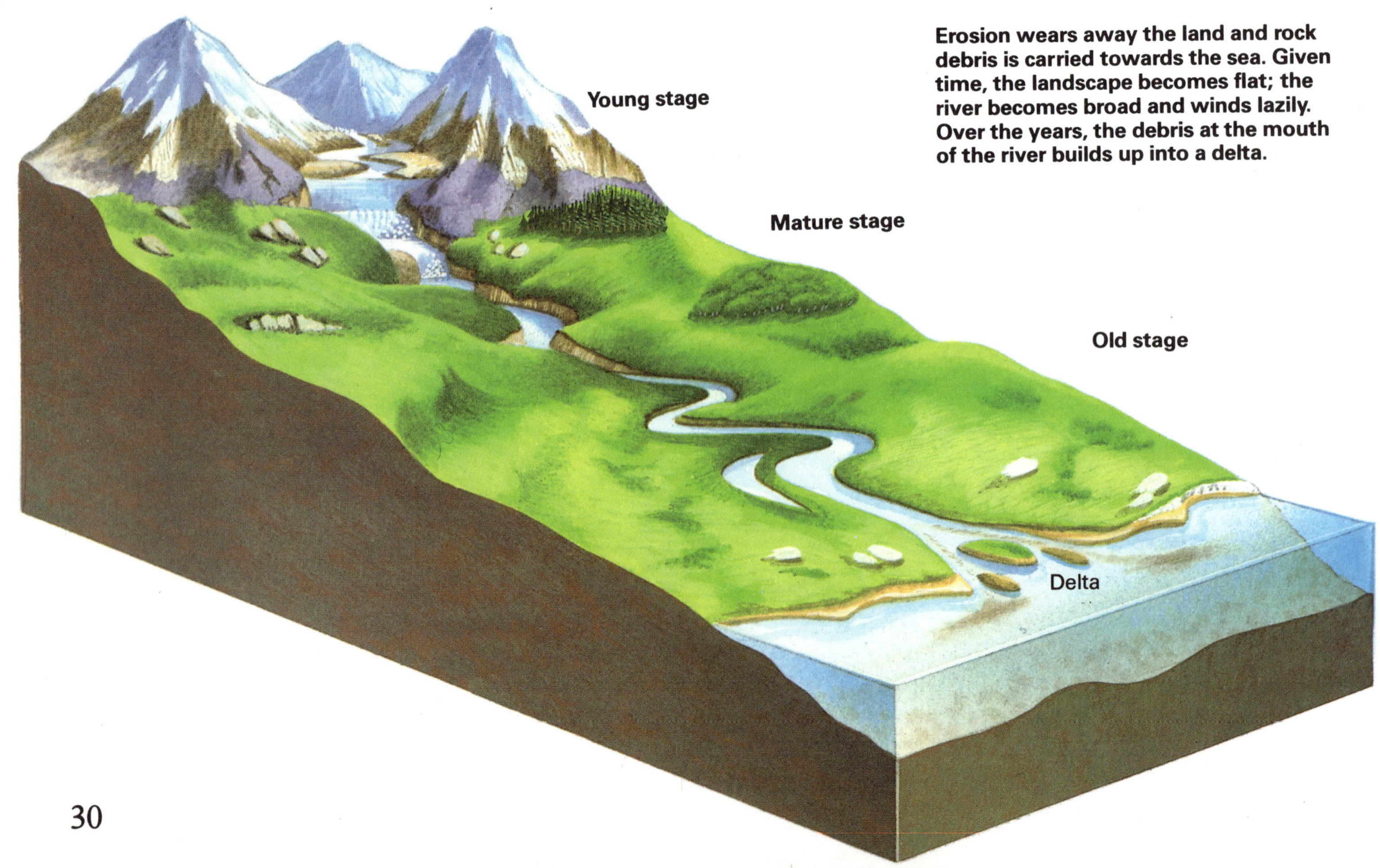

Erosion wears away the land and rock debris is carried towards the sea. Given time, the landscape becomes flat; the river becomes broad and winds lazily. Over the years, the debris at the mouth of the river builds up into a delta.

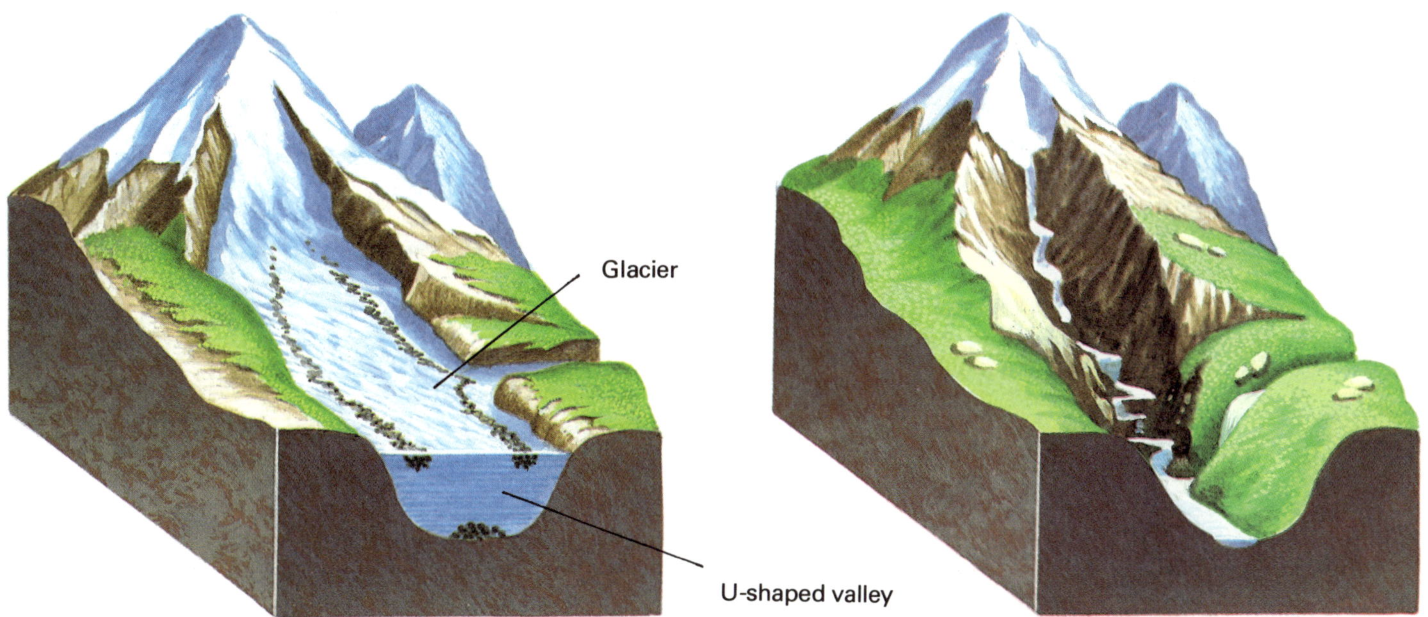

During the Ice Ages, rocks, firmly embedded in the glacier, turned the glacier into a giant 'file' which wore down the surrounding rocks into a deep valley.

When the Ice Ages passed, the glacier was replaced by a mountain river.

Frost Shattering

In cold places, ice is important in shaping the landscape. Water running down the mountain slopes seeps into cracks in the rock. As the water freezes, it expands with enough force to split the rocks apart. (The same thing happens when water freezes in our house pipes and bursts them.) Millions of tons of frost-worn rock litter mountain slopes.

Rivers of Ice

High in the mountains, snowfalls build up into solid ice, sometimes hundreds of metres thick. These are glaciers, great rivers of ice which slowly make their way down a valley at a rate of about a metre a day. Glaciers are very powerful. As they move along, they pick up boulders and debris and carve away the valley floor and sides.

After the Ice Ages, the land had been changed by glaciers. Great U-shaped valleys had been formed. Vast areas of land were covered with boulders, sand and clay that had been moved about by the rivers of ice.

Pounding waves wear away the land into steep cliffs.

The Sea Versus the Land

Another form of erosion is by the sea. Around our coasts, the sea is constantly eating away at the land. In some places it cuts steep rock cliffs. In others it carries sand and pebbles along the coast to dump them on gently sloping shores. So are born sand and pebble beaches. Sometimes the sand is dumped at the entrance to a bay, where it gradually forms a bar or spit which may cut the bay off from the sea.

Sandy beaches are built up from tiny fragments worn away from cliffs and rocky coasts.

A World of Atoms

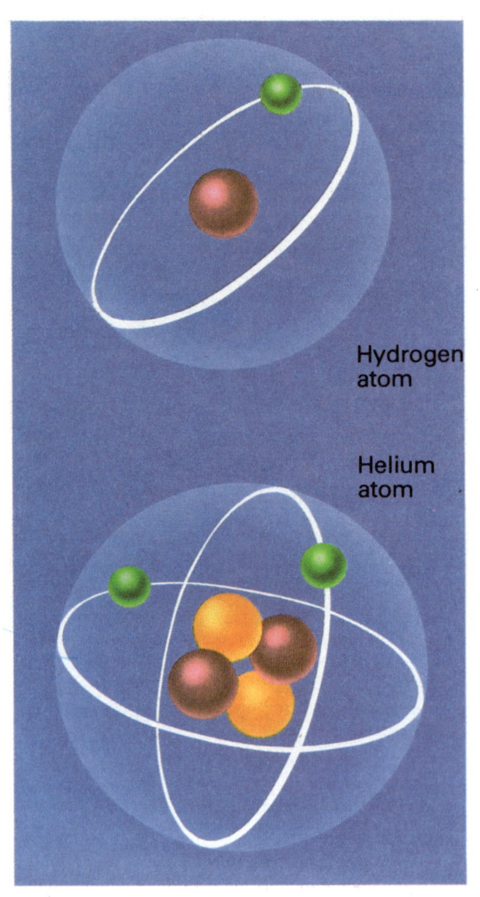

Everything in the universe is made up of atoms. Rocks, water, the air we breathe, plants, animals and people all contain millions upon millions of these tiny, invisible particles. About 30 million atoms placed side by side would stretch across the head of a pin.

But even the tiny atom is made up of even smaller pieces. The simplest atom is that of the light gas hydrogen. At the centre of the hydrogen atom is a tiny solid body called a *proton*. Around this spins an even smaller *electron*. The whirling electron makes billions of trips around the proton in a millionth of a second. Protons have a positive electric charge, electrons have a negative charge.

Other atoms are much more complicated than the hydrogen atom. An atom of another light gas, helium, has two protons, two electrons and there are two particles called *neutrons* with the protons at the centre or *nucleus* of the atom. Neutrons have no electrical charge. The most complicated atom is the uranium atom. It has 92 electrons, 92 protons and 146 neutrons.

Atoms are so small that if an atom were the size of a finger nail, then your hand would be big enough to grasp the Earth.

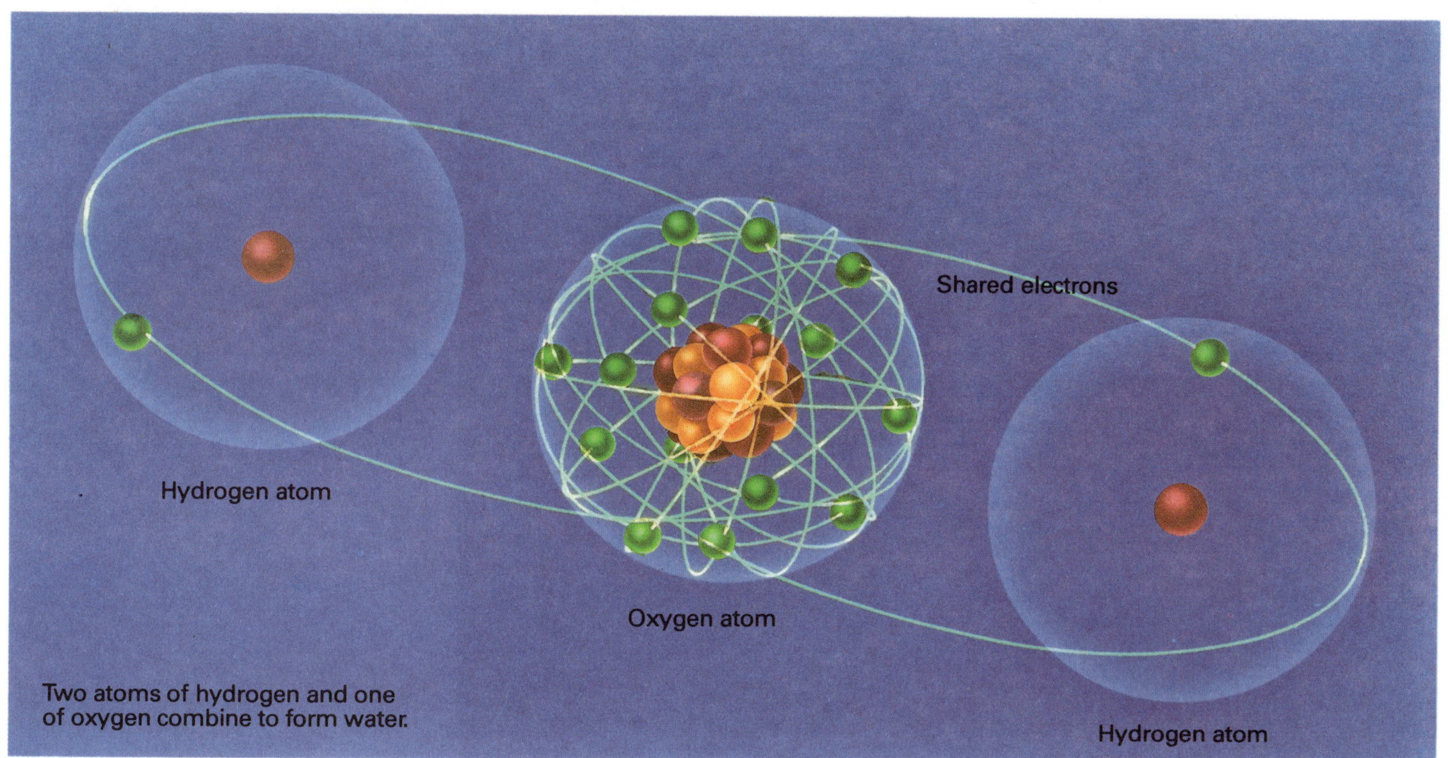

Two atoms of hydrogen and one of oxygen combine to form water.

The Elements

All the millions of substances in the world are made up from about a hundred simple substances called *elements*. Gold, silver and copper are elements; so are the gases hydrogen and oxygen. The atoms of different elements often join up to make different substances called *compounds*. The salt you put on your food is made up of atoms of the elements sodium and chlorine. Two atoms of hydrogen and one atom of oxygen join to make a *molecule* of water. A molecule is the smallest portion of a substance that can exist.

Every molecule of a substance is made up of the same number of atoms, joined together in exactly the same pattern. The main difference between the atoms of one element and those of another is in the number of protons in the nucleus. For example, every atom of aluminium has 13 protons; every atom of lead has 82. If an atom gains or loses protons, it becomes an atom of another element. The number of protons is called the *atomic number* of the element.

Although there are about a hundred elements, nearly all of the Earth's crust, the atmosphere and the oceans is made up of only eight elements. These are oxygen, the most common, aluminium, silicon, iron, calcium, potassium, sodium and magnesium. In the whole universe, there is more hydrogen than any other element. This is because the stars are made of hydrogen.

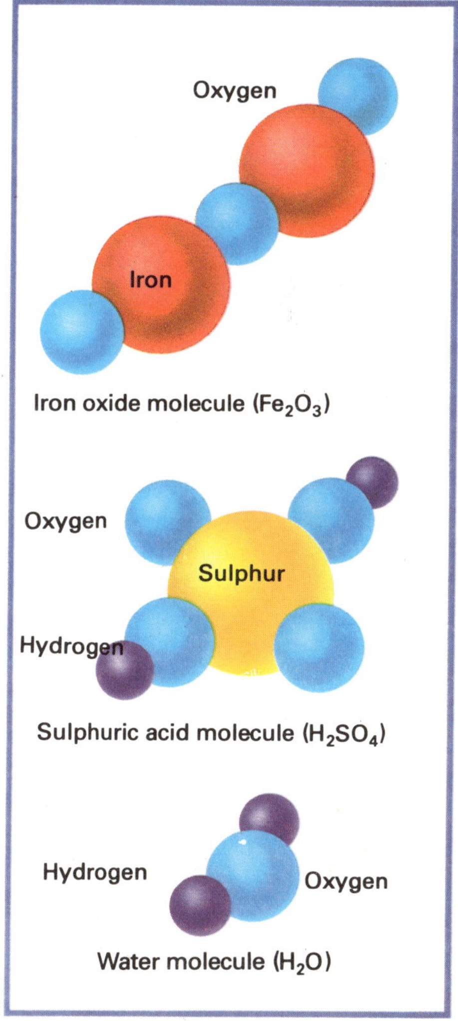

Iron oxide molecule (Fe_2O_3)

Sulphuric acid molecule (H_2SO_4)

Water molecule (H_2O)

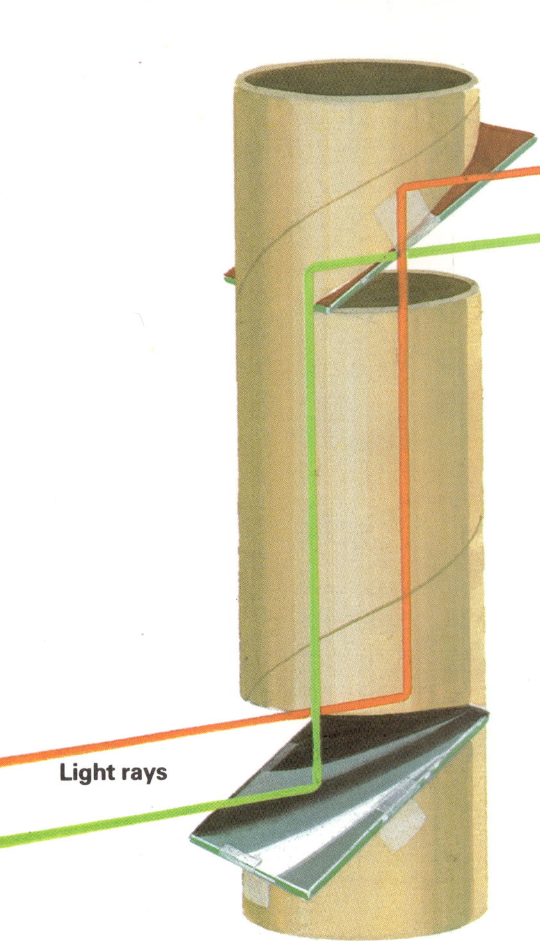

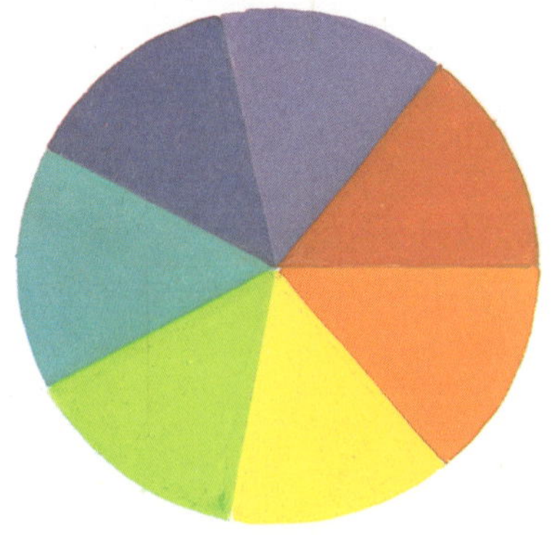

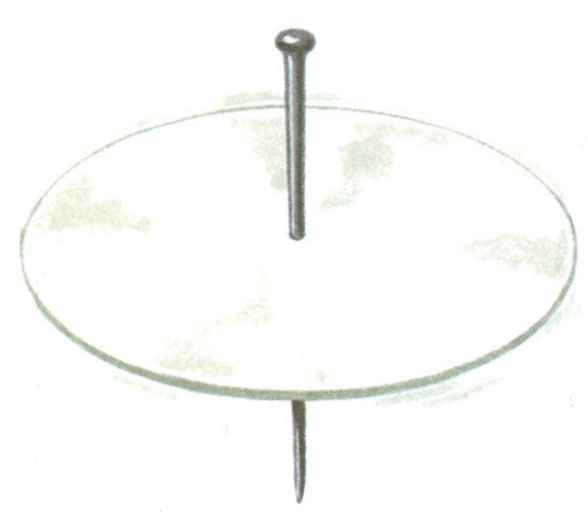

Left: You can use the property of mirrors to reflect light to help you make a periscope. Fix the mirrors in the tube exactly at an angle of 45°. Then you will be able to see over walls and look round corners.

Above: Ordinary white light from the Sun is actually a mixture of many different colours. You can show this by passing a beam of sunlight through a wedge of glass (a prism). The light emerges as a much broader beam, which forms a band (spectrum) showing all the colours of the rainbow. You can turn these colours back into white by means of a colour wheel. Paint the colours on the wheel as shown. Then spin it and watch the colours merge together to form white.

Simple Science

If you hold a pea in one hand and a golf ball in the other, and drop them, which hits the ground first? You will probably say 'the golf ball'. Try the experiment yourself, and you will be astonished to observe that both pea and golf ball hit the ground at exactly the same time!

If you measure the time they take to fall and the distance they fall, you can work out how much they accelerate under the pull of the Earth, or gravity. By carrying out this simple experiment and observing what happens, you have increased your knowledge of the world around you. You have been practising science.

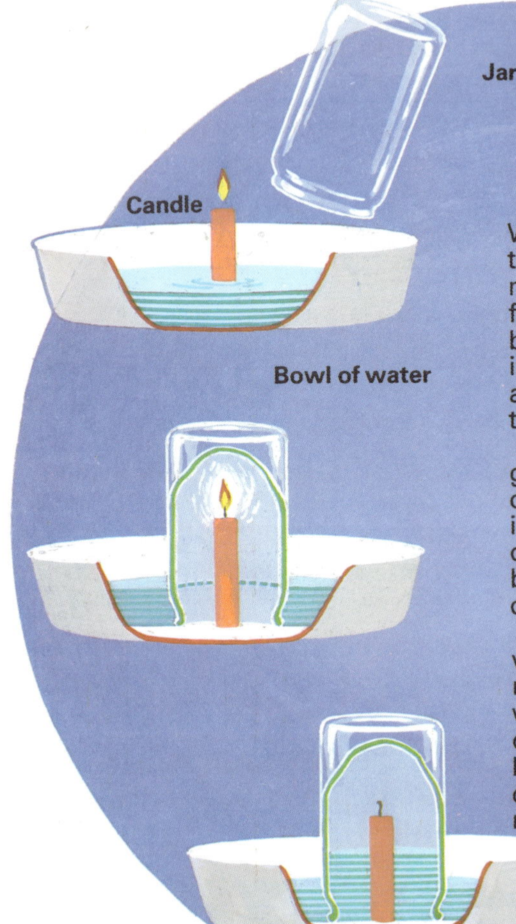

HOW MUCH OXYGEN?

We are able to live on Earth because the air contains oxygen which we must breathe to remain alive. You can find the amount of oxygen in the air by a simple experiment. Fix a candle in a bowl of water. Light the candle, and then place a jar over it down into the water. Watch what happens.

The water level inside the jar gradually rises. This shows that some of the air is being used up, and water is taking its place. In fact it is the oxygen in the air that is being used up because substances combine with oxygen when they burn.

Soon the candle goes out and the water level remains steady. Make a note of where the water level is. You will find that it has gone about one-fifth of the way up the jar. This is because air contains about one-fifth oxygen. Most of the other gas is nitrogen.

Every day of our lives we benefit from the knowledge gained by careful observation and experiment by dedicated men and women of science down the ages. One of the first true scientists was Galileo in the 1600s, who first carried out experiments with falling bodies like the one described.

There are two broad scientific fields – the physical sciences and the biological, or life sciences. The main physical sciences are physics and chemistry. Physics deals with such things as energy and forces, including light, heat and magnetism. Chemistry is concerned with the way substances are made up and how they react together. The biological sciences include zoology and botany. Zoology is the study of animals, while botany is the study of plants.

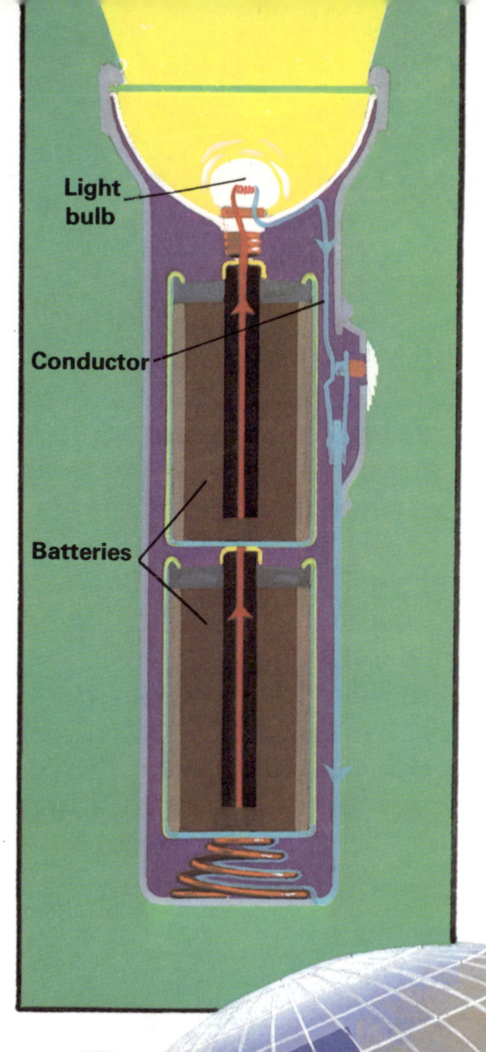

LIGHT BULB
The electricity flows into the light bulb and passes through a thin wire, or filament. It causes the filament to become white hot and thus give out light. The wire is made from a metal called tungsten which can resist the heat without breaking or melting.

CONDUCTORS
Brass strips carry the current from the battery to the bulb. Like most metals, brass is a good conductor of electricity. The rest of the torch is often made from plastic or rubber, which do not conduct electricity. They are insulators.

BATTERIES
In a torch battery, or dry cell, the electricity is produced by chemical action. This takes place between two electrodes and a paste containing ammonium chloride. The electrodes are a carbon rod (in the middle) and zinc, which forms the battery container.

Iron and a few metals like it are different from other metals because they can be magnetized – they can be made into magnets. Magnetism is a strange kind of force that we cannot see or feel, but we can see it in action. A horseshoe magnet, for example, readily attracts objects made from iron. But it will not attract objects made from aluminum or copper.

The magnetism in an object, say a bar, is not the same all over. It appears to be concentrated at the ends, at points we call the poles. The poles at each end are different from one another. When a bar magnet is suspended, one end always points north, the other south.

A suspended magnet (a compass) points north-south because the Earth itself acts like a magnet. And the magnet aligns itself with invisible lines of the Earth's magnetic force. But magnetic north-south differs slightly from 'true' north-south shown on maps.

If a south pole of one magnet is brought near the south pole of another, they push each other away. But if a north pole and a south pole come together, they attract one another.

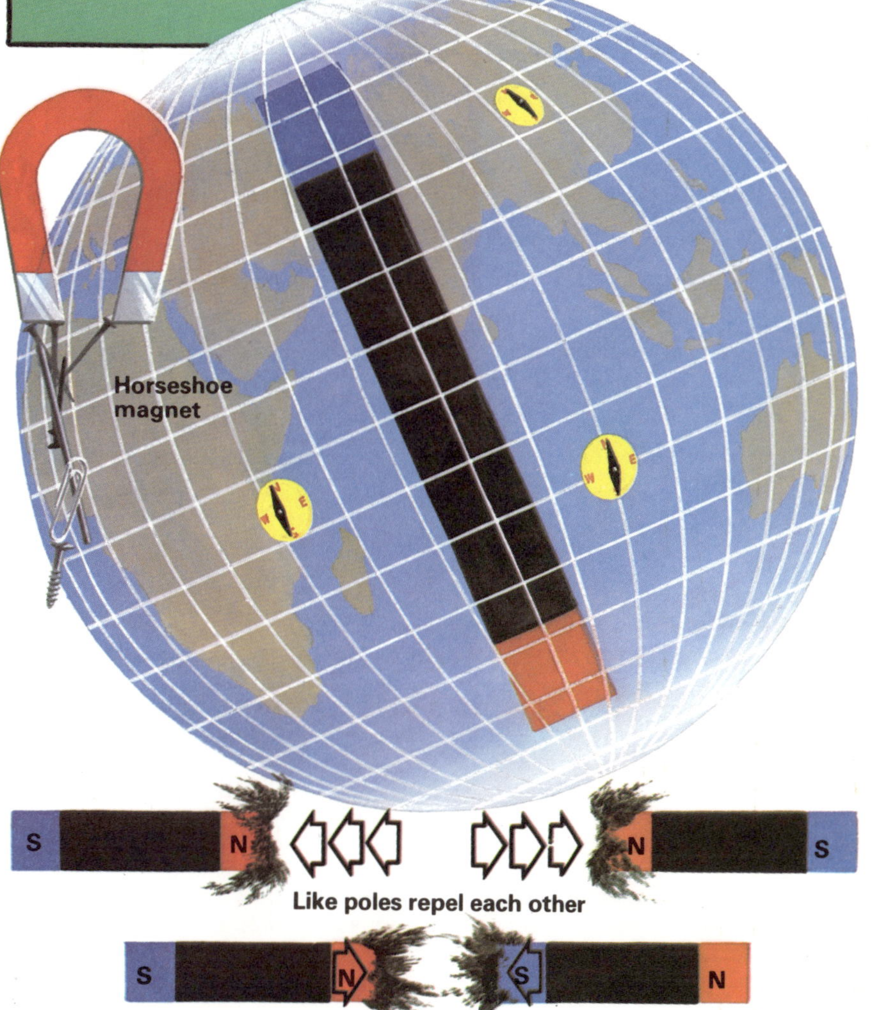

Solids, Liquids and Gases

When scientists talk about matter, they mean everything in the world. And all matter can be divided into three groups: solids such as iron or wood, liquids such as water and oil, and gases such as air or steam. Ice is solid water. When ice is heated it melts to become liquid water. When the liquid is heated to 100°C it boils and becomes a gas – steam.

Solids tend to resist being pulled or pushed out of shape; they usually keep the same size and shape, no matter where they are. Liquids have no shape of their own. They take the shape of any container they are poured into. Gases do not keep either their shape or their size. They expand to completely fill anything they are in.

The reason why different materials behave in different ways is because of the tiny atoms that make them up. Iron is different from gold because it is made up of a different kind of atom. The way in which the atoms are packed together decides whether a substance is a solid, a liquid or a gas.

Water is a strange liquid. It is one of the very few things that grows bigger (expands) when it freezes. That is why huge icebergs float, even though most of the bulk is under the surface.

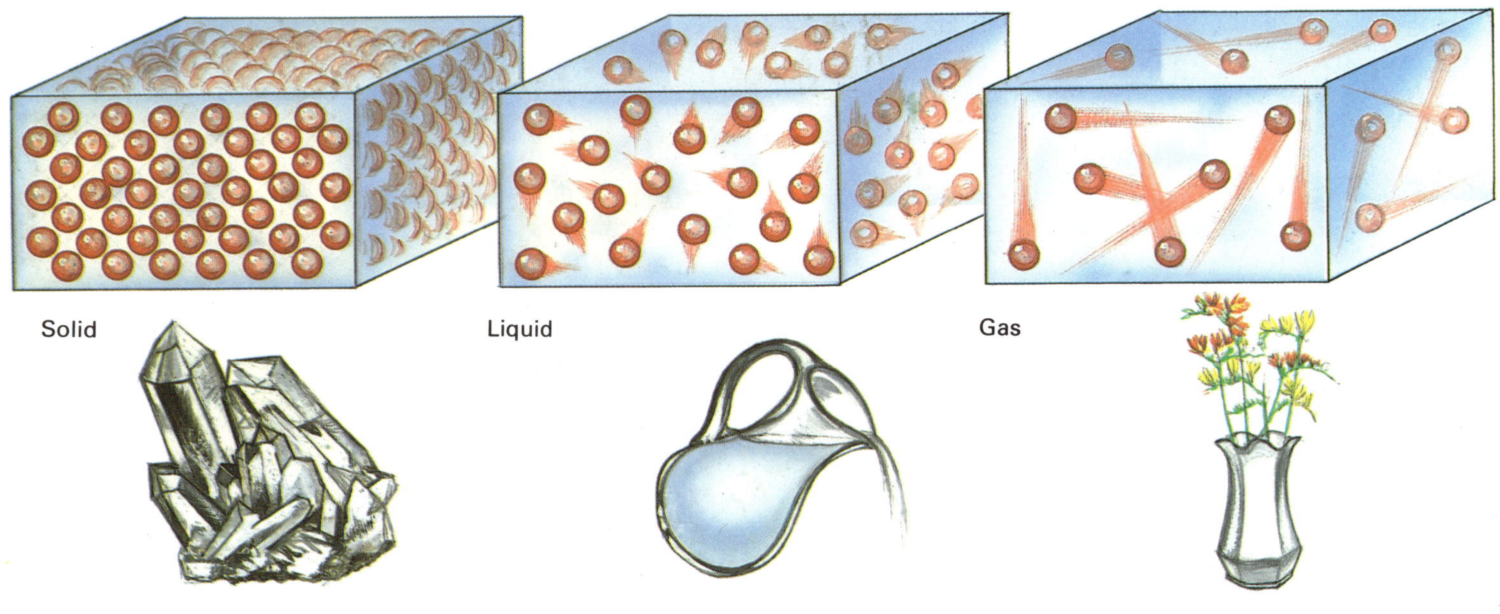

A solid keeps its shape

Liquids hold together but take the shape of a container

When gases are released, they expand for ever

How solid something is depends on how closely packed the atoms in it are. In a solid, the atoms are close together and fixed in position. This is why it is difficult for a solid to change its shape or its size. In a liquid, the atoms are less tightly packed and can move about a bit. When a solid is heated, the atoms in it move more and more until they form a liquid. They move apart but do not escape from each other completely. If we go on heating a liquid, the particles in it move faster and faster. After a while they move so quickly that they escape from the surface of the liquid and become a gas. This is called *evaporation.* When the liquid gets hotter still, the particles escape so quickly that the liquid bubbles. This is called *boiling.* When water boils it turns into the invisible gas, steam.

Solids

Solids are solid because of the way their atoms and molecules are arranged. Ice, water and steam are all the same from a chemical point of view – they all contain the same kind of atoms and molecules. The difference lies in the movement of the molecules. In ice, the molecules are held tightly in a definite pattern – what is called a *crystal lattice* – by strong forces between the neighbouring molecules. Snow is a mass of beautiful ice crystals, each six-sided and no two of them are alike (see above). Although molecules in ice do not move about, they still vibrate a little.

Liquids

Some substances such as water, oil and the metal mercury are liquid at ordinary room temperature. A liquid is similar to a gas because its atoms and molecules are not fixed together in any particular way. But it is also similar to a solid because it has a definite volume.

The molecules of a liquid are often attracted to the molecules of other substances. And this attraction is greater than the attraction between neighbouring molecules of the liquid. This is why liquids will rise up a narrow tube. It is called *capillary action.* Water also has a 'skin' called *surface tension.* This is why the pond-skater (above) can walk on the surface.

Gases

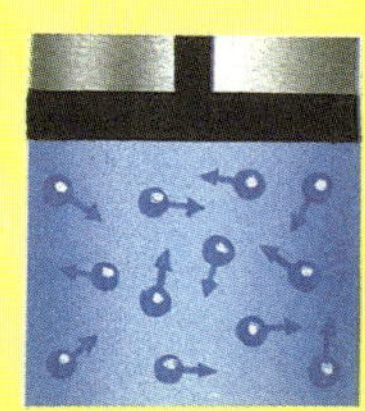

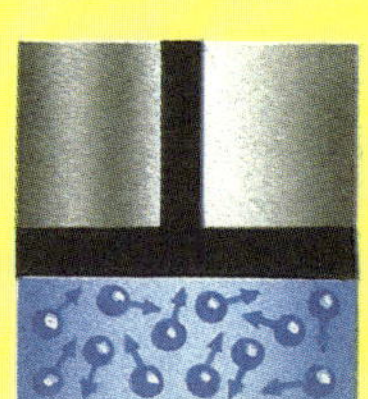

Gases behave quite differently from solids and liquids. They are the lightest and most movable form of matter. Any substance on Earth can be turned into a gas if it is heated above its boiling point. Iron becomes a gas if it is heated to about 2900°C. The temperature of the Sun is so high that all the matter in it is in the form of a gas.

Every gas consists of molecules flying about and colliding with each other. The pressure of a mass doubles if its volume is halved (above). But the temperature must remain constant.

Heat – Molecules in Motion

Centre of the Sun
15,000,000°C

Surface of the Sun
5500°C

Iron melts
1540°C

Sunlit side of Mercury
375°C

Paper catches fire
284°C

Water boils
100°C

Hottest shade temperature
on Earth 57.7°C

Water freezes
0°C

Coldest temperature on Earth
−88.3°C

Air becomes liquid at about
−200°C

Absolute Zero
−273.16°C

What is heat? Scientists say it is a form of energy – the energy of moving atoms and molecules, that everything is made up of. Atoms and molecules are always on the move, and the heat of anything is simply a measure of how fast they are moving. The faster they move, the hotter a body is.

We measure heat with *thermometers*. Water boils when the thermometer shows 100 on the Centigrade scale (100°C); it freezes at 0°C. Our bodies use the food we eat as fuel to keep our temperature at about 37°C. But temperature and heat are not quite the same thing. If we put two pots on the stove, one full of water, the other with very little water, it will take much longer for the full pot to boil. This means that much more *heat* has to be put into the full pot to get both pots to 100°C.

Heat passes from one place to another in three different ways. They are called *convection, radiation* and *conduction.*

Convection carries heat by circulating it in *convection currents.* A room heater, for example, warms the air around it. This heated air expands and rises and is replaced by cooler air. Then the new cooler air is heated and rises. This means that a constant current of air carries heat all over the room. Convection currents also occur in liquids (right).

With radiation, heat travels through empty space. When something gets hot, its moving atoms and molecules make invisible waves of radiant energy. These waves are also called *infra-red rays.* The heat that reaches us from the Sun has travelled by radiation rays at the speed of light. Heat waves and light waves are exactly the same except for their different wavelengths.

Conduction is the movement of heat through a material or from one body to another if the bodies are touching. If we place one end of a metal spoon in boiling water, the handle of the spoon soon becomes too hot to hold. The heat from the water has travelled up the spoon by conduction. Some materials such as metals are good conductors – they conduct heat easily; other substances such as wood are bad conductors.

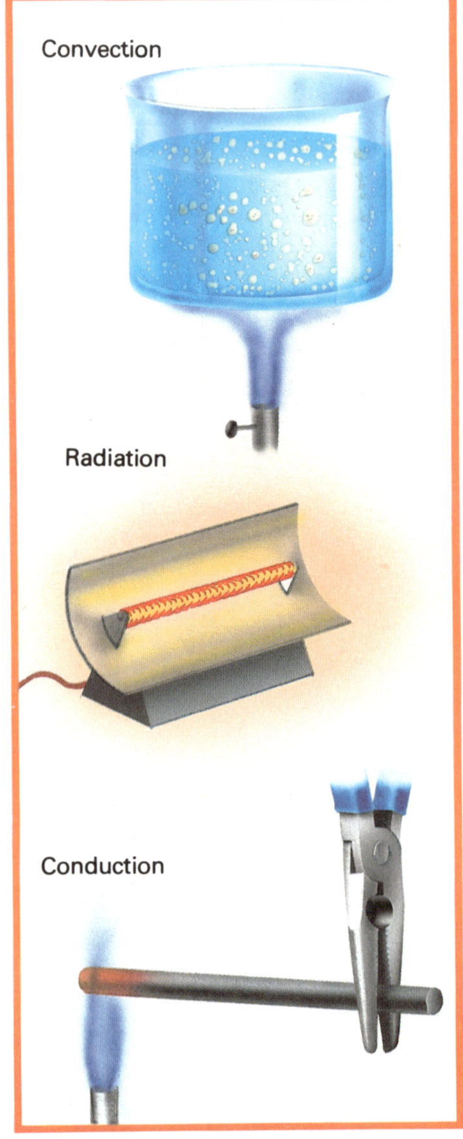

Left: An example of the tremendous range of temperatures experienced in the universe.

Hot and Cold

Steel begins to melt at a temperature of about 1500°C, but this is very chilly compared to the heat of the Sun. Inside the Sun the temperature is about 15 million degrees. Other stars are much hotter still. There appears to be no limit to how hot it can get.

Cold is different. The coldest place on Earth is a chilly −88°C (88 degrees below zero). But the thermometer would have to drop to −183°C before the air started to freeze. At −273°C, *absolute zero* is reached. At this temperature everything would be frozen solid. Nothing would move. Even the atoms would stop moving. But it is not possible to reach this temperature.

Nearly everything grows bigger when it is heated. If you place a thermometer in hot water, the atoms in the mercury move faster and faster and take up more space. The mercury expands and moves up the thermometer's stem.

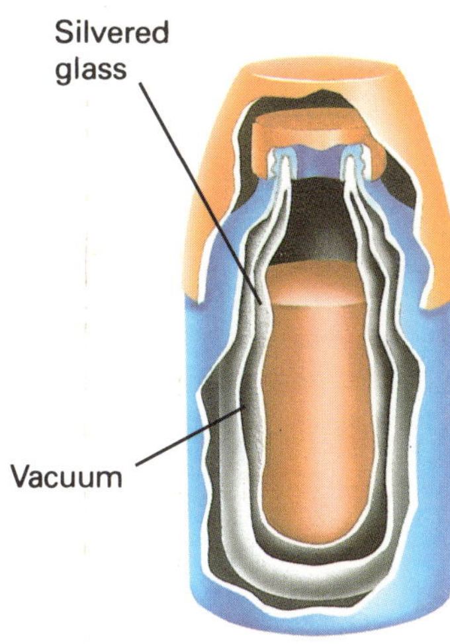

Vacuum flasks keep things hot or cold for a long time. There is a vacuum between the double walls of the flask to stop heat loss by conduction. The container is also silvered to help stop loss of heat by radiation.

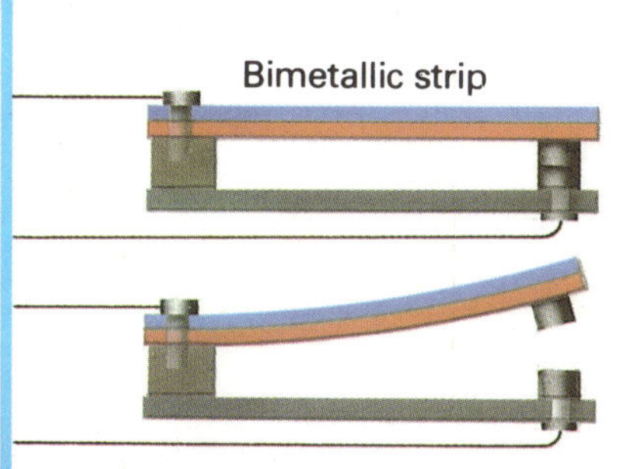

Thermostats make use of the fact that some substances expand and contract more than others when they are heated. They are used in heating systems, cookers and irons to switch the heat on when the temperature falls too low, and to switch it off again when the required temperature is reached. They are also used in refrigerators.

Many thermostats have a *bimetallic strip* made of two different metals such as brass and iron fastened together. As the temperature rises, the brass expands more than the iron. This makes the strip bend upwards. The electrical contact is broken and the heating current stops flowing. As the bimetallic strip cools down again the brass contracts until the two metals are the same size once more. The contact is made and the heating current flows once more.

A fire-fighter wears a special suit so that he can walk through flames and remain unharmed. The suit is made of asbestos, a substance that is a very poor conductor of heat. The silvery surface of the suit reflects heat away.

Chemical Reactions

Chemistry is the study of substances. It looks at what they are made of and how they split up or join together with other substances. Everything around us is made of chemicals. The water we drink, the salt and sugar we eat are chemicals. So are the proteins that make up most of all plants and animals.

There are just over a hundred basic chemicals called *elements*. Everything is made up of these. Iron, oxygen, carbon, gold and silver are all elements. And elements are made up of tiny atoms. Each element has its own kind of atom that is different from the atoms of all the other elements. When the atoms of two or more different elements join together, they form a chemical *compound*. Water is a compound of the elements of hydrogen and oxygen. Two atoms of hydrogen join with one atom of oxygen to make a *molecule* of water.

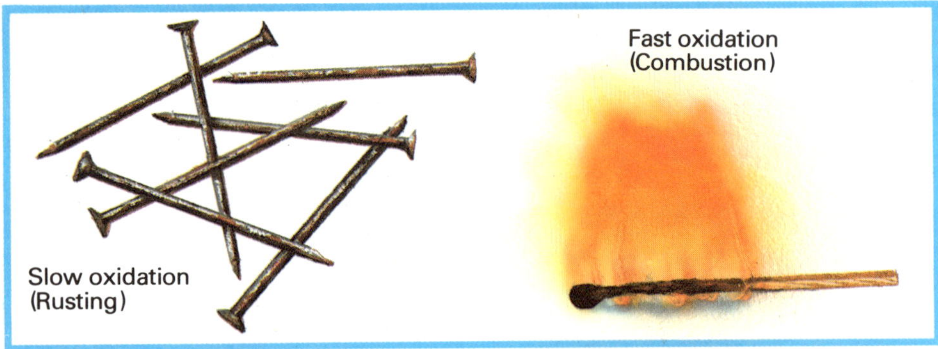

Some compounds are very complicated. Each molecule of sugar, for example, contains 22 hydrogen atoms, 11 oxygen atoms and 12 carbon atoms. Sugar, starch and alcohol all have molecules that contain hydrogen, oxygen and carbon, but in different proportions. It is the different proportions that make the three substances different.

Chemists use symbols to name substances. Chemical formulas show the elements that make up the substances. The symbol for the element hydrogen is H; for oxygen it is O. The formula for water is H_2O.

Vast quantities of chemicals are used in the modern world. Soaps and detergents, dyes and acids, polishes, artificial fibres and explosives – all these things and thousands more are products of the vast chemical industry.

When something burns very quickly indeed, we say it 'explodes'. The exploding force in fireworks (above) comes from the rapid burning of gunpowder. Gunpowder is a mixture of sulphur, saltpetre and charcoal. When an explosion happens, a quite small quantity of explosive such as gunpowder burns in a flash and turns into a large amount of hot gas. It is this expanding gas that sends rockets into the air. The brilliant colours of fireworks comes from metallic salts that are added. Calcium salts give a red colour; sodium, yellow; barium, green; and copper, blue and green.

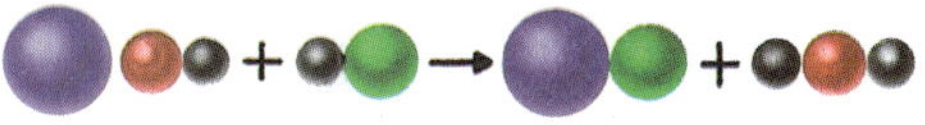

Acids turn litmus paper red. *Bases* turn litmus paper blue. Acids and bases neutralize each other – they cancel each other out. Bases that dissolve in water are called *alkalis.* When a base neutralizes an acid it makes salt and water only. If we take a solution of sodium hydroxide (a base) and add it to hydrochloric acid in the right quantities, the result is neutral. We are left with sodium chloride (table salt) and water (see above).

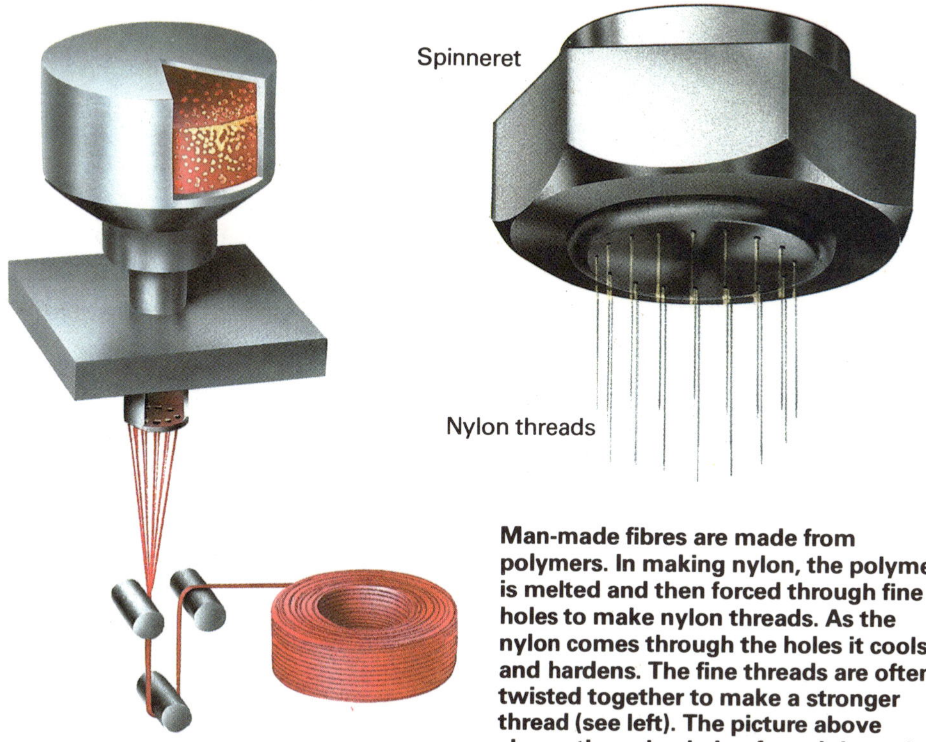

Man-made fibres are made from polymers. In making nylon, the polymer is melted and then forced through fine holes to make nylon threads. As the nylon comes through the holes it cools and hardens. The fine threads are often twisted together to make a stronger thread (see left). The picture above shows the nylon being forced through the holes in a *spinneret*.

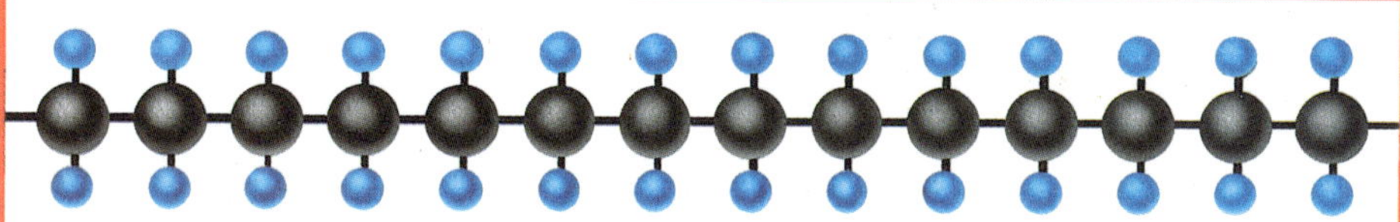

Substances that are made up of long chains of carbon atoms are often called *polymers.* Cotton is a natural polymer because the fibres of cotton are made up of a polymer called *cellulose.* Cellulose is a compound with long chains of carbon atoms. Nowadays, chemists make artificial polymers. For example, molecules of the gas ethylene join together in a long chain to make polyethylene – the plastic we call Polythene (see above). There are many different plastics that rely on the joining together of carbon atoms. Plastics have countless uses.

Slow and Fast Burning

Oxygen is the most plentiful of all the elements in nature. Although it is a gas we cannot see, it accounts for about half the weight of most rocks and minerals. A fifth of the air we breathe is oxygen, and nearly all living things need it.

Oxygen is a very active chemical. It combines with many other chemical elements to make a very large number of compounds. These compounds are called *oxides*. The process in which they are made is called *oxidation*. Slow oxidation happens when iron is in damp air. This produces *iron oxide,* which we call rust. When oxygen and another element are combined rapidly, light and heat are given off. We call fast oxidation *combustion,* or burning.

Iron and Steel

Imagine our world without metals – no metal cars, coins, saucepans, tools or machines. Our civilization just couldn't exist without them. Metals are useful because they have important qualities that other substances do not have. They vary a lot in appearance and how they behave, but most of them are silvery in colour and quite heavy. Many are shiny and conduct heat and electricity well. Most of them can be drawn out into wires and hammered into sheets.

But a few are different. Some are not silvery – gold and copper, for example. Others are quite light – potassium will even float on water. Mercury is a liquid at normal temperatures.

We also call mixtures of different metals 'metals'. These are *alloys* such as brass, bronze and pewter. Alloys and other metals that do not contain any iron are called *nonferrous* metals.

About a quarter of the Earth's crust under our feet is made up of metals.

Henry Bessemer invented the blast furnace. He found that if hot air was blown through molten iron, the carbon in the iron and other impurities were blown away as gases. The furnace is fed with ore and other substances. The charge melts in a fierce blast or air. It turns into molten iron, waste slag and hot gas. The waste hot gas is used to heat the air blast.

Smelting and Refining

Metals are seldom found in the earth in their pure form. They are usually mixed up with other elements and earth materials. These mixtures are called *ores*. Separating metals from their ores and preparing them for use is called *metallurgy*.

The metal ores coming from the ground are usually just lumps of rock. The rock must pass through several stages before pure metal is obtained. Unwanted material must first be removed. This can be done by crushing, washing, heating and floating the ore in a frothy liquid. Many of the common ores such as iron ore are then heated with coke in a huge furnace. This is called *smelting*. Smelting makes a metal that is still not pure. It still has to be *refined*.

There are several ways to refine metals. Sometimes the metal is heated with substances that remove the impurities. Steel is made in this way. Other metals, such as copper, have an electric current passed through them in a solution.

When the metal has been refined it can be used in its pure state or it can be mixed with other metals to form a useful alloy. It can be shaped in a *cast*, rolled into sheets or pulled out into wires.

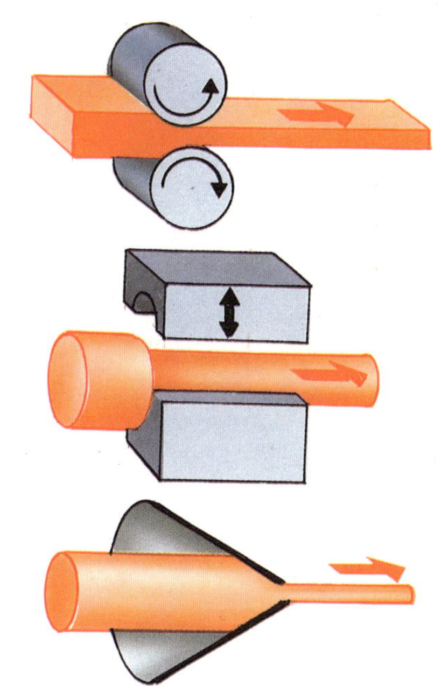

The diagrams above show three ways of shaping metals. *Rolling* (top) is a way of making sheets of metal by passing the hot metal between rollers. In *forging* (centre) the hot metal is pressed into shape between heavy blocks. In *cold drawing* (bottom) the cold metal is pulled through holes to make wire of various thicknesses.

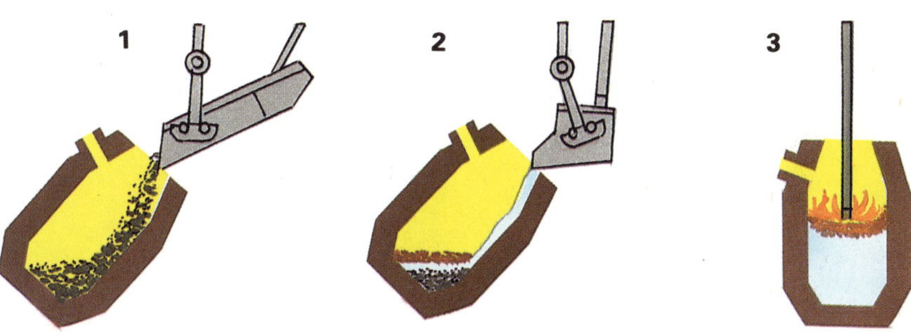

Steel is made by heating scrap steel (1) and mixing it with molten iron (2). All impurities are burned off by feeding in oxygen (3). The furnace is tilted and, after sampling (4), the molten steel is tapped off (5). Lastly, the waste slag is removed (6).

Left: Charging a steel furnace with molten iron. Steel is basically an alloy of iron and carbon, but small amounts of other metals are added during the steelmaking process to produce steels with particular properties. The addition of chromium and nickel produces stainless steel, while tungsten makes a very hard steel suitable for high-speed cutting tools.

The Force of Gravity

An astronaut, hundreds of miles above the Earth, is weightless because he is so far from the Earth's gravitational centre. He feels he is floating and not moving, but both he and his spaceship are travelling at about 30,000 km per hour. The pull of gravity holds him in orbit around the Earth.

Everything in Earth is pulled downwards by a strange force called gravity. The pull of gravity is always towards the centre of the Earth. A stone dropped from someone's hand in England falls to the ground in the same way it would fall in New Zealand on the opposite side of the world. Both stones fall towards the centre of the Earth. And gravity isn't a force that happens only on Earth. Everything in the universe is attracted towards everything else. It is only because the Earth is so big and so close to us that we notice gravity here. The more massive a body, the more material in it, the greater its gravitational pull on other bodies.

The Sun is much more massive than the Earth and all the other planets put together. So the Sun's enormous gravitational pull holds all the planets in place as they circle their big parent body. It is incredible to think that our mighty Earth, speeding along at 30 km per second, is held in its orbit by this invisible bond. In exactly the same way, Earth's gravity holds the Moon in place in its monthly journey around us.

Gravity decreases with distance from the Earth and the same object weighs less and less.

The Tides

Although the Moon's gravity is much less than the Earth's, it still affects us. Tides are caused mainly by the gravitational pull of the Moon, and, to a lesser extent, by the pull of the Sun. When the Moon is overhead, the oceans' waters are drawn towards it, causing a bulge, which is balanced by another bulge on the opposite side of the Earth. High tides are called *spring* tides. They happen when the Earth, Moon and Sun are in a straight line (see diagram). The combined gravitational pull of the Moon and the Sun makes high tides even higher and low tides even lower. The smallest tides – called *neap* tides – happen when the pull of the Moon is at right angles to that of the Sun. Spring tides happen about twice a month, about the time of the full moon and the new moon. Neap tides happen around the first and last quarters of the moon.

Tides occur twice every 24 hours 50 minutes, the time taken for one complete orbit of the Moon around the Earth.

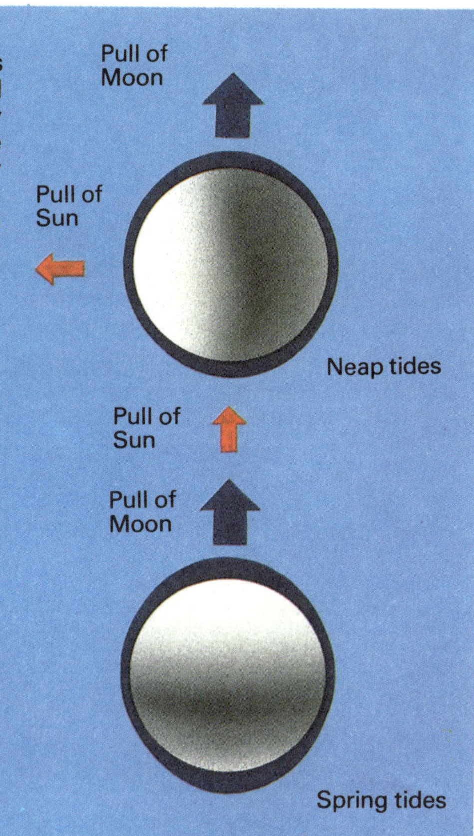

The great Italian 16th century scientist Galileo was the first to prove that all objects fall to the ground at the same speed. People knew that a cannon ball falls faster than a feather. But Galileo proved that this was because the feather was slowed down by air resistance. On the Moon, where there is no air, the cannon ball and the feather fall at exactly the same rate.

Losing Gravity

The force of gravity grows less and less the further apart bodies are. When people go up in a spaceship the pull of Earth gravity gets less the higher they go. After a while, the Earth's pull is so small the astronauts do not notice it. They are weightless and live in a strange floating state where there is no 'up' or 'down'.

But what happens if the spaceship goes further and gets close to the Moon? Then the astronauts and their ship begin to come into the pull of the Moon's gravity. With no rockets firing, the spaceship will be pulled faster and faster towards the Moon. If the astronauts land on the Moon they find they can do things they cannot do on Earth. They can lift rocks six times as heavy. Even in their bulky spacesuits they can jump much higher. This is because the gravity of the Moon is only a sixth of Earth gravity. The Moon has only a sixth of the mass of our Earth. If an astronaut who weighed 65 kg on Earth weighed himself on the Moon, the scales would show a weight of only 11 kg. On the other hand, if people ever reach the giant planet Jupiter they will find things much more difficult. If you can jump a height of one metre on Earth, you could only jump 28 cm on Jupiter. And if it were possible to stand on the surface of the Sun, you could not even jump to the height of 3 cm!

Magnets

A magnet is any piece of metal that will attract or pull towards itself iron, steel or a few other metals. Magnets can be of different sizes and shapes, and they can be strong or weak. The ends of magnets are called their *poles*. One end is called the *north-seeking pole* (N); the other is the *south-seeking pole* (S).

Magnets are very important. They are used every day in telephones and in the loudspeakers of television sets and radios. And they are a vital part of the big generators that make our electricity.

The magnet on the right is called a *horseshoe magnet*. If we hang chains of pins from it, each pin becomes a small magnet; each with its own north and south poles.

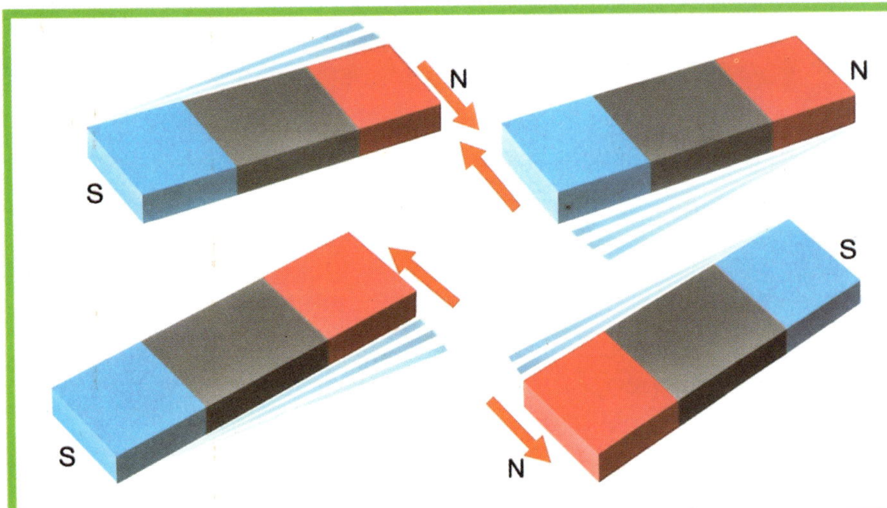

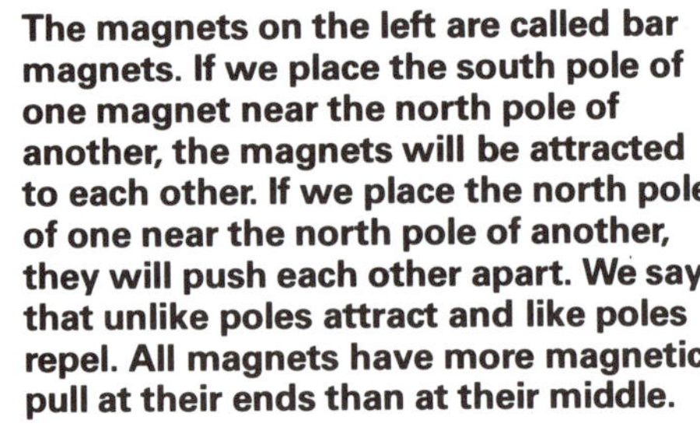

The magnets on the left are called bar magnets. If we place the south pole of one magnet near the north pole of another, the magnets will be attracted to each other. If we place the north pole of one near the north pole of another, they will push each other apart. We say that unlike poles attract and like poles repel. All magnets have more magnetic pull at their ends than at their middle.

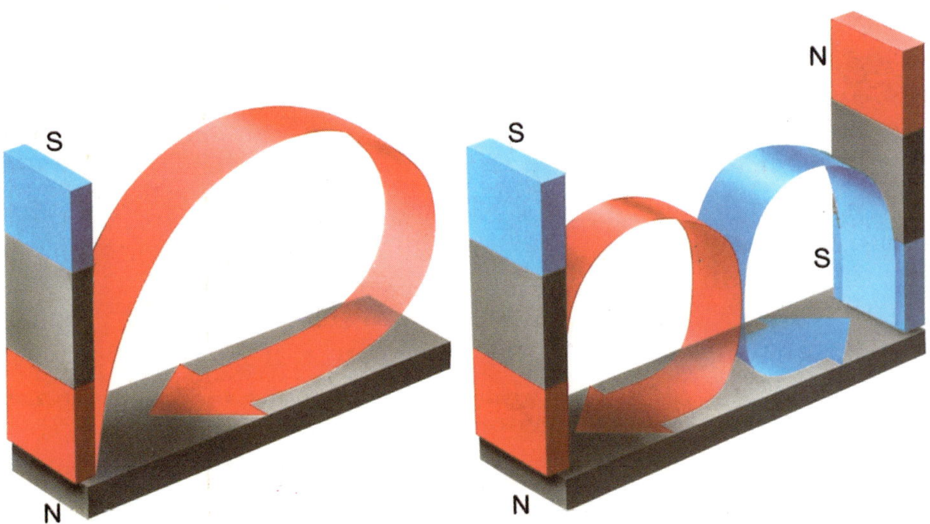

There are several ways of making magnets. One way is to stroke a permanent magnet across the metal to be magnetized, usually a piece of iron. (Soft iron is easier to magnetize than hard steel.) The iron must be stroked in one direction only, as shown in the pictures on the left.

A weak magnet can also be made by placing the iron in line with the Earth's magnetic field and hammering it. An electric current flowing in a coil around the metal will also magnetize it.

Magnets can be made to lose their magnetism by hammering them or by heating them in a flame.

Magnetic Fields

Every magnet has an invisible *magnetic field* going through it and around it. The field around a bar magnet can be seen if we lay a sheet of paper over the magnet and sprinkle iron filings on the paper. When the paper is tapped, the iron filings will move into lines, called *lines of force,* around the magnet. Most of the lines cluster round the ends of the magnet where the magnetism is strongest.

The magnet on the right is called a *horseshoe magnet.* If we move a small compass around in the horseshoe magnet's field and note the way the compass needle points, we can draw a pattern of lines as in the picture.

The Earth has a weak magnetic field, rather like that of an enormous bar magnet. Compass needles all over the world point north and south because of the Earth's magnetism.

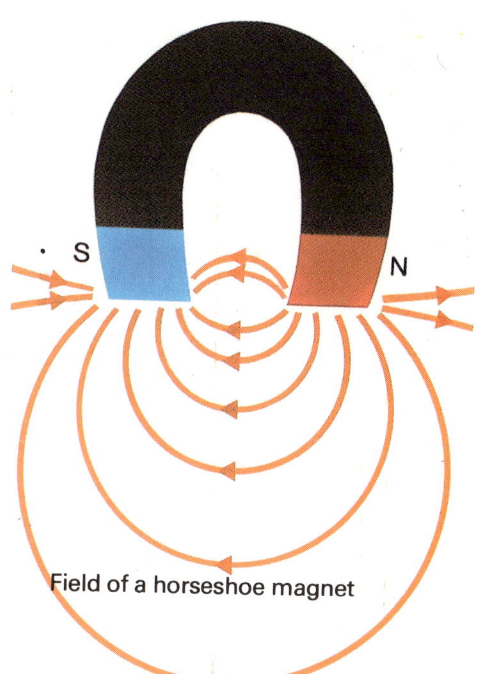

Field of a horseshoe magnet

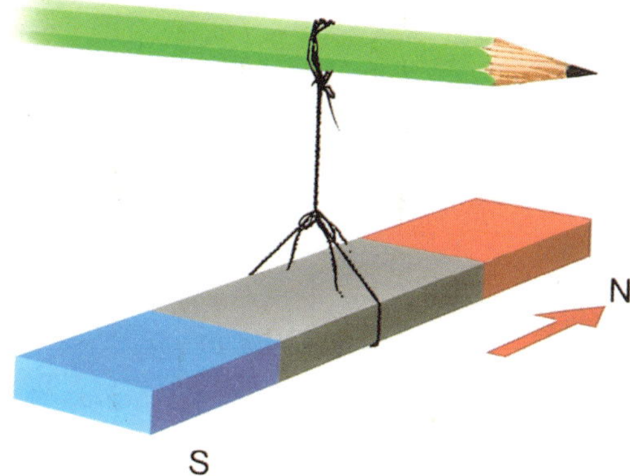

If a bar magnet is suspended as shown above, it will always come to rest pointing in a North–South direction. And always the same end of the magnet points North. A compass (below) is really a small, lightweight magnet. It is pivoted so that it can move freely. The Earth's North pole always attracts the magnet's South pole.

The end of the magnet that points North is called the magnet's *North-seeking pole*.

Compass

The Earth's magnetic field

Making Electricity

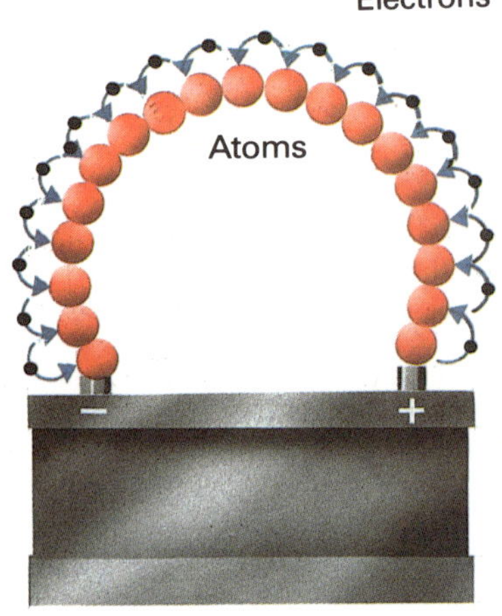

When the terminals of a battery are connected by a wire, an electric current flows from one terminal to the other. Most metals are good conductors of electricity – especially copper and silver. Wires are usually made of copper. The copper atoms have *free* electrons that can be pushed on to the next atom in the line. Another free electron is pushed from that atom, and so on to the other battery terminal. This is an electric current.

When ancient people saw lightning flashes in the sky, they thought the gods were angry. They did not know about electricity, but they noticed that some things seemed at times to attract other things. The ancient Greeks knew that if they rubbed a piece of amber with a woollen cloth, straw and dry leaves were attracted to it.

Today, we know that both the lightning and the amber's attraction are forms of electricity. Lightning happens when clouds store up too much electricity. Electric sparks which we call lightning shoot from the clouds to other clouds or to the ground.

An electric current is a movement, or flow, of tiny particles called *electrons*. Electrons are particles of negative electricity that circle around the centre of every atom. In some materials, a few of the electrons are only loosely held to their atoms. They are free to jump from atom to atom. When they do this, an electric current flows. An electric current is started by a battery or electric generator. If the

Electricity can be produced by separating two different metals with a solution that conducts electricity. A 'dry' cell is not really dry. It is filled with a damp chemical paste. The positive terminal is a carbon rod. The zinc container is the negative electrode.

An accumulator or battery contains cells made of lead plates in dilute sulphuric acid. Car batteries usually have six 2-volt cells. They are connected in series to give 12 volts.

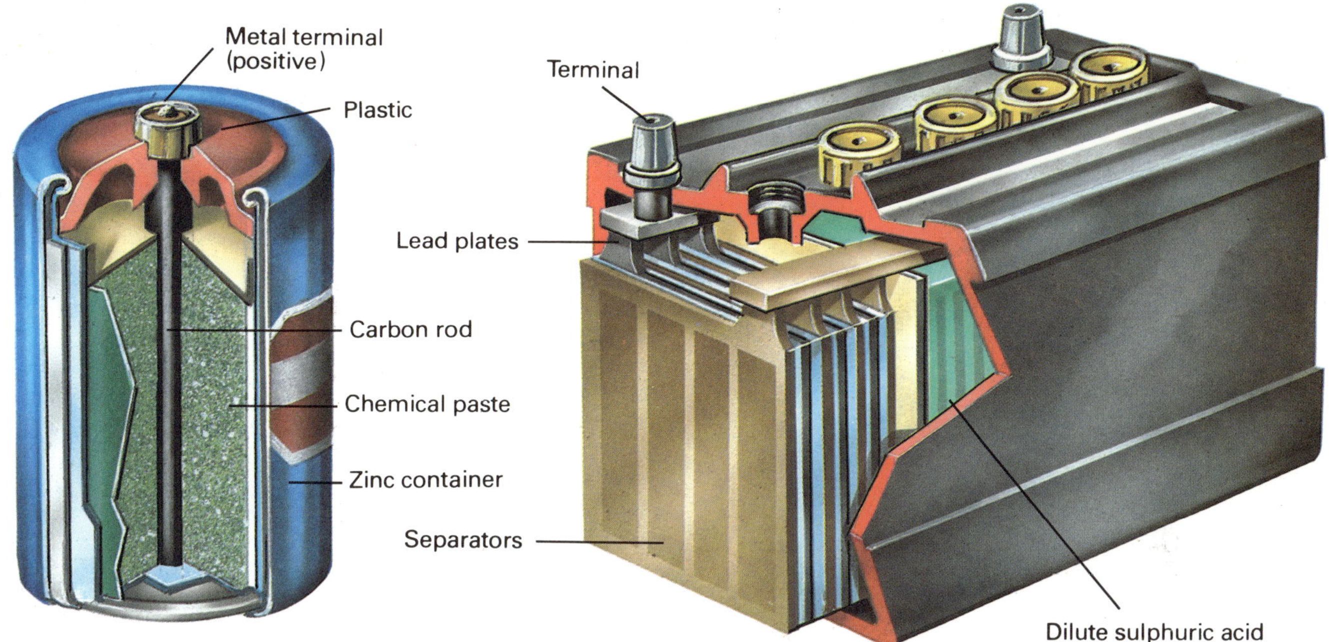

terminals of a battery are connected to each end of a piece of wire, electrons are pushed from the first atom in the line to the next, and so on along the wire – all in a flash of time. Wires which carry electric current are often made of copper. Copper, like most metals, is a good *conductor* of electricity. It has lots of free electrons.

Batteries and Generators

Batteries make electricity by chemical action. The most common kind of battery – the flashlight battery – is really a *dry cell.* When the chemicals in the cell are used up, the cell is dead and is thrown away. A battery is two or more cells working together.

A car battery is different. It is filled with dilute sulphuric acid in which are lead plates. When this kind of battery runs down it can be recharged by connecting it to an electric current. This makes the chemical action go backwards. The electrons are put back where they were and the battery can produce current again.

An electric generator is a machine that turns mechanical energy into electrical energy. The simplest generator is a loop of wire that is turned between the poles of a magnet. When the wire cuts the lines of force between the magnet's poles, an electric current is produced in the wire. This is the principle of the electric generator.

The diagram below shows a very simple electric generator. A loop of wire is turned between the poles of a permanent magnet. As the wire cuts the lines of magnetic force between the magnet's poles, an electric current is produced in the wire. The current is taken from the wire loop through carbon brushes that rub against metal rings. Large generators have thousands of loops of wire and produce a very large, steady current.

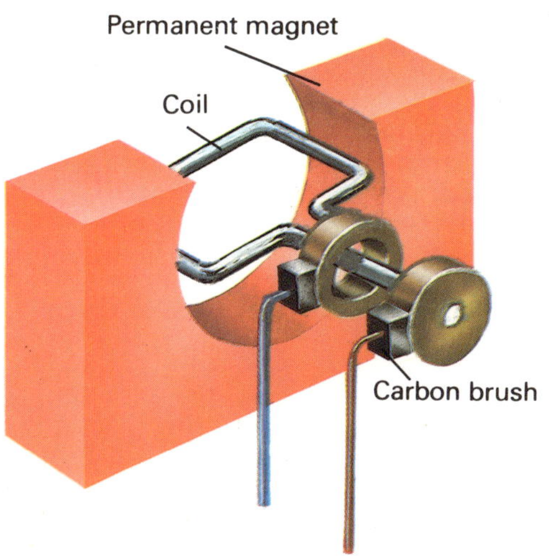

Putting Electricity to Work

When an electric current goes through the fine coiled wire *filament* inside a light bulb, the filament gets hot and glows with light. The filament is made of tungsten, a metal that does not melt easily when it is hot. The bulb has no air in it and has other gases to help stop the filament burning out.

Electricity is the most useful form of energy. It can be taken easily by cables to our homes, factories and offices and there used to produce light and heat or run machines.

The electricity we use is produced at power stations by large generators. These are machines that are turned by power from coal or oil to make electricity. Electricity flows along wires as a current. A current of electricity must have a completely unbroken path. If we could follow a current from the generator, it would travel across country through heavy overhead copper wires and along underground cables to our house. There it would go through a meter that would show how much current went through it; through fuses, to an electric light bulb. After the current has passed through the bulb and produced light, it goes all the way back through a separate wire to the generator in the power station. All this happens in a flash.

Most electricity is used to make things move. What do vacuum cleaners, food mixers and tape recorders have in common? They all have *electric motors* inside them to make things go round (see opposite page).

Some of the most powerful electric motors are used to drive electric trains. The electricity can be carried to the train's motors in different ways. Some railways have overhead wires above the track. A metal bar reaches up from the train and slides along the wire to collect the electric current. This is called a *pantograph.* Other trains get their power from a third rail placed beside the track.

HOW AN ELECTRIC MOTOR WORKS
The diagrams show how a simple motor works. When a current flows through the coil, a magnetic field is set up. The coil then has a north pole and a south pole as shown by the 'ghost' magnet drawn as though it were inside the coil. Permanent magnets give a magnetic field in which the coil turns. Forces of attraction and repulsion between the fields make the coil turn. As the coil turns *carbon brushes* rub against separate *commutator* segments to carry current to the coil as shown. When the poles of the coil are almost in line with the poles of the permanent magnet, the brushes are almost at the end of the commutator segments (1). But the moving coil cannot stop and carries on past this point. At the same time the commutator reverses the current flowing through the coil and in doing so reverses the poles of the coil (2). (This is shown in the diagram by the ghost magnet. The end with the black dot has changed from blue to red.) Forces of attraction and repulsion between the coil and the permanent magnet keep the coil turning (3) until the commutator changes the poles again (4). In this way the coil, or motor, keeps turning.

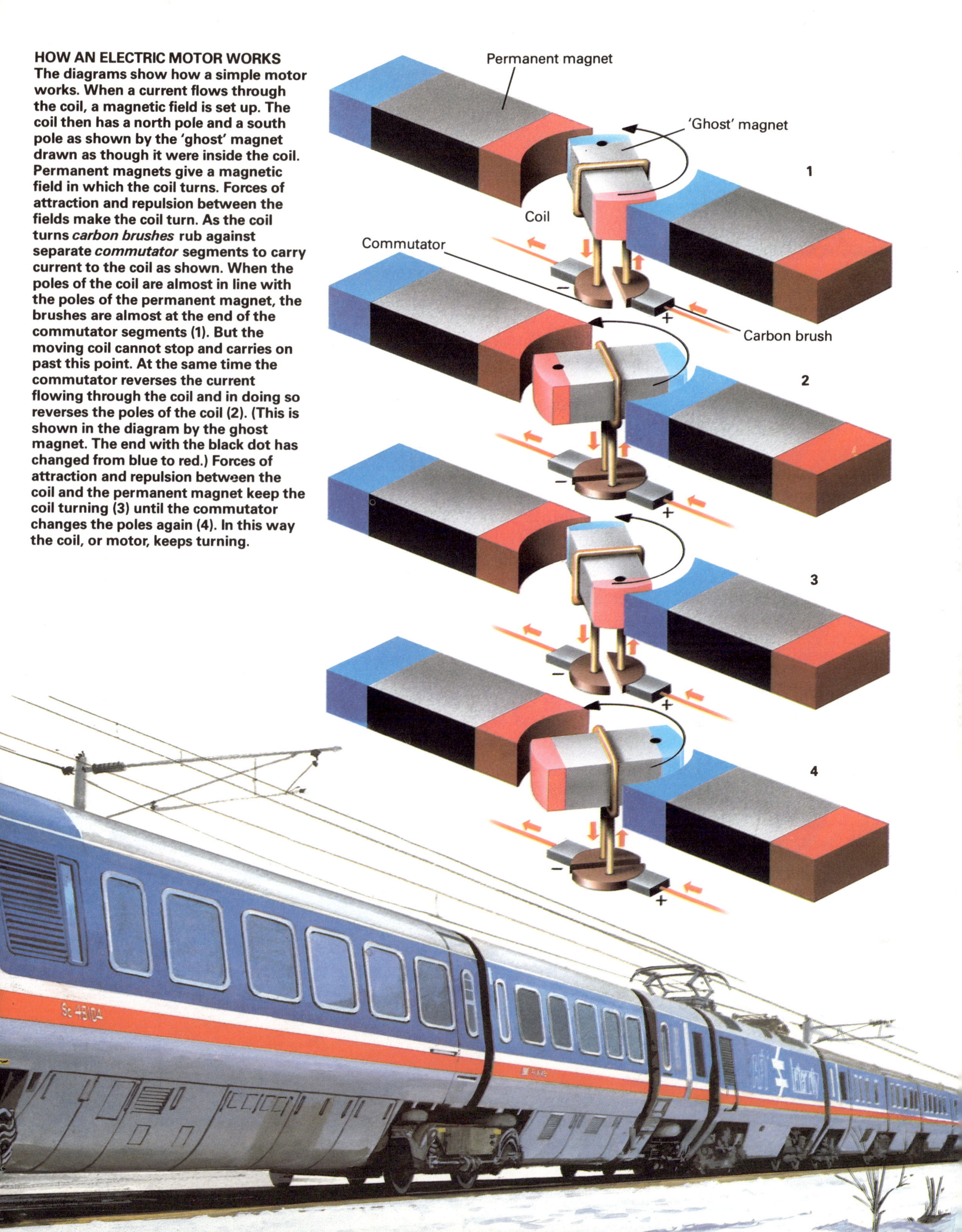

Man and Machines

The ancient Egyptians used the *inclined plane* to get the great stone blocks for the pyramids up to the height they needed. It was easier than lifting them straight up.

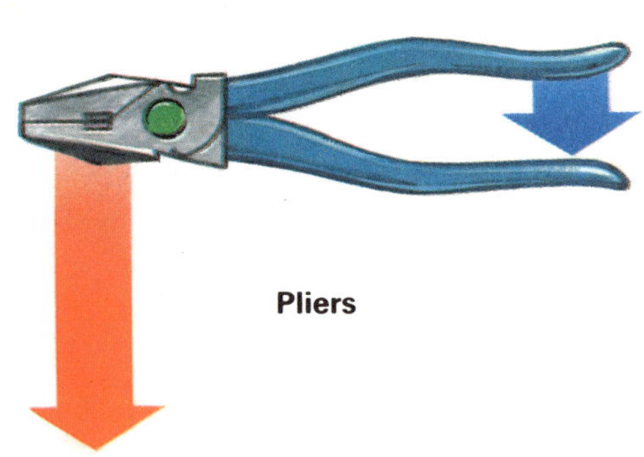

Pliers

A machine is something made by people to help them do jobs more easily. It may be large with masses of wheels and other moving parts like a locomotive or a motor car; or it may be very simple. A pair of scissors is a machine, and so is a screwdriver.

People began using machines centuries ago because they wanted to make their work easier. They wanted to harness power that was greater than the power of their own muscles or the muscles of animals.

Nowadays, machines are essential to everything we do. Industry uses giant machines; we use smaller machines such as washing machines, mixers and refrigerators in our homes. In fact, we depend on machines so much that a serious breakdown of machines at a power station can cut off light, heat, transport and industrial power generally.

Screw

Gear wheels

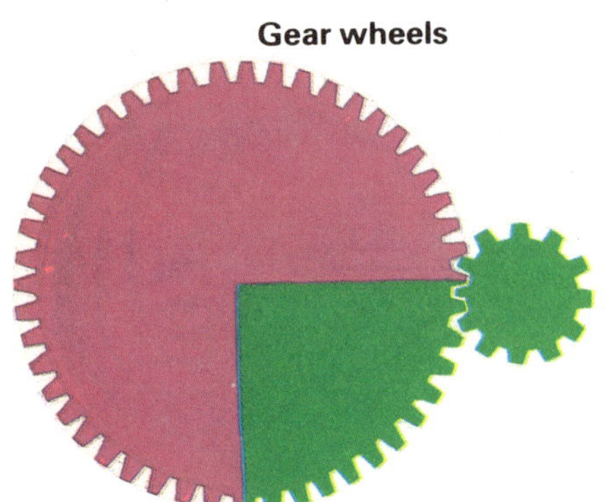

SIMPLE MACHINES

All the things in the pictures above are simple machines. The lever is a simple machine. There are lots of different kinds. Scissors are levers, so are nutcrackers. Pliers are levers. Because they are pivoted near one end, a small amount of pressure on the handle end gives a lot of pressure at the other end.

The spiral thread of a screw is a kind of inclined plane. As the screw is turned, the thread pulls it into the wall.

Gears are machines that change the speed of wheels and help to do work. If the small wheel with 12 teeth turns once, the big wheel with 48 teeth makes only a quarter turn – but with four times the turning force of the small one.

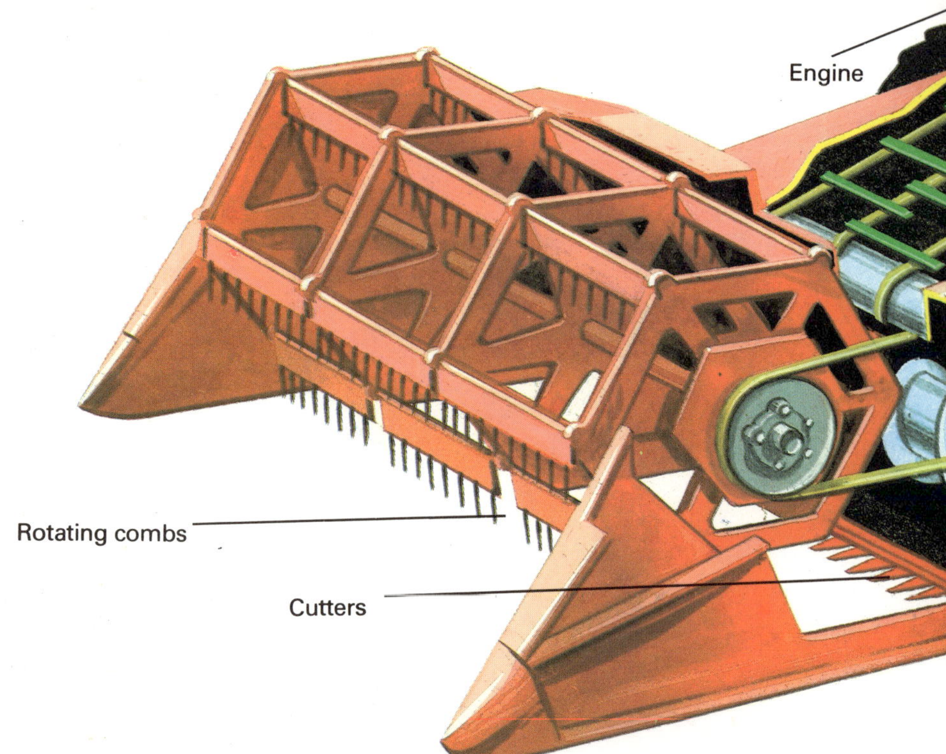

Machines give people the power to do much more work than they could with their strength alone. Suppose you wanted to shift a rock that weighed 50 kilograms from one place to another. To lift it and carry it would be impossible. You would have to exert a lifting force of 50 kg. But if you used a long board as a lever you might shift the rock by using a force of only 10 kg. The lever, which is a simple machine, makes your work easier.

A machine can never do more work than the energy put into it. It often turns one kind of energy, such as electricity, into another kind – mechanical energy that turns wheels or moves machine parts in some way. The efficiency of a machine is the ratio between the energy it supplies and the energy put into it. The perfect machine should have an efficiency of 100 per cent, but this is impossible because every machine has friction in its moving parts. Many machines have an efficiency of only about 10 per cent. Very few can do better than 30 per cent.

For centuries people have tried to make a machine that, once started, will work for ever without needing power – a perpetual motion machine. In the machine above the magnet was supposed to pull the ball up the slope. It fell through the hole, ran down and was pulled up again – for ever. But it didn't work because of friction.

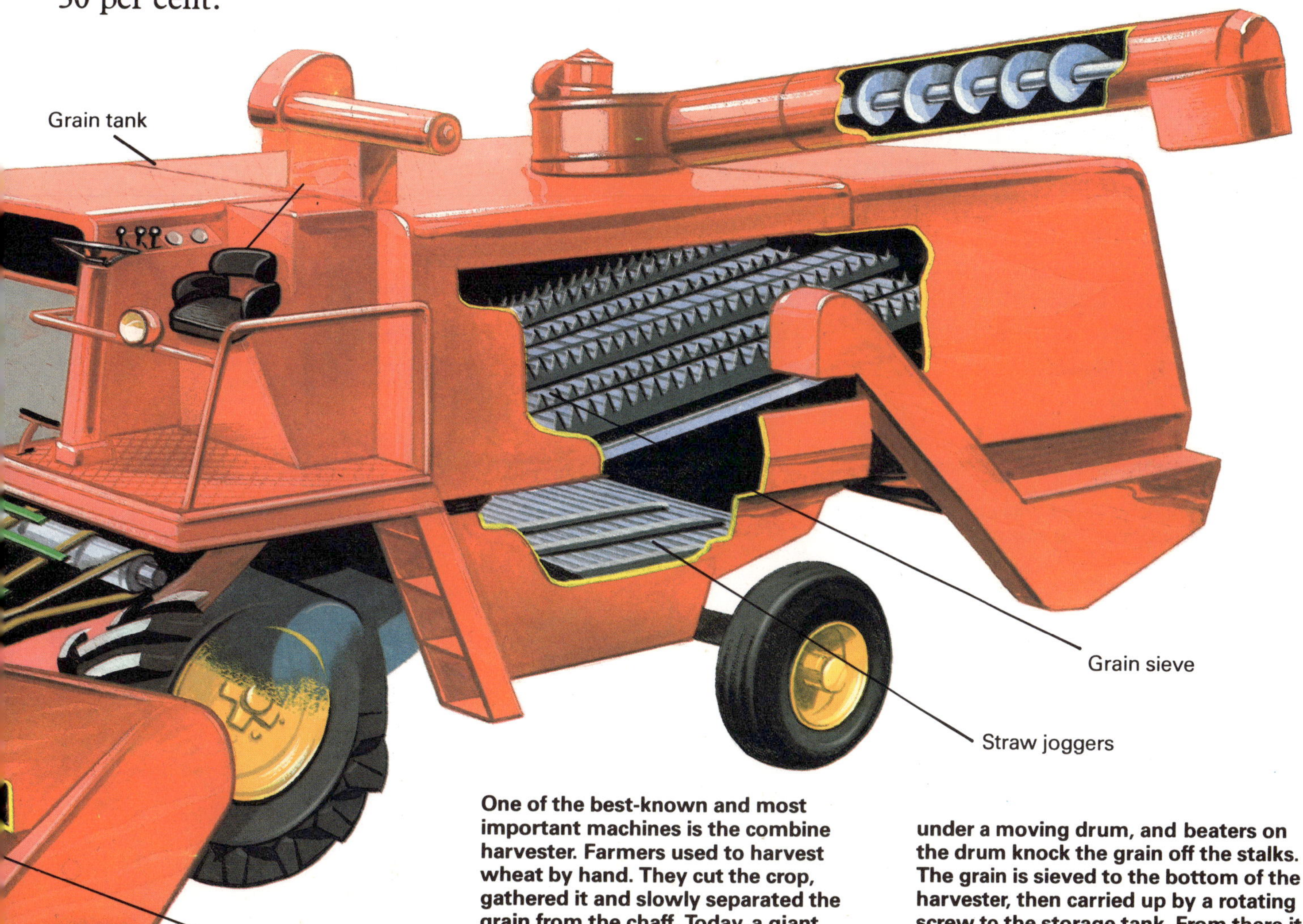

Grain tank

Grain sieve

Straw joggers

Rotating screw

One of the best-known and most important machines is the combine harvester. Farmers used to harvest wheat by hand. They cut the crop, gathered it and slowly separated the grain from the chaff. Today, a giant combine harvester does the whole job in a fraction of the time. Moving knives cut the stalks. The cut stalks are carried under a moving drum, and beaters on the drum knock the grain off the stalks. The grain is sieved to the bottom of the harvester, then carried up by a rotating screw to the storage tank. From there it is piped out into a truck. The straw stalks are shaken to the back of the harvester, where they fall to the ground.

Computers and Robots

Computers are playing a more and more important part in all our lives, whether we realize it or not. Businesses, large and small, are using computers to keep accounts, pay salaries, keep an eye on the stock position. They are used in schools, by the police, by banks, by the armed forces, by airlines and by scientists.

The strange thing is that computers can only do a few simple tasks. They can add. They can subtract. And they can compare one number with another. Why, then, are computers so special. The answer is that they can do these three things at lightning fast speed. They can do millions of calculations in a second.

Although the computer works with numbers, the information it uses does not have to start off as numbers. It can play chess with you, guide a spacecraft, check fingerprints and draw a map of Australia. But before it begins to work on any of these tasks it turns the information into numbers. And the numbers it uses are not quite the same as ours. We use the numbers 0 to 9. All the computer needs is 0 and 1. In fact, it can only count up to 1! This is called the *binary system*.

The computer uses the binary system because it has been designed to work with electrical currents. It can recognize the difference between a flow of current and no flow of current. If there is a current it registers 1; if there is no current it registers 0.

At the heart of every computer, pocket calculator or digital watch is the silicon chip. A tiny chip only 5 mm square, can be the main part of a computer. The number of microscopic transistors and other electrical parts that can be put on a chip has increased rapidly year by year. It is now possible to put more than a million of them on a single tiny chip.

Because the silicon chip is so small and cheap, computers have also become much smaller and cheaper. The home microcomputer can work very well with the household TV set.

As we press the computer's keys to give it commands, the computer translates our key commands into its own binary computer language and works on them. The result appears on the screen.

Communicating with the Computer

To instruct a computer to do something you have to write a program. Writing a program in binary numbers would take a lot of time and effort – the binary for our 8 is 1000 and to the computer the letter T is 01010100. So a simple solution has been found. The computer itself is programmed to translate our instructions into binary. We type in our program in a language we can understand. The computer then translates our language into its own language and starts work on it.

The computer does all its calculations in its main part – called the *central processing unit* or CPU for short. It also has a memory where it stores all the information that is fed into it. It stores little bits of information in separate memory locations or 'boxes'. All we have to do is give the computer the address of any memory location and the machine will find the information in that location in a millionth of a second.

To communicate with a computer we usually type in letters and numbers as on an ordinary typewriter, but using some special computer commands.

WHAT IS A ROBOT?

A robot is a machine that can be programmed to do different tasks. And most robots have an arm or arms that can do work for us. The robot's master is a computer.

More and more robots are working in factories all over the world. They spray paint, lift heavy loads and weld things together. And when they have been taught to do these things they usually do them better than human beings can. Switch on a robot and it will go on working 24 hours a day without stopping for a rest. It can work in places where people could not exist, and it hardly ever goes sick.

In the picture below, robots are welding cars as they move along an assembly line. Very careful programming lies behind a production system like this. A computer controls the robots so that they spot weld sections of each car without getting in each other's way.

Sound Recording

Compared with light, sound travels very slowly. In air, sound travels at about 330 metres per second. Light travels about a million times faster. This means that spectators at an athletics meeting see the smoke from the starter's gun about half a second before they hear the bang. And sound needs something to travel through – something such as air or water. On the Moon there is no air. There is therefore no sound. But light and radio waves can travel through empty space, so astronauts talk to each other by radio.

Sound is very useful underwater. A ship's echo sounder sends out bursts of sound waves from under the ship. The sound travels down to the seabed and bounces back up to the ship. The echo sounder calculates the time taken for the sound to go to the bottom and back to the ship. This gives the depth of water under the ship.

To make sound, we must make something vibrate – a violin string, for example. If something vibrates, it makes the surrounding air vibrate. These air vibrations reach our ear-drums and make them vibrate too. We hear the sound.

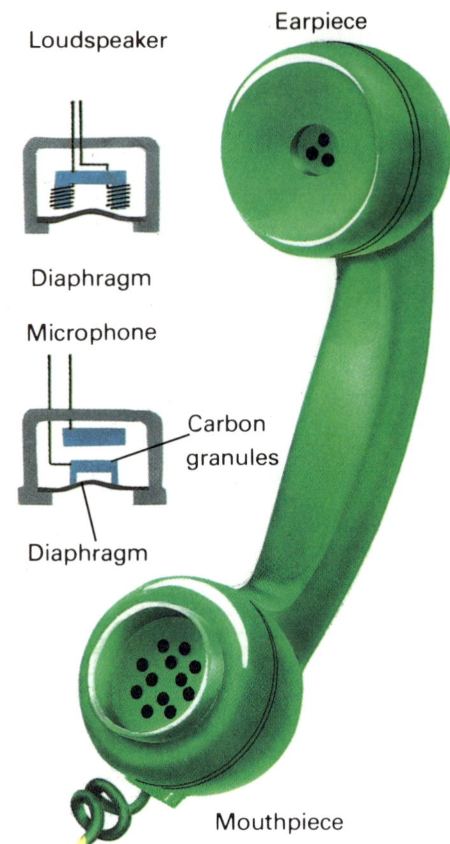

The mouthpiece of a telephone has a small microphone inside it. The sound waves from your voice make a thin diaphragm vibrate. This squeezes carbon granules in the microphone. An electric current flows through the microphone and the granules vary the strength of this current as you speak. This varying current flows through wires to the telephone exchange, from where it is sent on to the earpiece of the other telephone. There is a small loudspeaker in the earpiece which produces the sound of your voice.

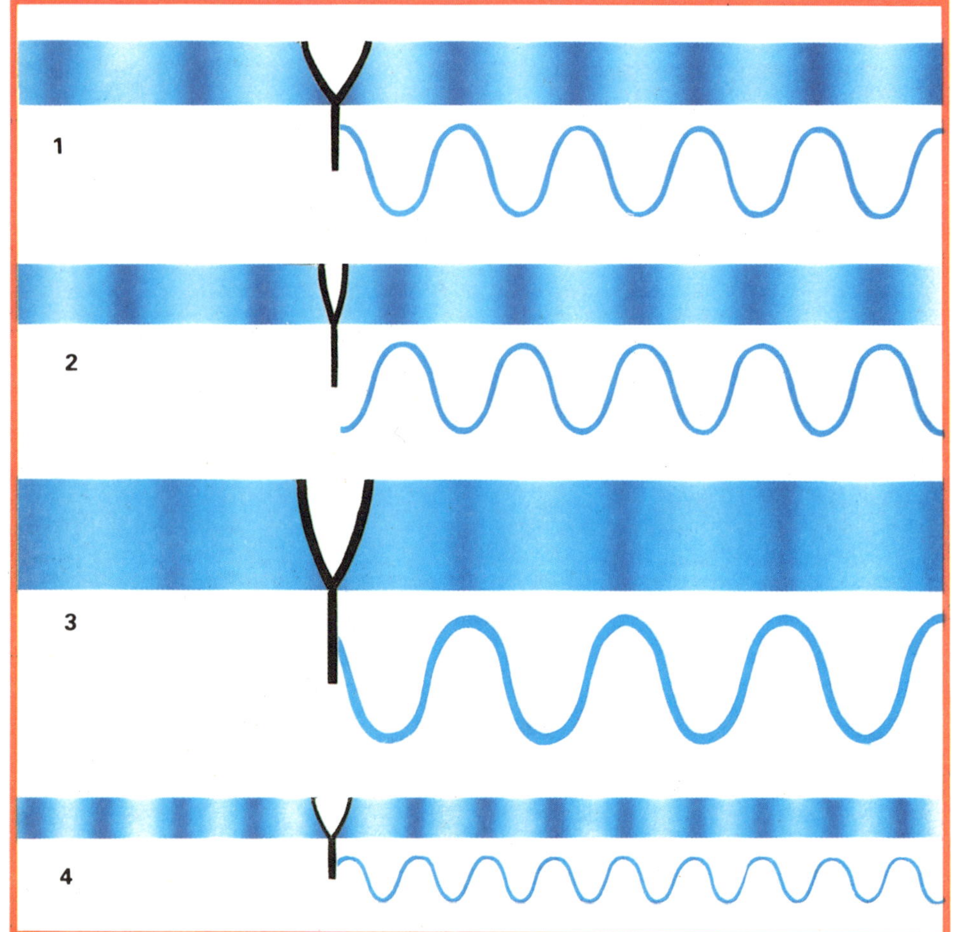

Sound is made when something vibrates. If we strike a tuning fork, the prongs of the fork vibrate. As they move outward in the air, the air molecules are squeezed. A region of *compression* forms (1). When the prongs spring back, the air molecules move apart. There is a region of *rarefaction* (2). These regions of compression and rarefaction move out through the air. We call them sound waves. If the tuning fork is struck harder, the compressions are greater and the sound is louder (3). If a smaller fork is struck, the vibrating frequency is higher. A higher pitched sound is heard (4).

RECORDING ON TAPE

In a recording, sounds are recorded as a magnetic pattern on plastic tape. The tape has a coating of magnetic iron oxide on one side. The capstan rotates, pulling the tape past the heads. The erase head wipes out any existing recording on the tape by making the tape pass through a rapidly changing current. The record head causes a varying current that corresponds to the voice or music to be recorded. This current magnetizes the tape. When the tape is played back, the playback head picks up the magnetic signals from the tape. These become an electric current that is amplified and is a copy of the original sound. Most home recorders have only two heads – an erase head and a record/playback head. Many professional tape recorders, however, have three heads as shown in the diagram at the bottom of the page.

We can think of a tape as having tiny magnetic particles. Before recording, the magnetic particles are arranged as in the top picture. After recording, they become arranged in a pattern that corresponds to the sound recorded.

Recording Sound on Disc

In 1877, Thomas Edison, the great American inventor, recited 'Mary had a little lamb' into a tube. At the end of the tube was a thin metal disc that vibrated as Edison spoke. Attached to the disc was a needle that vibrated with the disc. The vibrating needle was made to cut a wavy groove in a drum covered in tinfoil. This wavy groove was a copy of the loudness and pitch of Edison's voice. When Edison attached a horn to the tube and turned the drum again, a very scratchy voice said: 'Mary had a little lamb'. Edison had discovered how to record sound.

Today, records are made and played back by electricity. The grooves in the record are very fine and play for a long time. Sounds are picked up by a microphone which turns the sound waves into electrical waves. These electrical waves go to a sapphire needle that vibrates and makes grooves in a smooth lacquer disc. From this master disc many other records are made.

Stereo records are made with two microphones, each picking up different sounds. These separate sounds are cut into each side of the record's grooves. The result is a fuller, richer sound.

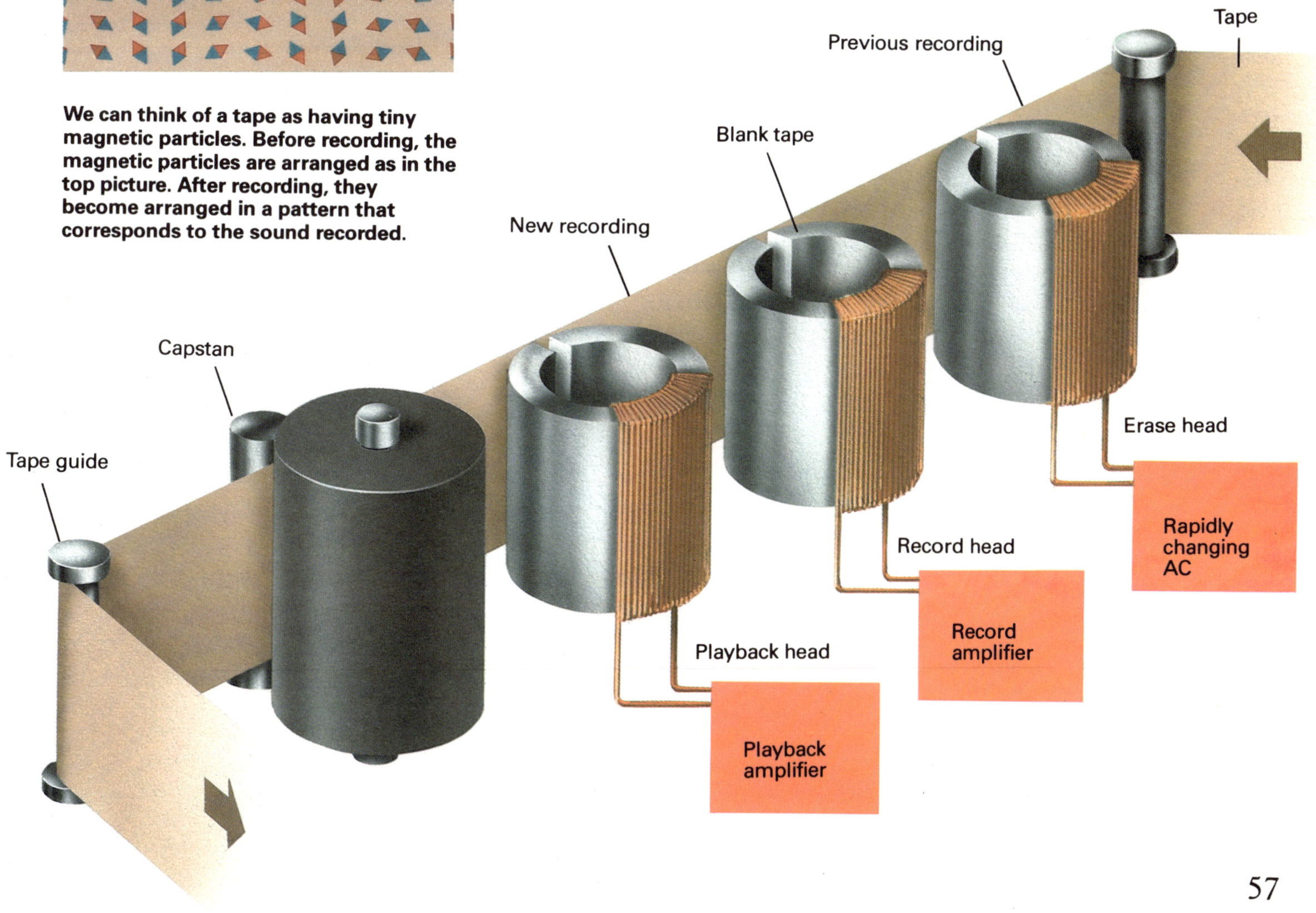

Across the Spectrum

Cosmic rays
Gamma rays
X-ray

The Sun is constantly giving out an enormous amount of energy in the form of waves. These waves include the visible light rays that we can see. Others are infra-red rays (heat), ultra-violet rays, radio waves, X-rays and gamma rays. All these waves are forms of *electromagnetic radiation* and they all travel at the same speed – 300,000 kilometres per second – the speed of light.

But there is one important difference between these various waves. They all have a different *wavelength* – the distance between the start of one wave and the beginning of the next. Gamma rays are only about a billionth of a centimetre long, radio waves can measure several kilometres.

When an atomic bomb explodes it gives off a vast quantity of heat waves and other dangerous radiation.

Bottom right: One of the many uses of ultra-violet radiation is in the detection of forgeries. Fluorescent substances are often present in materials such as inks, and even very slight variations show up under ultra-violet light.

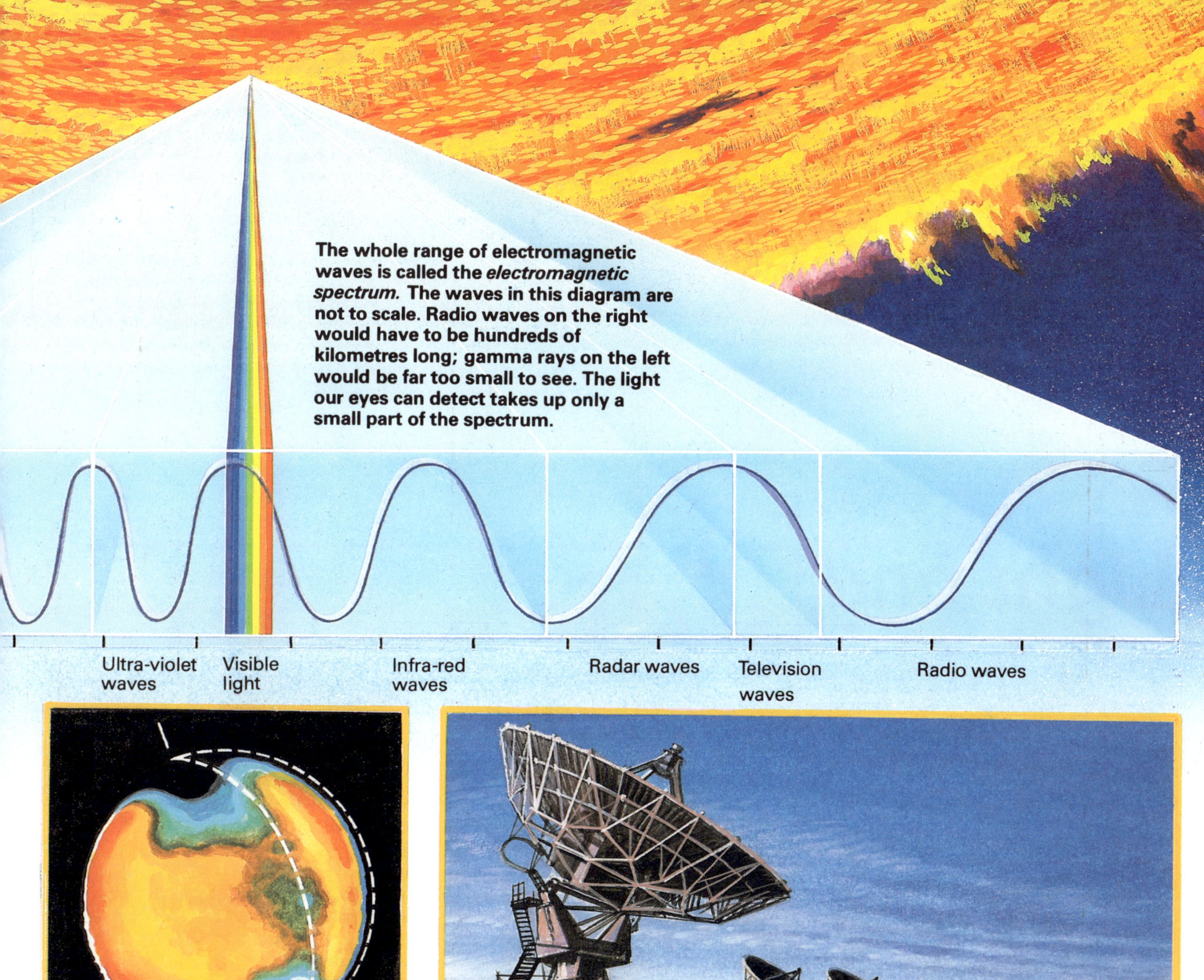

The whole range of electromagnetic waves is called the *electromagnetic spectrum.* The waves in this diagram are not to scale. Radio waves on the right would have to be hundreds of kilometres long; gamma rays on the left would be far too small to see. The light our eyes can detect takes up only a small part of the spectrum.

Above: An infra-red photograph of the Earth taken from space.

Radio telescopes are important in astromony. Their huge dishes capture radio signals from the heavens.

Left: When sunlight falls on rain or spray, we sometimes see a rainbow: the drops of water break up the Sun's light into the colours of the spectrum. The colours are always in the same order – from red to violet.

Doctors use X-rays to see inside our bodies. These very short waves pass right through some things more easily than others – bones, for example, stop the waves quite a lot. This means that when X-rays are passed through us on to a photographic plate, doctors can see broken bones and other things that are wrong inside us.

Visible light from the Sun can be broken down into the colours of the rainbow – from violet at one end to red at the other. The band of radiation immediately above red is called infra-red. It has a longer wavelength than red light and cannot be seen. But we can feel it as heat. Beyond infra-red come radio waves.

Below violet light comes ultra-violet radiation. Ultra-violet rays are sent out by the Sun. They pass through our skin and reach the nerves that lie under its surface. Below ultra-violet rays come the X-rays that doctors use to see right inside us.

The first man to study light and tell people how it worked was Isaac Newton. In 1665, the great scientist shone a beam of light through a glass *prism,* shaped like the one on the left. He found that the light that came out of the prism had been broken up into all the colours of the rainbow. Newton had discovered that ordinary white light is made up of all the rainbow colours added together. We see a band of colours because our eyes see different wavelengths of light as different colours. Each colour has its own wavelength.

Light and Colour

MIXING LIGHT
The three primary colours of light are red, green and blue. Any other colour can be made by mixing these colours. When red, green and blue lights are mixed, the result is white light.

MIXING PAINTS
When paints, inks or dyes are mixed, the basic colours are cyan blue, magenta red and yellow. Cyan and yellow give green. If the three basic colours are mixed, the result is black.

Without light, all life on Earth would come to an end because all the plants and trees would die. People have always realized how important light is, so they tried to find out what it was. Some thought it was made up of tiny particles, others thought it was a series of waves. Today, scientists think that light is neither completely a wave nor completely a stream of particles. It is a cross between the two. But they are still not quite sure what light really is. They do know that light waves are *electromagnetic,* just like radio waves and X-rays.

Radio waves can be kilometres long. Light waves are very short – about five-hundred-thousandths of a centimetre long. This wavelength is important because it limits the size of things we can see through a microscope. If we look at anything about the size of the wavelength of light through a powerful microscope, it is fuzzy.

Invisible Light

Different kinds of light can be seen by different animals. Most humans see all the colours from red through orange, yellow, green, blue to violet.

More than a hundred years ago, scientists tried to find out about the spectrum colours by putting a thermometer in each colour coming from a prism. It was found that as the thermometer was moved from violet to the red end, the temperature increased slightly. But, even more surprising, when the thermometer was placed beyond the red, where there was no visible light, the temperature was even hotter. There is a hot, invisible radiation just below the red. This radiation is called *infrared* radiation (*infra* means below). Some animals such as the pit viper can actually 'see' these infrared rays, which are really heat rays.

At the other end of the colour spectrum are other beams of 'light' that we cannot see. They are just above the violet, so they are called 'ultraviolet'. Bees can see ultraviolet light although humans cannot.

Light travels in a straight line at a speed of about 300,000 km per second. But there are ways of making light change direction. One way is to bounce it off the surface of something. This is called *reflection*. We can see the Moon and the other planets because they reflect the Sun's light. They have no light of their own.

Seems Straight

Place a coin in a cup and move your head back until the coin is just no longer visible. Now, keeping your head steady, pour some water into the cup. Hey presto! The coin appears. This magic is caused by *refraction*. Refraction causes a light beam to bend as it passes from one substance to another. When the light beam from the coin leaves the water and enters the air, it bends so that you can see the coin. The coin looks as though it is in the position at the end of the dotted line in the diagram below. The amount by which light is refracted depends on two things: the angle at which the light beam strikes the second material, and the speed at which the light is travelling. If the light beam goes straight from one substance to another at right angles there is no refraction. If you put the coin in the cup and look straight down on it as you pour in the water, the coin doesn't appear to move. Light travels at its fastest in a vacuum (empty space). In air it travels almost as fast. But in water and glass, light slows down. In fact, in going through some kinds of glass, light travels at only about half its speed in a vacuum – 300,000 km per second.

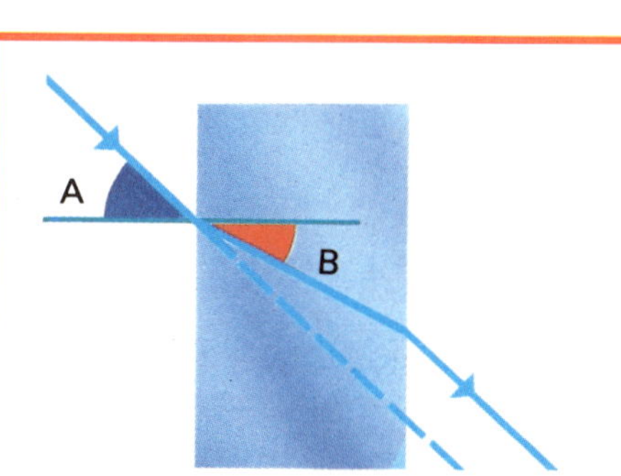

When light passes through a piece of glass it is *refracted*. Angle A is called the *angle of incidence*. Angle B is the *angle of refraction* (the angle by which the beam bends).

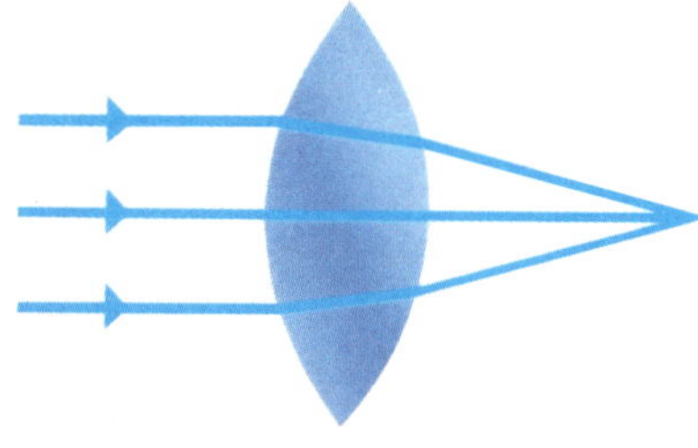

Light is bent in *lenses*. A lens shaped like the one above (convex) brings light rays together at a point called the *focal point*. A magnifying glass is a *convex lens*.

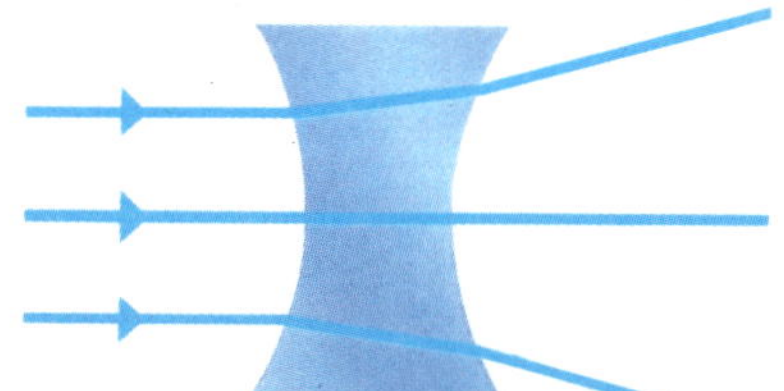

***Concave lenses* like the one above make light rays spread out. If you look through one, things look smaller. Lenses of this kind are nearly always used with other lenses.**

Very Special Light

The laser is one of the most important inventions of the 20th century. A laser beam is a beam of very pure light. We have seen that ordinary light is made up of all the colours of the rainbow. Each colour has a different wavelength. A laser beam has waves that are all the same. The waves rise and fall in step. This makes the laser's narrow beam very powerful. Because of the laser's power and accuracy, it is being used for more and more tasks. It can drill a tiny hole in a diamond, slice through steel plates, help in delicate surgical operations and carry thousands of telephone messages through fine fibres of glass.

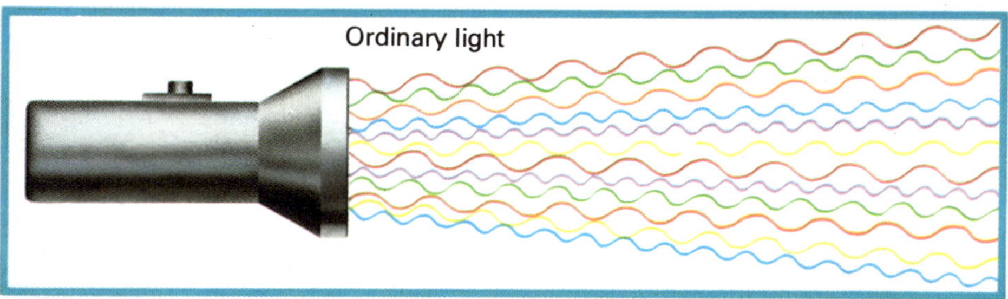

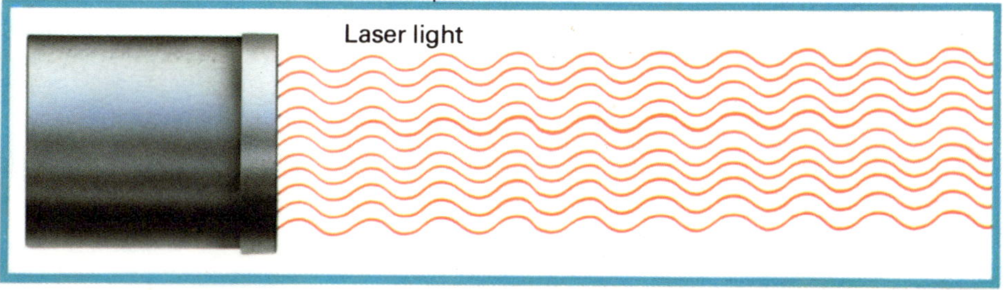

The camera on the left is a 35 mm single-lens reflex. A system of mirrors and lenses allows the person taking the picture to view the subject through the camera's lens. The lens of this camera can be unscrewed and replaced by another type of lens such as one for taking wide-angle views or a telephoto lens for taking pictures of distant objects.

Today's cameras often have several glass lenses (above). These are called compound lenses and they give a sharper image than a single lens. Most cameras have a focusing device. This makes the lens go nearer or further away from the object being photographed. We 'focus' on the object to get a clear, sharp picture by screwing the lens in or out. To take sharp pictures of close-up objects, the lens is further away from the film. When we focus on distant objects, the lens is closer to the film.

Photography

The word 'photography' means 'writing or drawing with light'. To take pictures we need two things – light and some material that is sensitive to light.

To take a black and white picture with a simple camera, we load a film into the camera. The film is usually a roll of plastic. The plastic is coated with a thin layer of substance that changes when light falls on it. The roll of plastic is stretched between two spools inside the camera. By pulling a lever or turning a key we wind an unexposed part of the film into the right position in the dark of the camera (see above). We are ready to take a picture. Just point the camera towards the subject and press the button. Pressing the button works a shutter that opens and closes very quickly to let just the right amount of light into the camera. The light is focused onto the plastic film by a glass lens.

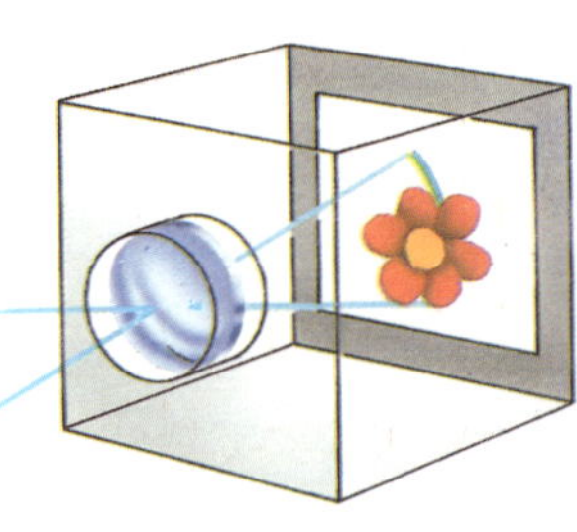

A simple way of capturing and controlling light is to use a pinhole camera. This is just a light-proof box with a tiny hole at one end. Light from the flower above goes through the hole and forms an upside down image at the back of the box. But this image is rather dim, so we need a lens to make it sharper. We also need a shutter and lens diaphragm to control the amount of light that reaches the film at the back.

Processing the Film

But when we have taken all the pictures possible on the roll of film, we still cannot see them. The film is now taken from its container in a dark room with perhaps only a dark red light. It is 'developed' by being placed in

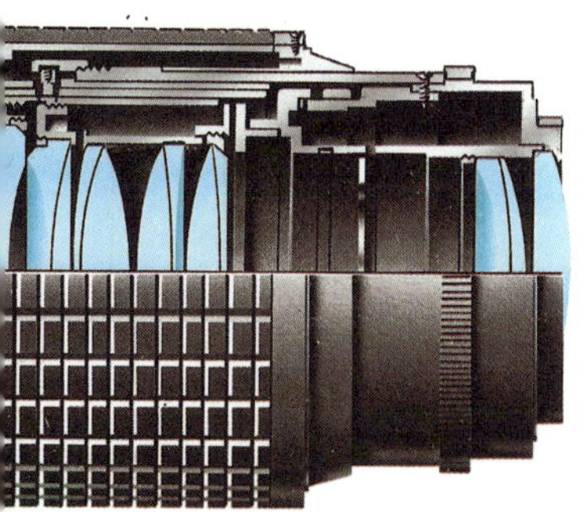

APERTURES
The aperture is the size of the opening of the diaphragm. In most cameras the size of the opening can be varied. The diaphragm can be closed to allow only a small amount of light into the camera (1). When it is fully open (4), a large amount of light passes through. Apertures are measured in 'f-numbers' – a low f-number such as 2 means that the aperture is very wide. A high f-number such as 16 means a small aperture. There are advantages in using a small aperture. An object far away from the camera will be quite sharp and clear – it will be in 'focus'. And so will an object quite close to the camera. If a large aperture is used, objects in the foreground and background will be fuzzy.

Once the photographs have been taken, they are processed in a darkroom – only a small red light called a safelight can be used. Three trays are usually needed. The first one contains the developer, the second the 'stop' liquid that stops the action of the developer, and the third the fixer chemical that stops the film being sensitive to light. The object on the left is a masking frame to hold the paper while printing. On the far left is an enlarger, used for making prints larger than the negative.

a special liquid that changes the chemicals on the film's surface. The pictures begin to appear. The film is now a 'negative' – dark areas in the picture are light, light areas dark.

To print the film, light is shone through the negative onto printing paper. Chemicals in the printing paper make our pictures appear as the camera saw them.

Radio and Television

Inside the Camera

The job of a television camera is to turn the image it sees into electrical signals that can be transmitted. In colour TV, the camera usually has three separate tubes inside it. These tubes split up the light from the image into three parts – a red part, a green part and a blue part. This splitting up is done by special mirrors called *dichroic mirrors*. You can see how this works in the diagram on the opposite page.

Each light colour goes through a special tube in the camera. These tubes make a pattern of electric charge as light falls on them. A beam of electrons in each tube moves quickly over the pattern of electric charge, going from left to right and top to bottom. This is called scanning. It makes a stream of electric signals, each signal telling how bright or dark a tiny part of the whole picture is.

From the Studio to Your Home

Several cameras are used to give different views of whatever is being televised. The cameras turn the image of what they see into electrical signals. These signals are fed to a control room where the programme director sits in front of a row of TV screens. Each screen shows the picture from one of the

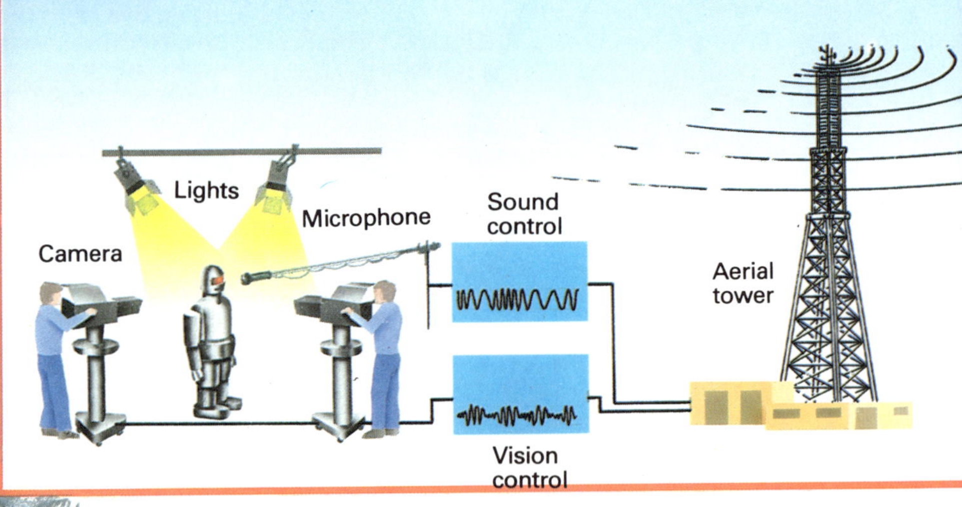

Radio Waves
Radio waves are quite invisible, but we know that they can be of many different wavelengths. (The wavelength is the distance between the top of one hump in the wave and the top of the next hump.) Some are very short – only a few centimetres long, others can be several kilometres long. Unlike sound waves, radio waves do not need air to travel through. We can talk to astronauts on the Moon because the radio waves travel quite easily through empty space. When a radio wave hits the aerial of your radio, it sets up a tiny electric current. If the set is tuned to the wavelength of the radio wave, the circuits in the set get rid of the carrier wave and send the signals of a person's voice or music to your loudspeaker.

cameras. The director chooses which picture he wants at a particular time, and the signals from this picture are fed to the transmitter. The transmitter may be quite a long way away from the studio.

Sound in the studio is picked up by microphones – again there can be several. The microphones turn the sound into electrical signals which go to a sound mixing position in the control room. There the sounds are selected or mixed as required before being fed to the transmitter.

The vision and sound signals are carried on radio waves sent out from the aerial at the top of the big tower. These radio waves are picked up by a receiving aerial and go into your TV set. The set turns the signals back into pictures and sound that you can see and hear.

Inside Your TV Set

When the picture signals go into your TV set they are removed from the radio wave that has carried them and go into a cathode ray tube. It is the front of this tube you look at when you watch TV. An electron gun for each colour shoots out electrons which strike the back of your screen. This is covered with different types of tiny phosphor dots that glow, blue, red or green when they are hit. The beams go through a perforated shadow mask that ensures that each beam strikes only one type of dot. As the beams travel over the screen very quickly, our eyes see a picture like that in the TV studio.

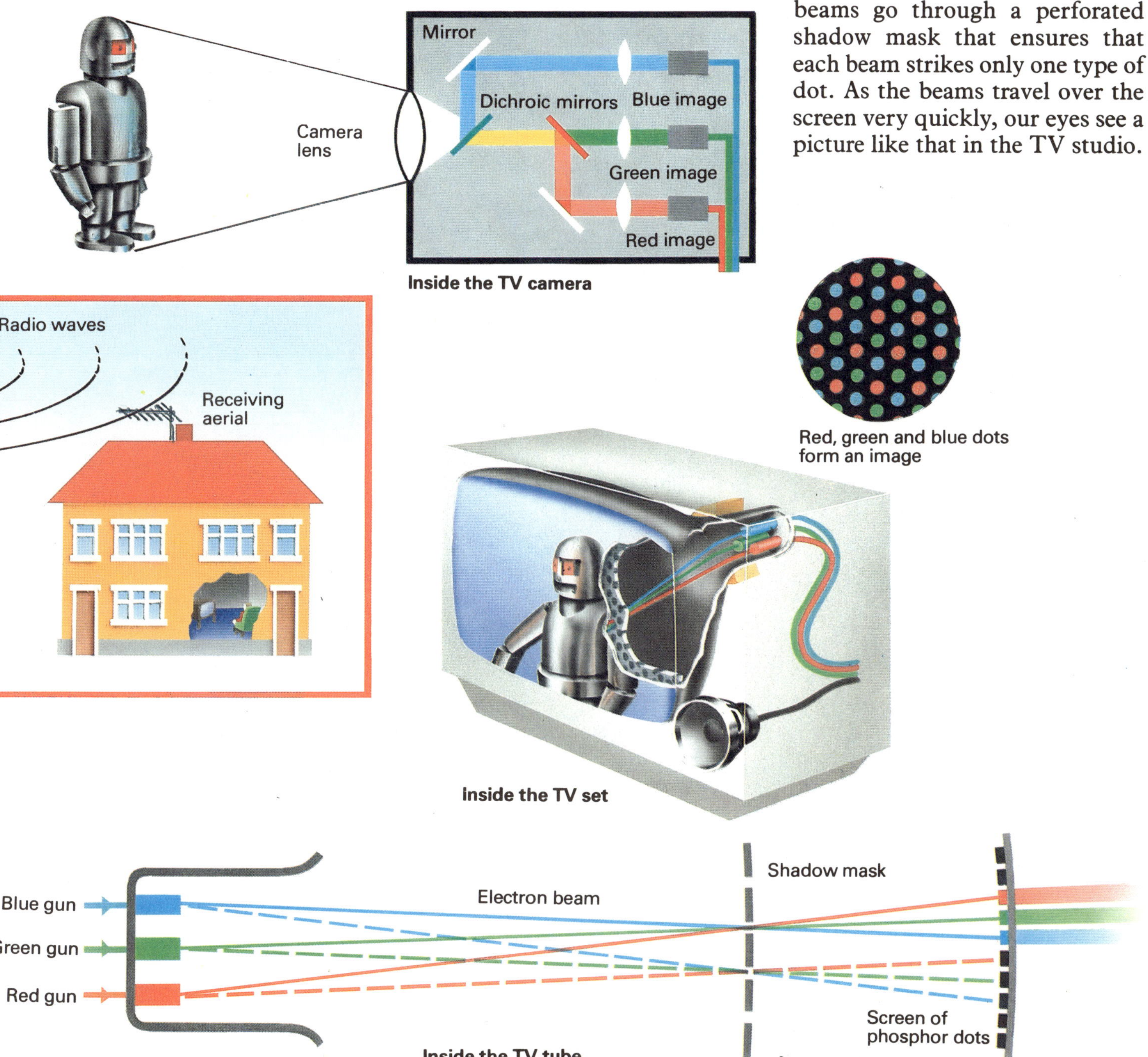

Inside the TV camera

Red, green and blue dots form an image

Inside the TV set

Inside the TV tube

Heat Engines

An engine is any machine that takes energy from heat, water or wind and makes this energy do useful work. The windmill and the waterwheel are simple kinds of engine, and people are still trying to make these engines more efficient. Steam engines took the place of the windmill and the waterwheel, and today we have petrol engines, diesel engines, jet engines and turbines.

A steam engine is a *heat engine*. Heat from burning coal, oil or gas is used to turn water in a boiler into steam. When water boils to become steam it expands to about 1,700 times its size. Steam engines use the energy of expanding steam to drive wheels or do other work.

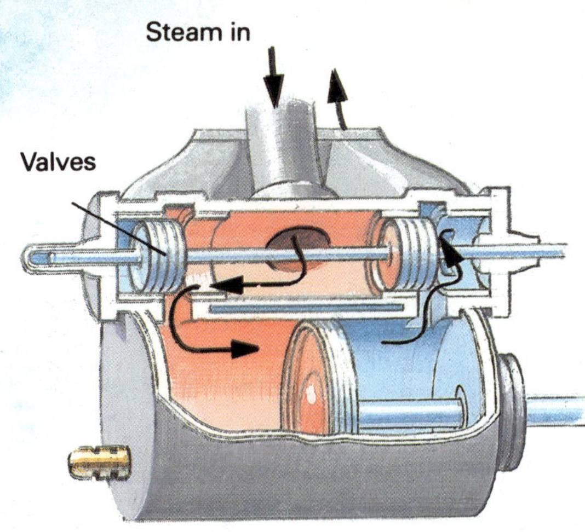

In a simple steam engine a piston slides to and fro inside a hollow cylinder. A system of valves allows steam into the cylinder at one end, then at the other, driving the piston back and forth.

How a Steam Engine Works

In a steam engine, the expanding steam pushes a piston to and fro inside a tube called a cylinder. The piston is attached to a piston rod that moves in and out with the piston. The piston rod is attached to another, longer rod called the connecting rod, which is joined to a driving wheel and makes it go round.

Various systems of valves allow the steam to shoot into the cylinder so that it drives the piston first one way, then the other. This kind of engine is called a *reciprocating* engine. At the beginning of the 1900s the reciprocating engine was the chief source of power. It ran locomotives, ships, factory machines and even motor cars. Today it has almost vanished because more efficient kinds of engines have been invented.

Another kind of steam engine is the *steam turbine*. A turbine is a large wheel with dozens of blades round it. A powerful jet of steam is made to hit the blades and cause the turbine to spin. Spinning turbines can be used to make electricity or drive a ship's propellers.

Internal Combustion

The motor car engine is called an *internal combustion* engine because the fuel is burned inside the engine. (In the steam engine the fuel is burned outside, away from the moving parts.) The internal combustion engine is more efficient than the steam engine. It gives more power for the energy put into it.

How it Works

The fuel – petrol or diesel oil – burns in a hollow cylinder. As the fuel turns to gas, it expands and

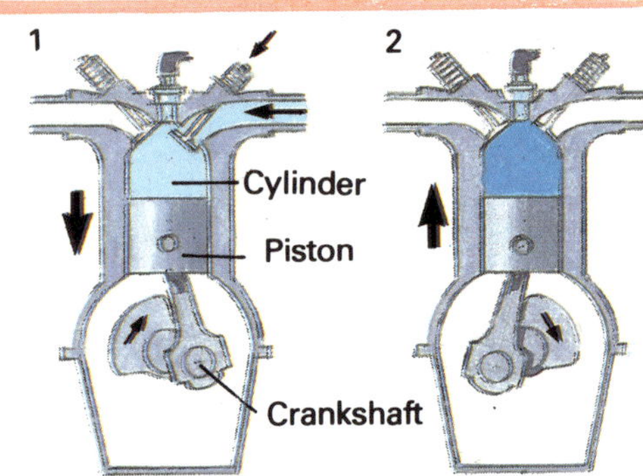

Petrol engines do not give power on every stroke of the piston. The diagrams above show what happens. At (1) an inlet valve opens and a mixture of petrol and air is sucked into the cylinder. Then the valve closes and as the piston goes

pushes a tight-fitting piston down the cylinder. When the piston is pushed down, it turns a *crankshaft*. The crankshaft is made to turn the car's wheels.

The Wankel Engine

The Wankel engine is an internal combustion engine like the ordinary petrol engine, but there are no pistons moving in cylinders. Instead of pistons, the Wankel has a central rotor in the shape of a triangle with curved sides. As the rotor goes round the combustion chamber, the engine goes through the intake, compression, power and exhaust stages of an ordinary engine.

Jet Engines

There are several kinds of jet engine. The first to be invented, and still very much used, is the *turbojet*, pictured in the diagram below. It works by eating up air in enormous quantities – it needs the oxygen in the air to make the fuel burn properly. As air is sucked in at the front by a series of fast-spinning blades, it is *compressed* – squeezed into a small space. The air has to be compressed to give a lot of oxygen in the combustion chamber.

Special paraffin is sprayed into the combustion chamber. This fuel spray goes on all the time the engine is working. It is first ignited by electric sparks. As the fuel burns, its temperature rises to well over 1000 °C. The hot gases expand and shoot out backwards into the atmosphere. This powerful stream of hot gas shooting out pushes the aircraft forward.

The hot gases turn another wheel called a *turbine*. A shaft connects the turbine to the compressor. This means that the compressor is kept turning and squeezing more air into the engine.

Jet speeds are sometimes increased by burning extra fuel between the turbine and the outlet nozzle. This is called *afterburning*.

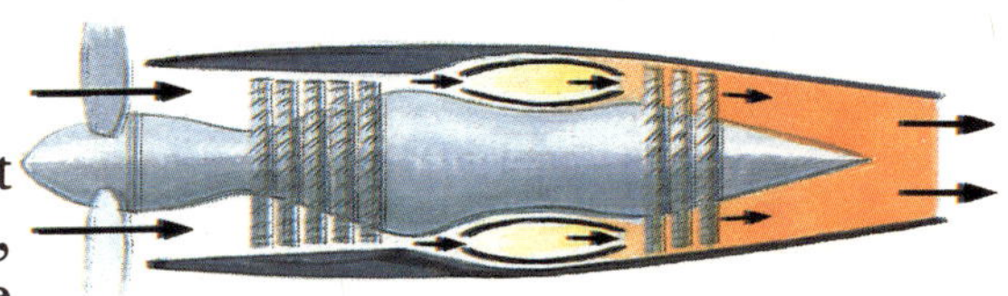

The engine above is a *turboprop*. In this engine the turbojet is used to turn a propeller which drives the aircraft forward. The turboprop is used on smaller aircraft, in which it is most efficient.

The *turbofan* engine pictured below is the one that powers most of today's big airliners. These engines have huge fans at the front to push enormous quantities of air back into the compressor. The air is divided into two streams; one goes through the combustion chamber, the other flows past the engine itself. The two streams combine at the back to give greater thrust.

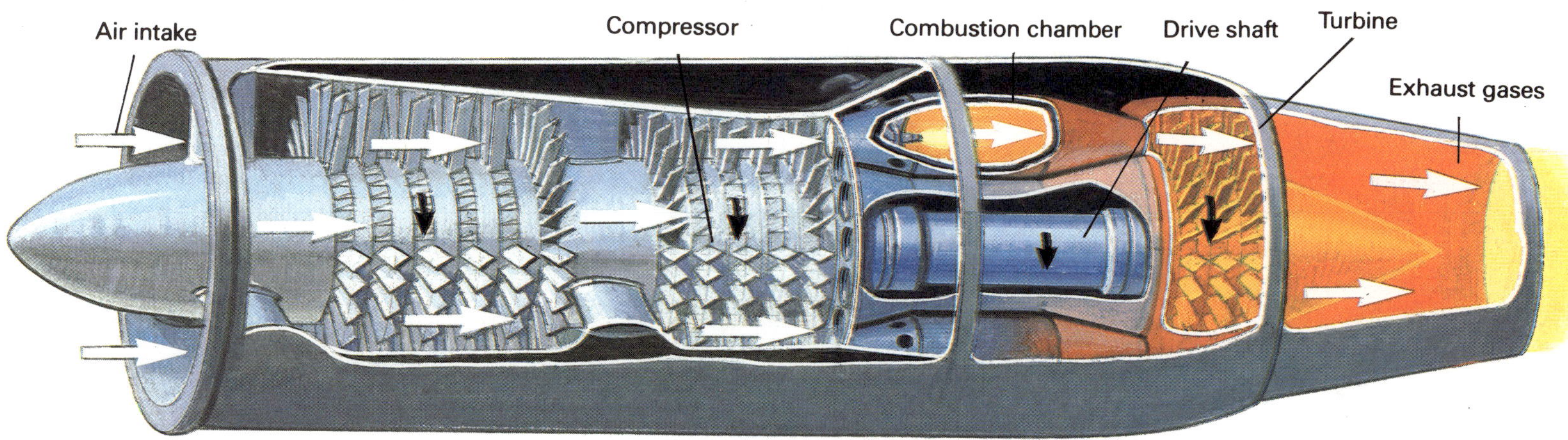

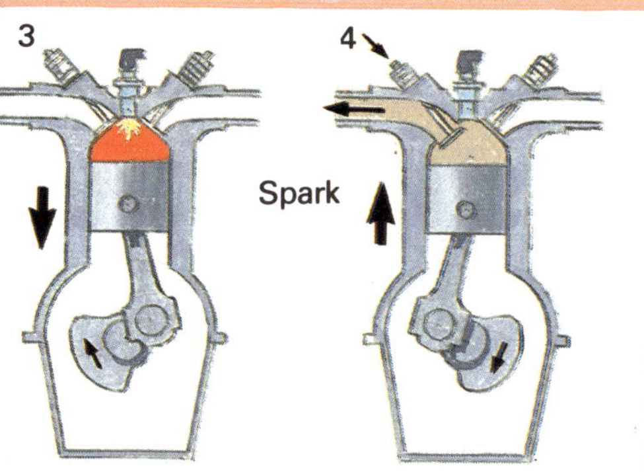

up it squeezes the fuel into the top of the cylinder (2). A spark takes place and the fuel mixture burns with great force and pushes the piston down the cylinder (3). Then an exhaust valve opens and the burnt gases are pushed out (4).

The Wankel engine

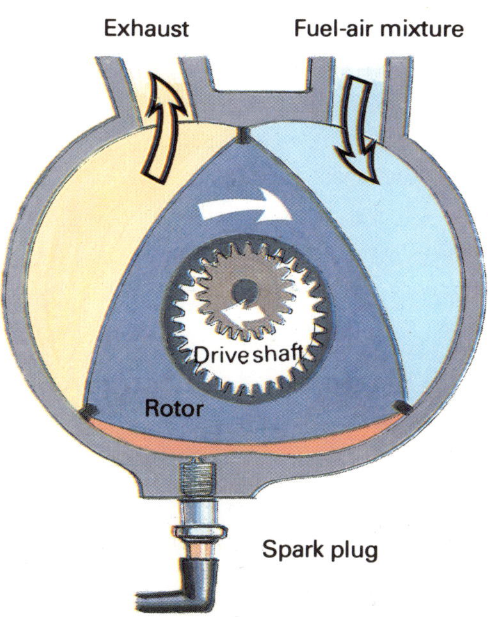

Science in the Air

The cockpit of a modern airliner is a mass of electronics. A dazzling variety of dials and warning lights face the pilot. They keep him informed as to how all the plane's systems are working, whether he is on course and so on.

As the aircraft approaches an airport an Instrument Landing System guides it in. Ground control supplies the pilot with direction of approach. Aircraft usually start to line up with the runway about 7 to 10 kilometres from the airport; then they follow radio beams until they land. Landing has become more and more automatic, and many aircraft can now land without the pilot touching the controls at all.

Despite all these electronic aids, aircraft still need pilots. In passenger planes, two sets of all essential equipment are carried, in case one fails. But even if both sets fail, the air crew are still there to bring the plane safely to land.

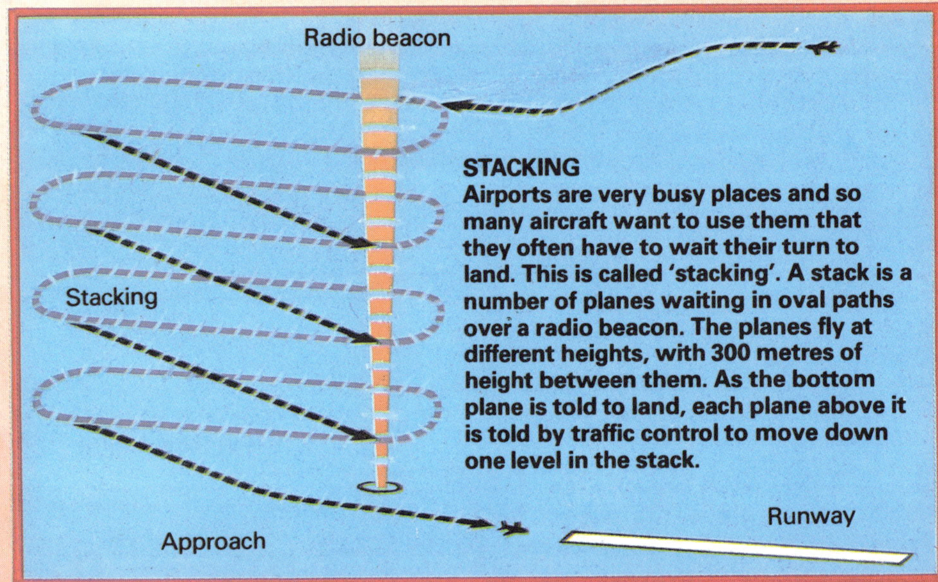

STACKING
Airports are very busy places and so many aircraft want to use them that they often have to wait their turn to land. This is called 'stacking'. A stack is a number of planes waiting in oval paths over a radio beacon. The planes fly at different heights, with 300 metres of height between them. As the bottom plane is told to land, each plane above it is told by traffic control to move down one level in the stack.

THE ALTIMETER
The pressure altimeter (opposite) tells the pilot how high he is above sea level. In the instrument is a sealed thin metal capsule filled with air. The pressure inside the capsule is always the same. But as the plane goes higher, the air pressure around it grows less. The air in the capsule can then push the thin metal outward. This turns a lever which works a pointer. Pipes connect the altimeter to the air outside the plane.

AEROFOILS
To fly, an aircraft must in some way lift itself off the ground against the pull of the Earth's gravity. This lift is produced by air flowing over the plane's wings. The wings have a special shape called an *aerofoil.* They are curved at the top and flat at the bottom. This means that the air passing over the top of the wing has to travel faster because it has further to go. So the air pressure is less above the wing than below it and the wing is lifted upward.

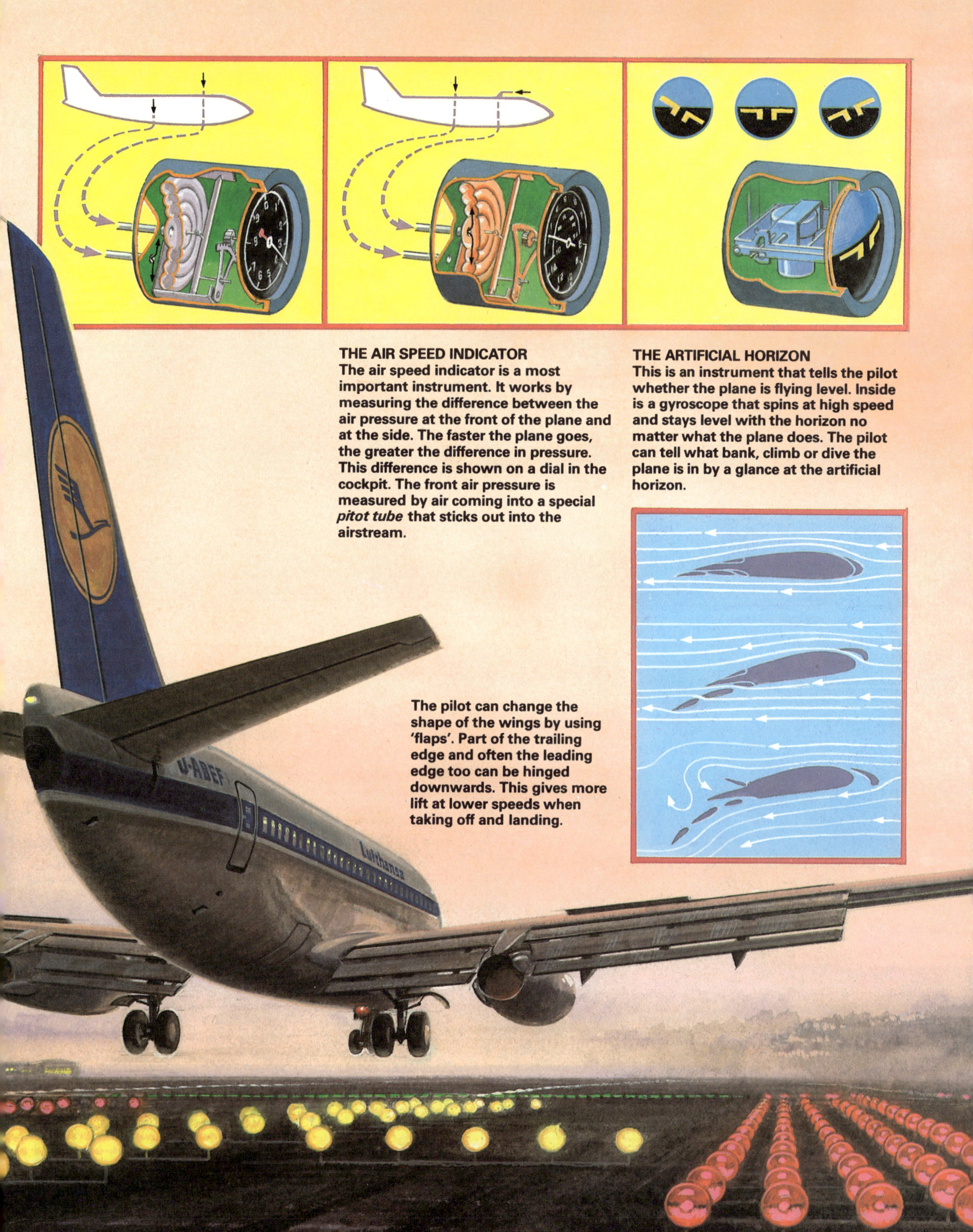

THE AIR SPEED INDICATOR

The air speed indicator is a most important instrument. It works by measuring the difference between the air pressure at the front of the plane and at the side. The faster the plane goes, the greater the difference in pressure. This difference is shown on a dial in the cockpit. The front air pressure is measured by air coming into a special *pitot tube* that sticks out into the airstream.

THE ARTIFICIAL HORIZON

This is an instrument that tells the pilot whether the plane is flying level. Inside is a gyroscope that spins at high speed and stays level with the horizon no matter what the plane does. The pilot can tell what bank, climb or dive the plane is in by a glance at the artificial horizon.

The pilot can change the shape of the wings by using 'flaps'. Part of the trailing edge and often the leading edge too can be hinged downwards. This gives more lift at lower speeds when taking off and landing.

Aircraft

Modern hot-air balloon

The highly successful fixed-wing, vertical-take-off Harrier warplane

The original Wright Flyer, 1903

Farman Goliath, 1919

Short Empire flying boat, 1936

Douglas DC-3, 1936. More than 13,000 were built.

The de Havilland Comet 1, 1952, the first jet airliner

The story of Man's conquest of the air began almost exactly two centuries ago, in 1783. In June of that year two French brothers, Joseph and Etienne Montgolfier, launched a hot-air balloon. But such balloons are now used only for sport. Today the skies belong to the aeroplane, commonly just called plane.

The first plane flight took place on 17 December 1903, at Kitty Hawk in North Carolina, in the United States. The plane was built by the Wright brothers, Orville and Wilbur. The first flight lasted for a mere 12 seconds, but it showed the way ahead. In 1909 Louis Blériot flew across the English Channel; ten years later John Alcock and Arthur Whitten Brown made the first non-stop flight across the Atlantic Ocean.

The Coming of the Airliner

During the 1920s and 1930s regular, or scheduled flights began, at first carrying airmail and later passengers. This was the era of the flying boat. By the end of the 1930s, as the world headed into World War II, a new type of plane was being developed: the jet. After the war the jet plane came into its own, first as a fighter, then as a commercial airliner.

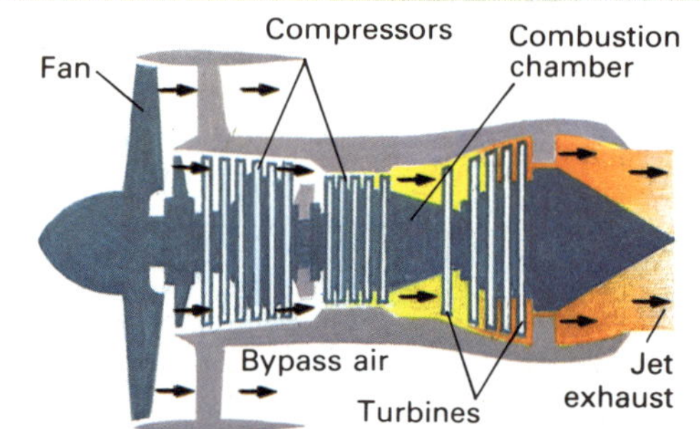

Above: A turbofan engine, used in most airliners. Air is taken into the engine and compressed. Fuel is burned in the compressed air in the combustion chamber. The hot gases produced spin the turbines before emerging as a jet. The by-pass air helps make the jet more efficient.

Below: A plane gets its 'lift' from the shape of its wings, a shape known as an aerofoil.

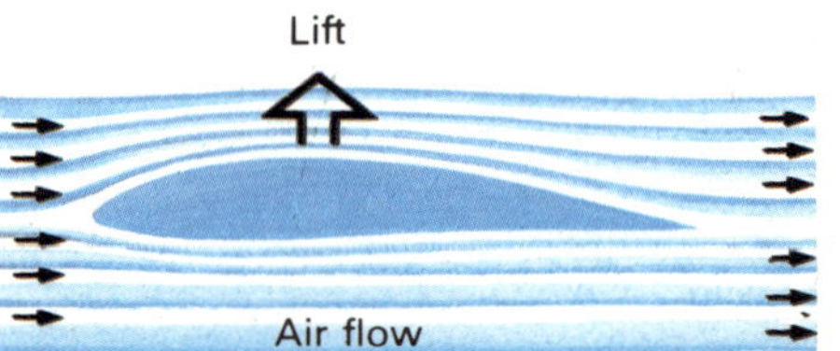

VERTICAL TAKE-OFF

One drawback of the ordinary plane is that it needs a long runway for taking off and landing. Over the years, different types of aircraft have been developed to overcome this drawback. The most successful has been the helicopter, developed in the 1930s, mainly by Igor Sikorsky in the United States. The helicopter obtains its lift by whirling blades on top of its fuselage. The only successful vertical take-off and landing (VTOL) fixed-wing plane has been the Harrier fighter (left). This moves vertically up and down by deflecting the jet exhausts from its engines.

In the 1960s jet planes became faster and bigger. In 1969 came the maiden flight of the supersonic airliner Concorde, developed jointly by Britain and France. It is still the fastest airliner in service, being capable of a speed of some 2,250 kilometres per hour. This is twice the speed of sound, and is faster than a rifle bullet.

In the same year came the maiden flight of the Boeing 747, the first of the big passenger jets, known as jumbo jets. The Boeing 747 can carry 400 passengers or more, but can operate efficiently only when most seats are filled. Its four engines use a lot of fuel. In recent years, as fuel costs have risen sharply, smaller planes have been developed for more economical airline operation. They include the European Airbus and the Boeing 757 and 767, which all have two highly efficient turbofan engines.

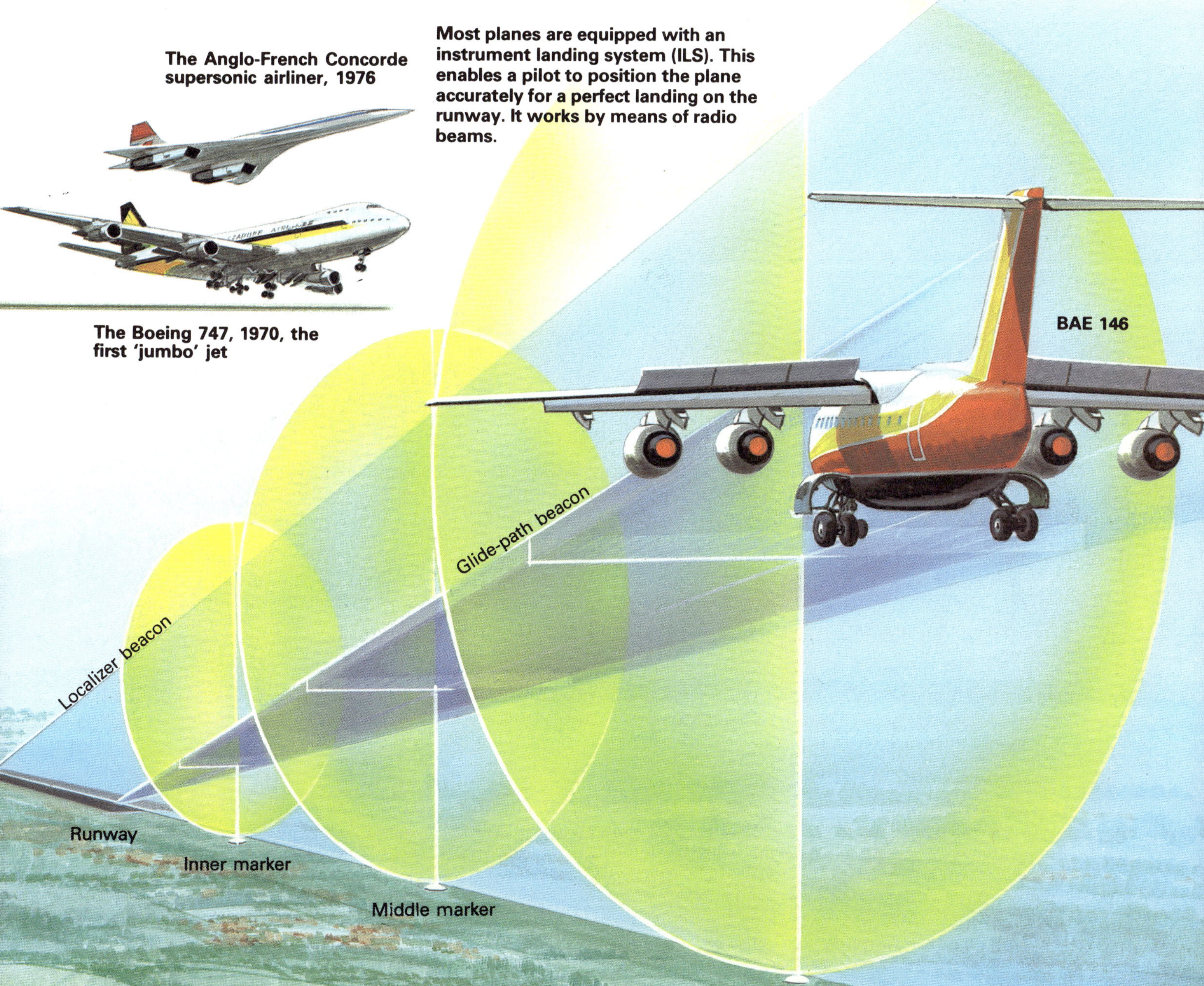

The Anglo-French Concorde supersonic airliner, 1976

The Boeing 747, 1970, the first 'jumbo' jet

Most planes are equipped with an instrument landing system (ILS). This enables a pilot to position the plane accurately for a perfect landing on the runway. It works by means of radio beams.

Under the Sea

Our Earth is the only planet in the Solar System that has oceans. And over three-quarters of its surface is water. For many centuries people have been diving down into the sea to hunt for things like sponges and pearls. The early divers plunged in and held their breath. Today, science is helping people to explore more and more of the great under-sea world. We are slowly finding out its secrets and beginning to extract its wealth.

But exploring the sea-bottom isn't easy. The average depth of the oceans is about 4,000 metres, with vast under-sea mountains and deep valleys. Only very special boats or unmanned vehicles can go down this far.

The oceans contain many substances that we need. There are vast deposits of metal ores on the Continental Shelf close to our shores. There are cricket-ball-sized lumps of the useful metals copper, nickel, manganese and cobalt lying on the deep-sea floors. But dredging useful quantities of these treasures has still to be achieved.

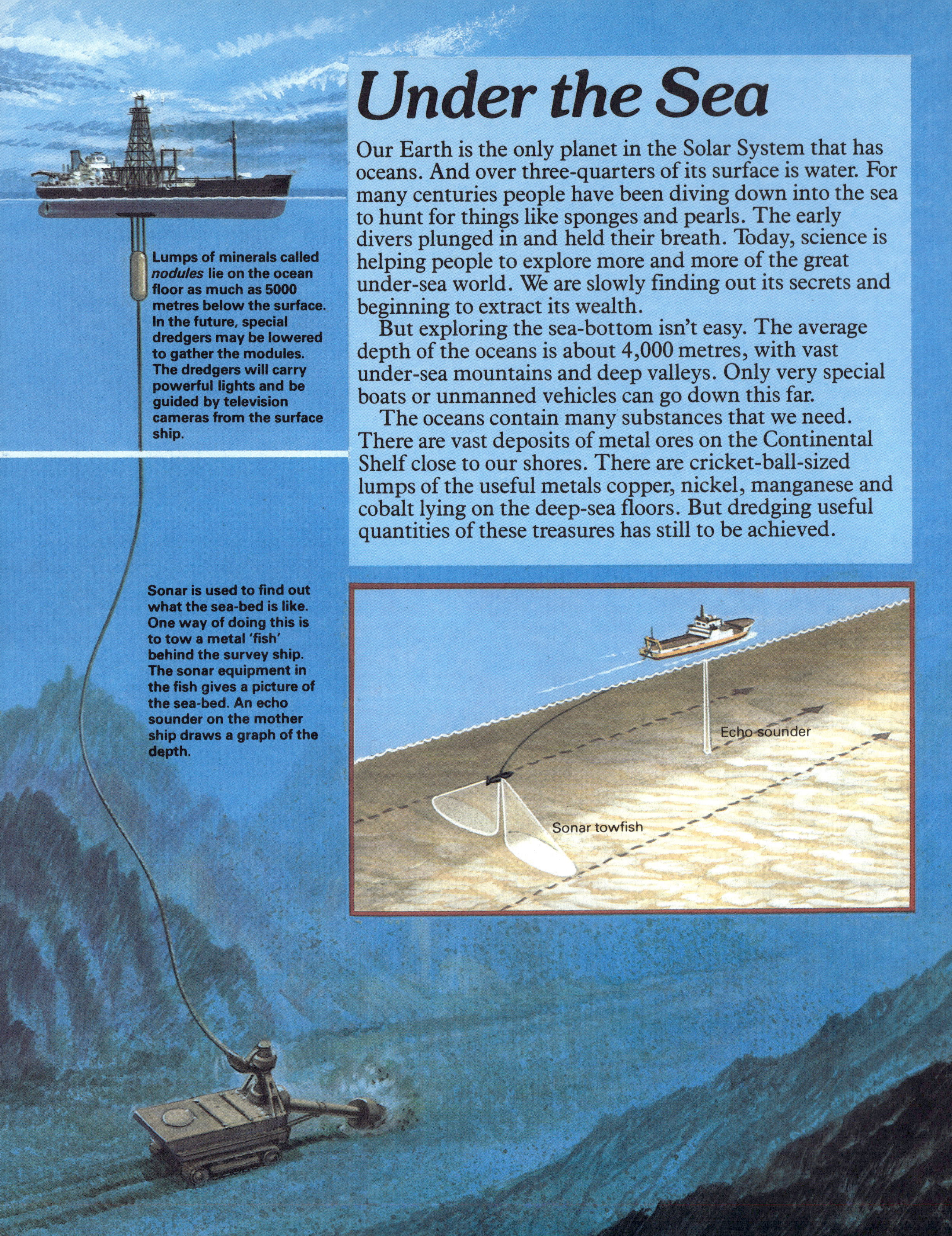

Lumps of minerals called *nodules* lie on the ocean floor as much as 5000 metres below the surface. In the future, special dredgers may be lowered to gather the modules. The dredgers will carry powerful lights and be guided by television cameras from the surface ship.

Sonar is used to find out what the sea-bed is like. One way of doing this is to tow a metal 'fish' behind the survey ship. The sonar equipment in the fish gives a picture of the sea-bed. An echo sounder on the mother ship draws a graph of the depth.

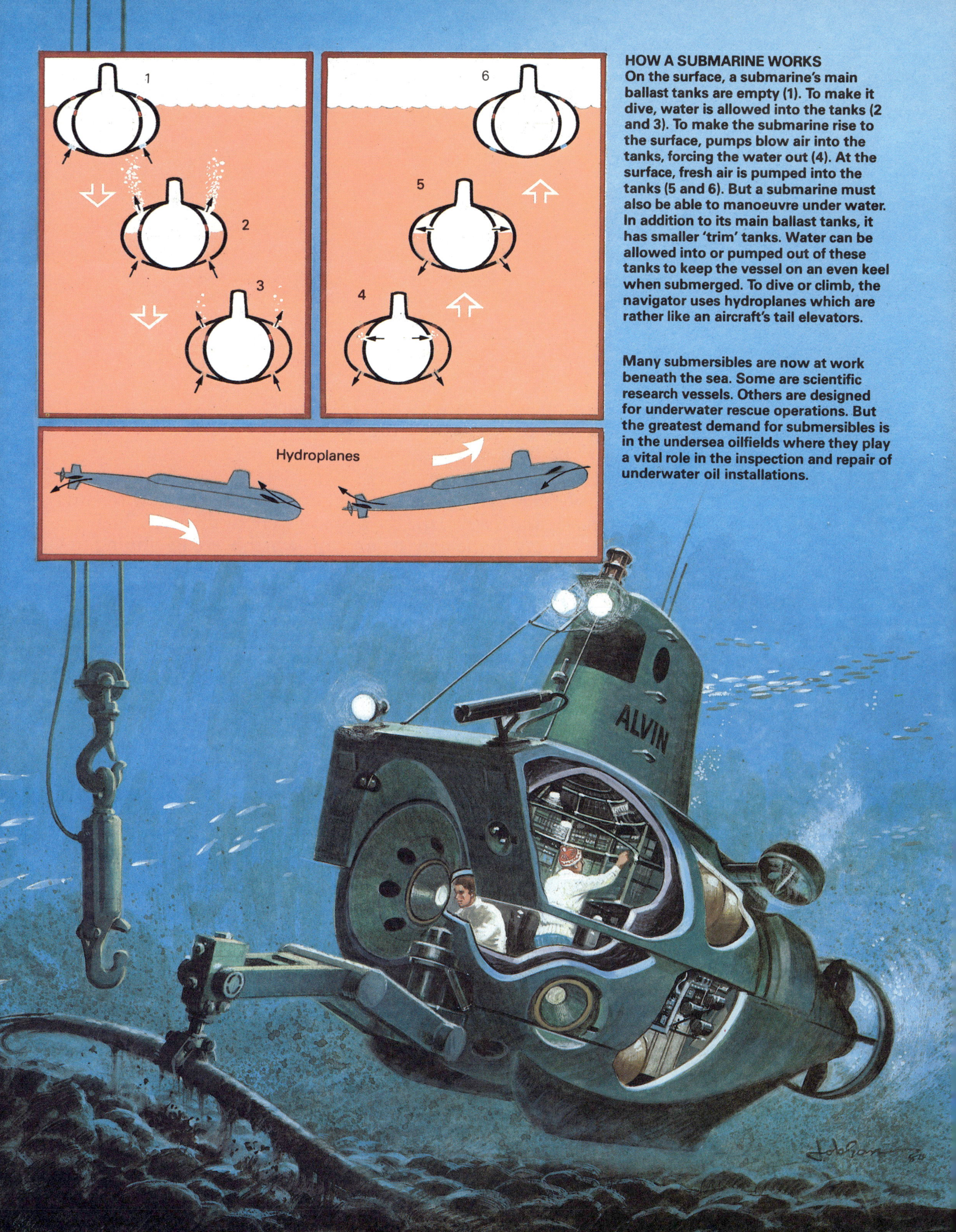

HOW A SUBMARINE WORKS
On the surface, a submarine's main ballast tanks are empty (1). To make it dive, water is allowed into the tanks (2 and 3). To make the submarine rise to the surface, pumps blow air into the tanks, forcing the water out (4). At the surface, fresh air is pumped into the tanks (5 and 6). But a submarine must also be able to manoeuvre under water. In addition to its main ballast tanks, it has smaller 'trim' tanks. Water can be allowed into or pumped out of these tanks to keep the vessel on an even keel when submerged. To dive or climb, the navigator uses hydroplanes which are rather like an aircraft's tail elevators.

Many submersibles are now at work beneath the sea. Some are scientific research vessels. Others are designed for underwater rescue operations. But the greatest demand for submersibles is in the undersea oilfields where they play a vital role in the inspection and repair of underwater oil installations.

Ships and the Sea

People first went down to the sea in ships about 7,000 years ago. Since then the seas have provided a major 'highway' for trade between countries. They have also been a battleground on which nations have won and lost empires.

Until the 1800s sails provided the main means of propelling ships. The most magnificent sailing ships were the swift and graceful clippers, which carried tea and later wool between the Far East and Europe. They were full-rigged ships with a huge sail area on three tall masts. In favourable conditions they could reach a speed of 20 knots (37 kilometres per hour).

The Age of Steam

However, even while the clippers were setting new records in the mid-1800s, the days of sail were numbered. The future lay in the new steamships which were beginning to cross the Atlantic Ocean. In 1845 the 'Great Britain' showed the way ahead. It was an iron steamship propelled by screw propeller. Within a few years metal hulls and screw propellers were standard.

The early steamships had piston steam engines, similar to those used in factories. In the 1890s a new steam 'engine' showed its superiority – the steam-turbine. Steam turbines still power most large ships. Many smaller ships have diesel engines similar to those in trucks, only much bigger.

A handful of ships are nuclear powered. They are mainly naval ships, such as aircraft carriers and submarines. Nuclear power has not yet proved economical enough for merchant ships.

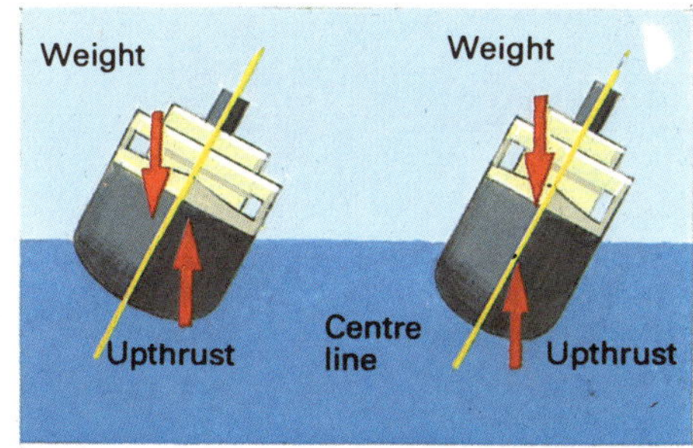

Above: Two main forces act on a ship floating in the water. One is its weight, which acts downwards. The other is an upward force, or upthrust. Ship designers design a ship so that the weight and upthrust act so as to right the vessel when it rolls (left). In a bad design (right) the weight and upthrust act so as to roll the vessel further and make it capsize.

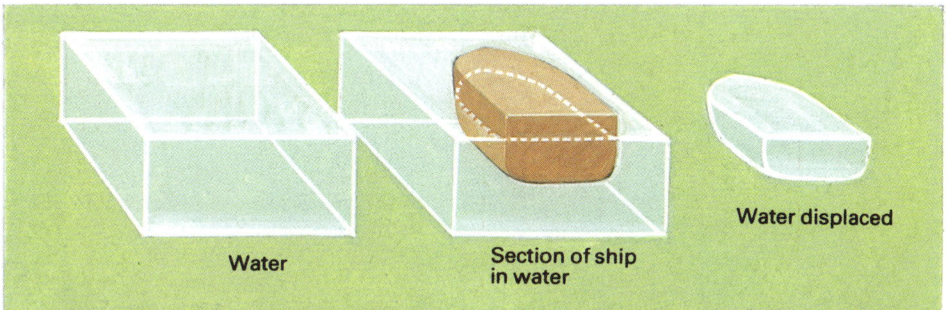

Water

Section of ship in water

Water displaced

When a ship sits in water, it displaces a certain amount of water. If the ship weighs the same or less than the water displaced, then it floats. If the ship weighs more than the water displaced, then it sinks.

Bottom: An interesting comparison of the sizes of ships through the ages. The 'Atlantic' is a giant supertanker and, with a length of 407 metres, is one of the largest ships now afloat. It transports crude oil from the Middle East oilfields.

Mid-19th century clipper

Mid-19th century steamship

1980 Esso 'Atlantic', 407 m

The World of Speed

The first aircraft were slow and clumsy. Their small engines gave them just enough speed to stay in the air. But as time went by, planes could fly faster and faster, until they reached speeds that were as fast as propeller-driven planes could go – about 1800 km/h. It was the jet engine that made higher speeds possible.

The first plane to fly faster than the speed of sound (about 1100 km/h) was the rocket-powered Bell X-1, in 1947. Today, planes like the Blackbird SR-71A (above) can fly at speeds of about 3500 km/h. They can also fly at very great heights. This plane has reached a height of over 24,000 metres.

About a hundred and fifty years ago, the fastest way to travel was on a horse. It had been like this for thousands of years until the invention of the steam engine. Stephenson's *Rocket* locomotive of 1829 had a top speed of 46 km/h, just faster than the top speed of a horse-drawn chariot. But during the 19th century, the steam engine was the 'king of speed' throughout the world. By 1850, trains could travel at more than 100 km/h and rail travel was available to everyone.

Nowadays, high-speed travel is part of our daily lives. Many people are fascinated by speed and enjoy speed sports such as motor racing. Modern electric trains hurtle along special tracks at over 300 km/h. The *Concorde* flashes across the Atlantic at twice the speed of sound. Good motorways allow us to get from place to place easily and quickly.

Wind tunnels are used to test the action of air against vehicles. Wind is blown through the tunnel at different speeds so that the scientists can see how the aircraft or train will react. In supersonic tunnels, special instruments show changes in the density of air as it flows around the model (below, left).

A ship travelling in water cannot go much faster than about 90 km/h. But craft that skim on or above the surface can travel much faster. A hydrofoil (right) sits on the water at low speed. But as it goes faster it is lifted until it is skimming along on long legs, rather like a person on skis. This cuts down the 'drag' of the water and hydrofoils can travel at around 110 km/h, provided the sea is not too rough. Most modern hydrofoils have 'surface-piercing' foils. These are shaped like a shallow V and they keep the craft stable as it turns sharply or speeds through the waves.

Hovercraft are also skimmers. They travel along on a cushion of air that lifts the craft clear of the water. Big passenger-carrying hovercraft can speed along at more than 140 km/h.

The world land speed record has advanced slowly over the years. In 1907 the record was held by a steam-driven car called *Wogglebug*. It reached a speed of 241 km/h. Today, the world's record is held by Britain's Richard Noble. In 1983 he reached a speed of 1019.47 km/h in his jet-powered *Thrust 2* (below).

By far the fastest travellers are astronauts. Their rocket-powered spaceships have to reach a speed of almost 40,000 km/h to get away from the Earth's gravity. We see pictures of Shuttle astronauts out in space, slowly and carefully edging themselves about with their spacepacks. But it is difficult to appreciate that they and their ship are still travelling at 20 times the speed of *Concorde*. Up in space there is no air or anything else to give the astronauts any idea of speed.

But even astronauts are very slow-moving compared to the fastest thing we know about – the speed of light. It travels 299,792 km in just one second!

The Story of Railways

Stephenson's Rocket opened the Liverpool and Manchester Railway in 1830.

The birth of the railways as we know them today can be traced to 1825. In that year George Stephenson built the world's first public railway, the Stockton and Darlington line, in northern England. He also built steam locomotives to run on it, beginning a revolution in transport that spread like wildfire throughout the world.

Above: 'Ellerman Lines', a preserved steam locomotive of the Merchant Navy class, built for mainline service in Britain in the 1950s. Weighing some 98 tonnes, it is a Pacific, or 4-6-2 type, having a 4-wheeled bogie in front, 6 driving wheels and 2 wheels beneath the cab. Preservation societies now exist in many countries to restore steam locomotives to their former splendour.

Goodbye to Steam

The age of steam on the railways lasted in most countries until the 1950s. Since then steam locomotives have been replaced by diesel and electric locomotives. Steam locomotives were magnificent machines and exciting to watch. But they were very inefficient, dirty and noisy.

The modern diesel and electric locomotives, on the other hand, are efficient, clean and quiet. They can also accelerate more quickly and have a higher top speed. The fastest diesel is British Rail's High Speed Train, which holds the world diesel record of 230 kilometres per hour.

A French electric TGV (Train à Grande Vitesse) holds the absolute rail speed record, with a speed of no less than 380 kilometres per hour. The TGVs now run on the Paris to Lyons line, specially built flat and straight for maximum speed. The other outstanding high-speed railway, the Shinkansen in Japan, also runs on specially built track.

In Canada, Italy, Spain and Britain railway engineers are experimenting with tilting body designs to allow high speeds on existing curved track.

Right: An example of a different kind of railway track, a monorail ('single-rail'). In this particular design, found at Tokyo Zoo, the passenger car is suspended from a wheeled trolley that runs along the overhead rail. In other kinds of monorails, the passenger car straddles the track.

Below: A conventional twin-rail track. The rails are clamped firmly to the sleepers, which are embedded in stone ballast. These days the rails are laid in very long lengths, made by welding short rails together.

Below: Currently the fastest trains in service are the TGVs, which run between Paris and Lyons in France. Like all the latest high speed trains, the TGVs are highly streamlined. They operate at speeds up to 260 kilometres an hour. They are designed as a complete unit, with two power cars and eight trailer cars making up each trainset.

The Motor Car

1902 Panhard Levassor

1909 Rolls-Royce 'Silver Ghost'

1930 Aston Martin

1960 BMC 'Mini'

1982 BMW Mi Coupé

In 1885 a new type of vehicle appeared on the roads in Stuttgart, Germany. It looked much like some of the small steam carriages seen in other towns. But it differed in one important respect – its engine used petrol as fuel. It was the ancestor of the modern motor car. Its inventor was named Karl Benz.

In less than a century the car has developed into our most important form of transport, which greatly affects the way we live. Something like 200 million cars now travel on the world's roads. The latest ones are sleek vehicles, carefully streamlined so that they slip through the air easily. Some are designed for speed, being able to travel over 200 kilometres an hour. Others are designed for economy, being able to travel over 20 kilometres on a litre of petrol. Many are built with the aid of robots.

Cars are a very comfortable and convenient form of transport, but they have their disadvantages. They cause accidents; they burn a fuel obtained from oil, which will soon be in short supply, and they are a major source of pollution. For these reasons car manufacturers are continually redesigning their cars to make them safer, use less fuel, and cause less pollution. They are also experimenting with new kinds of engines that run on steam, hot air, and electricity. These should cause no pollution at all.

THE FOUR-STROKE CYCLE

Below: Most car engines are piston engines. They contain pistons that move up and down in cylinders. A mixture of petrol and air is burned in the cylinders to produce hot gases. The gases expand and force the pistons down the cylinders to produce power to move the car. The diagram shows how the fuel mixture is taken into the cylinders (1), compressed (2), burned (3), and removed (4), according to a regular cycle, called the four-stroke cycle.

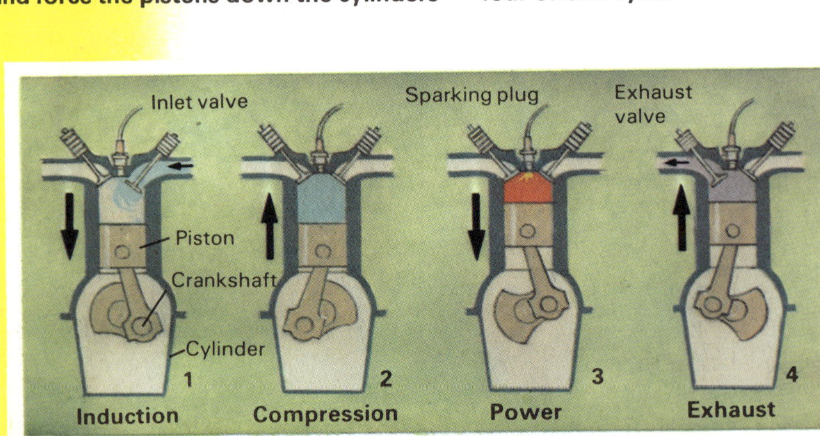

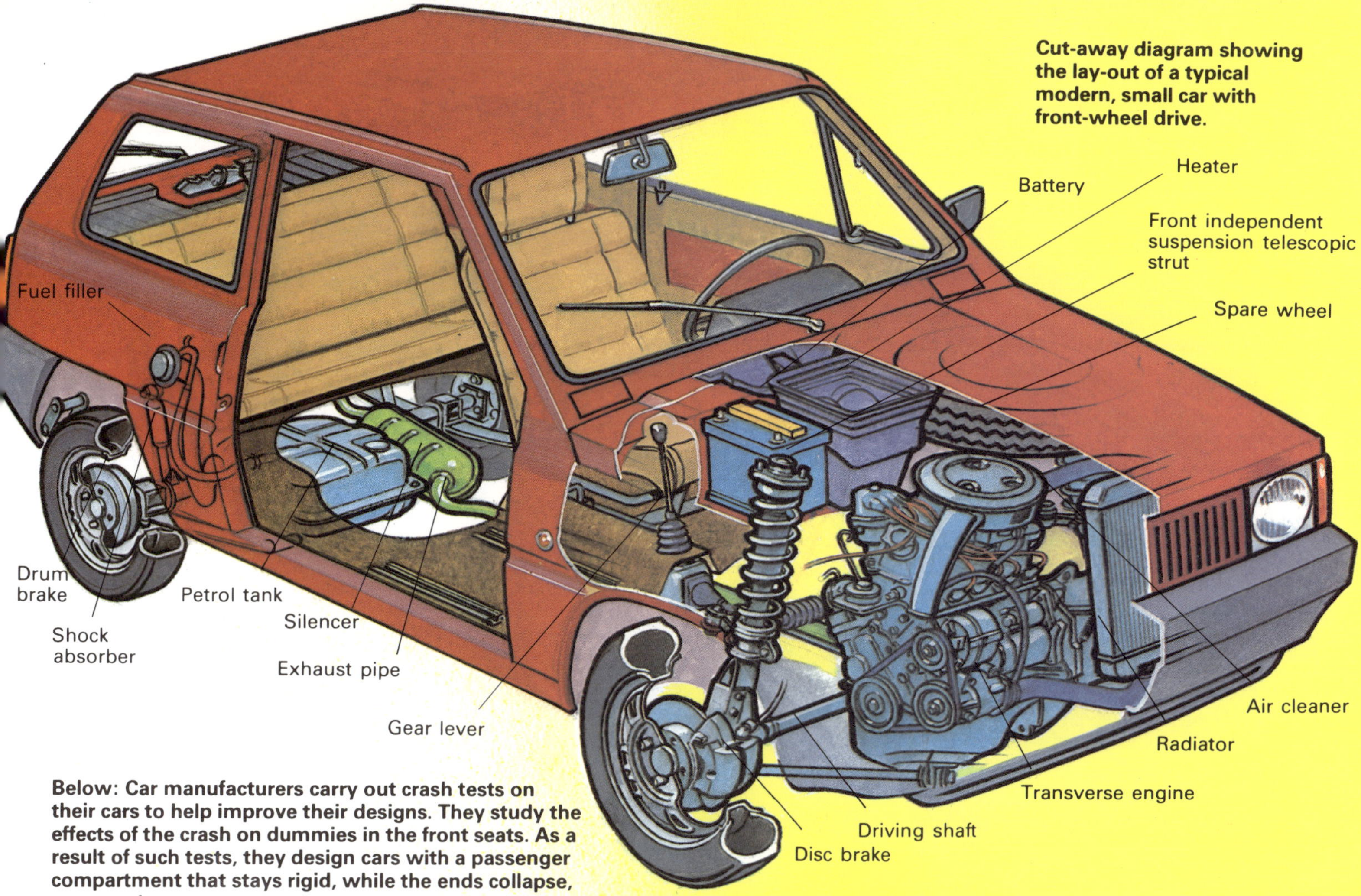

Cut-away diagram showing the lay-out of a typical modern, small car with front-wheel drive.

Below: Car manufacturers carry out crash tests on their cars to help improve their designs. They study the effects of the crash on dummies in the front seats. As a result of such tests, they design cars with a passenger compartment that stays rigid, while the ends collapse, or crumple.

CAR SYSTEMS

A car is a most complicated piece of machinery, made up of over 10,000 different parts. For simplicity we can group these parts into a number of different systems. Each system plays a particular part in the operation of the car.

THE ENGINE changes the energy in the fuel into mechanical motion.

THE TRANSMISSION SYSTEM carries, or transmits, the motion from the engine to the wheels. It consists usually of a clutch, gearbox, propeller shaft, and a final drive on the driving wheel axle.

THE STEERING SYSTEM allows the driver to turn the front wheels and so steer the car.

THE BRAKING SYSTEM gives the driver the power to slow down and stop the car.

THE SUSPENSION SYSTEM of springs and shock absorbers cushions the passenger from the effects of bumpy roads.

THE ELECTRICAL SYSTEM provides electricity from a battery to make sparks to ignite the fuel and power the lights, instruments, horn and other equipment.

Canals, Bridges and Tunnels

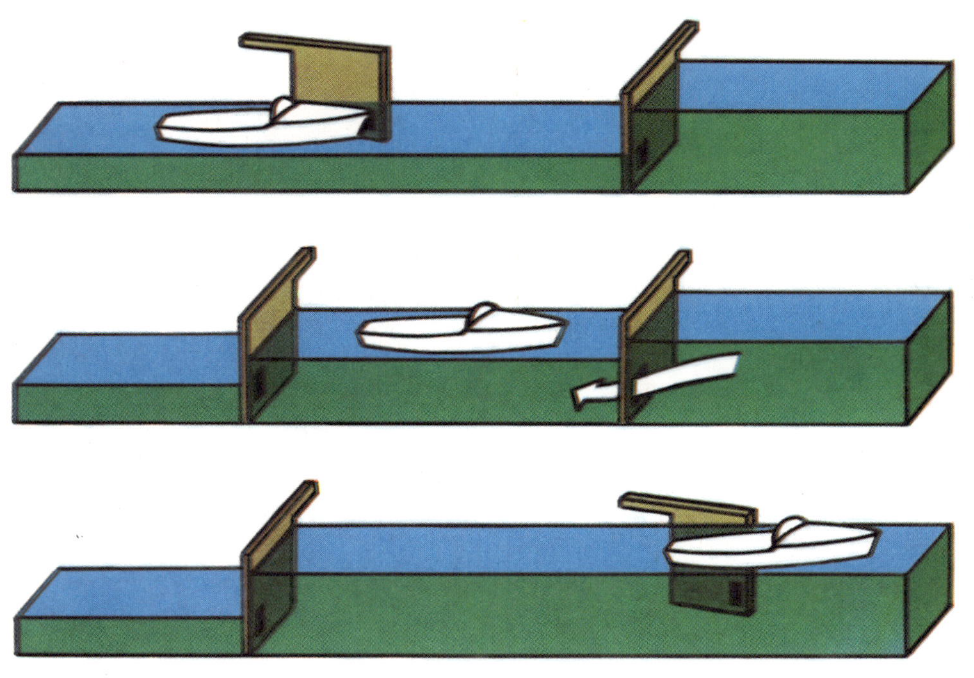

HOW LOCKS WORK
A lock is like a step. It raises ships and boats in a canal or river from one level to another. If a boat is climbing, it enters the first lock. The lower gate is open and the water inside the lock is at the same level as the lower part of the canal. When the boat is in the lock, the lower gate is closed. A small sluice (a flap) is opened in the upper gate and water flows down. The boat rises as the water level rises. When the water level is the same as the upper level, the upper gate is opened and the boat sails off. Ships can go through a series of locks to raise them to the required level. This happens in big canals such as that at Panama between North and South America. The Panama Canal has three sets of locks, built in pairs so that ships can pass through in both directions at the same time. Each lock is 300 metres long and 33 metres wide. Electric locomotives pull ships through the lock system.

Builders of roads and railways often reach mountains or rivers that they have to tunnel through or bridge. People who build bridges and dig tunnels and canals are called civil engineers.

Bridges are among the most spectacular of man-made structures. The simplest and oldest kind of bridge is the *beam bridge*. This is just a wooden or steel beam supported at either end by piers. The length or span of a beam bridge

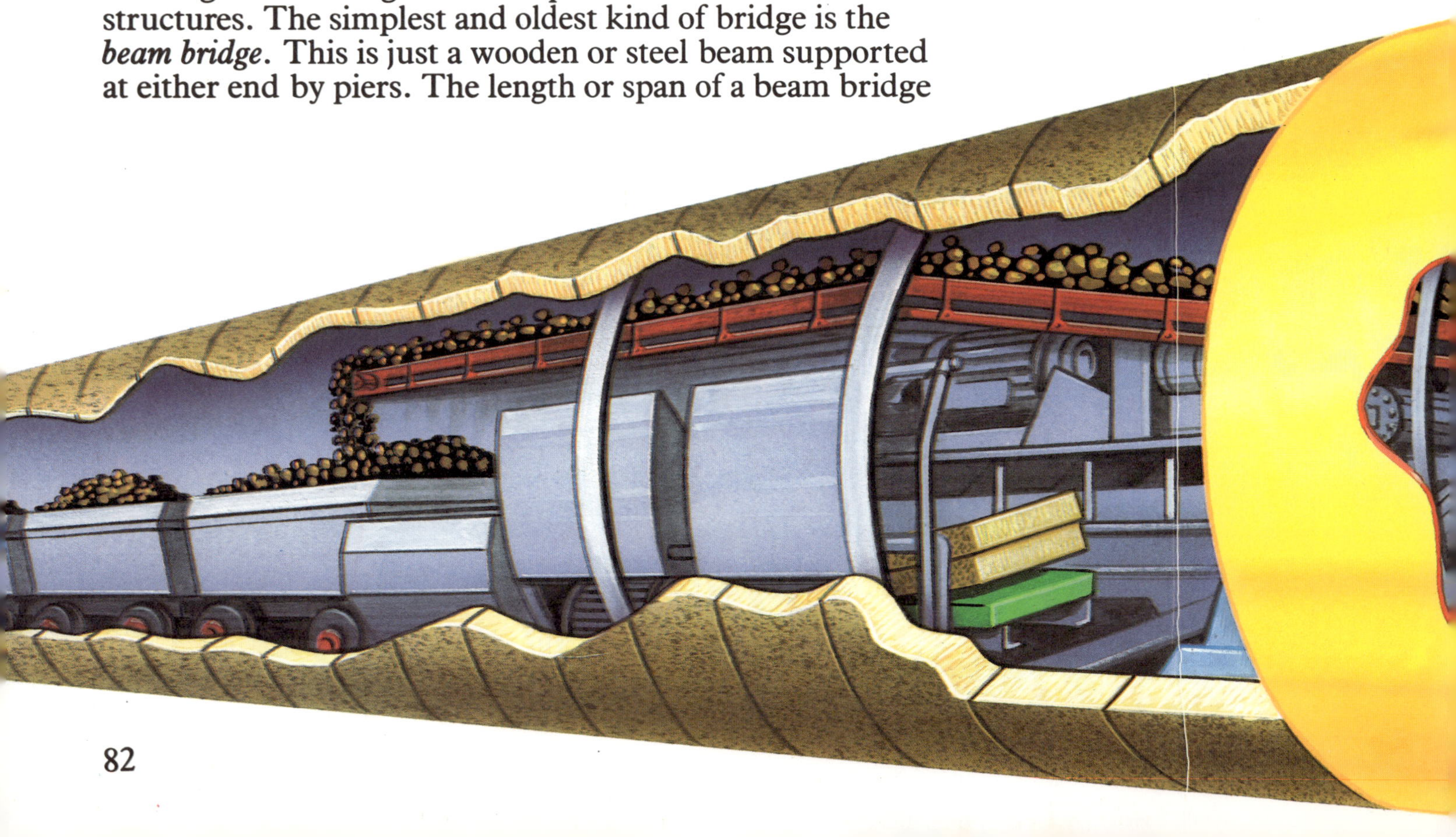

Beam bridge

Arch bridge

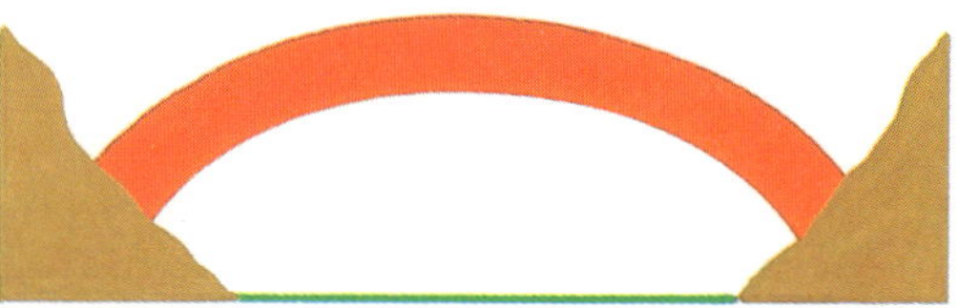

Suspension bridge

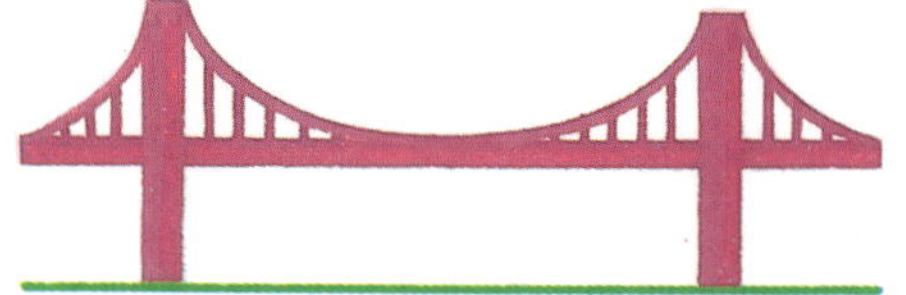

cannot be too great, otherwise the beam would sag and give way in the middle. Longer beam bridges have several piers along their length.

The *arch bridge* can have a longer span than a beam bridge. This is because the weight of the bridge travels down the sides of the arch to the supports at each end. The ancient Romans were expert builders of arch bridges.

The longest spans of all can be achieved with the *suspension bridge*. In this kind of bridge the road hangs in the air from a pair of heavy cables slung between high towers at either end. The cables are made up of thousands of steel wires bundled together until they make up a cable as much as a metre thick. These cables pass up and over the towers and then down to firm anchorage points on the ground.

Some Famous Bridges

The world's longest single bridge span is the main span of the bridge over the Humber estuary. It is 1410 metres long and is supported between two huge towers 162 metres high.

The longest suspension bridge, measured between anchorages at either end, is the Mackinac Straits bridge in Michigan, USA. It measures 2540 metres.

The longest steel arch bridge is the New River Gorge bridge at Fayetteville, West Virginia, USA. It has a span of 518 metres.

Probably the most famous bridge in the world is the Golden Gate bridge at San Francisco. Its span is 1280 metres.

The Verrazano Narrows bridge joins Brooklyn and Staten Island at the entrance to New York harbour. This great bridge has two decks, each with six lanes of traffic.

The world's widest long-span bridge is the Sydney Harbour bridge. It is 48 metres wide and has eight lanes of traffic and a footway.

Although we are seldom aware of it, the ground under our feet is often full of tunnels. Tunnels carry electricity cables, gas pipes, water and sewage. Other larger tunnels take underground railways, and tunnels through hills and mountains carry trains and cars. There are different ways of digging tunnels. If the tunnel is to be near the surface, the engineers can dig a deep trench, put a big tube in the trench and cover over the tube again. This method is called 'cut and cover'. The more modern way to dig a tunnel is to use a 'mole' like the one shown here. A powerful cutting head made of steel wheels is pushed and turned forward by powerful electric motors. The cutting head grinds up the earth and rock and this is passed back on conveyor belts to trucks that carry the rubble out of the tunnel. A steel shield protects the men working near the cutting head. As the head moves forward the tunnel is permanently lined with either steel or concrete.

Energy and Power

Warm swamps covered many regions of the Earth some 300 million years ago (main picture). In them grew huge ferns and horsetails. When these plants died, they fell into the swamp and began to decay. Over the years the remains dried and hardened into coal, now found sandwiched between the rock layers (inset above). The organisms that lived in ancient seas also died and decayed, and we find their remains today as oil and natural gas, trapped in the rock layers (inset below).

We could not live the way we do today without a plentiful supply of energy. Most of the energy we use comes from oil, coal and natural gas. These are known as fossil fuels because they are the remains of organisms – plants and animals – that once lived. And they are burned to release their energy.

Most oil, or petroleum, is made into fuels that are burned in engines, to power cars, trucks, locomotives and aeroplanes. These fuels include petrol, kerosene and diesel oil. Most coal is burned in power stations to produce electricity. The heat from the burning coal heats water in a boiler into steam. The steam then spins a turbine, which in turn spins a generator to make electricity. Electricity is a very convenient way of 'carrying' energy from place to place.

Some power stations use another kind of 'fuel' to produce heat for the boilers. This is nuclear fuel, such as uranium. Under certain conditions uranium atoms can be made to

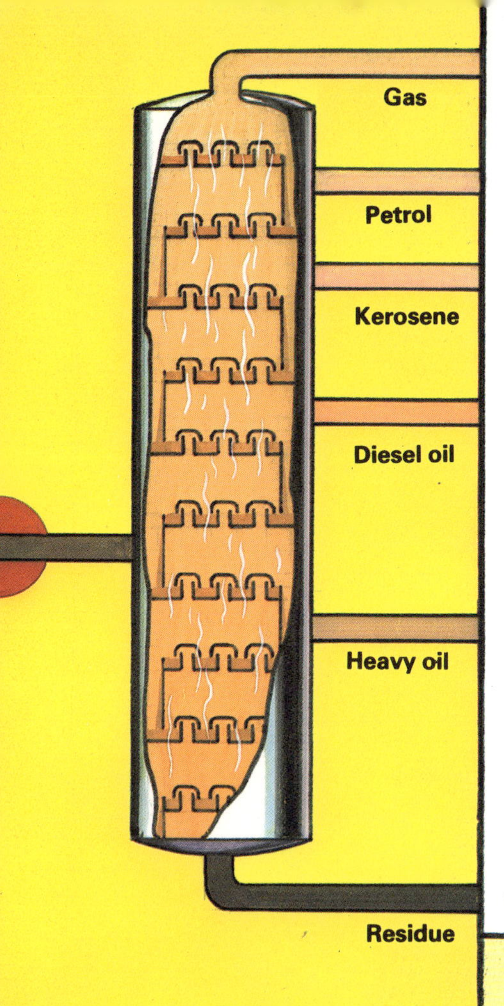

split, and this releases large amounts of heat (see page 69). There are now some 200 nuclear power stations around the world.

Alternative Energy Sources

Supplies of fossil fuels and uranium are obtained from the ground. Eventually these supplies will run out. Then we must find alternative sources of energy. We are already using one – flowing water. We harness this power in hydro-electric ('water-electric') schemes. The water spins water turbines, which drive the electricity generators.

Schemes to harness other natural energy sources are also well under way. Engineers are building huge wind turbines, wave-power devices and solar 'power towers'.

Left: Before it can be used, crude oil must be refined, or processed, in an oil refinery. The first stage is distillation, which takes place in this kind of tower. Oil vapour passes through the tower, and the various substances it contains separate out into various parts, or fractions.

Below: Some regions of the world are blessed with plenty of sunshine, a 'free' source of energy waiting to be tapped. This can be done with a solar power tower. Large numbers of mirrors reflect sunshine onto a boiler at the top of a tower. This heats water in the boiler into steam.

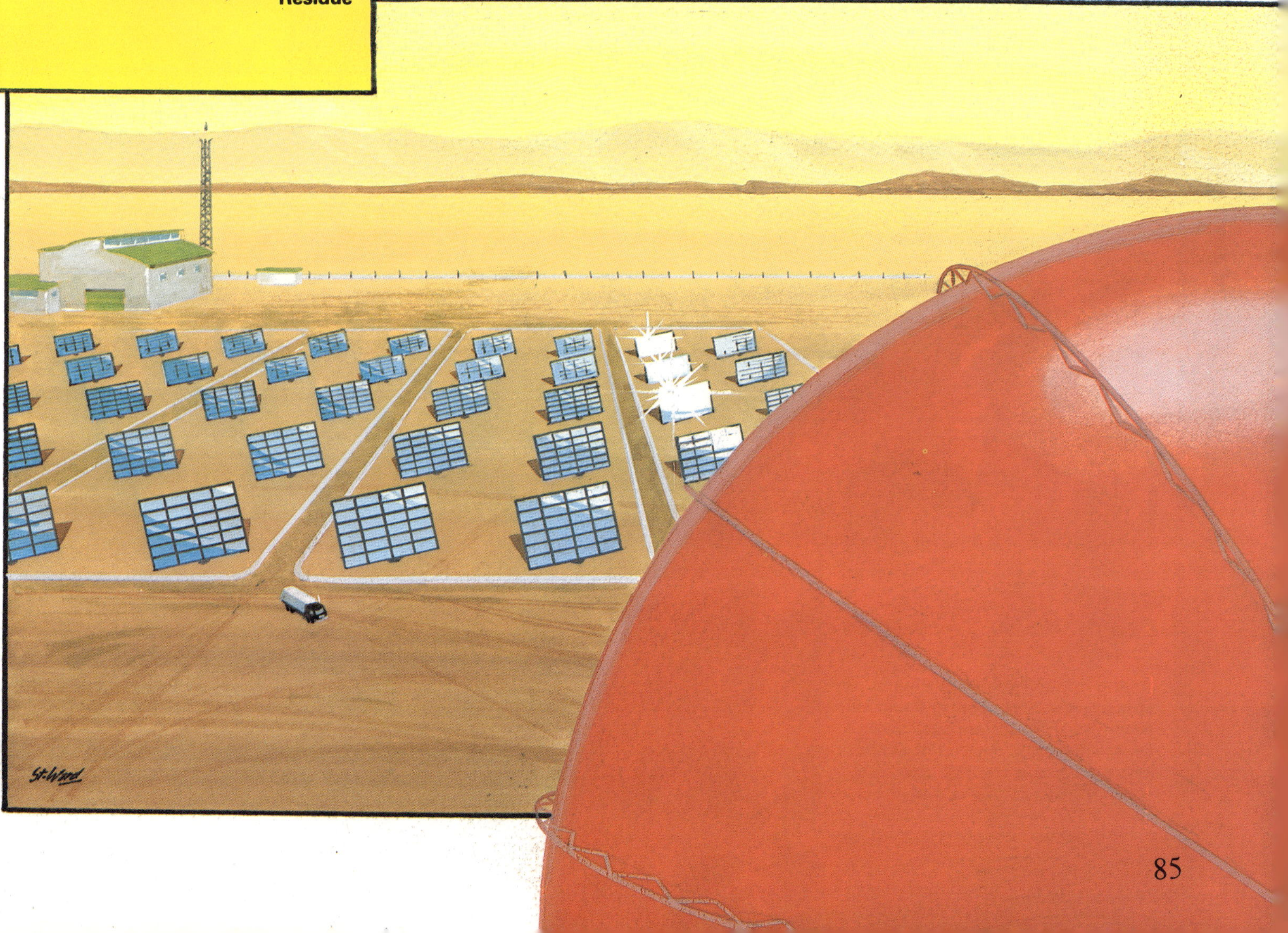

Fossil Fuels

A fuel is something that can be burned to give heat, light or power. It is a store of energy. The energy came in the first place from the Sun. Plants gather energy from the Sun. Oil, gas and coal were formed from plants that lived millions of years ago. They are called *fossil fuels*.

Drilling for oil is a very costly operation. First of all, the oil has to be found. Geologists spend a long time examining the layers of rock under the land or under the sea-bed. When they think there may be oil, an exploration well is drilled. If oil is found, then several more wells are drilled to find out if there is enough oil to justify a full-scale operation. A production platform is put in place, and only then does the valuable oil start to flow. In the stormy North Sea, the platforms may be in 300 metres of water. The oil itself can be 3000 metres below the sea-bed.

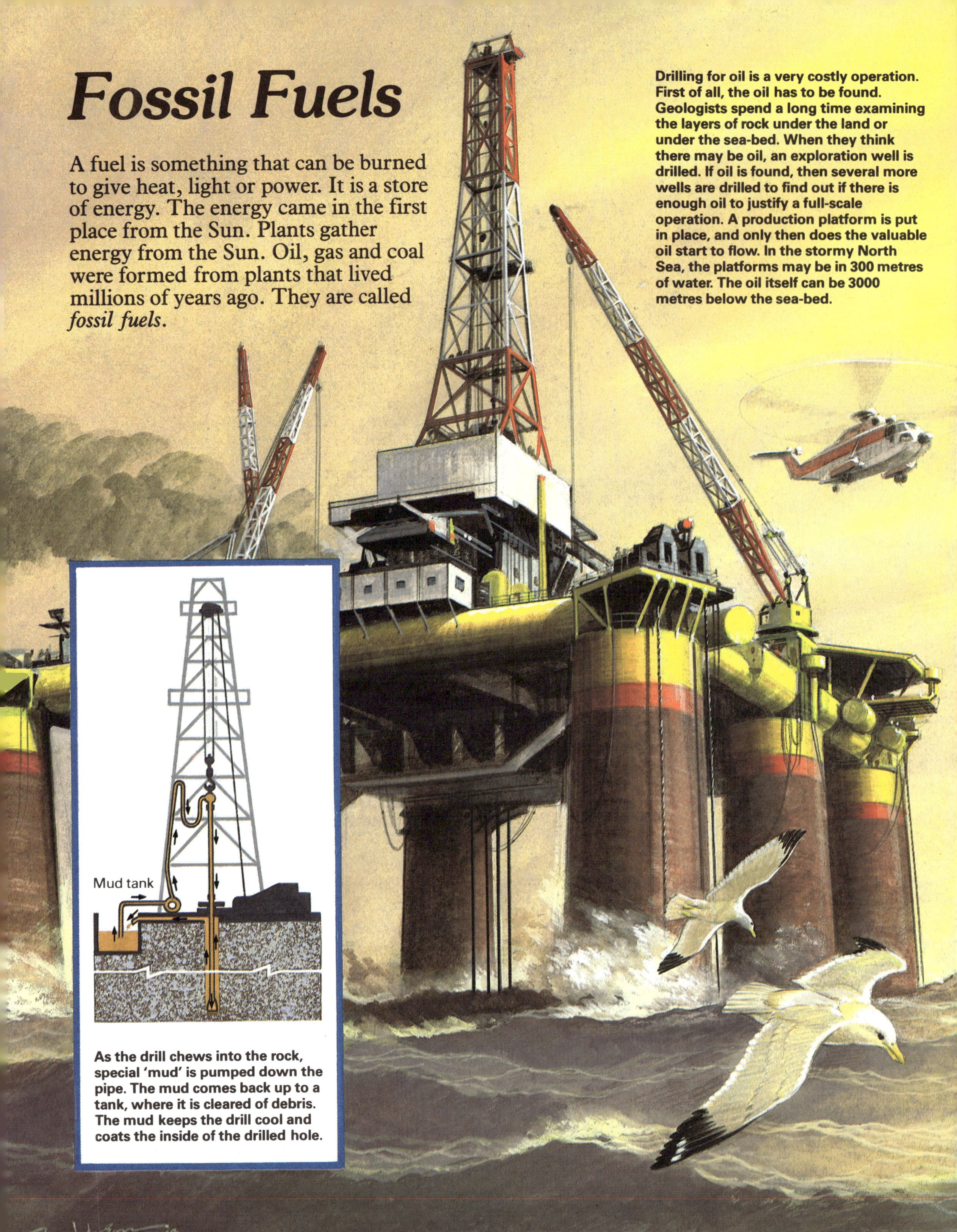

As the drill chews into the rock, special 'mud' is pumped down the pipe. The mud comes back up to a tank, where it is cleared of debris. The mud keeps the drill cool and coats the inside of the drilled hole.

How Coal is Formed

Like oil, coal is formed from living things. It started off millions of years ago as trees and plants in ancient forests. The forests slowly sank into swamps and were covered by layers of mud which later became solid rock. The pressure of this rock and the heat from the Earth began to change the plant remains.

The first stage in the formation of coal can be seen in some wet moorlands and bogs. There decaying plants form *peat,* a substance that can be cut and dried to make fuel that burns.

If peat is left in the ground for long enough it becomes *lignite* or brown coal. As more millions of years go by, the coal grows into *bituminous* coal, the black stuff we burn. The last stage in coal formation is *anthracite,* a shiny black rock that is clean to handle. Anthracite is almost pure carbon.

How Oil Forms Underground

The oil we use today was probably formed from decayed plants and animals that fell to the ocean floor 500 million years ago. Slowly, over thousands of centuries, the remains of the plants and animals were covered by layer upon layer of sand and mud. The pressure of these layers caused great heat. This heat, combined with chemical action, changed the ancient remains into the substances we call oil and gas. As more time went by, the oil and gas seeped slowly upwards through soft rock. After a while, they reached solid rock and they could go no further. They were in a *trap,* in which collected oil, gas and water. It is these traps which today's oilmen search for.

All Kinds of Oil

Petroleum from the ground is often called 'crude oil' because it is a complicated mixture of chemicals that has to be sorted out before we can use all the materials in it. This sorting out is done at an oil refinery. A refinery is a maze of steel towers and pipes, but among the main pieces of equipment are tall *fractionating columns.*

Crude oil is heated to a vapour in a furnace. A pipe carries the vapour to an entrance near the bottom of the column. Inside the column, trays are arranged one above the other (see below left). The trays are hottest at the bottom and coolest at the top of the tower. As the oil vapour rises, it passes through holes and is caught by *bubble caps* like upside-down cups (see inset below). The caps force the vapour down again through liquids that have already condensed in the trays. This makes more of the vapour condense.

The various oil products condense to liquid at different temperatures. The heaviest liquids collect at the bottom of the tower – substances such as asphalt for road-making. Above this comes diesel oil, and above this again paraffin for jet planes and home heaters. Near the top appears petrol for cars, while right at the top is gas for cooking and heating.

This kind of *bit* is used to drill through hard rock. Its steel teeth grind and crush the rock.

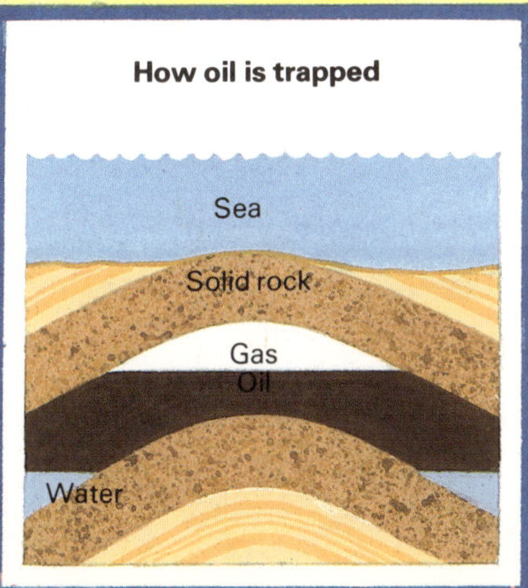

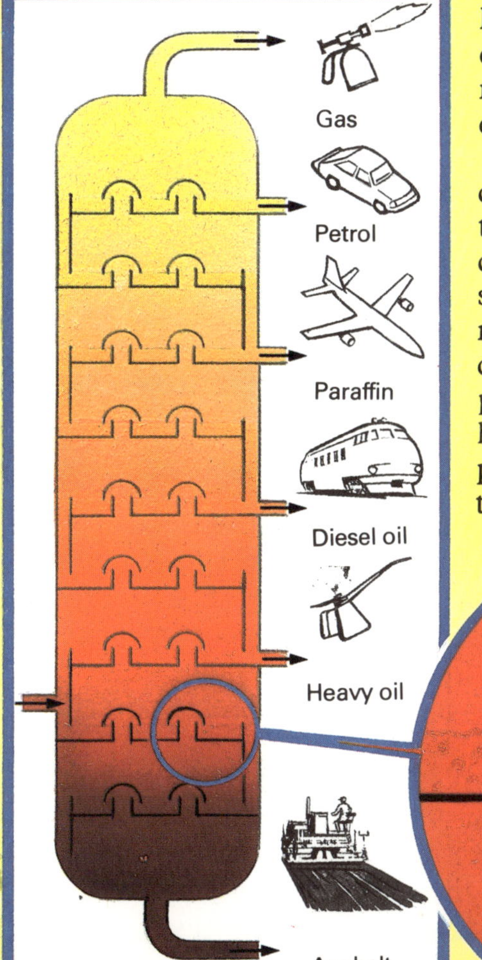

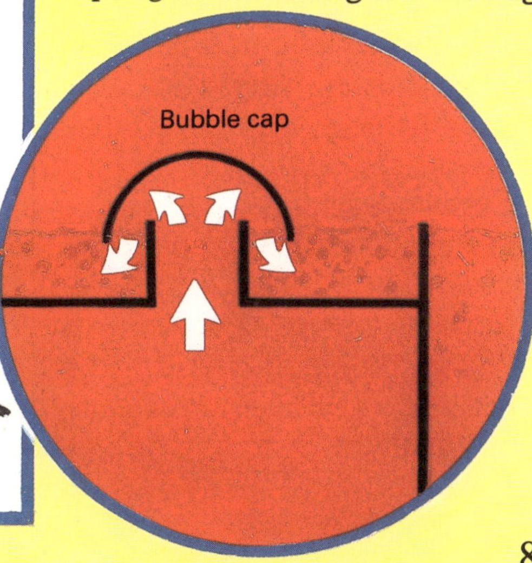

Power of the Atom

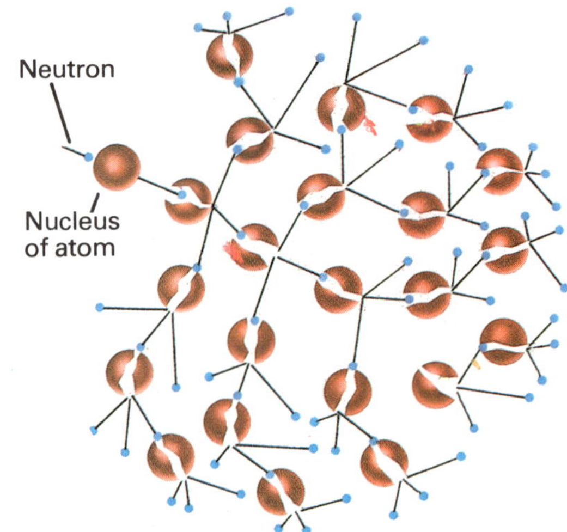

A chain reaction occurs when a neutron splits a uranium atom and produces at least two more neutrons which in turn split other atoms. An uncontrolled chain reaction produces a nuclear explosion.

Scientists have discovered how to get vast amounts of power from the atom. This knowledge can be used for the good of mankind – to make electricity. It can also be used to make nuclear weapons.

The nucleus (centre) of the atom is made up of particles called protons and neutrons, held together by powerful forces of attraction. When the nucleus is broken apart, these forces are released as energy in the form of radiation.

The atoms of some elements are constantly breaking up by themselves. They are called *radioactive elements*. Uranium is one of these. One kind of uranium has 92 protons and 143 neutrons in its nucleus. We add these numbers together and call this uranium 235 or U-235 for short. In U-235, a neutron sometimes shoots off from the nucleus. Sometimes this neutron hits another U-235 neutron and knocks loose another neutron. If this should happen often enough we have a *chain reaction* and a great deal of energy is let loose. If a piece of U-235 is large enough, a great many neutrons fly about at once. The reaction gets out of hand and we have a tremendous explosion – an atomic bomb.

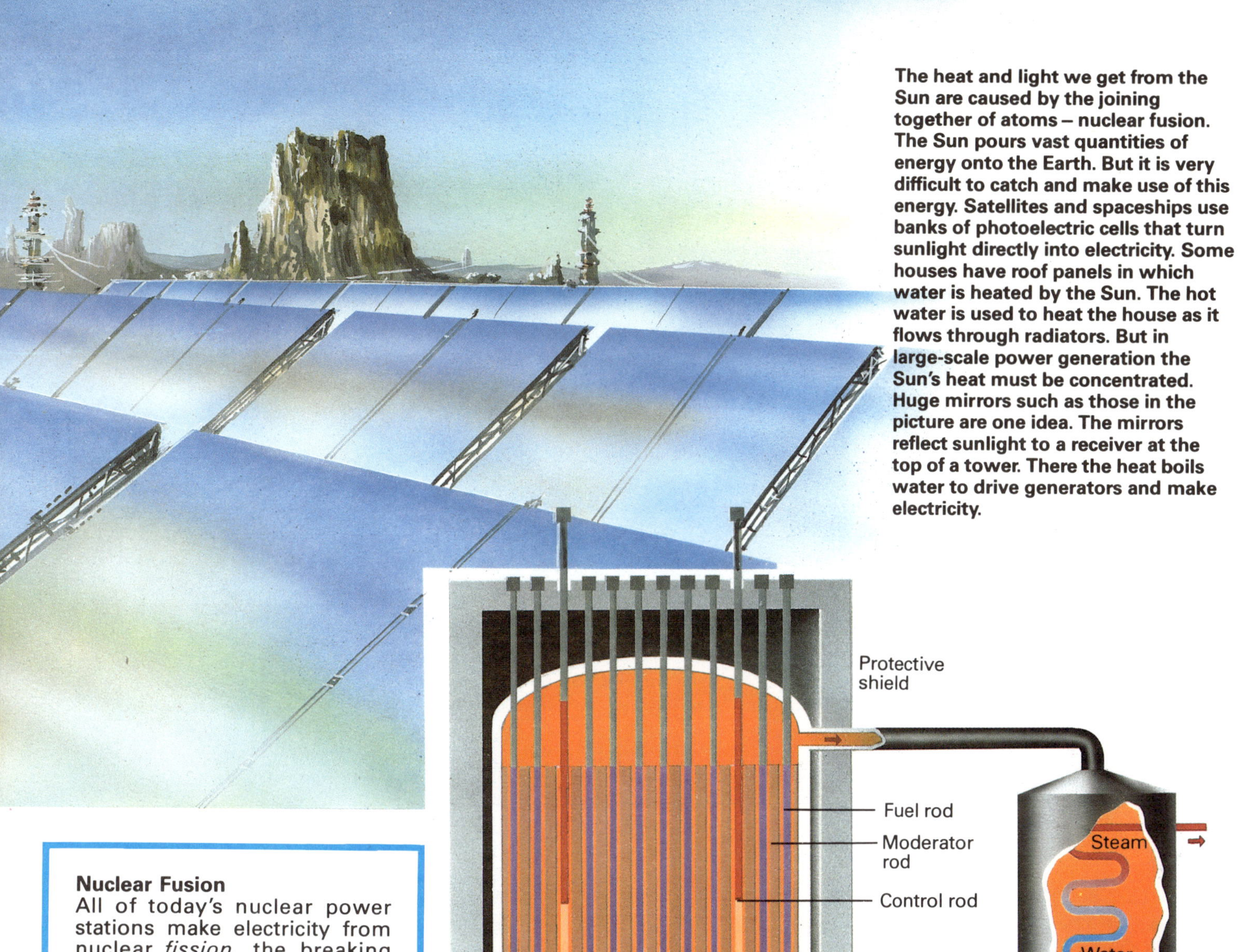

The heat and light we get from the Sun are caused by the joining together of atoms – nuclear fusion. The Sun pours vast quantities of energy onto the Earth. But it is very difficult to catch and make use of this energy. Satellites and spaceships use banks of photoelectric cells that turn sunlight directly into electricity. Some houses have roof panels in which water is heated by the Sun. The hot water is used to heat the house as it flows through radiators. But in large-scale power generation the Sun's heat must be concentrated. Huge mirrors such as those in the picture are one idea. The mirrors reflect sunlight to a receiver at the top of a tower. There the heat boils water to drive generators and make electricity.

Nuclear Fusion
All of today's nuclear power stations make electricity from nuclear *fission,* the breaking apart of atoms. But there is another kind of nuclear power – the power that is produced when atoms come together to form larger atoms. This is the powerful energy source that makes the Sun shine and keeps us all alive. It also produces the terrible power of hydrogen bombs. It is called nuclear *fusion.*

In nuclear fission the atoms of heavy elements such as uranium and plutonium are split apart. In nuclear fusion, the atoms of light elements such as hydrogen and helium are forced together. Inside the Sun, it is the turning of hydrogen into helium that produces our light and heat.

Scientists have been trying for many years to make nuclear fusion work safely to produce all the energy we need. If they succeed, all our fuel shortages and power problems will end.

In a nuclear power station, the chain reaction is controlled. A nuclear reactor has rods containing some U-235 placed in a *moderator.* The moderator is usually graphite or water. In case the chain reaction starts to go too quickly, *control rods* are inserted too. These are made of metals that absorb neutrons and can be moved in or out of the reactor.

Heat is produced by the nuclear reaction and a cooling liquid or gas passes through the reactor to take up the heat. This coolant goes to a *heat exchanger* where it makes steam to drive steam turbines. These turbines make electricity.

Power of the Sea

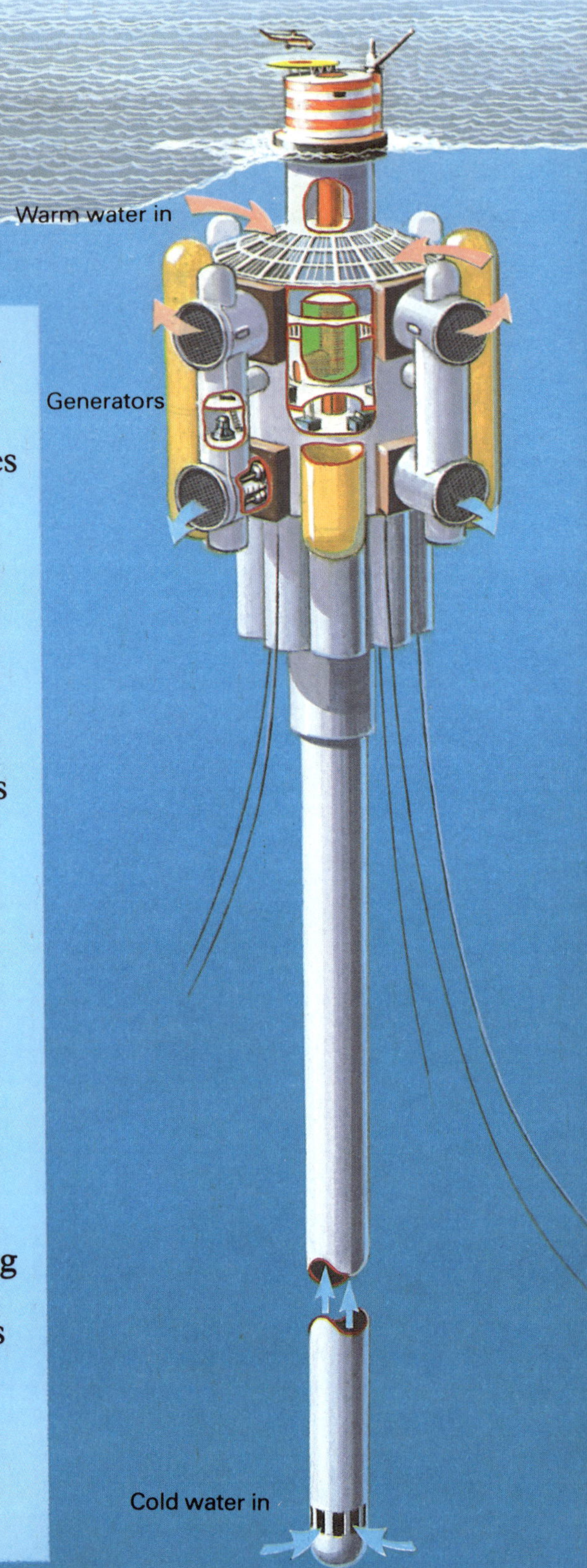

In a few years from now, the world's oil wells will begin to dry up. We will have to find other kinds of energy, and scientists are turning their attention to some of the Earth's 'free' energy sources. Among those 'free' sources is the energy that can be got from the sea.

If you have been at the seaside when big waves are coming in you will know the power behind these moving masses of water. There can, in fact, be 80 kilowatts of power for every metre of wave along its length. Many different ways of collecting power from the waves have been tried, but so far none of them has been completely successful. People have tried floating 'ducks' that move up and down in the waves. Machines inside the 'ducks' turn the bobbing motion into electricity. Others have tried hinged rafts which move with the waves and drive turbines.

The ocean currents are another possible source of power. Year in, year out, great masses of water move steadily through the oceans, always following the same path. The Gulf Stream that runs across the Atlantic Ocean towards northern Europe is such an ocean current. Scientists have been working on machines to make use of this vast mass of moving water. But the ocean currents move slowly, so the machines will have to be very big to work well (see opposite page).

Another idea, pictured on the right, is a huge floating power station. As the Sun beats down on the oceans, it heats the surface waters, but the water deep down stays very cold. This difference in temperature between the two layers of water can be used to work a heat engine. Cold water goes in at the bottom and warm surface water goes in at the top. The difference in temperature is made to drive turbo-generators to make electricity.

Above: Lines of hinged rafts are moored facing the direction from which the wind usually blows. As the waves pass under them, the rafts move up and down, making the hinges work as pumps. The pumps produce liquid at high pressure to drive an electric generator.

At the right above is a floating power station. It is here that the energy from the rafts is turned into electricity before being sent ashore by cable.

Right: A possible scheme to get power from the Gulf Stream or other ocean currents. It is a huge underwater turbine, with blades hundreds of metres across. The turbine has to be very big because ocean currents move quite slowly. You can tell the size of the turbine by comparing it with the submersible.

Another wave-power machine is called the *oscillating water column.* This is simply a long vertical tube open to the air at the top, with the bottom below the surface. When a wave passes, the water inside the tube rises and falls. The rise and fall of water is like a piston in a cylinder which can drive an air turbine to make electricity.

Left: A floating thermal power station in which differences in water temperature are used to drive electricity generators.

All of these schemes are future possibilities. The way that the energy of the sea has been harnessed already is in tidal power stations where the difference in water level between high and low tides is used to power turbines.

Measuring Time

Sundials were first used by the Egyptians. As the Sun moves across the sky, its shadow shows the time of day.

For centuries, people used the Sun, Moon and stars to tell the time by. It takes a year for the Earth to go right round the Sun once. The Moon's monthly phases give us the 12 divisions into which the year is divided. But, more important, the Earth rotates once on its axis every 24 hours, giving regular day and night.

For thousands of years, these rough divisions of time were accurate enough. Then came the sundial, the water clock and the sandglass.

The first mechanical clocks appeared about the end of the 13th century, but they were not very accurate. It was not until the pendulum clock was invented in 1656 that people could really tell the time with any certainty. The pendulum clock is based on something discovered earlier by the great Italian scientist Galileo. When Galileo was a boy, he watched the swinging of a hanging lamp in Pisa cathedral. He found that each swing of the lamp as it moved back and forth took exactly the same time, whether it was a big swing or a small one. Many accurate pendulum clocks are still in use today.

Today's very accurate clocks and watches are not mechanical. Electric watches run off tiny batteries. There are quartz clocks, driven by the tiny vibrations given off by quartz crystals when an electric current is applied to them. Atomic clocks are driven by the movement of atoms and molecules. These can be accurate to less than one thousandth of a second a year.

So that dawn and sunset fall at about the same time on the clock all over the world, there are many time zones. Most of them are one hour apart. Large countries such as the United States have many time zones. When you go from west to east, you have to advance your watch every time you enter a new time zone. If you cross the International Date Line on the 180° meridian your watch goes back 24 hours to make up for the time difference.

Concorde crosses the Atlantic so quickly, it 'beats' the clock.

The Egyptians developed the water clock in about 1400 BC. This clock had holes in the bottom that allowed water to drip slowly out. Levels were marked inside to show the time.

The early mechanical clocks were powered by weights. The weights were attached to a cord that was wound round a drum. As one weight fell, the drum turned. This worked a set of toothed wheels called gears. One of these gears turned the clock hands. Another toothed wheel drove a lever called an escapement. The escapement rocked back and forth and controlled the speed of the gears.

Clocks driven by springs appeared in the 15th century. These were more accurate than the weight-driven timepieces.

The sand-glass had two containers joined by a narrow stem. It took a fixed length of time for the sand to trickle from one container to the other.

Very accurate time-keeping was needed at sea. The first accurate chronometers were made by John Harrison. The one above was regulated by a balance spring.

The modern digital watch shows the time in numbers. At the heart of the watch is a quartz crystal. An electric current from a tiny battery is fed to the crystal. This makes it vibrate at a steady frequency. The crystal gives out electric signals at this frequency which go to the microchip part of the watch. The microchip counts the signals and every second, minute and hour sends another signal to the digital display. It may also display the date.

The inside of an electronic watch.

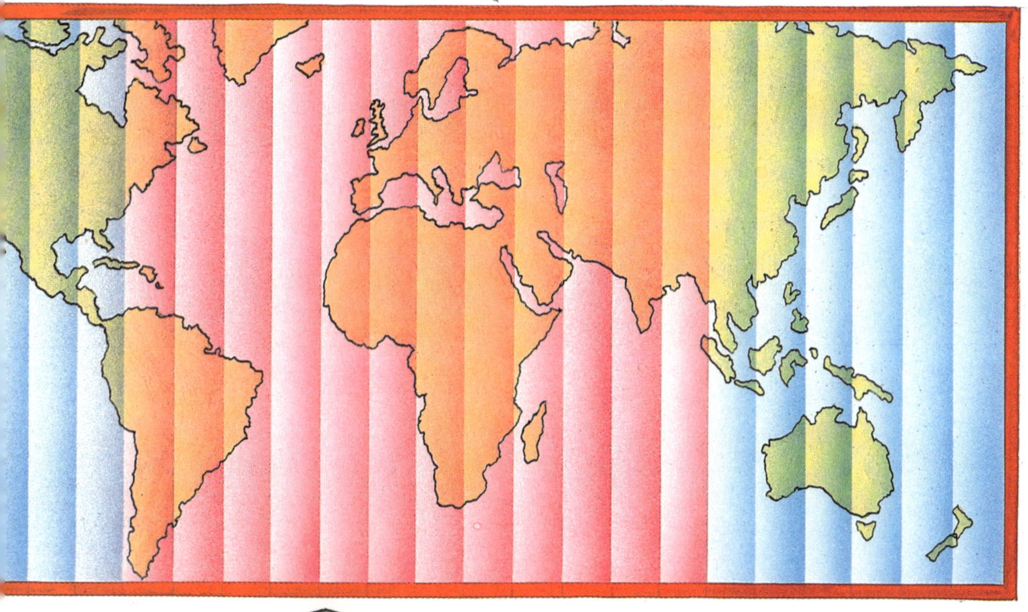

The early clocks were driven by a falling weight and regulated by a rocking bar. The bar allowed a wheel connected to the hands to move round one tooth at a time.

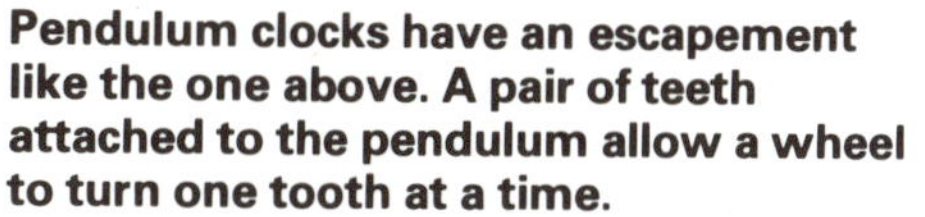

Pendulum clocks have an escapement like the one above. A pair of teeth attached to the pendulum allow a wheel to turn one tooth at a time.

A clock made in 1580.

Science in the Home

Science has played a big part in making our homes comfortable and easy to operate. Even forgetting such things as television sets, radios, refrigerators and food mixers, there are many other ways in which science works for us. Many of the home inventions of the past hundred years are now so much a part of our daily lives that we seldom stop to think about them. The first canned food, for example, went on sale in the 1820s. But it was not until the 1860s that the first can-opener was invented. Before then, people opened cans with a hammer and chisel!

Cleaning and washing used to be hard work, often needing servants armed with mops and brooms. Then science came to our aid. The carpet sweeper was invented in

It is very seldom we have to think about all the wires, pipes and tanks that are hidden behind the walls, under the floors and in the lofts of our homes. Some of them are shown in the picture below. The big tank feeds all the water pipes throughout the house. The smaller tanks are fed from it and are for the hot water system. The hot water boiler on the ground floor may use gas, coal or oil to heat the water. The electricity supply comes in through a main fuse box. You can see how the wires run from a fuse through all the electric sockets in a room back to the fuse box.

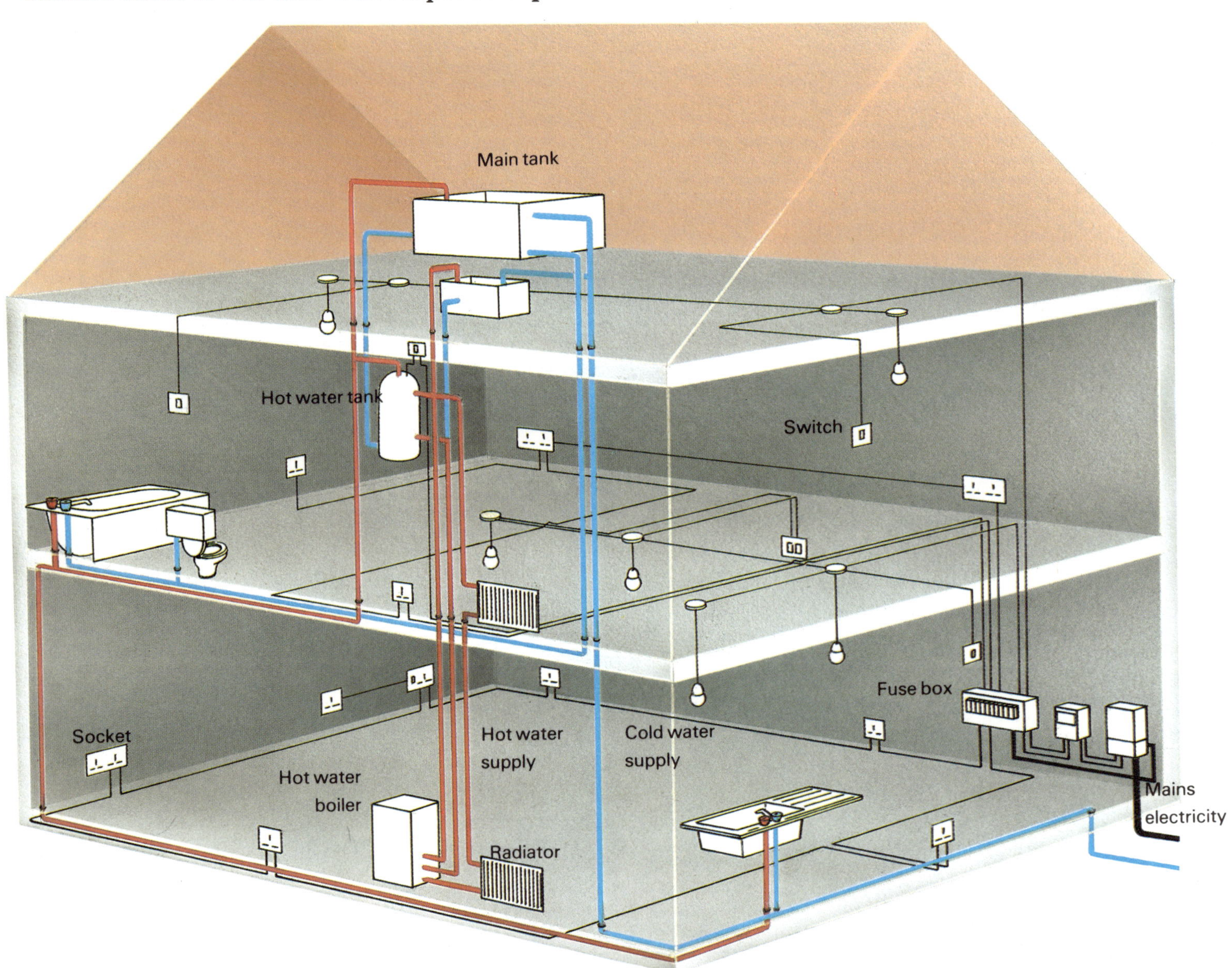

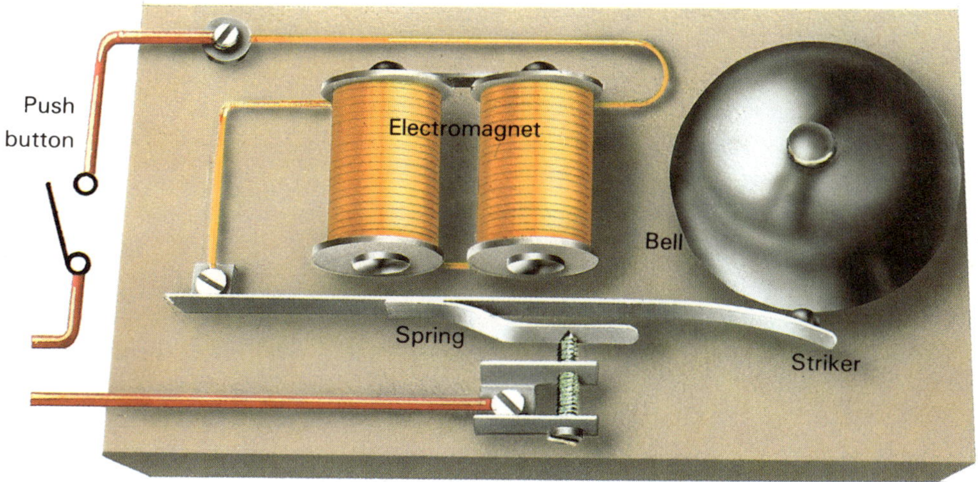

THE ELECTRIC BELL
When you press the button of an electric bell you close a switch that makes an electric current flow through an electromagnet. This magnetism moves a striker which hits the bell. As the striker moves, it opens the contact that passes current to the electromagnet. There is no magnetism, so a spring pulls the striker back. This closes the contact again and current passes again to the electromagnet. The bell rings and opens the contact again. In this way, the bell keeps on ringing as long as the button is pressed.

1876, soon followed by the hand-cranked vacuum cleaner, worked by bellows. In 1901 an electric motor and an air filter turned it into the vacuum cleaner.

The first washing machines were also worked by turning a handle. By 1914, electric motors were being used. Although detergents were invented as long ago as 1916, it was not until 1945 that they came into general use.

The oil lamp, like the candle, was one of the earliest and most useful inventions. Then came gas in the early 1800s. But gas light was rather poor until the invention of the incandescent mantle in 1885. The mantle was a sleeve of fine cotton soaked in chemicals. This fitted over the gas flame and burned to increase and spread the light. The carbon-filament electric lamp, invented around 1878, was the forerunner of today's tungsten-filament lamp and the fluorescent tube. Many other inventions, big and small, help to make our lives easier; things like safety pins, zip fasteners, sewing machines, safety razors, water closets and non-stick frying pans.

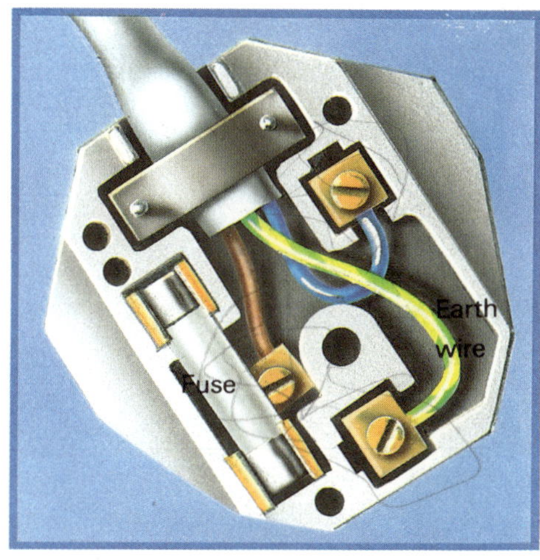

Electric plugs (above) should have a fuse inside them for safety. Inside the tube is a thin wire which melts if too much current passes through it. This cuts off the electricity before any damage is done. Without a fuse, an electrical fault could cause the current to rise and cause overheating and start a fire. Fuses are graded in amperes (amps) – an amp is the unit of electric current. The number of amps printed on a fuse is the amount of current that the fuse will allow through to whatever appliance is being used without 'blowing'.

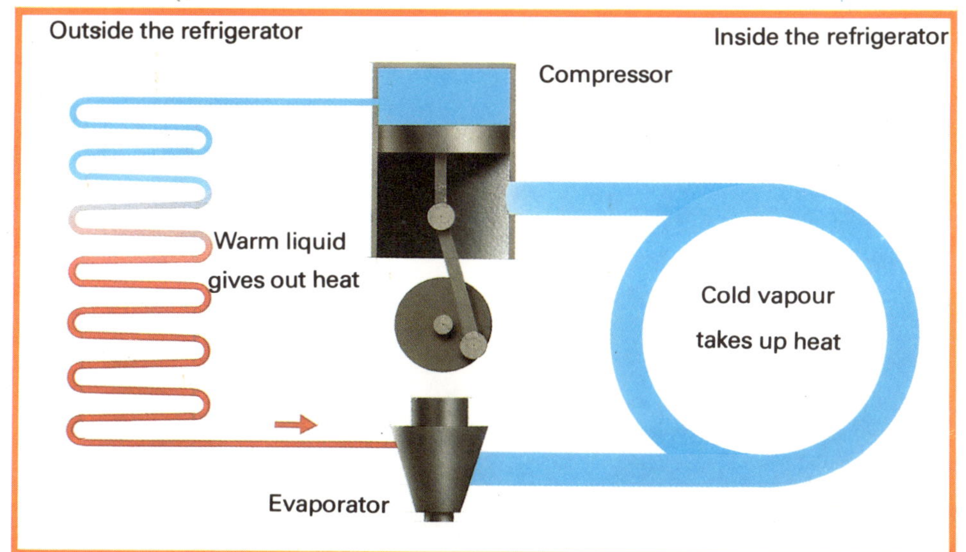

A refrigerator has pipes inside it that contain a cold fluid. This fluid easily changes from a liquid to a vapour. As it goes into the refrigerator it is liquid and is pumped through an evaporator. This lowers the liquid's pressure and it becomes vapour. The change from liquid to vapour makes the vapour cold. This cold vapour flows through pipes inside the refrigerator. After it leaves, it goes to a condenser. This increases its pressure and it changes back to liquid, giving out heat. In this way, heat is taken from inside the refrigerator to the outside.

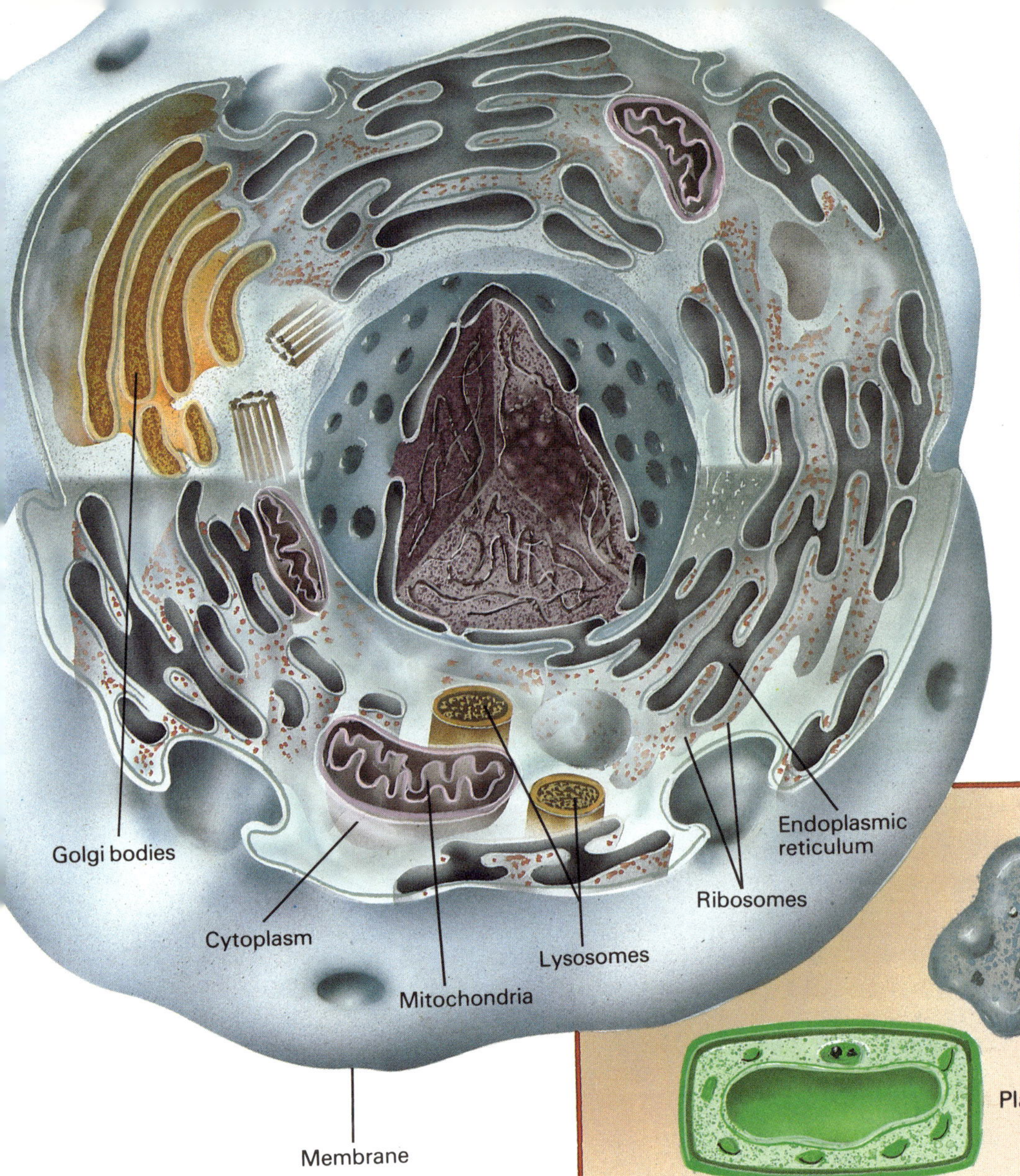

Golgi bodies
Cytoplasm
Mitochondria
Lysosomes
Ribosomes
Endoplasmic reticulum
Membrane

Parts of the Cell
The *membrane* is the cell's skin. It holds all the parts together. The *cytoplasm* is all the inside of the cell except the nucleus. The *nucleus* is the contol centre that orders all the cell's activities. The *mitochondria* are the energy-producers of the cell. They take in food and give out energy for all the cell's parts. *Lysosomes* are round bodies that break down the food that comes into the cell. *Golgi bodies* are stacks of thin discs. Scientists are not sure what they do. *Ribosomes* are dot-like objects that make proteins for the cell. The *endoplasmic reticulum* is a channel that joins the cell's membrane to the membrane around the nucleus.

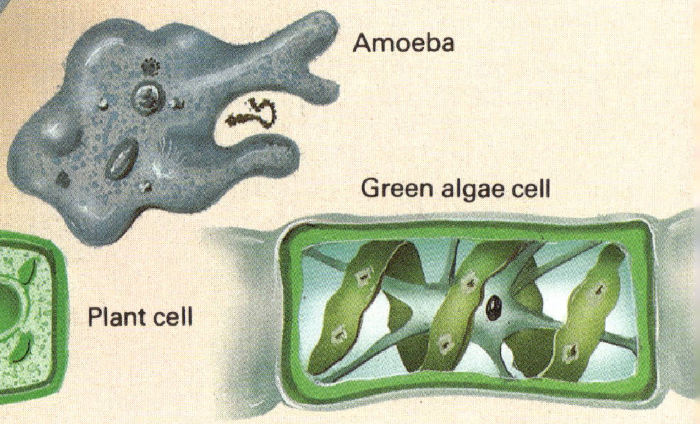

Amoeba
Green algae cell
Plant cell

The Science of Life

Our bodies are made up of millions upon millions of tiny cells. All these cells grow from only two cells that join together at conception, when a new life begins. The cells come in all shapes and sizes. Some brain cells are only $\frac{1}{200}$ mm across. Other cells, such as muscle and nerve cells, are long and thin. Nerve cells can be as much as a metre long.

But all cells are similar in some ways. They are all enclosed in a thin membrane. Inside the membrane is the *cytoplasm*. This jelly-like stuff contains several different structures, and each has its own job to do. At the cell's centre is its *nucleus*. The nucleus is the cell's 'brain', controlling everything that the cell does.

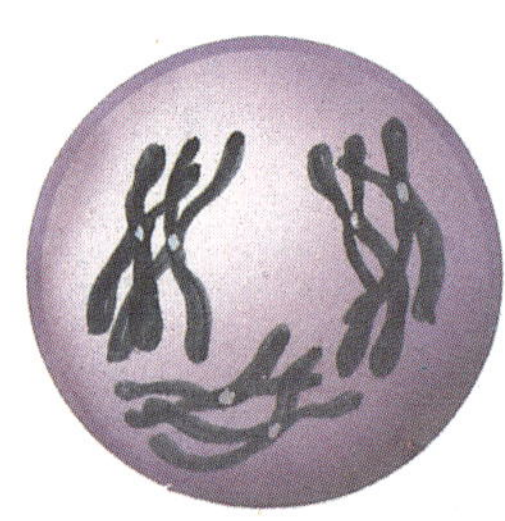

The nucleus is the cell's control room. Fine strands called *chromosomes* are scattered inside it. Chromosomes are made up of two kinds of substances – DNA and *proteins*. DNA is a chemical that controls all the things that are passed on from one generation to the next. It rules whether we will have fair or dark hair, blue eyes or brown. DNA does this by controlling the production of other substances called proteins.

Cells at Work

Below you can see some of the different kinds of living cells. *Red blood cells* are those that make our blood look red. They carry oxygen from the lungs all over our bodies. *White blood cells* are those that we need to protect us from disease. *Nerve cells* are shaped as they are so that they can carry messages to different parts of the body. *Lymphocytes* and *phagocytes* are two kinds of cell which 'eat' harmful bacteria in the body. When we cut ourself, bacteria often attack the wound. Then phagocytes come along and attack and surround the bacteria. If the invading bacteria or micro-organisms are still not beaten, the lymphocytes come along and secrete *antibodies* that make the invaders harmless.

Amoebas are tiny creatures that consist of only one cell. All the machinery for life is held inside them. Despite their small size, they are able to move about, feed themselves and reproduce.

Passing On the Information
A new life begins when two cells join to make a new one. This new cell must have in it all the characteristics that a person inherits from his or her parents. The cell must also contain all the information needed to build up a human body.

Each chromosome in the cell's nucleus is a chain of things called *genes*. There may be 1000 of them on each chromosome. The genes govern our hair colour, eye colour and all our other characteristics. The genes are made of DNA. Each DNA molecule is arranged in two spirals linked by chemicals, rather like the rungs of a ladder (see below). There are only four different chemical rungs but they can be arranged in a huge variety of combinations to give all the different characteristics that people have.

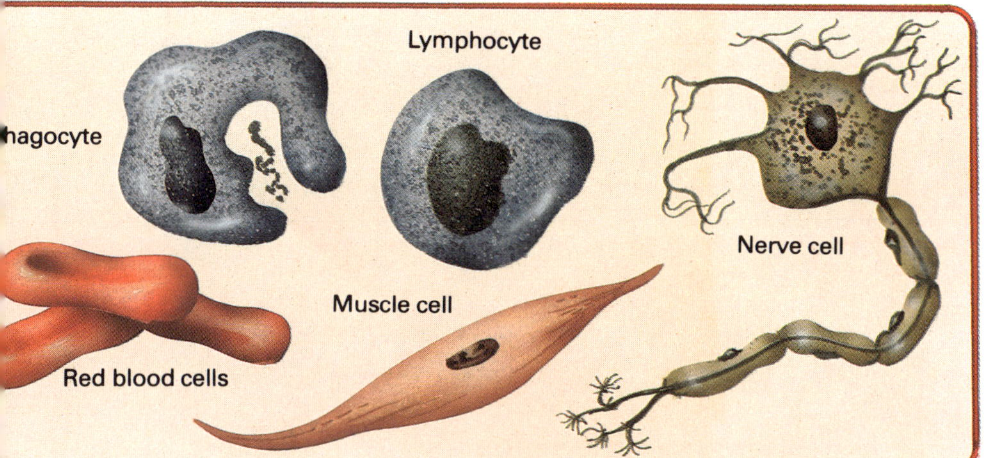

Making New Cells
The only way new tissue can be formed is from the division of cells. The nucleus splits in half to make two identical nuclei, each with a full set of chromosomes. Then the cell itself divides to make two cells.

There is another kind of cell division which takes place in *sex* cells. In this process, the parent sex cell, male or female, divides in such a way that each new cell has only half the number of chromosomes of the parent cell. So when the sex cells meet, each gives a half set of chromosomes to the new cell, which must therefore have a complete set of chromosomes, half from the father and half from the mother.

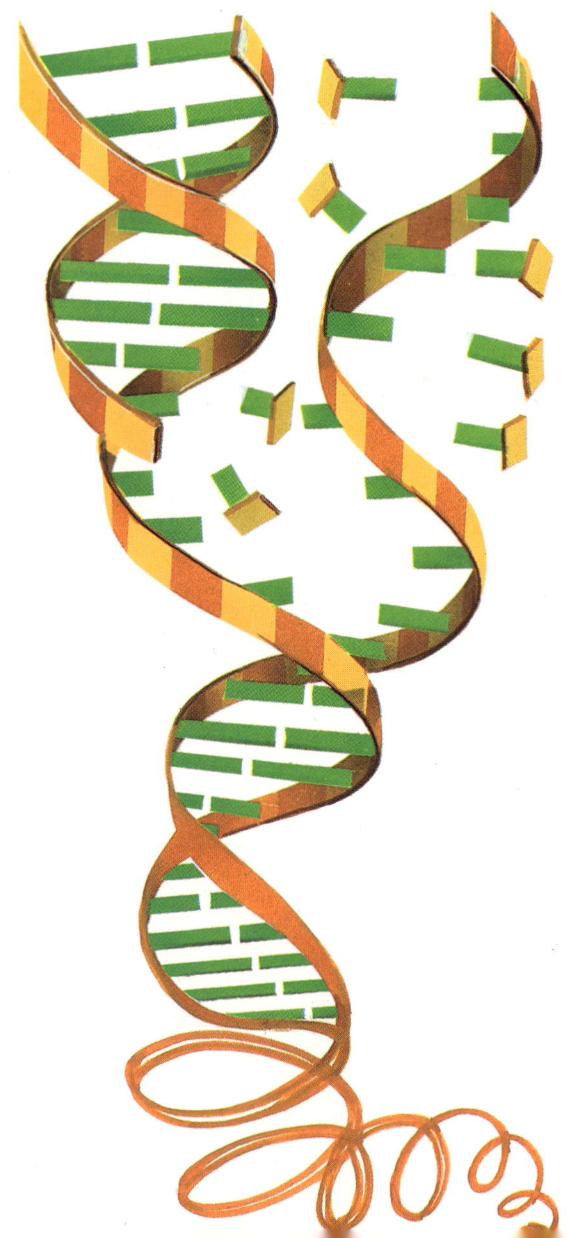

The Body Machine

The human body is a wonderful machine. It is made up of millions upon millions of tiny cells which group together to form organs such as the heart and lungs. Inside a thin covering of skin and a framework of bones are all the different parts that allow us to move, breathe, speak and eat. Our eyes, ears and other senses tell the brain what is going on outside our bodies. The brain controls everything that we do.

We breathe in air so that our bodies can have a constant supply of oxygen. Without this gas, all our cells would quickly die. We eat to give our bodies fuel.

Our lungs are like a pair of bellows in our chest. We have a sheet of muscle called the *diaphragm* stretched across the bottom of our chest. When this and the rib muscles contract, the space in our chest grows bigger. Air rushes in through our nose and into our lungs. When air goes into our lungs, it passes through finer and finer tubes until it enters tiny air sacs called *alveoli*.

The alveoli are covered with a network of fine blood vessels. Oxygen passes from the air into the blood and the blood gives back carbon dioxide gas to the lungs. The blood carries oxygen to all parts of our bodies.

Air in

Carbon dioxide out

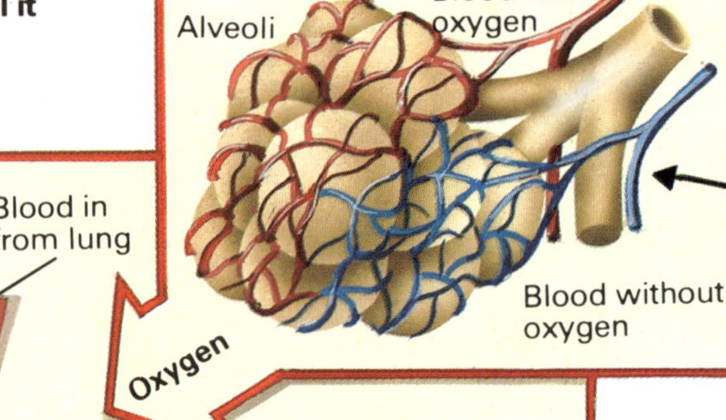

Lung

Oxygen

Blood out to body

Blood out to lung

Blood in from lung

Blood in from body

Heart

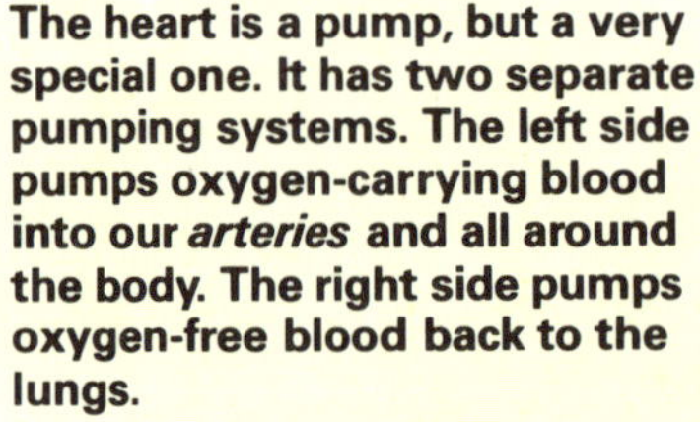

The heart is a pump, but a very special one. It has two separate pumping systems. The left side pumps oxygen-carrying blood into our *arteries* and all around the body. The right side pumps oxygen-free blood back to the lungs.

Food

Blood is red because it contains millions of tiny discs which we call the red blood cells. It is these cells that carry the oxygen around our bodies. Blood also contains white cells that help to defend the body against disease. The red and white cells float in a watery liquid called *plasma*.

Oxygen

Blood travels all over the body through a vast network of blood vessels. First of all it goes through our arteries. Then it travels through finer and finer tubes until it reaches very fine vessels called *capillaries.* The capillaries give food and oxygen from the blood to all the body's cells. In return, the cells give the capillaries carbon dioxide and other waste materials that travel back to the heart through our *veins*.

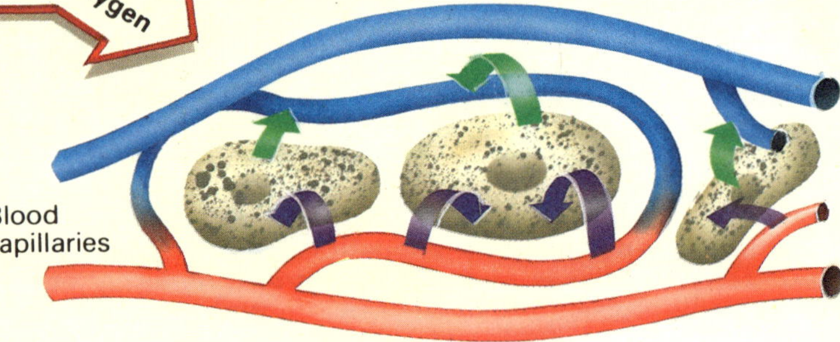

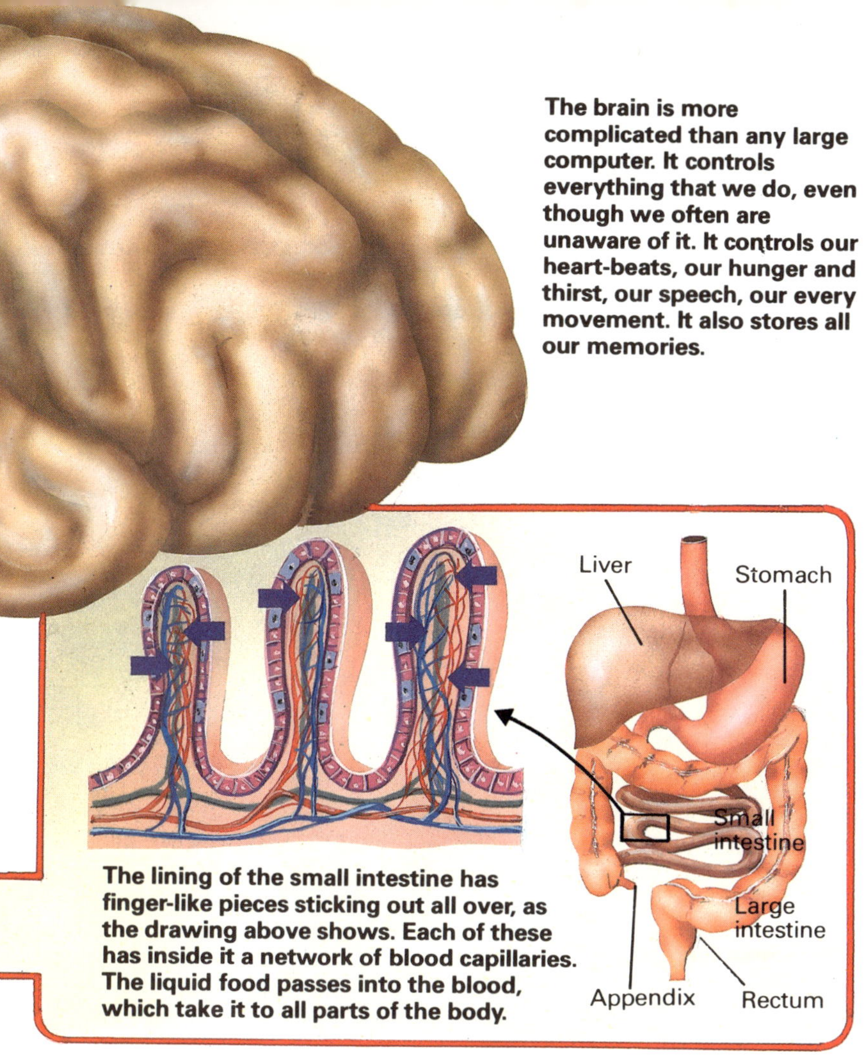

The brain is more complicated than any large computer. It controls everything that we do, even though we often are unaware of it. It controls our heart-beats, our hunger and thirst, our speech, our every movement. It also stores all our memories.

The lining of the small intestine has finger-like pieces sticking out all over, as the drawing above shows. Each of these has inside it a network of blood capillaries. The liquid food passes into the blood, which take it to all parts of the body.

The Nervous System

The nervous system controls all the other systems in our body. It has two main parts. The first part is made up of the brain and the spinal cord that runs down our back inside the backbone. The other part of the nervous system is made up of nerves that go out from the spinal cord and the brain to the various parts of the body.

The nerves are rather like telephone wires. When the doorbell rings, a message goes from our ears to our brain. The brain decides what we should do about it and sends messages to various parts of our body, telling them to work together and get out of our chair. Our muscles contract in the right order; we go to the door and open it.

Reflex Actions

But not all our actions have to be ordered by the brain. If you touch a very hot plate, you pull your hand away instantly without having to think about it. This is called a *reflex action*. Nerves in our hand detect the heat and shoot a message to a nerve centre in the spinal cord. The nerve centre immediately sends back a message to the hand to draw itself away.

Our food stays in the *stomach* for some time. There it is squeezed and churned and mixed with juice. Then it passes slowly into the *small intestine,* a coiled tube about 6 metres long. Two glands, the *liver* and the *pancreas,* are connected to the small intestine. The liver pours a liquid called *bile* into the intestine. This helps to digest fat. The pancreas sends in substances called *enzymes* that also help to break down the food.

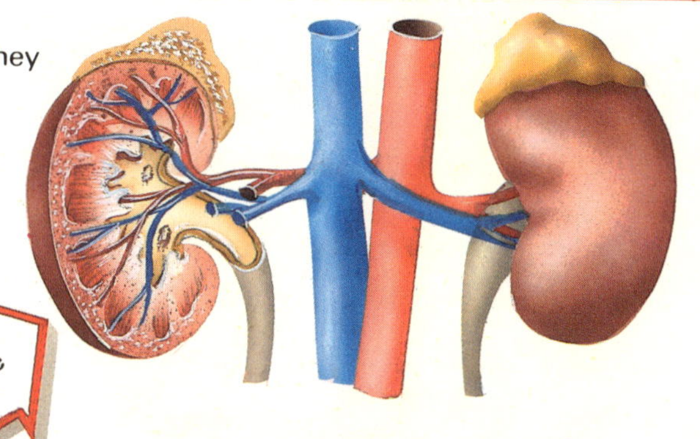

The removal of waste from our bodies is called *excretion.* Several important organs work to get rid of waste. We lose water as sweat through our skin. We breathe out carbon dioxide and water from our lungs.

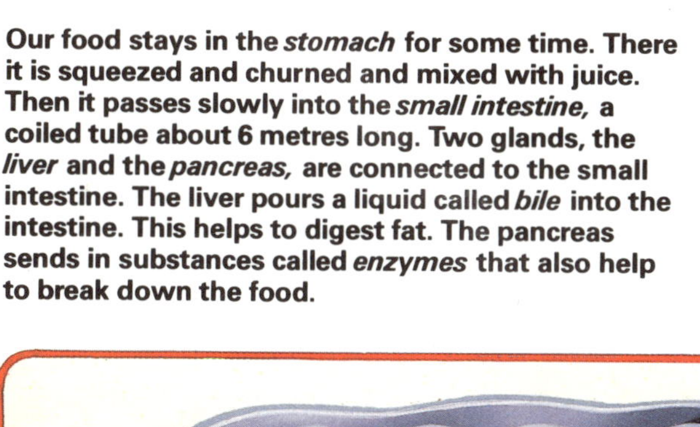

The cells in our bodies have inside them hundreds of tiny sausage-shaped objects called *mitochondria.* (The one in the picture above is very much enlarged.) Mitochondria are power stations. They burn up the food we eat to give us energy. There may be as many as 800 of them in one tiny cell.

Our two *kidneys* (pictured above) get rid of most of our unwanted water and other waste. They filter our blood and we get rid of the waste as urine. The *liver* is the largest gland in our body. As our blood passes through the liver, its poisons and waste are removed. The liver also stores substances that our body uses when they are needed.

Animals in Motion

If we had to think about all the things that happen to our bodies when we run, we would never be able to do it! Think about just a few of them. We bend and unbend joints in our feet, ankles, knees, hips, shoulders, elbows and wrists. Muscles pull in the right order to make all these joints work at just the right moment. Other muscles make us breathe more deeply. In fact, when we run we use more than a hundred different muscles.

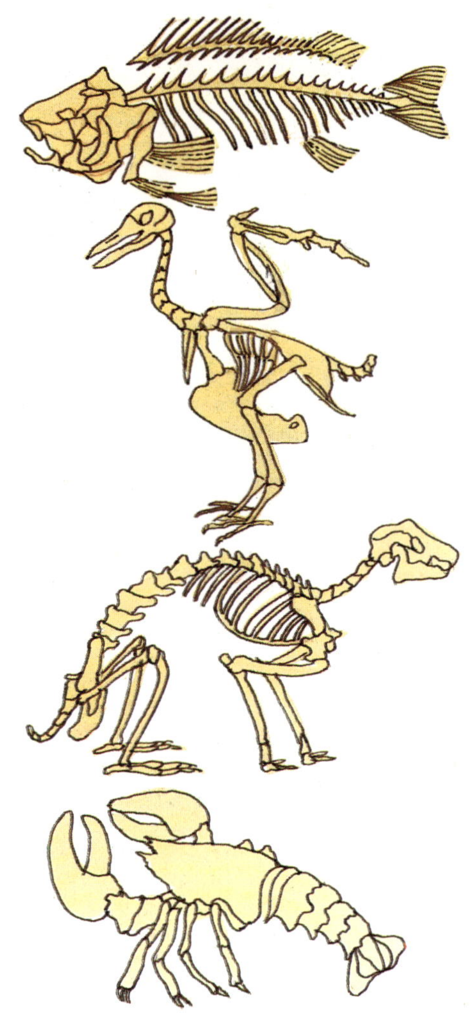

The skeletons of all animals are suited to their way of life. The fish has a 'bendy' backbone. The bird has light bones for flying. The dog has limbs that can move forward and backward, bend and straighten and twist. The lobster has a hard outside skeleton.

The Skeleton

Our skeleton is built up of more than 200 living bones. These bones support our body, protect the organs inside us, but allow us to move about freely. Bones meet at movable joints and are held together by bands of tough tissue called *ligaments*. To let the bones move smoothly against each other, their ends are covered with a pad of tissue called *cartilage* (gristle). And the joint is kept 'oiled' by a special liquid.

The Muscles

All our movements depend on muscles. Muscles work our arms and legs, make us smile, turn our eyes and chew our food. They also pump the blood around our bodies and churn the food in our digestive system.

Muscles are made up of thousands of long, thin fibres. The fibres are arranged in bundles enclosed in a sheath. These muscle fibres contract when they get a signal from a nerve. Muscles work in pairs; one pulls one way and the other pulls the opposite way.

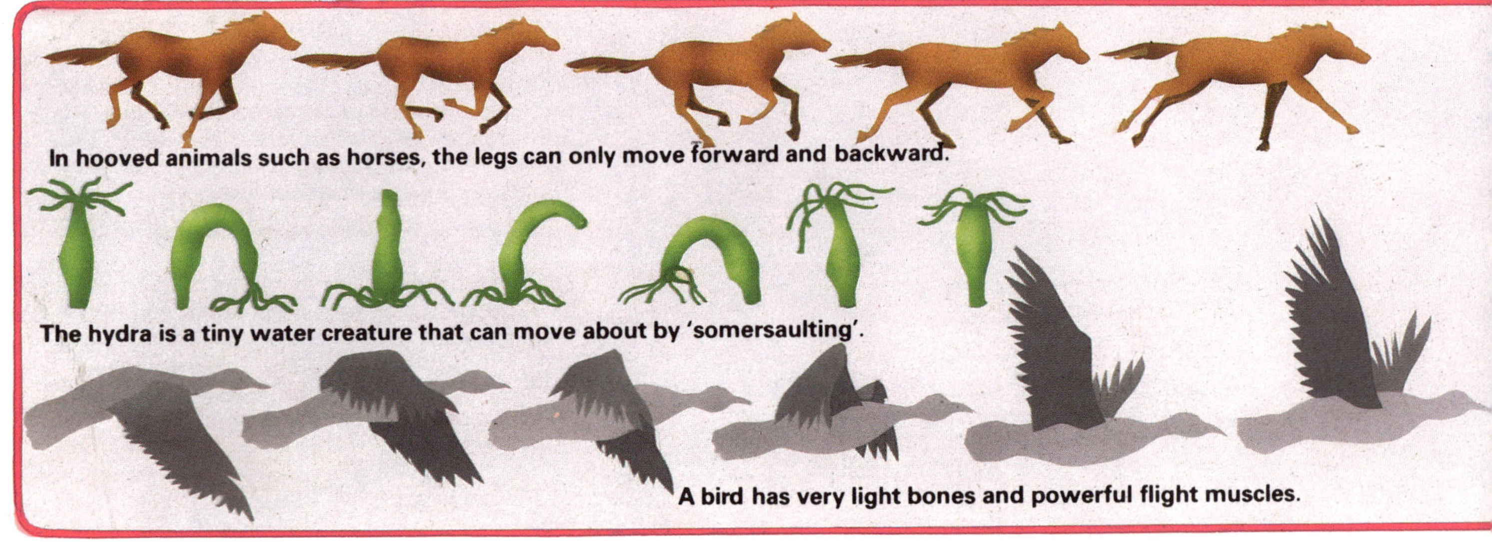

In hooved animals such as horses, the legs can only move forward and backward.

The hydra is a tiny water creature that can move about by 'somersaulting'.

A bird has very light bones and powerful flight muscles.

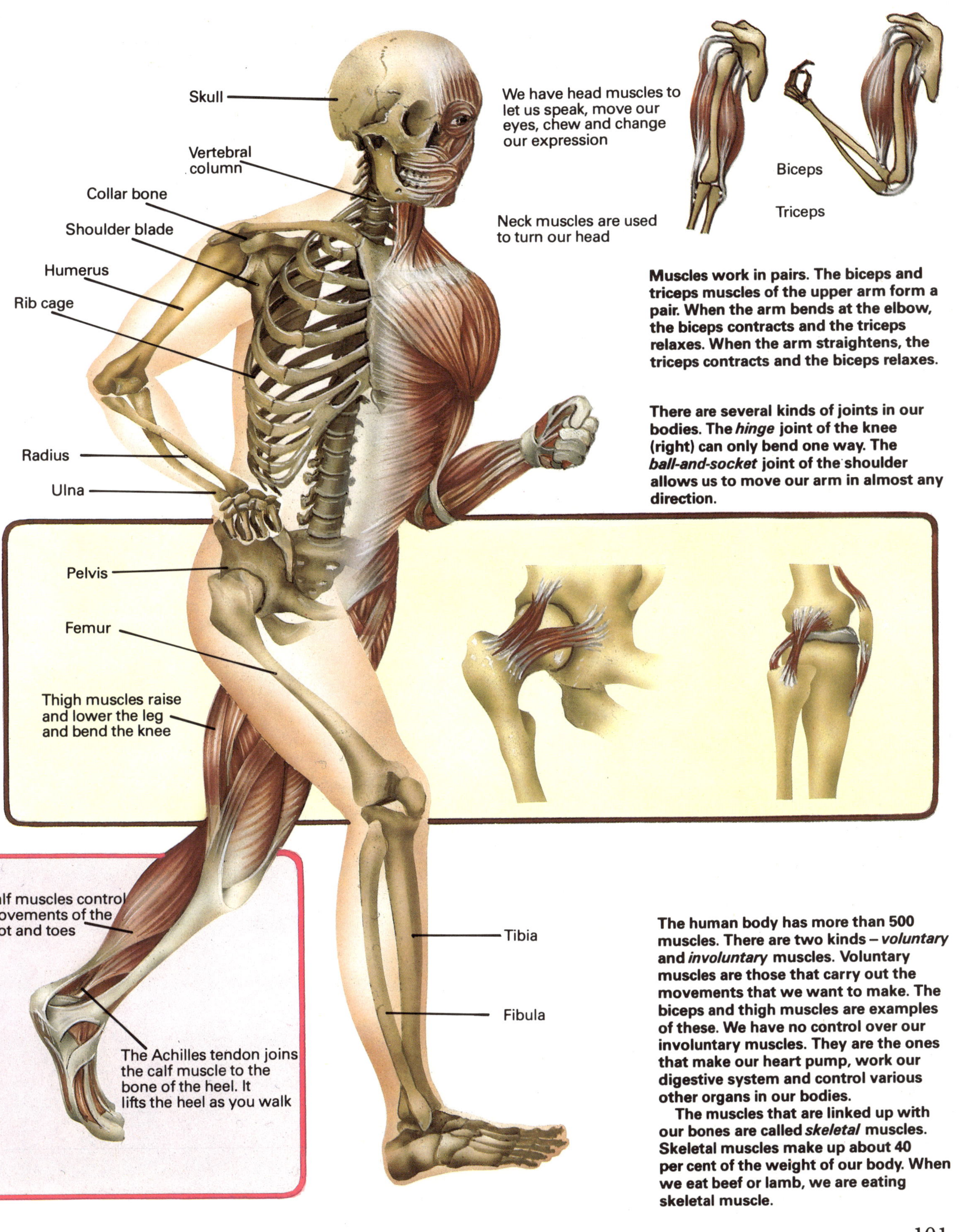

Muscles work in pairs. The biceps and triceps muscles of the upper arm form a pair. When the arm bends at the elbow, the biceps contracts and the triceps relaxes. When the arm straightens, the triceps contracts and the biceps relaxes.

There are several kinds of joints in our bodies. The *hinge* joint of the knee (right) can only bend one way. The *ball-and-socket* joint of the shoulder allows us to move our arm in almost any direction.

The human body has more than 500 muscles. There are two kinds – *voluntary* and *involuntary* muscles. Voluntary muscles are those that carry out the movements that we want to make. The biceps and thigh muscles are examples of these. We have no control over our involuntary muscles. They are the ones that make our heart pump, work our digestive system and control various other organs in our bodies.

The muscles that are linked up with our bones are called *skeletal* muscles. Skeletal muscles make up about 40 per cent of the weight of our body. When we eat beef or lamb, we are eating skeletal muscle.

How Plants Live

All living things are divided into two great groups – the Animal Kingdom and the Plant Kingdom. Animals and plants have several things in common – they grow, they are able to reproduce themselves and make new animals or plants, and they are all made up of tiny cells.

The main difference between animals and plants is in the way they feed. Animals take in ready-made food in the form of plants or other animals. Plants make their own food from simple substances in the air and water. This is called *photosynthesis*. The plants need light for making food. They also need a green substance called *chlorophyll*. This is why most plants are green.

Green plants are food factories. Without them there would be no life on Earth. The most important part of the plant factory is the leaves. These are arranged so that they get as much sunlight as possible. The green chlorophyll in the leaves traps the light energy, which the plant then uses to combine water and *carbon dioxide* gas. Simple sugars and other living matter are formed to give the plant food. Any plant that contains chlorophyll can make its own food.

Plants take in carbon dioxide gas from the air and water and minerals from the soil through the roots. Water from the soil travels up the plant's stems to the leaves through a system of tiny vessels. Other vessels carry food down the stem to the roots.

Oxygen and water are left over after photosynthesis. The plant gets rid of them through small openings in the leaves. These openings are called *stomata*. The oxygen we breathe in never runs out because it is always being renewed by the plants. All living things use oxygen to get energy from their food.

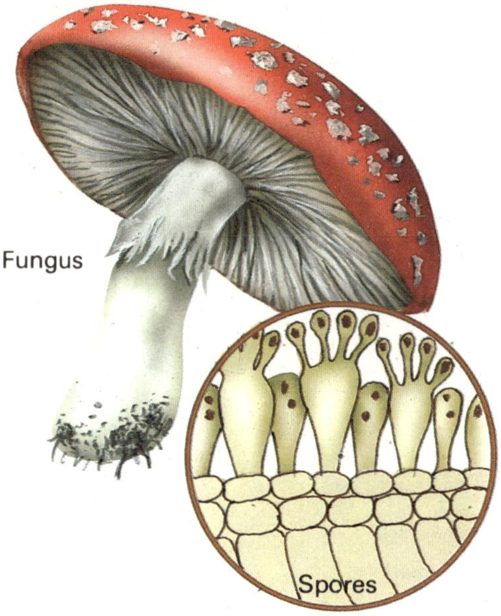

Pine cone and seeds

Fungus

Flowering plant

Stamen

Pistil

Spores

Growing seeds

Flowers produce seeds that can grow into new plants. They often have brightly coloured petals to attract insects and other animals. The insects carry the pollen from one flower to another. The fruit of the pine tree is a woody cone that takes two years to mature. Fungi such as mushrooms are simple plants that have no green colouring matter. They produce spores that are scattered by the wind and grow into new plants. Plants such as the strawberry send out runners that take root and become new plants.

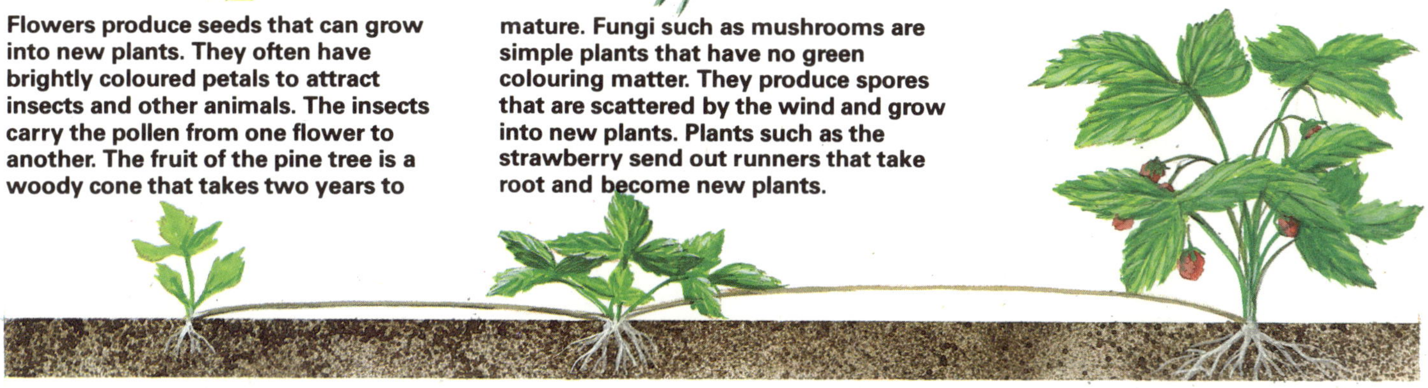

New Plants from Old

Most plants have flowers. The flowers are there to make new plants. Some plants have male and female parts in separate flowers. Other plants have the male and female parts in the same flower. The male parts are called the *stamens*. Male cells – tiny yellow grains called *pollen* – are made in a part of the stamen called the *anther.* The female part of the flower is the *pistil*. It is here that the *ovules* or female egg cells are made.

In *pollination,* pollen grains must be carried from an anther to a pistil. Most plants, including all flowering and cone-bearing plants, reproduce in this way. In some plants, the pollen goes from the anthers to the pistil of the same flower or another flower in the same plant. But in most plants the pollen grains go from one flower's anthers to the pistil of another flower of the same species.

Sometimes the wind carries the pollen from one plant to another. Sometimes an insect such as a bee gets pollen stuck to its body and carries it to another flower.

After pollination, the seeds grow in the flowers and become surrounded by the fruit. The fruit helps to scatter the seeds far and wide so that they have room to grow.

The leaves of some plants have grown in such a way that they can catch insects. These plants live in places where they cannot get enough food from the soil. Insects are attracted by the nectar of the pitcher plant below, but slip down the smooth sides of the pitcher into a pool of liquid which dissolves them.

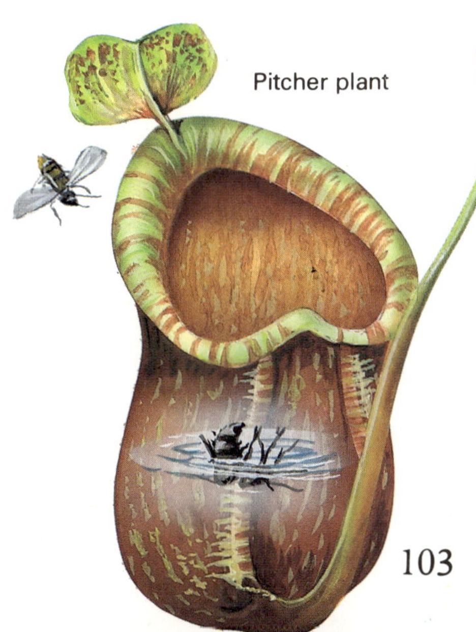

Great Inventions

The story of civilization can be traced in the inventions that Man has made. Among the early inventions of greatest importance were metal smelting, in the 4000s BC; the wheel and the plough, in the 3000s BC; and the harnessing of water power, in Roman times. But the pace of invention was slow until the 1400s, the time of the Renaissance, or 'rebirth of learning'.

Hot air balloon, 1783

Year	Invention	Inventor
1450	**Printing Press**	Johannes Gutenberg, Germany
1590	**Compound Microscope**	Zacharias Janssen, the Netherlands
1608/9	**Refracting Telescope**	Hans Lippershey, the Netherlands, and Galileo Galilei, Italy
1668	**Reflecting Telescope**	Isaac Newton, Britain
1698	**Steam Pump**	Thomas Savery, Britain
1712	**Beam Engine**	Thomas Newcomen, Britain
1733	**Flying Shuttle**	John Kay, Britain
1767	**Spinning Jenny**	James Hargreaves, Britain
1780s	**Improved Steam Engine**	James Watt, Britain
1783	**Hot-air Balloon**	Montgolfier Brothers, France
1785	**Power Loom**	Edmund Cartwright, Britain
1792	**Cotton Gin**	Eli Whitney, United States
1800	**Electric Battery**	Allessandro Volta, Italy
1800	**Lathe**	Henry Maudslay, Britain
1804	**Steam Locomotive**	Richard Trevithick, Britain
1815	**Safety Lamp**	Humphry Davy, Britain
1815	**Stethoscope**	René T. H. Laënec, France
1836	**Revolver**	Samuel Colt, United States
1837	**Telegraph**	William Cooke and Charles Wheatstone, Britain; Samuel Morse, United States
1839	**Steam Hammer**	James Nasmyth, Britain
1845	**Sewing Machine**	Elias Howe, United States
1856	**Bessemer Process**	Henry Bessemer, Britain
1867	**Dynamite**	Alfred Nobel, Sweden
1872	**Typewriter**	Christopher L. Scholes, United States
1876	**Telephone**	Alexander Graham Bell, United States
1877	**Phonograph (Gramophone)**	Thomas Alva Edison, United States
1878	**Cathode-Ray Tube**	William Crookes, Britain
1878/9	**Electric Lamp**	Joseph Swan, Britain, and Thomas Alva Edison, United States
1880s	**Machine Gun**	Hiram Stevens Maxim, United States
1884	**Steam Turbine**	Charles Algernon Parsons, Britain
1885	**Petrol Engine**	Karl Benz and Gottlieb Daimler, Germany
1888	**Pneumatic Tyre**	John Boyd Dunlop, Britain
1892	**Diesel Engine**	Rudolf Diesel, Germany
1895	**Radio**	Guglielmo Marconi, Italy
1903	**Powered Aircraft**	Wilbur and Orville Wright, United States
1926	**Television**	John Logie Baird, Britain, and Vladimir Zworykin, United States
1930	**Jet Engine**	Frank Whittle, Britain
1944	**Digital Computer**	Howard Aiken, United States
1947	**Polaroid Camera**	Edwin H. Land, United States
1955	**Hovercraft**	Christopher Cockerell, Britain
1971	**Microprocessor**	Intel Corporation, United States

The wheel was invented about 3000 BC

Motor cycle, 1885

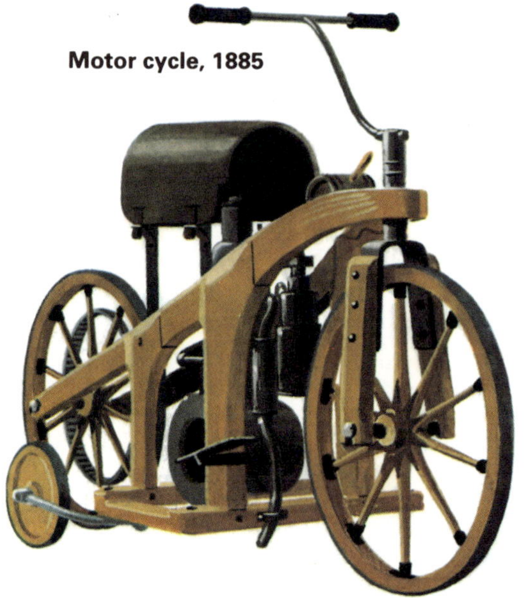

The Wright brothers' 'Flyer'
The windmill was invented in Persia about AD 600
Telegraph, 1837
The bowdrill was invented about 50,000 years ago
Early telephone
Early TV tube
Early phonograph
Stephenson's Rocket, 1830
ROCKET
Early Scholes typewriter
Early Colt revolver

Amazing Machines

Man is not a very strong creature, yet he can move mountains. He has no wings, yet he can fly. He cannot breathe under water, yet he can venture into the ocean deeps. He can even beat the pull of gravity and travel into space, surviving there for months at a time, and return safely. He can do these things – and many more – because he has the brain power to invent machines.

The modern Age of Machines began in the 1700s when several people invented machines to speed up textile making. Then a reliable steam engine was developed to run the machines. This mechanization led to a great change in the way things were made – to an Industrial Revolution.

At the present time we are in the grips of another industrial revolution, brought about by what is called automation. This means the use of machines that work automatically, with little need for human workers. The 'brains' behind the operation of these machines are the 'electronic brains' of the most amazing machine of all – the computer.

UNDERSTANDING THE COMPUTER

The word computer means calculator. And whatever job they do, computers work by carrying out a series of simple arithmetic calculations on sets of numbers. The numbers can represent all kinds of different information, or *data.* Computers are so marvellous because they can carry out such calculations at incredible speed, often performing hundreds of thousands of operations every second. But they cannot 'think' for themselves. They need a human being to tell them what to do.

The ordinary computer is properly called a digital computer, because it handles data in the form of numbers, or digits. It does not use ordinary decimal digits (0–9), but just the two digits 1 and 0. These are called binary digits, or *bits.*

So all instructions and data must thus be coded into bits before the computer can work on them. The computer does most of this coding itself. But first the computer operator writes his instructions, or program, in a simplified 'language' that the computer can 'understand'. It is called a computer language.

The program and data form what is called the software of the computer. The computer equipment is called the hardware. The software is fed into the computer through an input device such as a keyboard or a magnetic disc or tape unit. Inside the computer it is stored in a memory unit. Calculations are carried out by an arithmetic unit under the control of a control unit. After calculations have been completed, the control unit directs the results to an output device. This may be a video display unit (VDU) like a television screen, or it may be a high-speed printer.

How a hovercraft works

Fans blast air downwards

Flexible 'skirt' holds in air

Cushion of air

The hovercraft is equally at home on water as on land, gliding along on a cushion of air. It makes an excellent amphibious landing craft for the armed services. The largest hovercraft, such as the SRN4, are used as car ferries across the English Channel.

Right: The laser produces a narrow beam of pure light containing immense energy. It can be focused into a point of intense heat that can slice through metal like a knife through butter. Lasers have many other uses in the modern world from guiding tunnelling machines to 'playing' the latest compact record discs.

Left: Among the most powerful man-made machines are the turbogenerators used at power stations to produce electricity. The picture shows a massive generator rotor for a hydro-electric power plant.

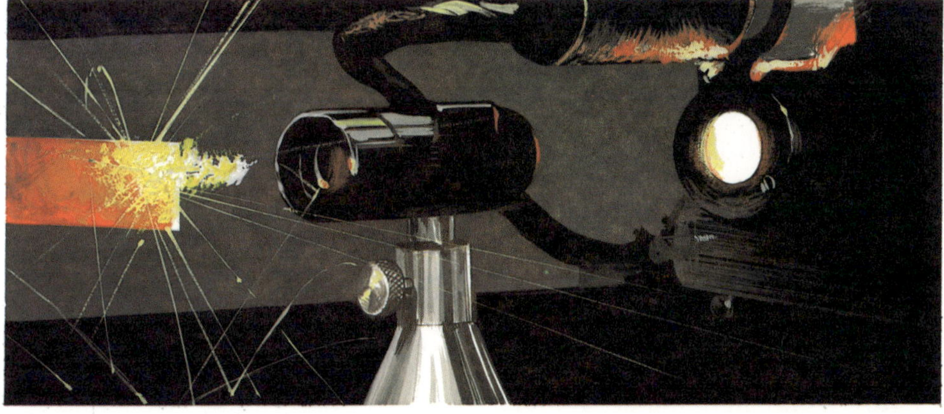

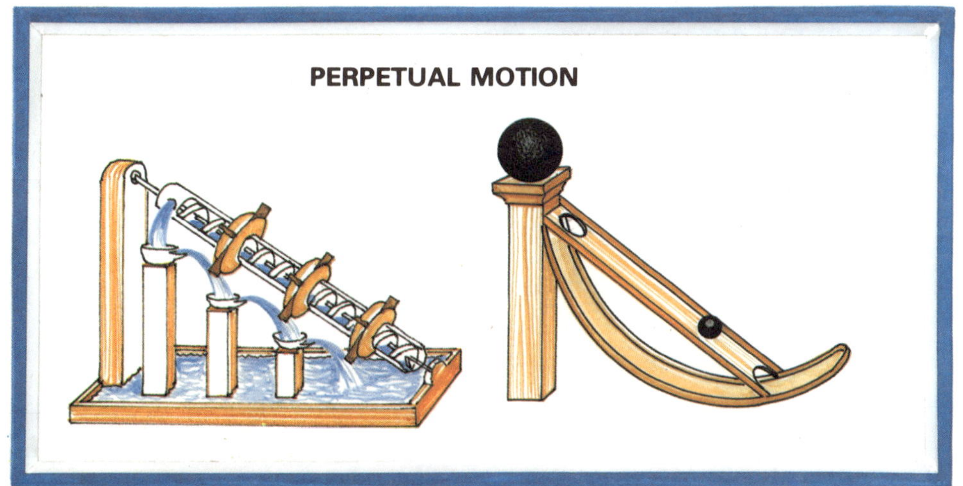

Many people have tried to invent machines that, once set moving, would carry on moving by themselves, in endless, or perpetual, motion. The pictures show two ideas. The Archimedean screw raises water as it turns. At the top the water spills out and cascades downwards and turns paddle wheels that turn the screw. It does not work because too much energy is lost in friction. In the ball-and-magnet machine, the idea is that the magnet attracts the ball up the slope. Near the top, the ball falls through the hole and back to the bottom, and is attracted up again. The drawback is that the magnet attracts the ball directly to it.

Glossary

Absolute zero The lowest temperature that there can be in theory. It is $-273.15°C$. Scientists have got to within a few millionths of a degree of this temperature, but will probably never reach it.

Accumulator A device for storing electricity. A common type, the lead-acid accumulator, consists of a container filled with dilute sulphuric acid, in which are lead plates. When a small current is passed through terminals attached to the plates, chemical changes take place in the plates, and the accumulator is 'charged'.

Acid A chemical substance that has a sour taste. Some acids such as sulphuric acid are dangerous, others are harmless, such as the citric acid in oranges and lemons. All acids turn a special sort of paper called litmus paper from blue to red.

Alkali The opposite of an acid. When acids and alkalis are mixed they make a neutral solution to give salt and water. Alkalis turn litmus paper from red to blue.

Alloy A metal made up of more than one element. A dentist's amalgam, for example, is an alloy of 70 per cent mercury and 30 per cent copper.

Alternating current Electric current which rapidly reverses its direction. Mains electricity is usually alternating current (AC) at 50 cycles per second.

Amplifier An electronic device that increases the strength of a signal.

Archimedes' Principle When a body is immersed or partly immersed in a liquid, the liquid buoys up the body with a force that equals the weight of liquid displaced by the body.

Boiling point The temperature at which a liquid changes into a gas.

Capacitor A device for storing charge. It has two metal plates separated by some kind of insulator. It will not allow a direct current to pass, but will allow an alternating current to pass, especially if it alternates very rapidly.

Catalyst A substance that is able to alter the speed of a chemical reaction without itself being changed.

Combustion The chemical reaction in which a substance joins with oxygen and gives off heat and light and burns with a flame.

Compound A substance made up of two or more elements that are combined chemically.

Conductor A substance that allows a free flow of electricity through it.

Cosmic Rays Radiation, mainly in the form of charged particles, that strikes the Earth from outer space.

Crystal A solid substance that has a definite geometrical shape. Most pure solids exist as crystals.

Diffraction The spreading out of light as it passes through a narrow slit or past the edge of an obstacle.

Electric field The region around an electrically charged body.

Electrolysis The conduction of electricity between two electrodes through a solution (electrolyte). Chemical changes take place at the electrodes.

Electromagnet A magnet with an iron core surrounded by a coil of wire that carries an electric current. The core is only a magnet when the current is switched on.

Electron Negatively charged particle that circles the nucleus in all atoms. In every neutral atom there are as many electrons as there are positive protons in the nucleus.

Element A substance that is made up of exactly similar atoms. An element cannot be split up into simpler substances.

Energy The ability to do work. Energy exists in many forms: heat energy, electrical energy, mechanical energy, chemical energy, etc.

Fission The splitting of the nucleus of an atom which releases vast amounts of energy. Fission takes place in atomic bombs and nuclear reactors. Usually uranium atoms are split.

Friction The force that opposes any attempt to move one surface over another touching it.

Fusion, nuclear The combining of light atoms such as hydrogen to give out vast amounts of energy. Fusion happens in hydrogen bombs and in the stars.

Gravity The force that pulls all masses towards every other mass. Gravity keeps us on the surface of the Earth and the planets circling the Sun.

Infra-red rays Invisible radiations with wavelengths just longer than those of visible light. These are heat rays.

Insulator A material that is a poor conductor of electricity, heat or sound.

Ion An electrically charged atom or group of atoms.

Laser An intense beam of light with all its waves in step.

Lens A shaped piece of glass or other transparent material which makes things look larger or smaller by gathering together rays of light or spreading them apart.

Mass The mass of an object is the amount of matter in it. We measure mass in kilograms and grams. (See also *weight*.)

Microwaves Radio waves with wavelengths less than about 20 cm.

Molecule The smallest amount of a substance that can exist alone. It is made up of one or more atoms.

Neutron An atomic particle which has no charge. Neutrons are found in the nuclei of all atoms except hydrogen.

Nucleus, atomic The centre of an atom. It contains protons (positively charged particles) and neutrons (uncharged particles). The nucleus itself is positively charged. Nearly all the weight of an atom is in its nucleus.

Photon A quantum or packet of light.

Plastics Solid materials that at some stage of their manufacture are plastic (pliable) by heat and pressure. They can then be given a new shape.

Prism A triangular block of glass that can split up white light into all the colours of the rainbow.

Proton A positively charged particle that is found in the nucleus of every atom. The positive charge of a proton is equal to the negative charge of an electron.

Radioactivity A substance whose atoms are always breaking up is said to be radioactive. A radioactive substance usually gives out alpha-particles and beta-particles.

Reaction A chemical process that involves two or more substances and which results in a chemical change.

Reflection The bouncing back of light rays, sound waves or any kind of electromagnetic radiation after it strikes a surface.

Refraction The bending of a light ray as it crosses the boundary between two substances of different optical density.

Resistance The property of an electrical conductor that makes it oppose the flow of current through it. Resistance is measured in ohms.

Salt A chemical compound that is formed with water when a base reacts with an acid. A salt is also formed when a metal reacts with an acid.

Semiconductor A substance such as silicon that is neither a good conductor nor a good insulator. Transistors are made from semiconductors.

Specific gravity The density of a given volume of a substance, at a given temperature, compared with that of a similar volume of water at 4°C. Also called relative density.

Spectroscope An instrument for splitting up light into its various colours by means of a prism or a diffraction grating. The colours produced can then be studied.

Surface tension The property of the surface of a liquid that makes it behave as though it were covered with a thin elastic skin. It is caused by the forces of attraction between molecules in the surface of the liquid.

Temperature The degree of hotness of a substance which is measured on a temperature scale such as Centigrade or Fahrenheit.

Thermostat A device that regulates temperature. It cuts off the heating source if the temperature rises beyond a certain value, and vice versa.

Transformer A device for changing alternating current at one voltage to alternating current at a different voltage.

Transistor A semiconductor device that can amplify and control electric current. Transistors have taken the place of thermionic valves.

Ultra-violet rays Light waves that are of smaller wavelength than the visible light at the violet end of the spectrum. The Sun's radiation is rich in ultra-violet rays. They may also be produced artificially by special lamps.

Vacuum Empty spaces in which there are no atoms or molecules. A true vacuum cannot be obtained in practice, but the word is used to describe a space in which there is very little gas.

Vapour A gas that can be turned into a liquid by squeezing it without cooling.

Wavelength The distance from the crest of one wave to the crest of the next. Radio wavelengths are measured in metres.

Weight The downward force exerted by the gravitational pull on an object. The mass of an object does not vary, but the weight depends on how much gravitational pull there is. On Earth, for example, an object weighs more than it does on the Moon, where the gravitational pull is not so strong.

Science Index

THE CHILDREN'S FIRST GEOGRAPHY ENCYCLOPEDIA

The CHILDREN'S FIRST GEOGRAPHY ENCYCLOPEDIA

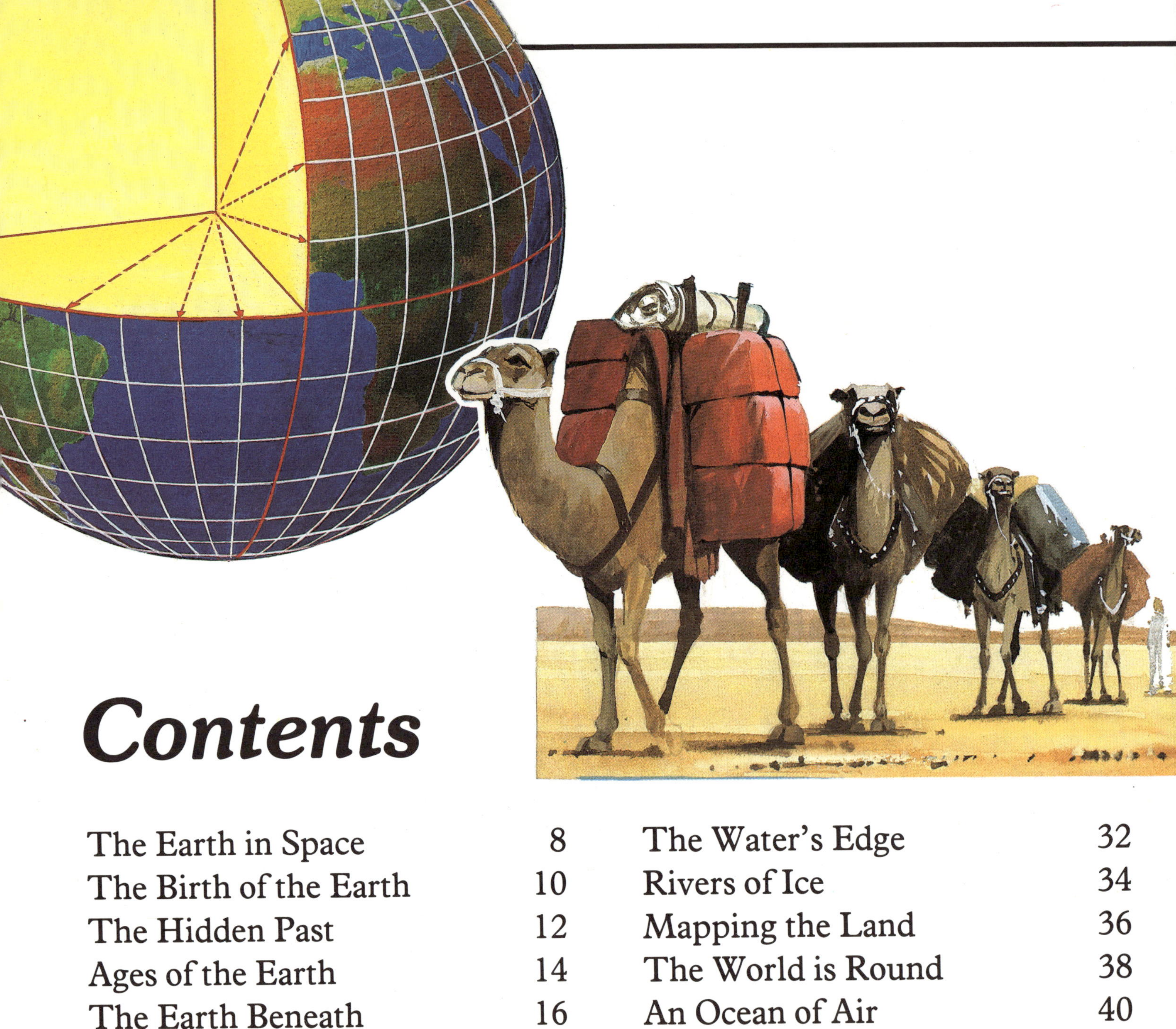

Contents

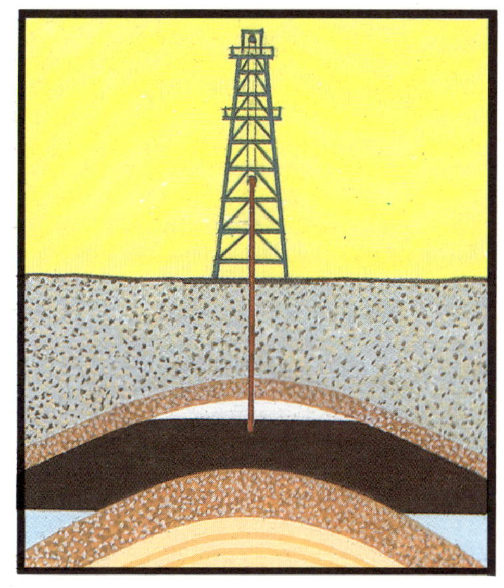

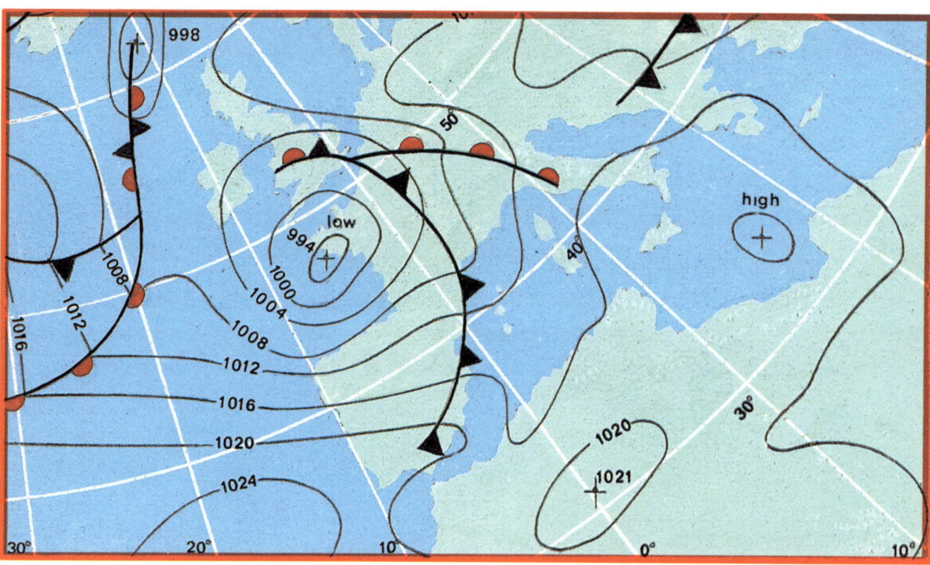

998
low
994
1000
1004
1008
1012
1016
1020
1024
high
1020
1021
50°
40°
30°
30°
20°
10°
0°
10°

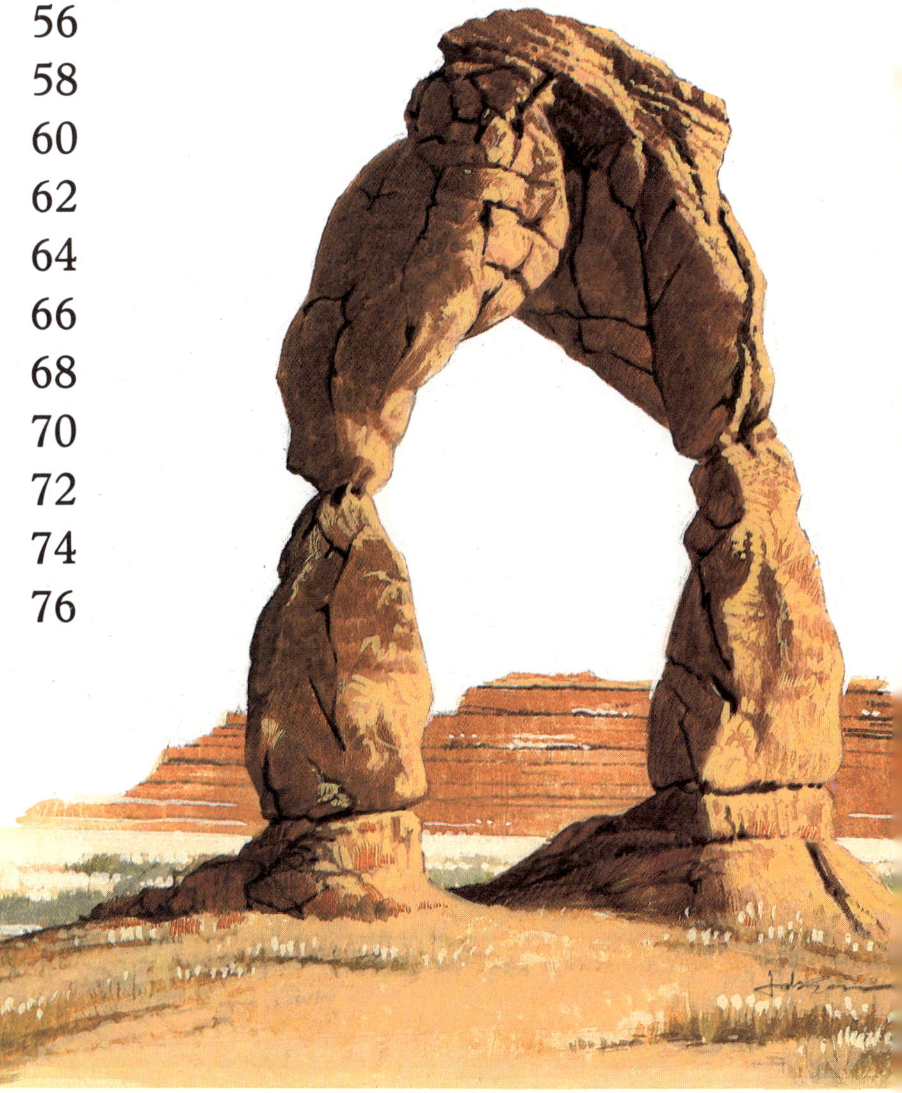

The Earth in Space

Our Earth is like a giant spaceship and we are space travellers. The Earth moves in three ways. First, it spins on its axis, making one turn in 24 hours. Second, it rotates around the Sun at an average speed of 106,200 km/h takes 365 days, 48 minutes and 46 seconds, or one *solar year*, to complete one orbit. Because this is longer than our 365-day *calendar year*, we have leap years of 366 days to stop the solar and calendar years getting out of step.

The Earth also moves with the Sun, the planets and the other bodies that form the Solar System around the Milky Way galaxy. It takes about 200 million years to complete one circuit around the galaxy.

Looking After Planet Earth

Spaceship Earth has all the resources we need and its resources are constantly but slowly renewed. The study of planet Earth is extremely important. Only by understanding our Earth will we be able to ensure that it remains a good home for future generations.

Right: The Earth rotates on its axis, the imaginary line joining the North Pole, the centre of the Earth and the South Pole. At the equator, where the speed of rotation is greatest, the Earth is spinning at a speed of 1670 km/h. The speed of rotation decreases away from the equator towards the poles. When a place on Earth faces the Sun, it enjoys daylight. When that same place turns away from the Sun, it is night. The Earth takes 23 hours, 56 minutes and 4 seconds to complete one full turn on its axis. This is the *sidereal day*. But while the Earth is spinning on its axis, it is also moving forward on its 365-day orbit around the Sun. Hence, the time taken for a point on Earth to face the Sun on two successive occasions is slightly longer than the sidereal day. In fact, the Earth must turn 1/365th more than one complete rotation before the point exactly faces the Sun. The time taken for this extra turn gives the *mean solar day* a length of 24 hours. The hours of daylight vary throughout the year.

Above: The diagram shows the orbits of the nine planets in the Solar System. In order of distance from the Sun, they are Mercury, Venus, Earth, Mars, Jupiter, Saturn, Uranus, Neptune and Pluto are small, rocky terrestrial planets. The others — the giant planets — are huge balls of gas. Between the orbits of Mars and Jupiter lies the asteroid belt where countless pieces of rock circle the Sun.

Below: The Sun measures 1,392,000 km across. It is 109 times as big as the Earth and nearly 10 times the size of the planet Jupiter – the largest planet. The Sun has an average surface temperature of 6000°C. It bakes the surfaces of Mercury and Venus. But the average surface temperature on Earth is 22°C. On Jupiter, however, the surface temperature is down to –150°C.

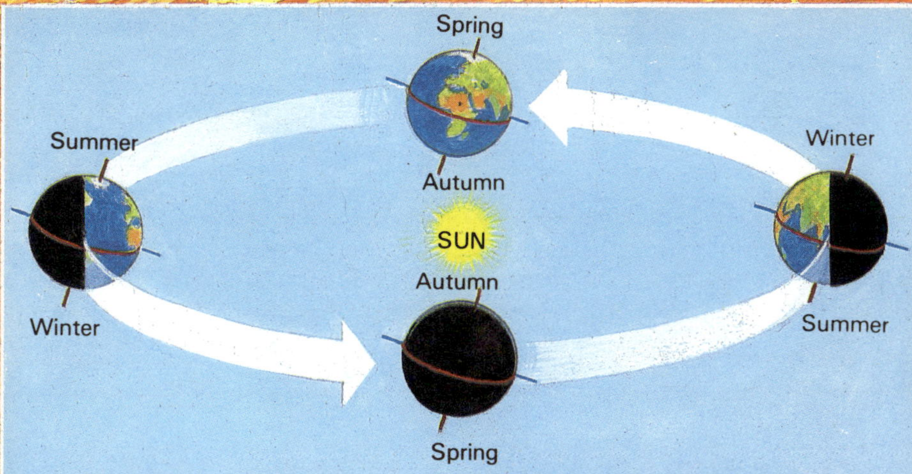

Above: Because the Earth's axis is tilted by 23½ degrees as it orbits the Sun, the northern and southern hemispheres lean towards and away from the Sun, causing seasons. On June 21, the summer solstice, the northern hemisphere leans towards the Sun to its greatest extent. On September 23, the autumn equinox, the Sun is overhead at the equator and the length of day and night is equal everywhere in the world. The southern hemisphere then tilts towards the Sun until December 23, the winter solstice, which is followed by the spring equinox on March 21. (The seasons are reversed south of the equator.)

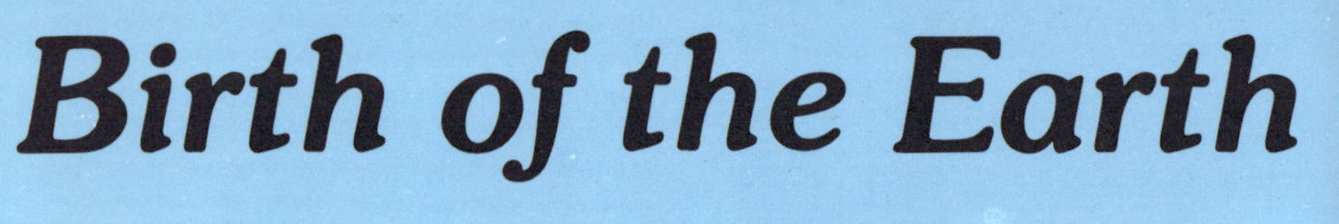

Birth of the Earth

Most scientists now agree that the Earth was formed from a cloud of gas and dust. This cloud was drifting through space about 5000 million years ago. Gradually, more and more particles were drawn to the centre by gravity. There, about 4600 million years ago, they formed a star, the Sun. The material left over formed the planets, moons and other bodies that make up the Solar System

Above: The Earth is made up of three parts. The thin crust varies between 60-70 km thick under the highest montains to about 5 km thick under the oceans. Beneath the crust is the denser (heavier) mantle. The mantle is about 2900 km thick. It encloses the extremely dense core, which measures about 6920 km across. The inner core is solid, but the outer core is probably liquid.

The Earth's Early History

The youthful Earth was probably a huge ball of gas, rather like Jupiter or Saturn. But eventually, because of gravity, heavier elements, notably iron, sank towards the centre, forming a dense core, while lighter elements stayed near the surface. As a result, the Earth now has a very dense (heavy) core, made up largely of iron and nickel, a dense mantle and a relatively light crust.

The Earth slowly shrank into the rocky planet we know today. At first, the surface was hot and molten. Geologists have not found any rocks much older than about 3800 million years, although the Earth itself is about 4550 million years old. Rocks formed in the first 700 million years were probably all broken up and remelted.

The Earth's first atmosphere was poisonous, but it contained water vapour released from the rocks by volcanoes. It contained little oxygen, the gas we need to breathe. The oxygen content began to increase about 1900 million years ago, when oxygen-producing plants first developed.

Below: For many millions of years after its formation, the Earth's surface must have been blazing hot. Constant volcanic activity released gas and water vapour from the rocks inside the Earth. The gases formed a primitive and poisonous atmosphere. Later on, when the surface started to cool, there were great thunderstorms. Rain started to fill up hollows in the early crust. It was perhaps in these warm pools that the first living things, bacteria, appeared.

THE EARTH'S DIMENSIONS

DIAMETER: The equatorial diameter is 12,756 km, but the polar diameter is shorter, 12,713 km.

CIRCUMFERENCE: The equatorial circumference (the distance around the equator) is 40,075 km. But if you travel around the Earth via the poles (the polar circumference), the distance is only 40,007 km.

AREA: The Earth has an area of 510,066,000 km^2.

LAND AND SEA: The oceans cover 361,740,000 km^2. This is nearly 71 per cent of the Earth's surface.

The Hidden Past

Fossils are evidence found in rocks of animals and plants which once lived on Earth. They range from animal footprints to animal bones, plants turned to stone and insects preserved in amber.

The pictures above show how a fossil is formed. When an animal dies (1), it must be buried quickly in underwater sediments. The flesh soon decays, but the bones survive (2).

Why Fossils are Important

Fossils occur in rocks all over the world. Because rock layers are folded and pushed upwards, fossils of seashells are found even at the tops of mountains. The study of fossils helps geologists to date rocks. It also helps us to understand the evolution of plants and animals throughout Earth history.

1 2 3 4 5

Above: The diagram shows how fossil moulds and casts are formed. A dead ammonite (1) is buried by sediment. The sediment is slowly compressed into rock (2). Water seeping through the rock dissolves the ammonite. This cavity is a mould of the ammonite (3). Later, minerals may be deposited from water in the cavity (4) to produce a fossil cast (5).

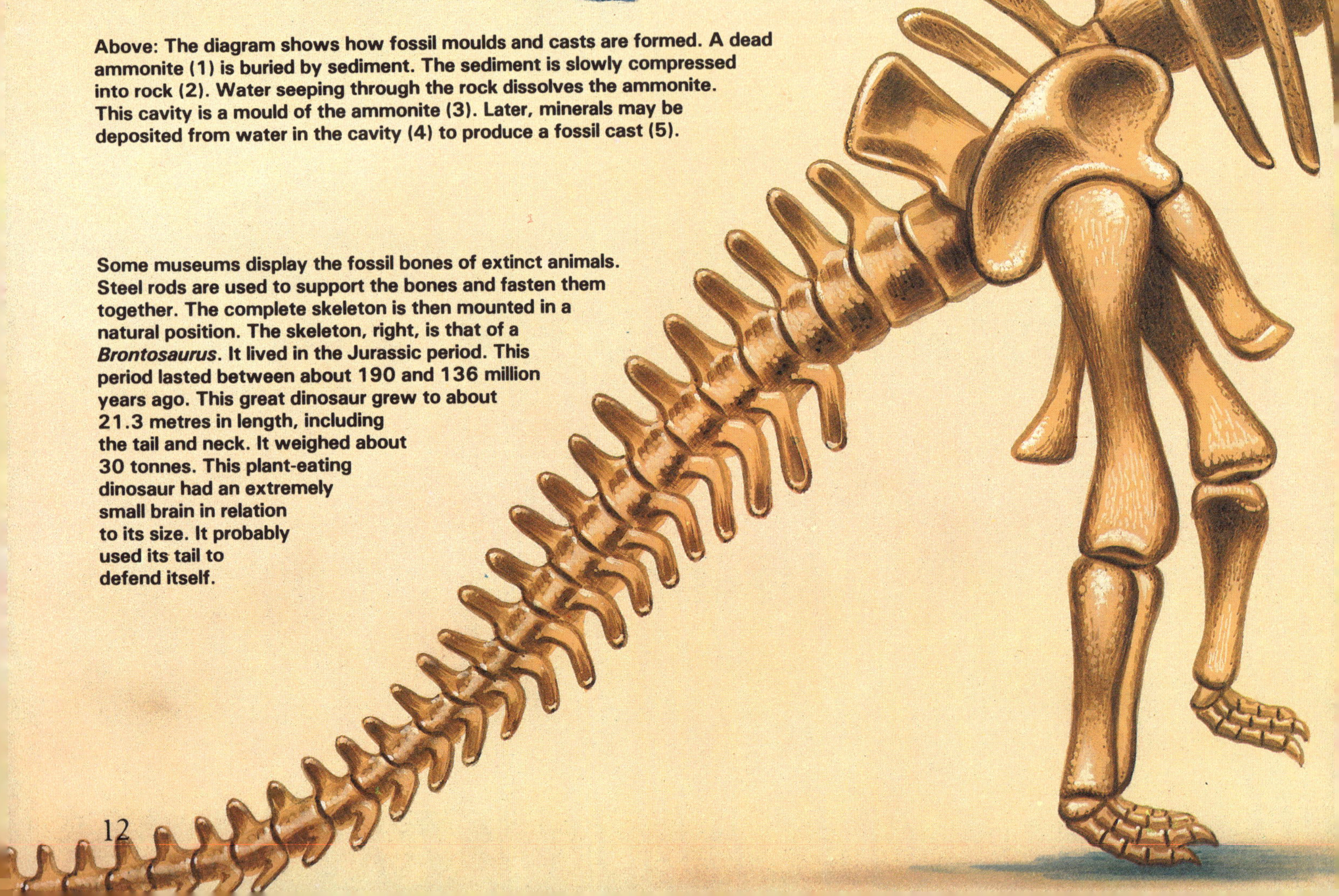

Some museums display the fossil bones of extinct animals. Steel rods are used to support the bones and fasten them together. The complete skeleton is then mounted in a natural position. The skeleton, right, is that of a *Brontosaurus*. It lived in the Jurassic period. This period lasted between about 190 and 136 million years ago. This great dinosaur grew to about 21.3 metres in length, including the tail and neck. It weighed about 30 tonnes. This plant-eating dinosaur had an extremely small brain in relation to its size. It probably used its tail to defend itself.

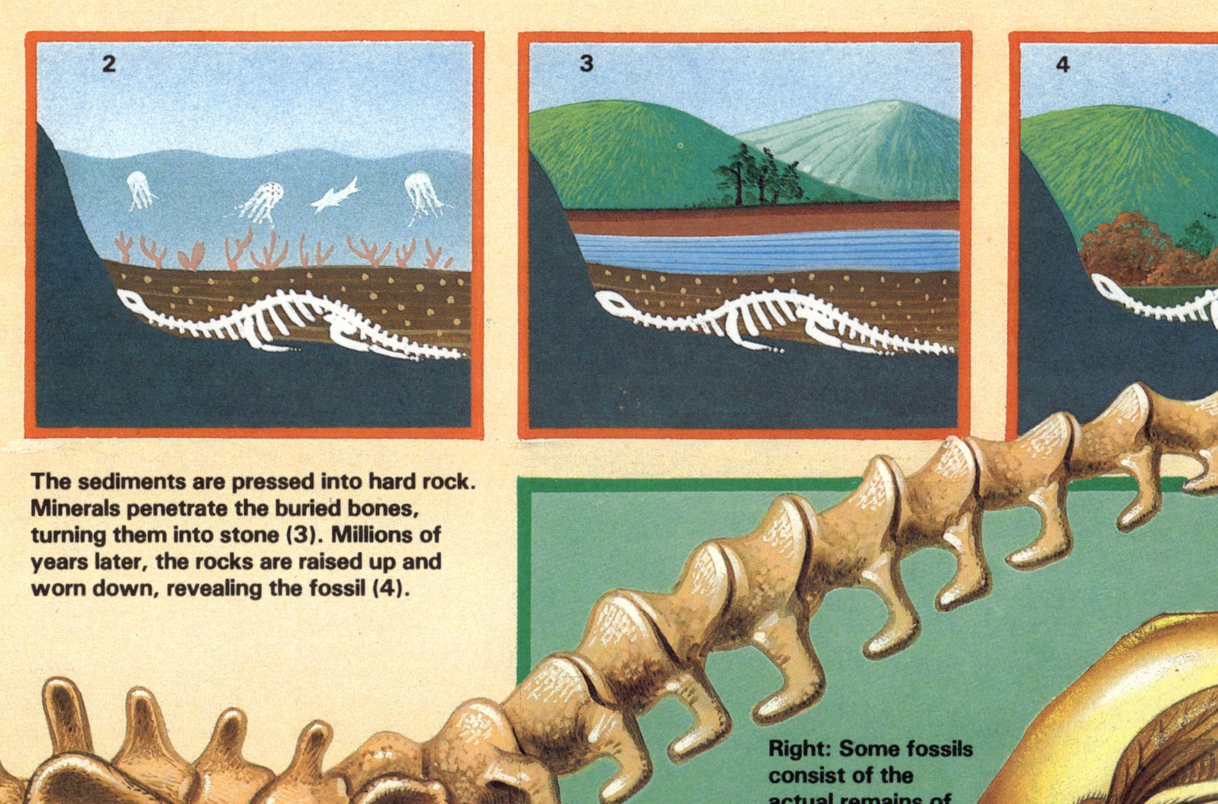

The sediments are pressed into hard rock. Minerals penetrate the buried bones, turning them into stone (3). Millions of years later, the rocks are raised up and worn down, revealing the fossil (4).

Right: Some fossils consist of the actual remains of ancient organisms. For example, insects may be trapped in sticky resin from ancient trees. The resin hardens into amber.

The Formation of Fossils

For fossils to form, the remains of animals and plants must be buried quickly. Otherwise, they would rot on the surface. Burial usually takes place in the mud, silt and sand on sea, lake and river beds. After burial, the flesh of a dead animal usually decays. Hard parts, such as bones and shells, are preserved. The sediments are gradually turned into solid rock. Water seeping through the rock often deposits minerals in the pores of bones and shells, slowly turning them into stone. Sometimes, every tiny molecule of a buried log is replaced by minerals. This process forms *petrified* logs. Leaves preserved in rocks sometimes form thin films of carbon which show the shape of the leaf.

Other fossils are moulds or casts of the original hard parts (see the diagrams on the facing page). A few fossils include the actual bodies of animals, such as woolly mammoths which lived 30,000 years ago. These have been preserved in the frozen ground of Siberia. But such fossils are extremely rare.

A person compared in size with Brontosaurus

Ages of the Earth

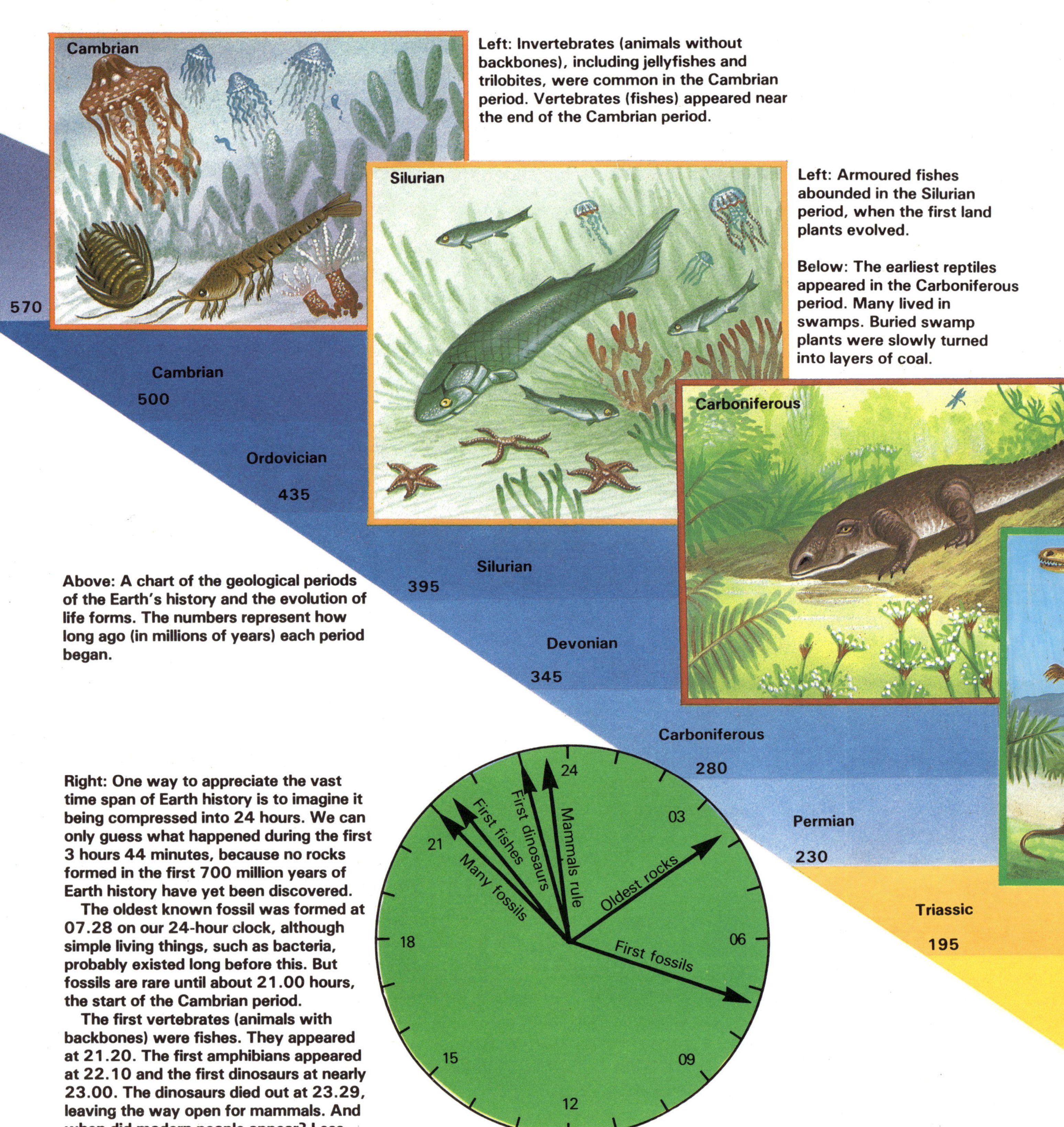

Left: Invertebrates (animals without backbones), including jellyfishes and trilobites, were common in the Cambrian period. Vertebrates (fishes) appeared near the end of the Cambrian period.

Left: Armoured fishes abounded in the Silurian period, when the first land plants evolved.

Below: The earliest reptiles appeared in the Carboniferous period. Many lived in swamps. Buried swamp plants were slowly turned into layers of coal.

Above: A chart of the geological periods of the Earth's history and the evolution of life forms. The numbers represent how long ago (in millions of years) each period began.

Right: One way to appreciate the vast time span of Earth history is to imagine it being compressed into 24 hours. We can only guess what happened during the first 3 hours 44 minutes, because no rocks formed in the first 700 million years of Earth history have yet been discovered.

The oldest known fossil was formed at 07.28 on our 24-hour clock, although simple living things, such as bacteria, probably existed long before this. But fossils are rare until about 21.00 hours, the start of the Cambrian period.

The first vertebrates (animals with backbones) were fishes. They appeared at 21.20. The first amphibians appeared at 22.10 and the first dinosaurs at nearly 23.00. The dinosaurs died out at 23.29, leaving the way open for mammals. And when did modern people appear? Less than a second before midnight.

Dating Rocks

The study of fossils made possible the fixing of the relative ages of rocks. And in the early 20th century, the discovery of radioactivity enabled scientists to fix the absolute ages of rocks. This is because some rocks contain bits of radioactive material which decays, or breaks down, at a fixed rate. Therefore, when scientists measure the proportion of a radioactive substance that has decayed, they can establish its age.

Eras and Periods

The last 570 million years are divided into the Palaeozoic (ancient life), Mesozoic (middle life) and Cenozoic (recent life) eras.

The Palaeozoic era (570-230 million years ago) is divided into six periods, although US geologists divide the Carboniferous period into two: the Mississippian and Pennsylvanian periods. The first period of the Palaeozoic era is the Cambrian. Cambrian rocks are rich in fossils. But in Precambrian rocks, formed before the Cambrian period began, fossils are rare. The Palaeozoic era saw the appearance of the first vertebrates (fishes), amphibians and reptiles.

The Mesozoic era (230-65 million years ago), contains three periods. It saw the rise of reptiles, including huge dinosaurs. Most reptiles became extinct at the end of the era.

The Cenozoic era in the last 65 million years saw the rise of mammals. This era contains two periods: the Tertiary and the Quaternary. Mighty mountain ranges such as the Alps and Himalayas were born during this era.

Above: The British Isles would look like this if the sea level rose or if the land sank by only 60 metres. The land and sea have changed many times throughout Earth history.

Triassic

Jurassic

Tertiary

Left: The first dinosaurs appeared in the Triassic period. The first mammals also evolved at this time.

Below left: The Jurassic period saw the emergence of such dinosaurs as *Brontosaurus* and *Stegosaurus*. There were flying reptiles, called Pterosaurs, and the first bird, *Archaeopteryx*.

Below: The Tertiary and Quaternary periods were dominated by mammals, such as giant ground sloths, huge grazing animals, sabre-toothed tigers and many birds. Primates date back 60 million years. Modern people (who are primates) appeared about 50,000 years ago.

Jurassic

Cretaceous

65

Tertiary

1.8

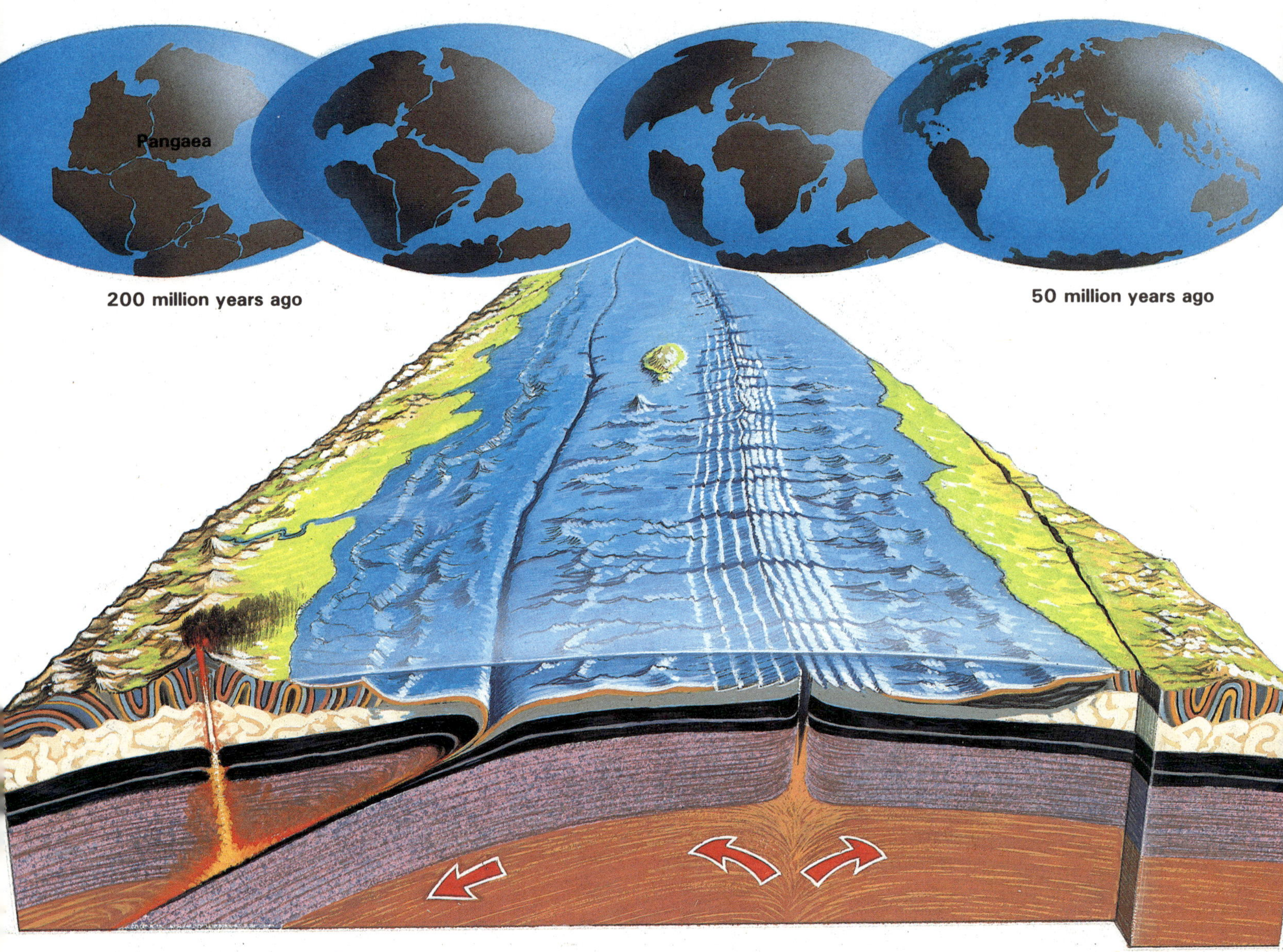

The Earth Beneath

Top: the maps show how the world has changed over the last 200 million years.

Above: The diagram shows an ocean ridge rising from the sea floor. In the centre of these ridges are valleys. These valleys are the edges of plates. Semi-molten material in the upper mantle is rising beneath the ridges. Under the plates it divides and flows sideways, pulling the plates apart. As the plates move, molten material wells up to fill the gap. It hardens into new crustal rock.

Along the deep ocean trenches, the fluid material sinks dowards and one plate is pushed beneath another. The diagram shows plates moving apart and plates colliding. Other plates move alongside each other. Such plates are separated by cracks called transform faults.

Look at a map of the Atlantic Ocean. You will see that North and South America look as though they would fit together with Europe and Africa, like pieces in a jigsaw. About 70 years ago, some scientists suggested that the continents were once joined together.

A German, Alfred Wegener (1880-1930), found similar rock structures on the edges of the facing continents. Fossils of the same land animals, which lived around 200 million years ago, were dug up in South America and Africa. How did they get there? They could not have swum the ocean. Wegener was convinced that the continents had been joined together 200 million years ago. But how do continents move?

Ocean Ridges and Trenches

The study of the oceans in recent years has helped to explain how continents move. No rocks in the oceanic crust are much older than 200 million years. This shows that the oceans are young features, unlike the continents, which have rocks dating back 3800 million years. The youngest rocks are in the middle of long, mostly underwater mountain ranges, or ocean ridges. The rocks in the crust become progressively older away from the ridges in both directions. The ocean ridges are earthquake zones. Earthquakes also occur along the deep ocean trenches, near the edges of the oceans.

THE EARTH'S CHANGING FACE

A space traveller passing the Earth 200 million years ago would have seen one large landmass and one vast blue ocean. But around 135 million years ago, the landmass, called Pangaea, had started to break up and the pieces were slowly drifting apart. The modern oceans were created between them. Some plates were large. Others, like the one carrying what is now India, were smaller. The Indian plate had been attached to Africa. But around 50 million years ago, it was pushing against the large Eurasian plate. Between the two plates was an ancient ocean. The rocks formed from sediments piled up on the bed of the ocean were squeezed up into the Himalayas, which form the world's highest mountain range.

Moving Plates

Boundaries between large blocks in the Earth's surface, called plates, run through the ocean ridges. Plates consist of the thin crust, including the continents, and part of the upper mantle. Under the ridges, hot fluid material is rising in the mantle and spreading sideways beneath the plates. These movements are pulling the plates apart by 1 to 10 cm a year. When the plates move, molten material rises to plug the gaps. It then hardens into new crustal rock.

Along the ocean trenches, however, plates are colliding and one plate is being pushed down beneath another. As it descends, the front edge of the plate is melted. Some plates move apart and some collide with each other. A third kind of movement occurs when plates move alongside each other. They move along long cracks in the surface, called transform faults.

Above: Plates move past each other like two blocks of wood being pushed in opposite directions. But the movement is not smooth. The plate edges are jagged and the plates are usually locked together. But pressure finally breaks the locks. The plates then move suddenly in a violent jerk.

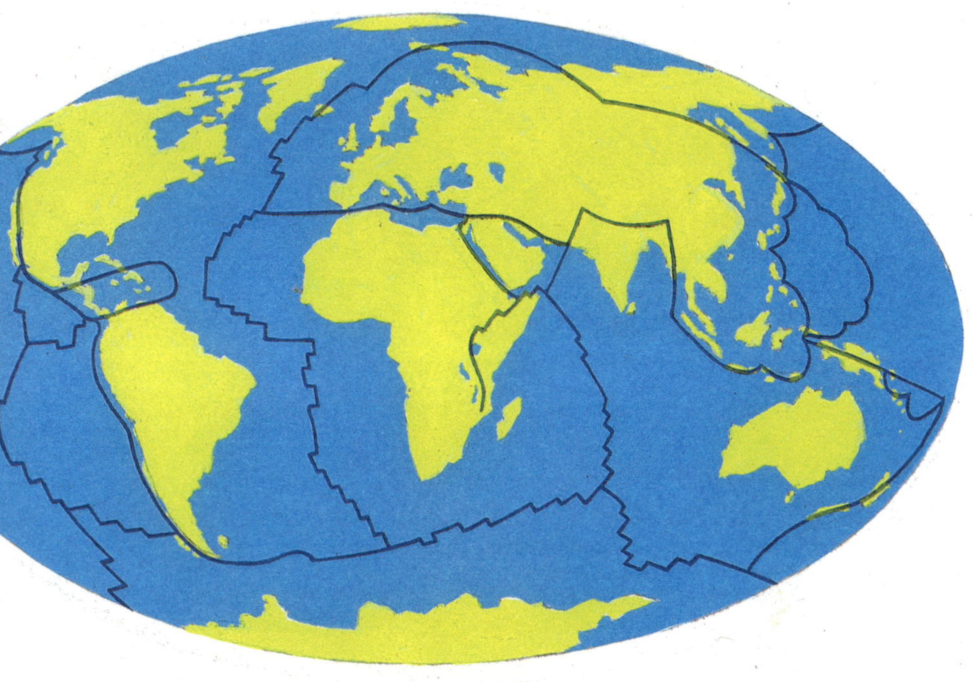

Right: The map shows the plates into which the Earth's surface is divided. The plates are all moving very slowly. The movements cause earthquakes, volcanic eruptions and the creation of mountain ranges.

Minerals and Mining

The sand on many beaches is composed largely of a mineral called quartz. Minerals make up all the rocks in the Earth. There are nearly 3000 minerals in the Earth's crust. Some, such as calcite and feldspar, are common. Others, such as diamonds, are rare.

Minerals are made up of elements. Elements are simple substances which cannot be broken down into other substances by chemical methods. Some 92 elements occur naturally in the Earth's crust. But only 22 are ever found in a pure state and samples of them are rare. Elements which occur on their own are called native elements. The other 70 elements all occur in chemical combinations. Minerals which are combinations of elements are called compounds. Metallic minerals contain metals. For example, galena is a metallic mineral containing lead and some silver. Other minerals, such as quartz, are non-metallic.

Below: Open-cast mining is used to remove the ores of valuable minerals that are found on or close to the surface.

Right: Minerals occur in many colours. Mineral collecting is a popular hobby. Beautiful crystals are prized by collectors.

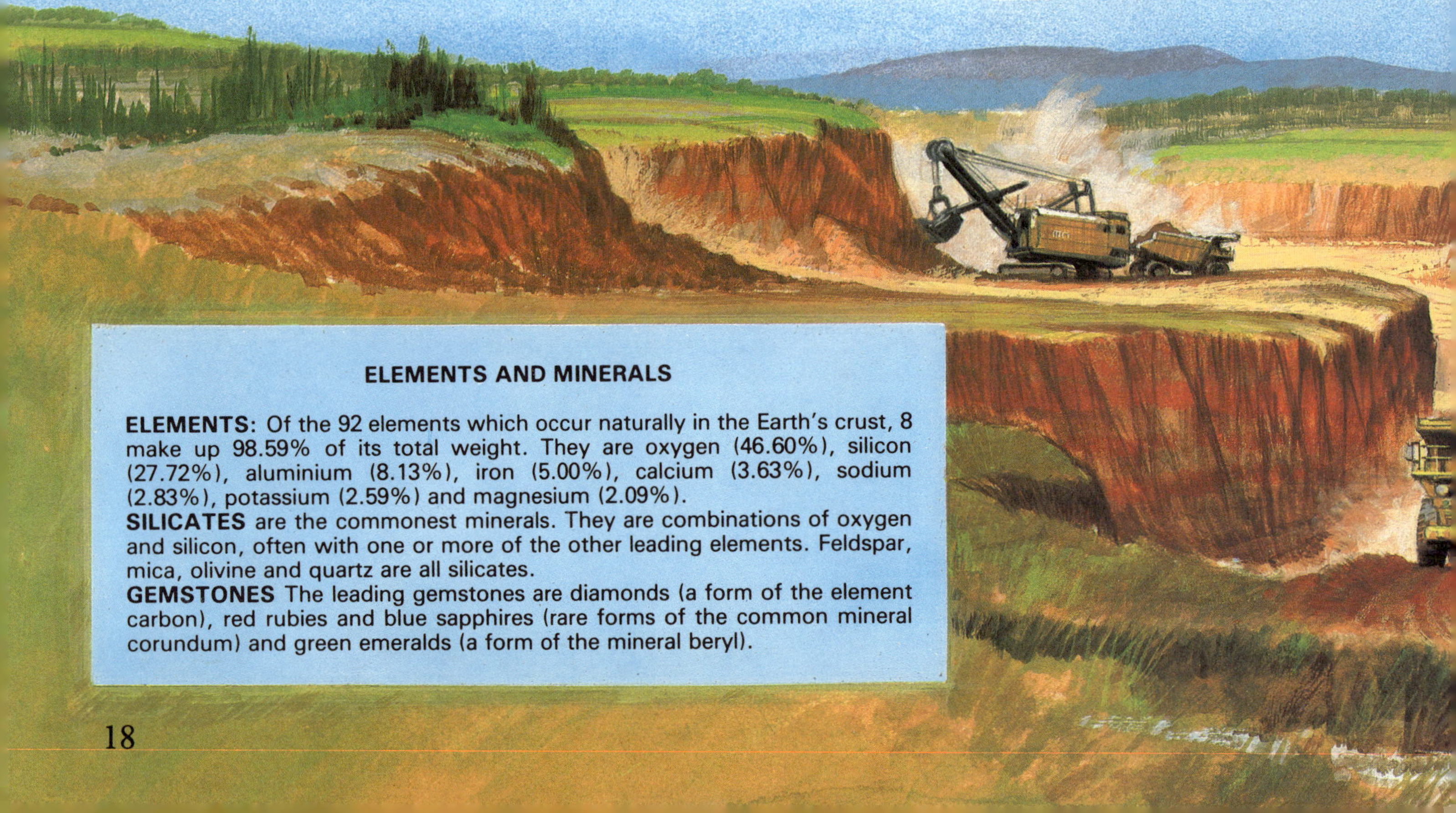

ELEMENTS AND MINERALS

ELEMENTS: Of the 92 elements which occur naturally in the Earth's crust, 8 make up 98.59% of its total weight. They are oxygen (46.60%), silicon (27.72%), aluminium (8.13%), iron (5.00%), calcium (3.63%), sodium (2.83%), potassium (2.59%) and magnesium (2.09%).

SILICATES are the commonest minerals. They are combinations of oxygen and silicon, often with one or more of the other leading elements. Feldspar, mica, olivine and quartz are all silicates.

GEMSTONES The leading gemstones are diamonds (a form of the element carbon), red rubies and blue sapphires (rare forms of the common mineral corundum) and green emeralds (a form of the mineral beryl).

MINERAL ORES

NATIVE ELEMEMENTS: Some valuable substances are found in a pure or almost pure state. They are called native elements. They include gold, diamond, silver and sulphur.

MINERAL ORES: Other substances occur in chemical combinations with other elements. Important metals and their ores include:

ALUMINIUM: Bauxite is the chief source of the metal aluminium. It is not a mineral. Instead, it contains several minerals: boehmite, diaspore and gibbsite.

COPPER: The most common copper ore is chalcopyrite. Other copper minerals are azurite, bornite, chalcosine, cuprite and malachite.

IRON: Hematite, magnetite and siderite.

LEAD: Galena and anglesite.

MANGANESE: Psilomelane, pyrolustie.

TIN: Cassiterite.

TUNGSTEN: Wolframite.

ZINC: Sphalerite (or zinc blende).

Rocks of the Earth

Rocks consist of minerals and most rocks contain several minerals. There are three kinds of rocks: igneous rocks, metamorphic rocks and sedimentary rocks.

Igneous Rocks

The term igneous comes from a Latin word meaning 'fire', and all igneous rocks are formed from hot magma. When magma cools slowly underground, coarse-grained igneous rocks are formed. The grains (or mineral crystals) in the rock are visible with the naked eye. The commonest igneous rock formed in this way is granite.

Other igneous rocks form when magma cools quickly in the air or in water. Fast cooling prevents the formation of crystals and so these rocks are fine-grained. To see the minerals in fine-grained rocks, you must study them through a microscope. The commonest fine-grained igneous rock is basalt.

Metamorphic Rocks

When magma rises upwards, it heats the other rocks. Heat changes rocks, just as wet dough is turned into bread in a hot oven. Rocks are also changed by pressure and by chemical action caused by hot steam and liquids.

Rocks changed by heat, pressure or steam are called metamorphic rocks. The hard metamorphic rock slate (used for roofing) was formerly the soft rock shale or mudstone.

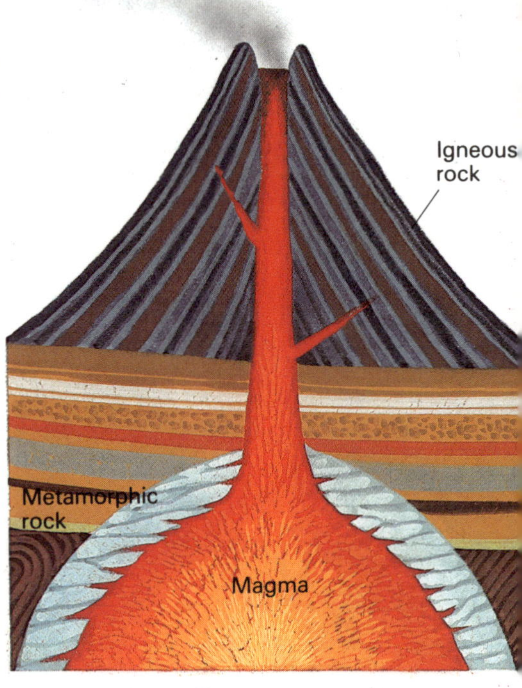

Below: The Grand Canyon is one of the most impressive sights in the world. This vast gorge in Arizona, USA, was cut out by the Colorado river, and in places it reaches a depth of more than 1.5 km. The successive layers of different coloured rocks give its steep walls a striped effect.

Marble is a metamorphic rock formed from limestone. Other metamorphic rocks include gneiss, hornfels and quartzite.

Sedimentary Rocks

Igneous and metamorphic rocks make up 95 per cent of the rocks in the top 16 km of the Earth's crust. But sedimentary rocks cover 75 per cent of the Earth's land surface.

Many sedimentary rocks consist of worn fragments of other rocks. These fragments are piled up, usually in water, and pressed into layers. The loose grains are later cemented together by minerals deposited from seeping water. Such rocks include sandstone and shale. Some sedimentary rocks are deposited from water. They include flint, rock salt and some kinds of limestone. Other limestones consist largely of the remains of dead sea creatures. Coal is another sedimentary rock. It consists of the remains of ancient plants.

Above: The diagram shows the main kinds of rock. Igneous rocks are formed when molten magma is pushed upwards through the Earth's crust and cools and hardens. Some magma reaches the surface and some cools underground. Metamorphic rocks are rocks that have been changed by great heat or by pressure. The third type is called sedimentary rock. Many sedimentary rocks are formed from fragments of sand, mud or the remains of dead sea creatures which pile up in water.

Right: Mountaineers have climbed most of the world's highest peaks, including Mount Everest. Everest is in the Himalayas, on the border between Nepal and China.

Mountains

The four main kinds of mountains are fold mountains, block mountains and volcanic and dome mountains.

Fold Mountains
Folds are bends in layers of rock caused by sideways movements in the Earth's crust. Upfolds are called anticlines and downfolds are called synclines.

Fold mountains rise when two plates in the Earth's crust push against each other. Flat layers of rock between the plates are then buckled upwards into huge loops. For example, the Himalayas are fold mountains caused by a collision between a plate bearing India and another plate bearing the rest of Asia (see pages 16-17). The Alps started to rise when, about 26 million years ago, the African plate pushed a small plate bearing Italy against the underside of Europe.

Block Mountains
When plates move, they crack nearby rocks. Long cracks are called faults. Plate movements cause faults to open up and push the cracked rocks up and down along the faults. Large blocks of land squeezed upwards along faults are called horsts or block mountains.

Volcanic and Dome Mountains
Volcanic mountains are made up of erupted magma. Sometimes magma rises upwards but does not reach the surface. It pushes the overlying rocks up into domes. When the overlying rocks are worn away, the hardened magma is exposed as a dome mountain.

Fold mountains are formed by lateral (sideways) pressure. Flat layers of rock are arched up into folds. Fold mountain ranges include the Himalayas in Asia, the Alps in Europe, the Rockies in North America and the Andes in South America.

Fast-flowing rivers in mountainous regions wear out deep, V-shaped valleys.

Valleys and Slopes

Even as mountains are pushed upwards, so the forces of erosion start to wear them down. Weathering breaks up rocks. Rivers and glaciers carry worn material away. In doing so, they wear out deep valleys. Rift valleys are not eroded. They are formed when blocks of land slip down between faults.

Steep slopes are the main feature of mountain areas. Rocks on steep slopes are unstable. They may be dislodged by earthquakes to cause landslides, earth flows (movements of fine soil and clay), mud flows (made of dust and sand or volcanic ash mixed with water), and avalanches (falls of ice, snow and rock).

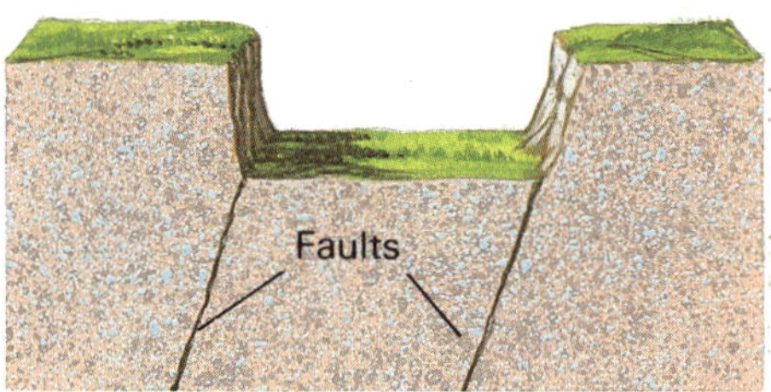

Rift valleys form when blocks of land sink downwards between two sets of faults.

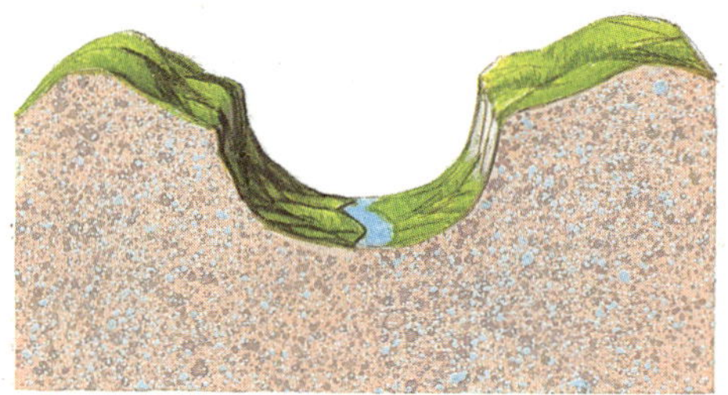

Steep-sided U-shaped valleys are worn out by glaciers (tongues of ice) in mountain regions.

Landslides are movements of soil and rock down a cliff or mountainside. Landslides can do much damage and cause loss of life.

KINDS OF MOUNTAINS

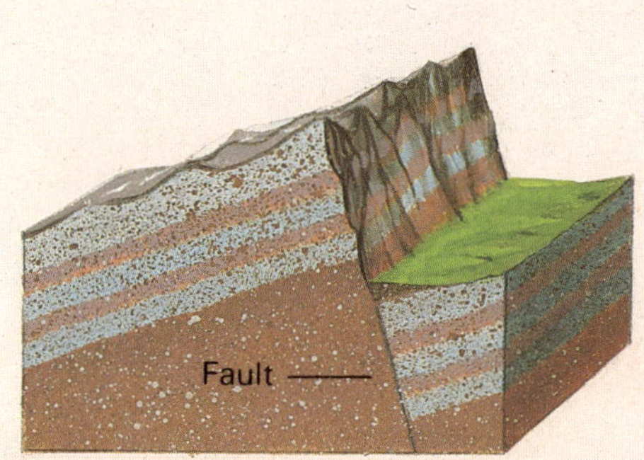

Block mountains are formed when a large block of land is pushed upwards along a fault (crack) or between two faults in the Earth's crust. The Sierra Nevada range in California in the south-western United States is an example of a block mountain.

Some volcanic mountains consist of volcanic ash and other fragments of magma which have been exploded into the air. Others are huge piles of hardened lava. Most volcanoes contain layers of ash alternating with layers of lava.

LANDSLIDES AND AVALANCHES

Some of the most destructive landslides and avalanches are caused by earthquakes.

For example, an earthquake in 1840 caused a landslide in the Himalayas. Rocks crashed down a gorge into the Indus River. The rocks dammed the river and a 40-mile long lake formed behind the rocks. When the dam burst, a flood destroyed everything in its path for hundreds of miles downstream.

A landslide in Italy in 1963 sent many rocks crashing into a man-made lake. Water surged over the dam, wiping out the resort of Longarone.

In 1970, an avalanche in Peru killed 18,000 people.

Volcanoes

Volcanoes are vents (holes) in the ground where magma reaches the Earth's surface. The magma may appear in flows of molten lava or as fragments, including volcanic ash and sizeable volcanic bombs. Mountains built of magma are also called volcanoes.

There are more than 500 active volcanoes. Active volcanoes have erupted in historic times. Between eruptions, they are dormant (sleeping). Volcanoes that are unlikely to erupt again are extinct.

Where Volcanoes Occur

Most volcanoes lie near the edges of the moving plates in the Earth's crust (see pages 16-17). Some are on the ocean ridges. Others are near places where one plate is descending beneath another. The descending plate is melted to produce magma. A few volcanoes, like those in Hawaii, lie far from plate edges. They are probably above hot spots in the Earth's mantle.

Right: This diagram of a volcano shows that magma rises from an underground chamber (1) to the crater (2) during eruptions. Ash is sometimes exploded into the air while lava (3) flows from the crater. The ash and lava pile up to form a volcanic mountain. Sheets of magma are forced into nearby rocks. Some called dykes (4) cut across existing layers, while sills (5) run between existing layers. Some magma may be forced through secondary vents (6) in the side of the mountain. Runny lava may rise through long faults (7) and spread out over the land. Extinct volcanoes (8) have not erupted in historic times. Magma heats water in the rocks. Some water appears in hot springs and geysers (9), which are high jets of hot water and steam.

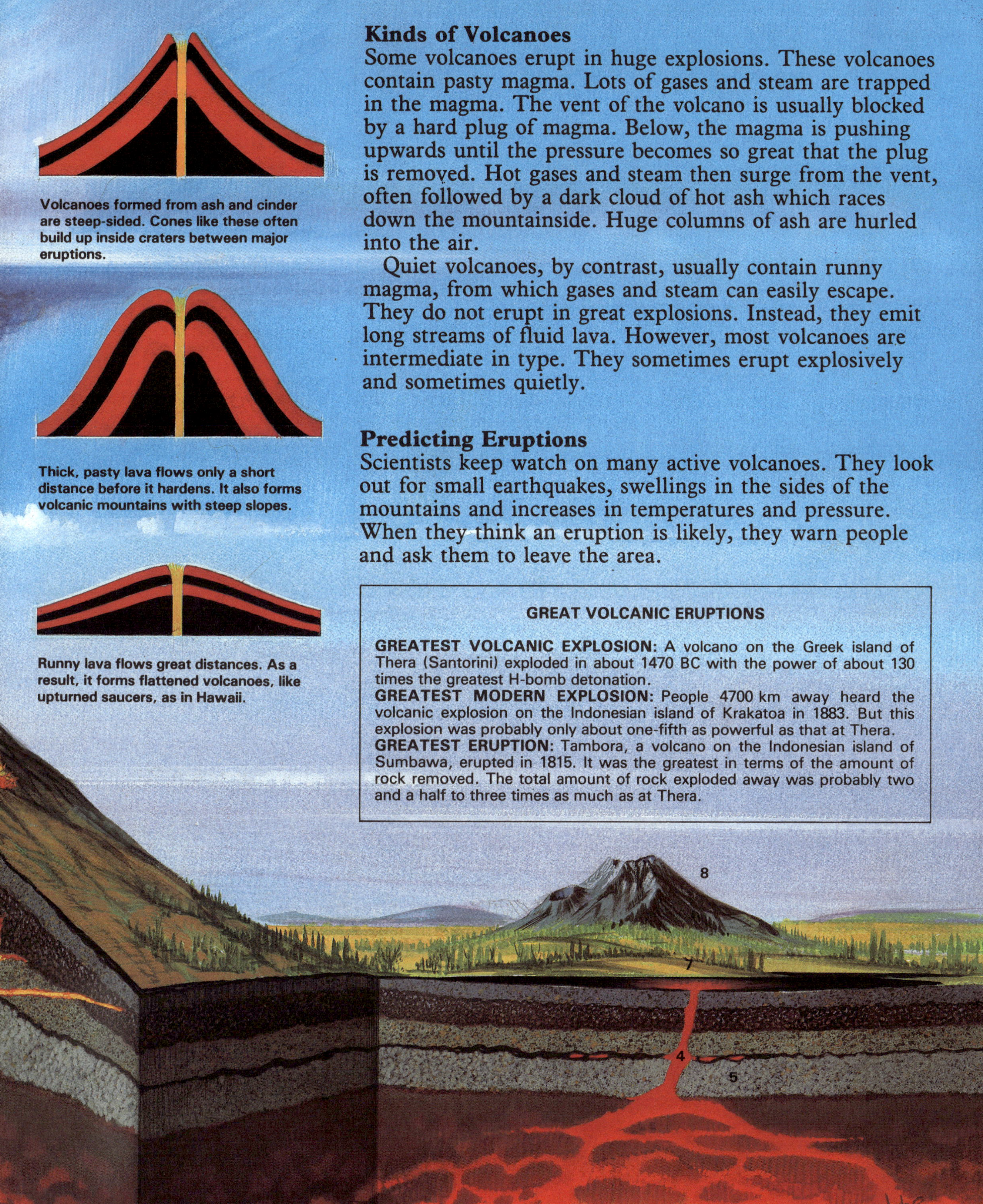

Volcanoes formed from ash and cinder are steep-sided. Cones like these often build up inside craters between major eruptions.

Thick, pasty lava flows only a short distance before it hardens. It also forms volcanic mountains with steep slopes.

Runny lava flows great distances. As a result, it forms flattened volcanoes, like upturned saucers, as in Hawaii.

Kinds of Volcanoes

Some volcanoes erupt in huge explosions. These volcanoes contain pasty magma. Lots of gases and steam are trapped in the magma. The vent of the volcano is usually blocked by a hard plug of magma. Below, the magma is pushing upwards until the pressure becomes so great that the plug is removed. Hot gases and steam then surge from the vent, often followed by a dark cloud of hot ash which races down the mountainside. Huge columns of ash are hurled into the air.

Quiet volcanoes, by contrast, usually contain runny magma, from which gases and steam can easily escape. They do not erupt in great explosions. Instead, they emit long streams of fluid lava. However, most volcanoes are intermediate in type. They sometimes erupt explosively and sometimes quietly.

Predicting Eruptions

Scientists keep watch on many active volcanoes. They look out for small earthquakes, swellings in the sides of the mountains and increases in temperatures and pressure. When they think an eruption is likely, they warn people and ask them to leave the area.

GREAT VOLCANIC ERUPTIONS

GREATEST VOLCANIC EXPLOSION: A volcano on the Greek island of Thera (Santorini) exploded in about 1470 BC with the power of about 130 times the greatest H-bomb detonation.

GREATEST MODERN EXPLOSION: People 4700 km away heard the volcanic explosion on the Indonesian island of Krakatoa in 1883. But this explosion was probably only about one-fifth as powerful as that at Thera.

GREATEST ERUPTION: Tambora, a volcano on the Indonesian island of Sumbawa, erupted in 1815. It was the greatest in terms of the amount of rock removed. The total amount of rock exploded away was probably two and a half to three times as much as at Thera.

Earthquakes

The Trembling Earth

Earthquakes can occur anywhere. They may be caused by landslides or by volcanic eruptions. But most are caused by movements along faults in rocks which shake the land. Most do little or no damage. But a few earthquakes cause great destruction.

The place inside the Earth where an earthquake occurs is called the focus. The most destructive earthquakes have a focus that is within about 60 km of the surface. Earth movements at much deeper levels have less effect at the surface. The point on the surface above the focus is called the epicentre. The epicentres of many earthquakes are in the oceans. The tremors may set off fast moving waves called tsunamis. Tsunamis can cause great damage far away from the epicentre.

Below: The map shows that most earthquakes occur in clearly defined zones. Earthquakes can occur anywhere, but most of them, including the most intense, are concentrated around the edges of the moving plates into which the Earth's crust is divided.

Bottom: During severe earthquakes, like the one that hit Anchorage and other towns in Alaska in 1964, large cracks may open up in the shaking ground. Buildings collapse and landslides often cause great damage. Other hazards include fires, which often do even more damage than the earthquake, and tsunamis (high waves) that strike coastal areas, sweeping ships inland.

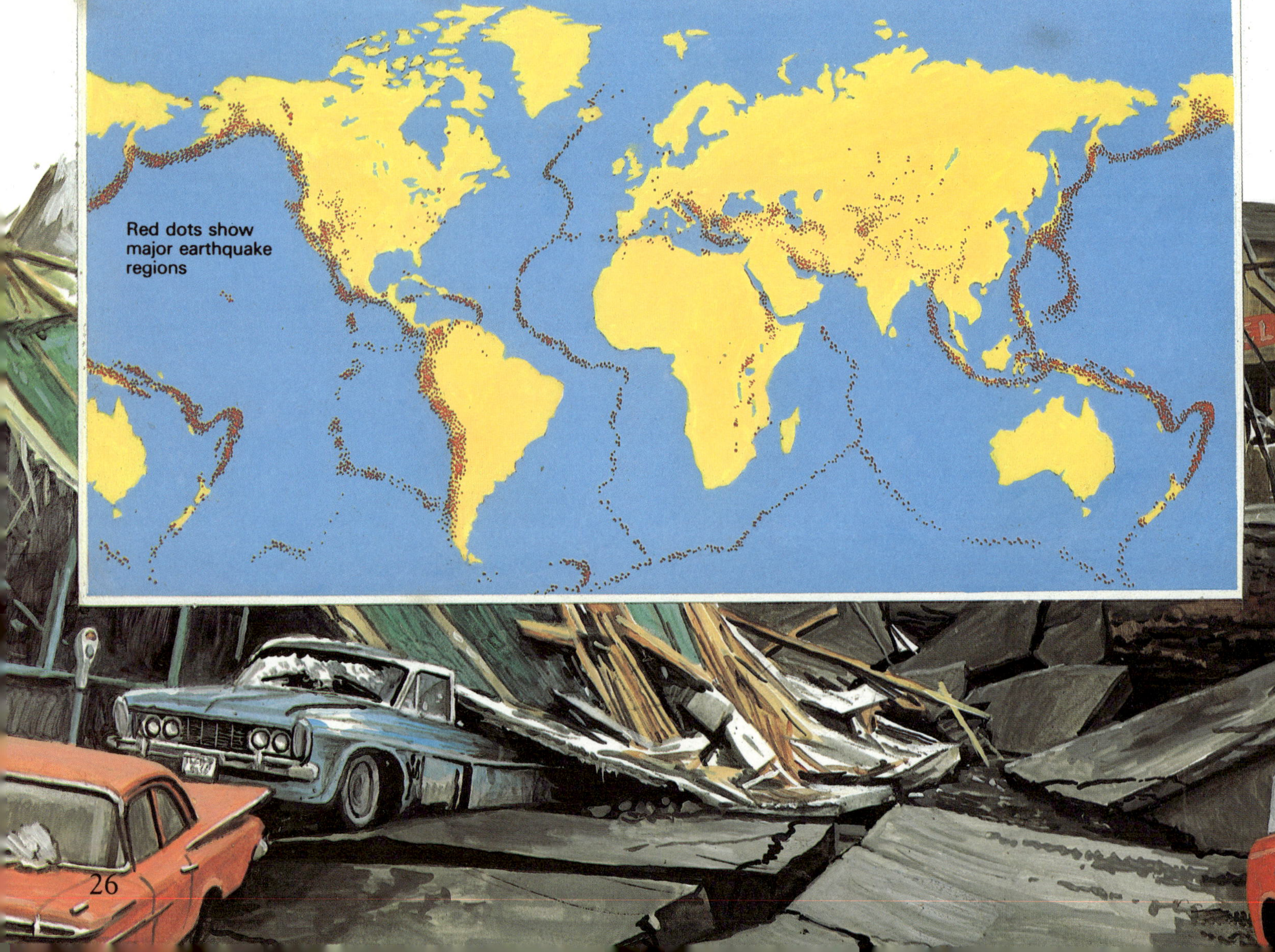

Where Earthquakes Occur

The chief earthquake zones follow the edges of the plates in the Earth's crust, namely the ocean ridges, zones where one plate is descending beneath another, and transform faults. Earthquakes occur when plates move in sudden jerks. The San Andreas (transform) fault runs through California, in the south-western USA. A movement along this fault in 1906 shook the city of San Francisco. Fires destroyed much property. Since 1906, scientists have found ways of building houses that will not collapse during 'quakes.

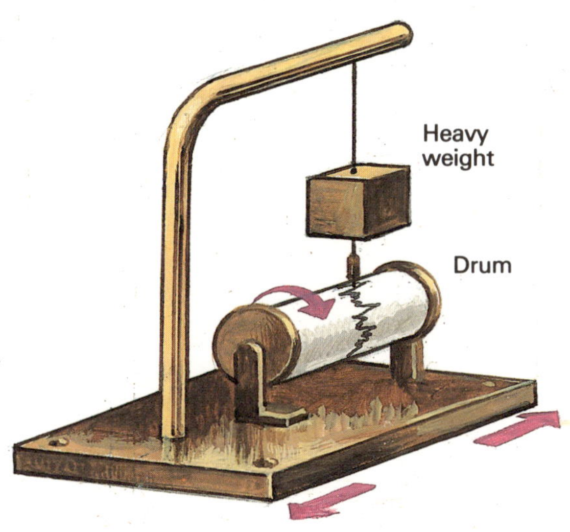

Above: Seismographs are sensitive instruments used to record earthquakes. When an earthquake occurs, the heavy weight suspended from the frame stays almost still while the support shakes. The vibrations are recorded on a piece of paper wrapped around a slowly revolving drum.

Earthquake Prediction

Scientists want to find ways of predicting earthquakes. They have discovered that rocks may be deformed as pressure builds up before a 'quake. Other changes in rocks and even unusual behaviour by animals, which seem to sense danger, are also being studied. But earthquake forecasting is still a young science.

Shaping the Land

Right: Limestone caves are worn out by rainwater. Limestone consists mostly of calcium carbonate. This substance reacts chemically with rainwater, which eats away the rock along the horizontal and vertical cracks in the rock. Water seeping through the caves is highly charged with calcium carbonate.
Water dripping from the roof of a cave is often agitated and evaporated by air currents. Thin films of the mineral calcite are then deposited from the water. Layer upon layer of such deposits build downwards to form the icicle-like stalactites. Water splashing onto the floor of a cave also deposits calcite. These build upwards into stalagmites.

Although it is difficult to see, the land in your home area is slowly changing. American scientists have worked out that about 0.3 metres of land is removed from the eastern USA every 9000 years. This may not seem much. But if you remember that we measure Earth history in millions of years, you will realize that mountains can be worn down to plains. The main forces that shape the land are weathering, winds, rivers, ice and, along coasts, sea waves.

Weathering occurs in several ways. For example, rain is important, because some minerals, such as rock salt, dissolve in water. Some rocks, such as limestones, do not dissolve in pure water. But limestone dissolves in water which contains carbon dioxide dissolved from the air or soil. The dissolved gas changes the water into a weak acid. This acid wears out limestone caves.

Rainwater also affects the hard rock granite. This is because water combines with some kinds of feldspar and turns them into clay. The quartz and mica in granite are not affected. Grains of these minerals are washed away by rain and rivers. The quartz grains often form sandy beaches along coasts.

Above: Plants contribute to the break-up of rocks. Here, a seedling has taken root in a crack in a boulder. As the tree grows, the roots exert great pressure, pushing the boulder apart.

Weathering in Mountains and Deserts

In mountain areas, water seeps into cracks in rocks during the day. At night, temperatures often fall below zero and the water freezes. Ice occupies nine per cent more space than the same amount of water and so, when water freezes, it expands and the ice pushes against the sides of cracks. When this happens night after night, the cracks are widened and the rocks are finally split apart. This is called frost action. The shattered rocks tumble downhill. They often pile up in heaps called talus or scree.

In deserts, rocks are heated by the Sun by day. In the evening, temperatures fall quickly, often to below freezing point. The fast cooling of the rocks cracks the surfaces, making sounds like pistol shots. Layers of rock then peel away.

DESERT LANDSCAPES

There are three main kinds of desert landscapes: sandy deserts called *erg*; stony deserts called *reg*; and bare rocky deserts called *hammada*.

Deserts have little rain, but the main land features in most deserts were carved out by running water at a time when the climate was very different from that of today. Even now, a rare thunderstorm can drown areas which have been dry for years. *Wadis* (dry valleys) fill up with rushing torrents that sweep huge amounts of sand and rock away.

But wind-blown sand is the main natural form of erosion in deserts today. It can strip the paint off cars and undercut telegraph poles and boulders. It is responsible for mushroom-shaped boulders with a large top resting on a narrow stem. Wind-blown sand also grinds out deep hollows in rocky surfaces.

In sandy deserts, the wind blows the sand into dunes. *Barchans* are crescent-shaped dunes, while *seif dunes* are long sand ridges.

Sand covers about one-fifth of the world's deserts. Winds blow the grains of sand around, piling them up into hills called dunes. Dunes move in the direction of the prevailing (usual) wind. Grains of sand are blown up the gentle windward slopes and then topple down the steep slip faces. In this way, the dune slowly advances from position 1 to 2, 3, 4, 5 and so on.

Plants and Animals

As shown in the picture on the facing page, the roots of trees and shrubs can split rocks apart and so they also contribute to weathering. But plants also protect the land, especially when grass roots bind loose soil particles together.

Worms, which eat vast amounts of soil, and burrowing animals, such as rodents and termites, also play their part, because churned up soil is easily removed by rain and wind.

Right: Many desert features were carved by water at times in the past when the desert had a moist climate. Today, wind-blown sand eats away rocks along lines of weakness and polishes rocks, such as this natural arch.

The Work of Rivers

Running water is a major force in shaping the land. In itself, water has little power to erode (wear away) rock. But rivers push loose boulders, stones and sand along their courses. As they do so, the loose material scrapes the river bed and loosens other rocks. In this way, rivers can wear out deep valleys. River water also dissolves some rocks. Of all the material carried by rivers, about 30 per cent is dissolved rock and 70 per cent is solid material. Most rivers can be divided into three distinctive stages. They are called youth, maturity and old age.

Above: Youthful rivers rise in glaciers, lakes or springs. They flow swiftly downhill and wear out deep V-shaped valleys. Erosion occurs when the river is in flood.

Youthful Rivers

Rivers originate in several ways. Some flow from melting glaciers. Some drain out of lakes. Others start in springs where water bubbles to the surface.

In mountain areas, youthful rivers flow rapidly straight down steep slopes. After rains or when snow melts in spring, they become raging torrents. They then wear away their beds and carve out deep, V-shaped valleys.

Above: In middle age, rivers develop meanders (bends) and so lateral (sideways) erosion becomes more important than downward erosion. As a result, the valleys become broader and broader.

Right: The diagram shows features of a river in old age. On straight stretches, the channel is symmetrical (1). On bends, the outer bend is undercut, but sediment is dumped on the inner bend (2). In old age, when a river floods, particles are dumped on the river banks to form mounds called levees (3). Other features are oxbow lakes (abandoned meanders) and deltas where the river divides into channels.

Left: In dry areas, fast-flowing rivers carve out deep gorges, as in the Big Bend part of the Rio Grande's course in Texas, USA.

Below: A section through a waterfall showing how the water undercuts the base of the rock face.

Mature Rivers

When rivers emerge from mountains, they slow down as they flow over less steep slopes. They develop large, sweeping bends, called meanders. Mature rivers do not deepen their valleys like youthful rivers. But the strong currents constantly widen the valleys.

Old Age Rivers

In old age, rivers flow slowly across nearly flat plains. There is little erosion, although the rivers carry huge amounts of fine sediment. When the rivers overflow, the sediment is spread over the land. Large particles are dropped on the river banks, where they pile up to form mounds called levees. Fine particles are swept long distances from the river.

In old age, rivers sometimes change course. They cut through the necks of bends and so straighten their courses. The bends then become 'abandoned meanders', or oxbow lakes, which later dry up. Some rivers dump much of their load of sediment at their mouths in areas called deltas. But in places where tidal currents are strong, the sediment is swept out to sea.

WATERFALLS

Many waterfalls, including Niagara Falls in North America, occur where rivers flow over hard rocks that resist erosion. The diagram, above, shows a waterfall of this kind. The softer rocks below are undercut so that, occasionally, parts of the overlying rock break off and crash down. Such falls gradually retreat upstream. On average, Niagara Falls is retreating by about 0.9 metres a year.

Other falls occur along steep escarpments that separate highlands from lowlands. Others occur in glaciated regions, where rivers plunge into deep U-shaped valleys.

The world's highest waterfall is Angel Falls, Venezuela. It is 979 metres high.

The Water's Edge

The sea is never still and, on stormy days, high waves crash against the shore. The waves trap air in cracks in rocks and compress it. When the pressure is released, the air expands again with considerable force, which may enlarge the cracks and shatter the rock. Waves also pick up loose rocks and throw them at the shore. This bombardment undercuts cliffs and breaks up loose rocks into smaller and smaller pieces.

Wave erosion removes soft rocks, such as the loose material deposited by ice sheets, far faster than hard rocks, such as granite or limestone. Rapidly eroded areas form bays, while hard rocks may remain as headlands. But, as shown in the picture on this page, caves and arches are worn into headlands. When the arches collapse, rocky islands, called stacks, are left behind. They, too, are eventually removed.

Longshore Drift

Waves and currents drag some of the eroded material out to sea. But in places they carry material along the coast, often in a zig-zag direction, as shown in the diagram on the next page. This is called longshore drift. It is responsible for various land features which are built up by wave action.

STORM WAVES

Storm waves batter coastal areas, hurling shingle into the air and dumping it on coastal roads. The most powerful waves in the Atlantic Ocean have shifted concrete blocks weighing 1000 tonnes. Lighthouses on rocky islands or coasts must be carefully designed to withstand the fury of the waves.

Storm waves can greatly change coastlines in a short time. A storm in the North Sea in 1953 removed 11 metres of land near Lowestoft, in eastern England, in barely two hours. On the far side of the North Sea, the waves broke through the sea walls guarding the Netherlands. About 200 people were drowned in the floods.

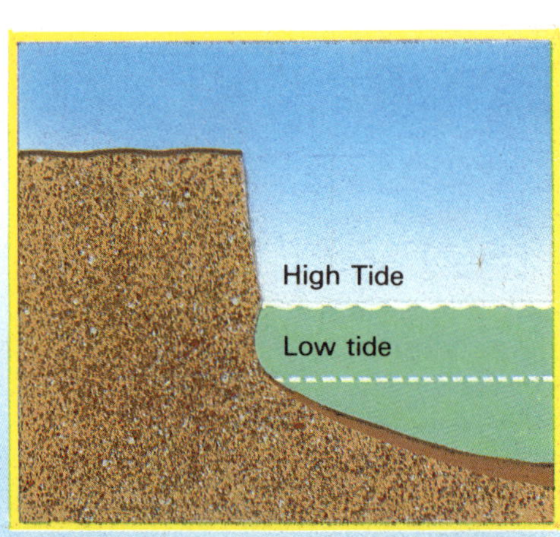

Below: Waves wear away soft rocks to form bays, while harder rocks form headlands. Wave action wears caves into the sides of headlands. Blow-holes are holes in the roofs of caves through which spray is thrown. When two caves meet, an arch is formed. When the arch collapses, the end of the headland becomes a stack.

Blow-hole
Stacks
Cave
Arch

VANISHING COASTLINES

Cliffs on Martha's Vineyard, an island in Massachusetts, in the USA, are being cut back by about 1.7 metres a year. A lighthouse has had to be rebuilt three times.

When the Romans conquered Britain in AD 43, the Holderness coast of Humberside, in northern England, stretched 3-5 km farther out to sea than it does today. Many towns shown on old maps have vanished beneath the waves.

The coasts of Holderness and Martha's Vineyard have something in common. They are both composed of loose rocks deposited by ice sheets. These soft rocks are more easily removed by waves than harder rocks.

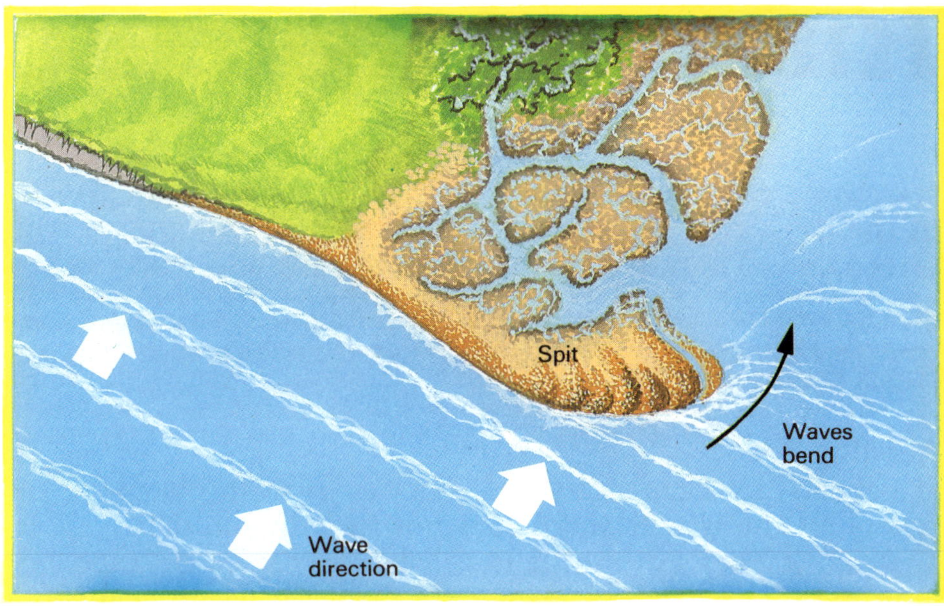

Spits are low ridges of sand and pebbles built up by waves and currents. They usually occur at places where the coast changes direction. Spits often develop curved hooks at the ends.

Opposite and above: Wave erosion occurs between high and low tide level. In this zone, storm waves hurl loose rocks at the shore and wear out hollows in the cliffs.

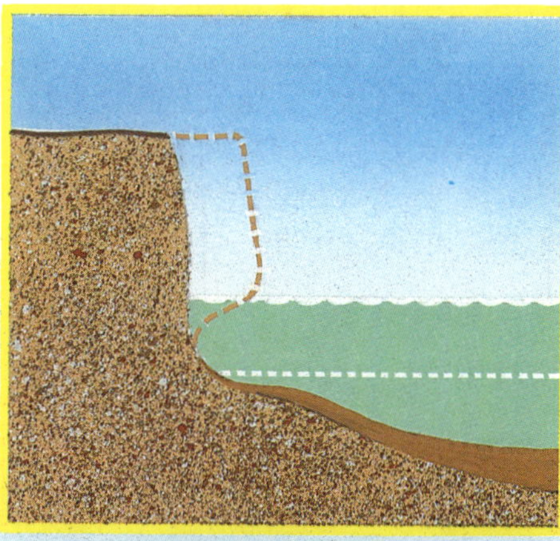
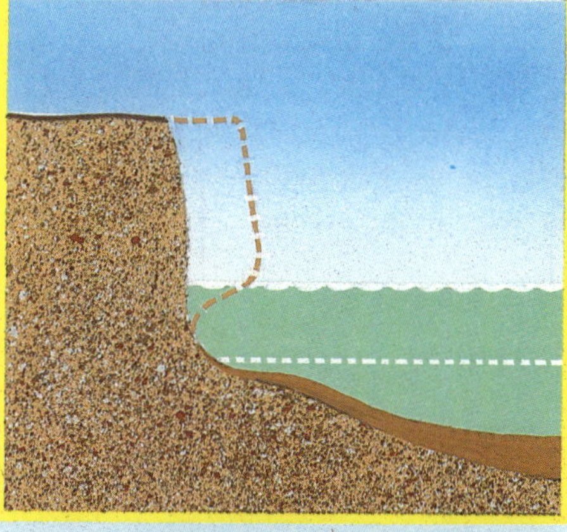

Above: The hollowing out of the bottom of cliffs continues until part of the cliff collapses. The shattered rocks on the shore are broken up and carried away.

Bars and Spits

Material carried along a coast is often dumped to form low ridges in the sea. Some, called bars, are not connected to the land. But spits extend outwards from the coast. Some extend across bays. They may seal off large areas of water to form lakes called lagoons.

A spit that links an island to the mainland is called a tombolo. For example, Chesil Beach in Dorset, England, is a long tombolo.

Other spits build up from two facing headlands, meeting up at an angle. Spits of this kind are found on the coasts of the eastern USA.

Longshore drift removes sandy beaches at seaside resorts. In order to keep the beaches, sea walls called groynes are built into the sea at right angles to the shore.

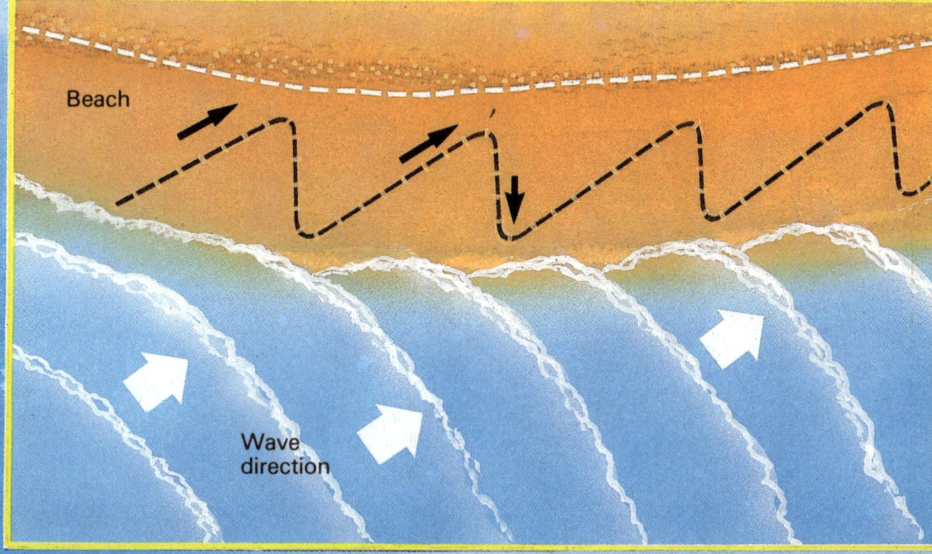

Left: Waves usually surge up the shore at an angle. But, because of gravity, the backwash returns at right angles to the shore. This zig-zag motion is responsible for the movement of sand and pebbles along a coast. This movement is called longshore drift.

Rivers of Ice

Ice covers about one tenth of the world's land areas. Most of the ice is in two great ice sheets covering Antarctica and Greenland. There are also smaller ice caps and many valley glaciers (rivers of ice) in mountain regions. But around 12,000 years ago, during the Ice Age, ice covered three times the present area.

Moving Ice

Ice sheets, ice caps and valley glaciers form in places where all the winter snow does not melt in summer. Instead, it piles up until it is slowly compacted into ice.

In mountain regions, glacier ice forms in basins, called cirques. It spills out of these basins and flows downhill, often joining up with other glaciers. The moving ice carries loose weathered rocks on its surface. The surface is pitted with cracks called crevasses. Many rocks fall into the crevasses and are frozen within the ice. Some glaciers end at a 'snout', where the ice melts and dumps the debris, or moraine. Others reach the sea and icebergs break off and float away.

Above: The map of the world shows the parts of the northern hemisphere that were covered by ice during the recent Ice Age. Mountain regions in central and southern Eurasia also had far more ice than they have today.

Below: Animals with plenty of hair, such as the woolly mammoth, were well equipped to survive the cold during the Ice Age. But the woolly mammoth was hunted to extinction by prehistoric hunters.

Glaciation

Moving bodies of ice have rocks frozen into their sides and bottoms. These rocks scrape against the land and wear away the underlying rocks. They deepen the basins (cirques) where the ice is formed. They carve out U-shaped valleys and other features shown in the diagrams on this page. Many of the world's lakes occupy ice-worn basins or basins dammed by moraine.

At the snouts of glaciers, some moraine piles up in long ridges. Other material, ranging from sizeable boulders to fine 'rock flour', is carried away from the ice by streams formed from meltwater.

Below: After an Ice Age, special land features reveal that this area was once glaciated. For example, pointed peaks (horns) form where three or more cirques occur back to back. U-shaped valleys are other features. Hanging valleys are tributary valleys that lie above the over-deepened U-shaped valleys. Streams often descend in waterfalls from the hanging valleys.

Above: The effects of glaciers can be studied in mountain regions. Glaciers transport loose rocks broken up by frost action. The rocks carried by glaciers are called moraine. Rocks frozen into the sides and bottoms of glaciers scrape against the land, eroding even more rocks.

THE GREAT ICE AGE

An Ice Age occurred between about 1.75 million and 10,000 years ago. It was not cold all the time. Between extremely cold periods, when ice spread over much of the northern hemisphere, there were times when it was warmer than it is today. In the last 900,000 years, there were 10 long, cold periods separated by warm periods. The warm periods lasted about 10,000 years. We may be living in a warm interval between cold periods. But there is not enough evidence to prove this theory. Why do climates change? Many theories have been put forward. It seems possible that changes in the Earth's orbit around the Sun and variations in the Earth's axis may be among the factors that caused the Ice Age.

Mapping the Land

Maps show the world or parts of it on flat surfaces. Accurate maps are drawn to scale. At a scale of 1:50,000, 1 cm on the map equals 50,000 cm or 0.5 km on the ground.

Surveying the Land

The first job of land surveyors (people who measure the land) is to fix as accurately as possible the positions of a network of points, by measuring the angles and distances between them. Surveyors use telescopic instruments, theodolites, to measure angles. Measuring distances was once a slow process, using metal tapes. But surveyors can now use electronic instruments. When the positions of the points are known, their heights are measured. These fixed points, which are often marked on the ground by concrete pillars, form the skeleton of a map.

MAP SYMBOLS

CONTOURS are lines joining places with the same height. They are usually brown lines, but underwater contours are blue.

CULTURAL FEATURES are man-made things, such as towns, churches, historical sites, including battlefields (crossed swords), lighthouses, roads and railways. They usually appear in red or black.

HACHURES are fine lines that show land forms three-dimensionally.

LAYER TINTING is the use of colours and shades of colours to show the various levels of the land.

SPOT HEIGHTS are black dots or solid black triangles. A figure in metres or feet alongside the point shows the exact height.

VEGETATION FEATURES, such as forests and swamps, are usually depicted as green symbols.

WATER FEATURES, such as rivers, lakes and coasts, are shown in blue.

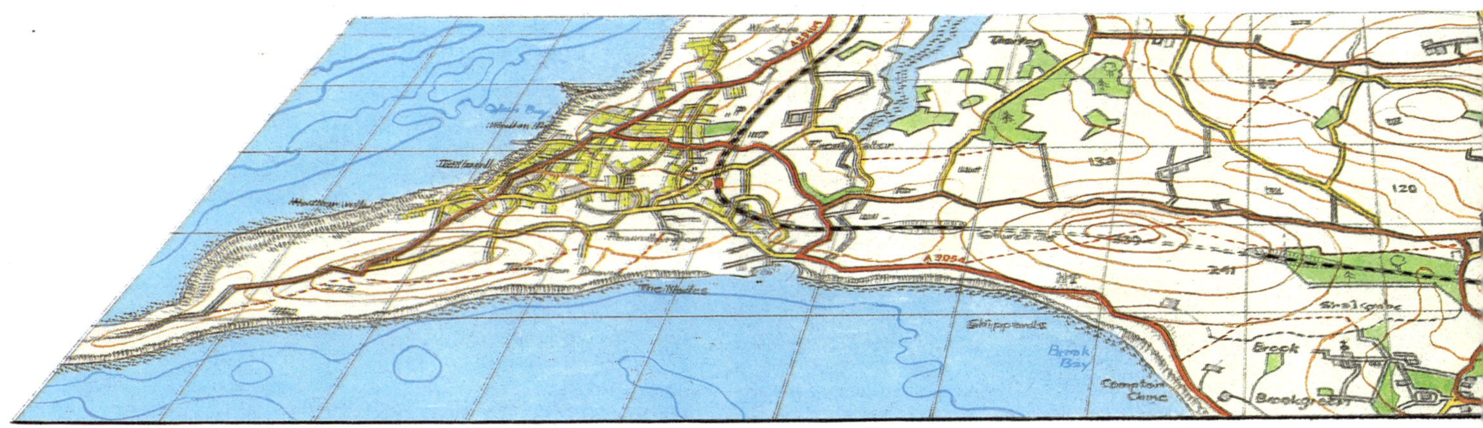

Detailed Mapping

When the network of points is fixed, surveyors must measure all the details of the land between them. This work was once done on the ground. But, today, mapping from air photographs has largely replaced ground mapping.

Aircraft take long strips of photographs of the land. Each photograph overlaps the next by 60 per cent. The fixed ground points are identified on the photographs. Because the distances between them are known, other distances can be measured on the photographs.

Heights can also be measured. This is because overlapping photographs viewed through a stereoscope appear as a three-dimensional model of the land.

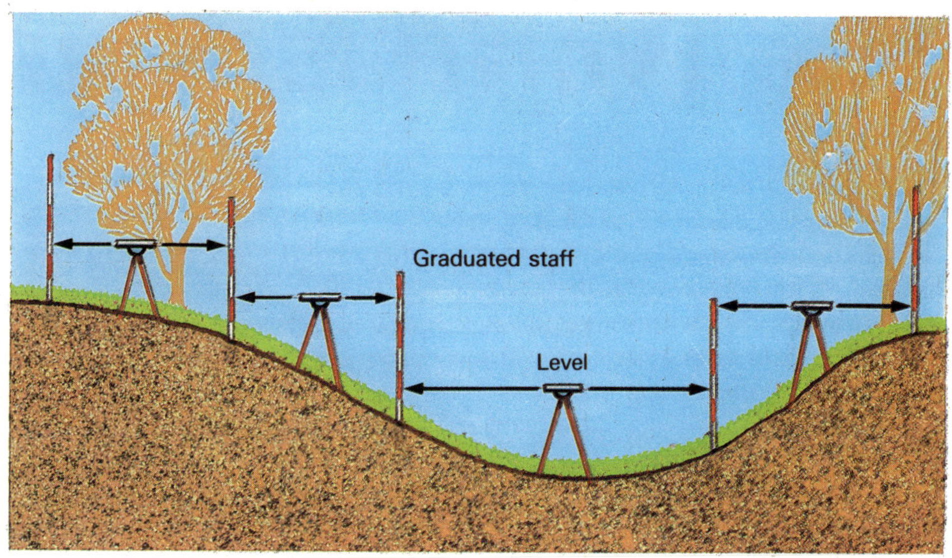

Above: To fix heights, surveyors use a telescopic instrument called a level, which is mounted on a tripod, and a graduated staff. The difference between the height of the level and a reading on the staff is the height difference between the two points.

Below: Topographic maps, or general reference maps, show the main features of the land over fairly small areas. They are drawn to scale so that any distance on the map represents a distance on the ground. In order to include as many details as possible, map-makers use symbols like those shown below. You will find a legend (key), containing all the symbols used on a map in the margins of most topographic maps.

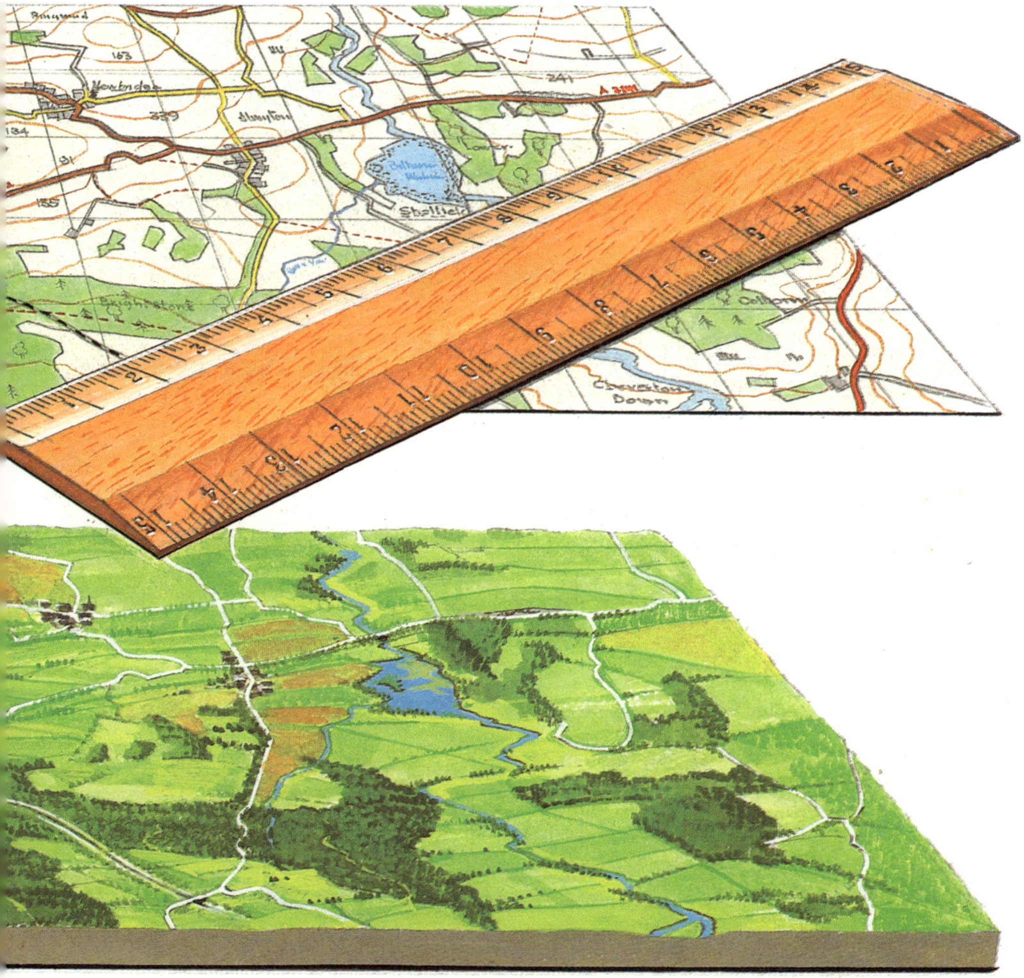

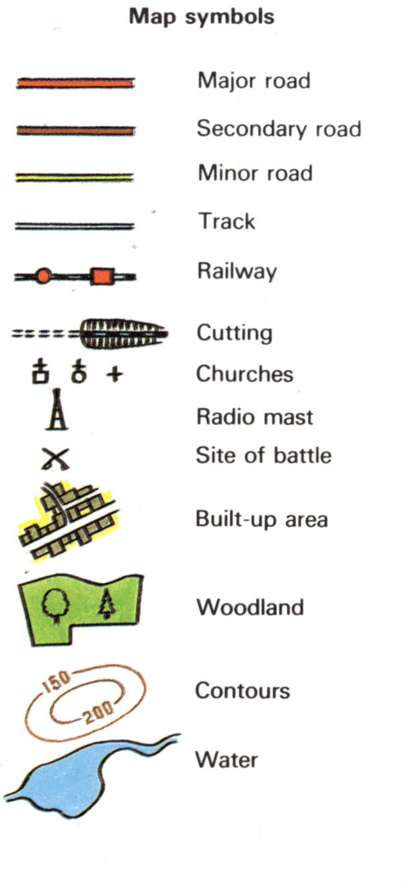

Map symbols

Major road
Secondary road
Minor road
Track
Railway
Cutting
Churches
Radio mast
Site of battle
Built-up area
Woodland
Contours 150 200
Water

The World is Round

Geographers are interested in features on the Earth's surface and how the features are related to one another. The best way to present the information which geographers need is a map. The facts on a map would often fill a book.

Types of Maps

Apart from topographic, or general reference, maps, there are many special kinds of maps. For example, weather maps show the weather conditions over a large area, and population maps show where people are most concentrated. Special maps are now often produced by computers. They can be a great help to planners.

Some maps are large-scale, covering small areas. Maps with extremely large scales are called *plans*. But small-scale maps cover large areas. Such maps appear in atlases. Small-scale maps create problems for map-makers.

Curved Surfaces, Flat Maps

A major problem faced by map-makers is that the Earth is nearly a sphere. Its surface is curved, not flat. To understand the problem, think of another sphere, an orange.

If you peel an orange, keeping the peel in one piece, you are left with a hollow sphere. It is impossible to turn this sphere into a flat surface without breaking it and crushing the pieces. To deal with this problem, map-makers have devised various solutions — map projections.

Map Projections

Map projections are ways of *projecting* details on a curved surface onto a flat surface.

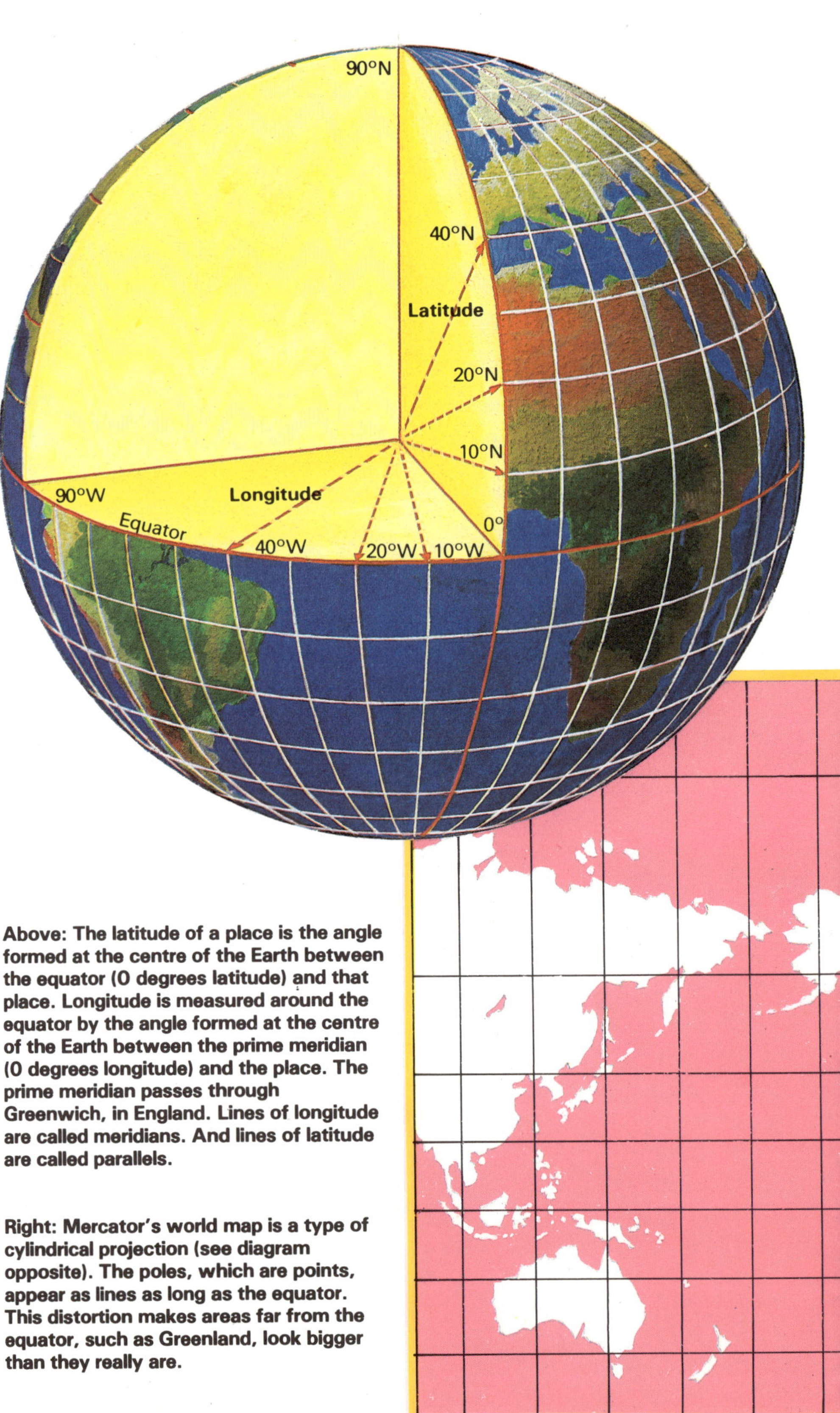

Above: The latitude of a place is the angle formed at the centre of the Earth between the equator (0 degrees latitude) and that place. Longitude is measured around the equator by the angle formed at the centre of the Earth between the prime meridian (0 degrees longitude) and the place. The prime meridian passes through Greenwich, in England. Lines of longitude are called meridians. And lines of latitude are called parallels.

Right: Mercator's world map is a type of cylindrical projection (see diagram opposite). The poles, which are points, appear as lines as long as the equator. This distortion makes areas far from the equator, such as Greenland, look bigger than they really are.

Some projections are devised as though the Earth is a glass sphere with all the details and lines of latitude and longitude engraved on it. If you place a light at the center of the globe, the engraved lines are projected as shadows onto flat surfaces. A cylindrical projection of this type is shown below. But most projections are worked out by mathematics.

No one map can show shapes, areas, distances and directions correctly at the same time. Only a globe can do that. Some map projections preserve some features and some preserve others. Equal area maps, for instance, ensure that all countries are the right *size*. Conformal maps make sure that the *shape* of the countries is correct. The type of projection depends on the purpose of the map.

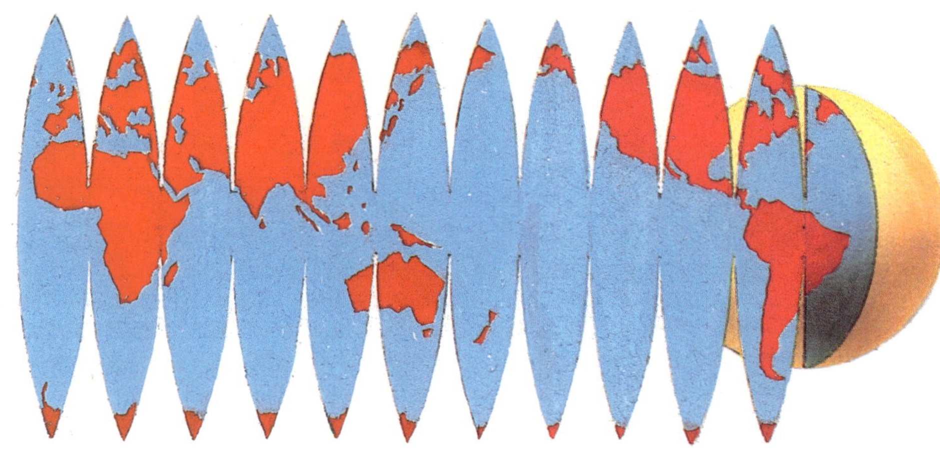

Above: The problem of showing a curved surface on a flat piece of paper is revealed when globes are made. The world map is first printed on a series of thin, lens-shaped pieces of paper, called gores. The gores are fitted together on the globe and pasted down. Some map projections are drawn in separate sections, resembling gores. Such projections are said to be interrupted. Maps based on interrupted projections are of little use, however, because they split up land masses.

Below: Cylindrical map projections are developed as though a light was placed at the center of an engraved glass globe. Around the globe is a cylinder of paper, touching the globe along the equator. The light casts shadows of the engraved meridians and parallels, together with the shapes of the continents, onto the paper. This creates a map. But you can see that the distances between lines of latitude increase towards the poles. On a true map, these distances should be the same.

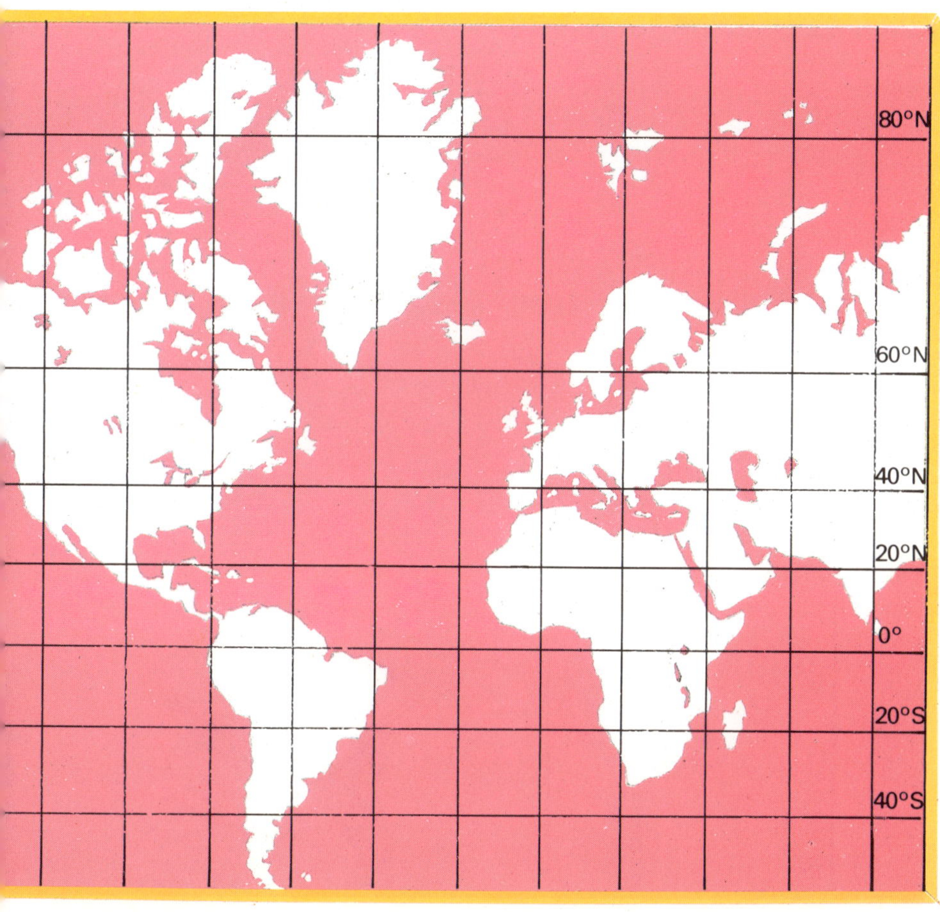

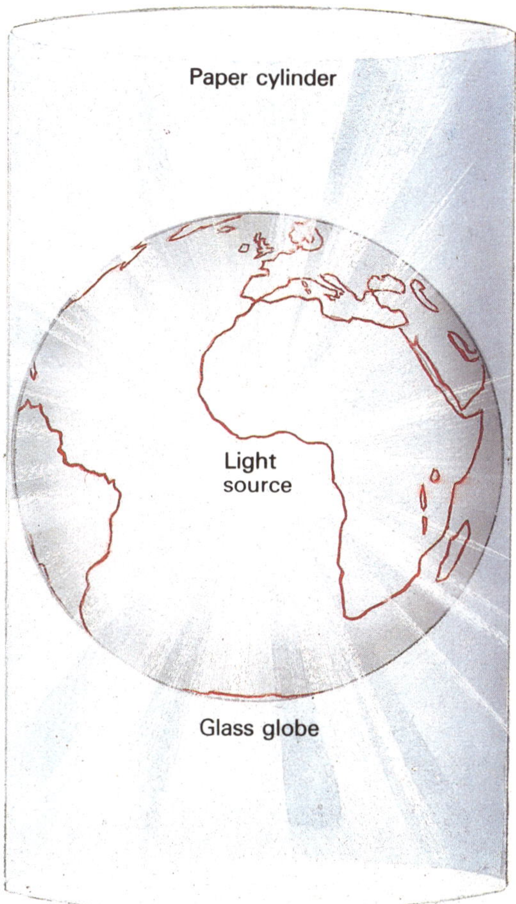

An Ocean of Air

We live in an ocean of air which envelopes the Earth. This thin layer, called the atmosphere, contains the oxygen which people and animals need to breathe and the carbon dioxide that plants need in order to grow. The air also contains moisture in the form of invisible water vapour or visible clouds and fog.

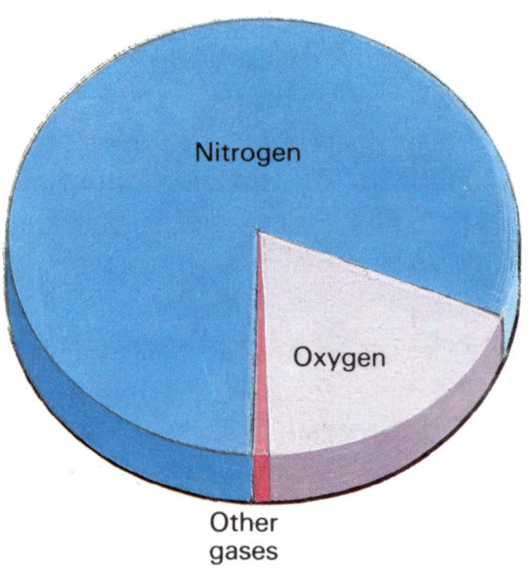

Above: Nitrogen and oxygen make up 99.04% of the air, while argon makes up 0.93%. The other gases, including carbon dioxide, make up 0.03%.

A Protective Shield

The atmosphere is also a shield. It is divided into several layers, which are more and more rarefied as one travels upwards. In the stratosphere, the second layer of the atmosphere, the air is much thinner than at the surface. But this layer contains a gas called ozone. This gas filters out harmful ultraviolet radiation emitted from the Sun. If this radiation were to reach the ground, life on land would be impossible. The atmosphere also stops the Earth from becoming too cold. When the Sun's rays warm the surface, heat is radiated back into the air. If there were no atmosphere, this heat would escape into space. We would then have hot days and bitterly cold nights. But the atmosphere absorbs some of the radiated heat, acting much like a greenhouse.

Opposite: The atmosphere contains several layers. Most of the mass of the atmosphere is in the troposphere, the lowest layer. Temperatures fall when one goes upwards. But the temperature stops falling about 18 km up above the equator and 8 km up above the poles. This is the tropopause, or the top of the troposphere. Here the temperature is about −57°C. Above is the stratosphere, which extends up to 50 km above the surface. Temperatures rise again, reaching 0°C at the top of the stratosphere. In the mesosphere, between 50 and 80 km up, temperatures fall again. In the ionosphere, temperatures rise steadily. At about 500 km, the exosphere merges into space.

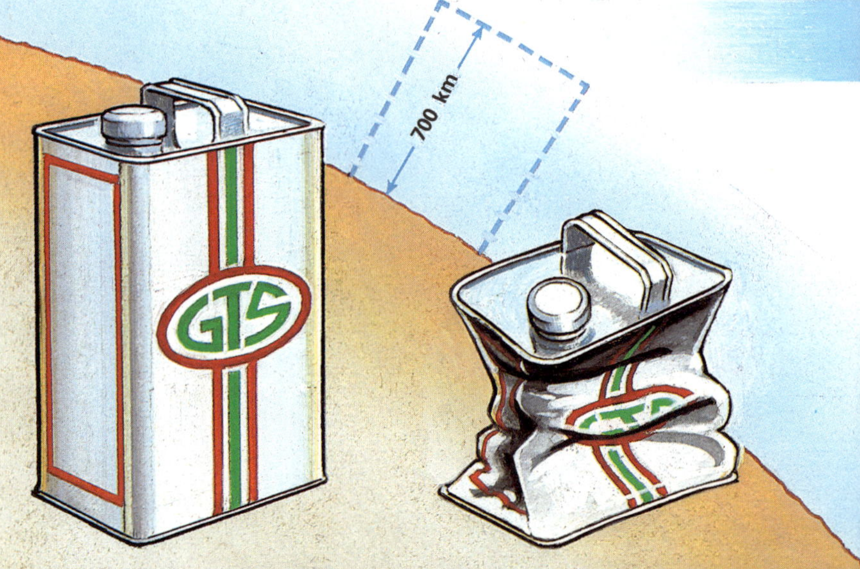

The atmosphere is a thin layer of air that surrounds the Earth. Although we cannot see it, the air has weight. In fact, at this moment, a column of air weighing about a tonne is pressing down on your shoulders. But you cannot feel this pressure, because there is an equal pressure inside your body. The air inside a metal can weighs about the same as a tablet you might take for a headache. If you pump this air out of the can, creating a vacuum inside it, then the air pressure is powerful enough to crumple the can.

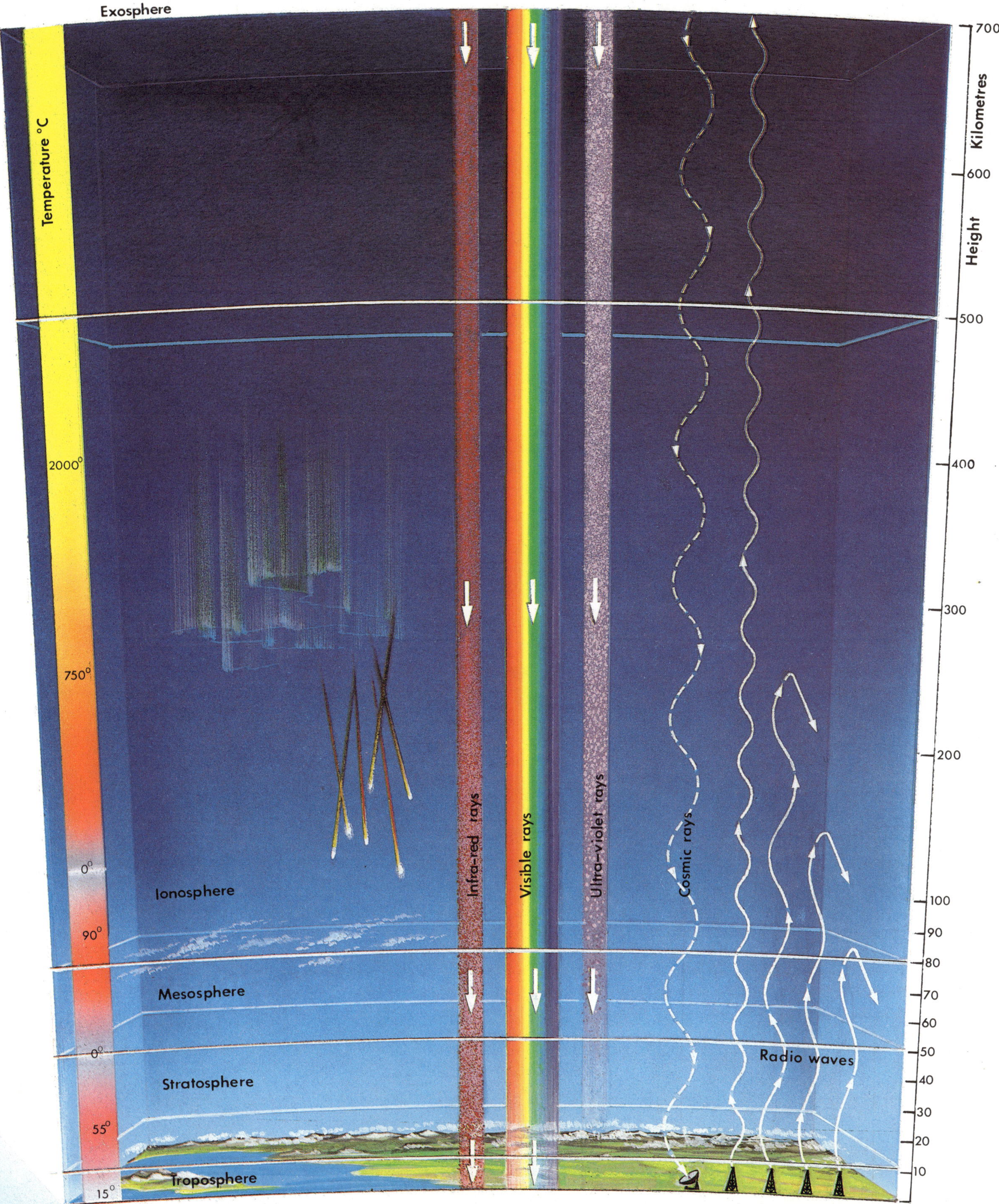
Exosphere
Temperature °C
2000°
750°
0°
90°
0°
55°
15°
Ionosphere
Mesosphere
Stratosphere
Troposphere
Infra-red rays
Visible rays
Ultra-violet rays
Cosmic rays
Radio waves
Height Kilometres
700
600
500
400
300
200
100
90
80
70
60
50
40
30
20
10

Cloud, Wind and Rain

Air is always moving because of the Sun's heat. At the equator, hot air rises. This creates a zone of low air pressure at the surface, called the *doldrums*. The rising air eventually cools and spreads out north and south. It finally sinks back to the Earth at around latitude 30° North and 30° South. These are the *horse latitudes*. Regions where air is sinking are high air pressure zones. From the horse latitudes, trade winds blow towards the equator and westerly winds blow towards the poles. From the poles — also high air pressure regions — come the polar easterlies. The trade winds, westerlies and polar easterlies are the prevailing (chief) winds of their various regions.

The Sun evaporates water from the oceans. Warm air can hold more water vapour than cold air. But when warm air rises and cools, it finally reaches *dew point*, when the air contains all the vapour it can at that temperature. More cooling makes water vapour *condense* (liquefy) into water droplets or ice crystals, which form clouds. In clouds, water droplets collide to become raindrops. The ice crystals also grow in size. They fall as snow or, in warm air, as raindrops.

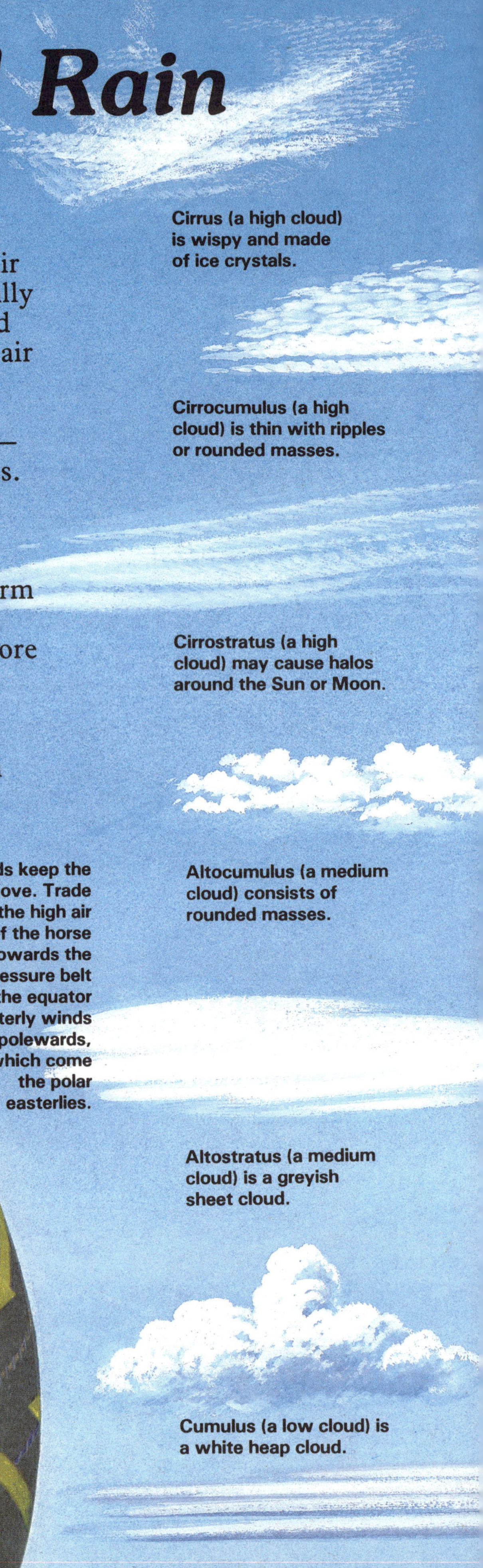

Cirrus (a high cloud) is wispy and made of ice crystals.

Cirrocumulus (a high cloud) is thin with ripples or rounded masses.

Cirrostratus (a high cloud) may cause halos around the Sun or Moon.

Altocumulus (a medium cloud) consists of rounded masses.

Altostratus (a medium cloud) is a greyish sheet cloud.

Cumulus (a low cloud) is a white heap cloud.

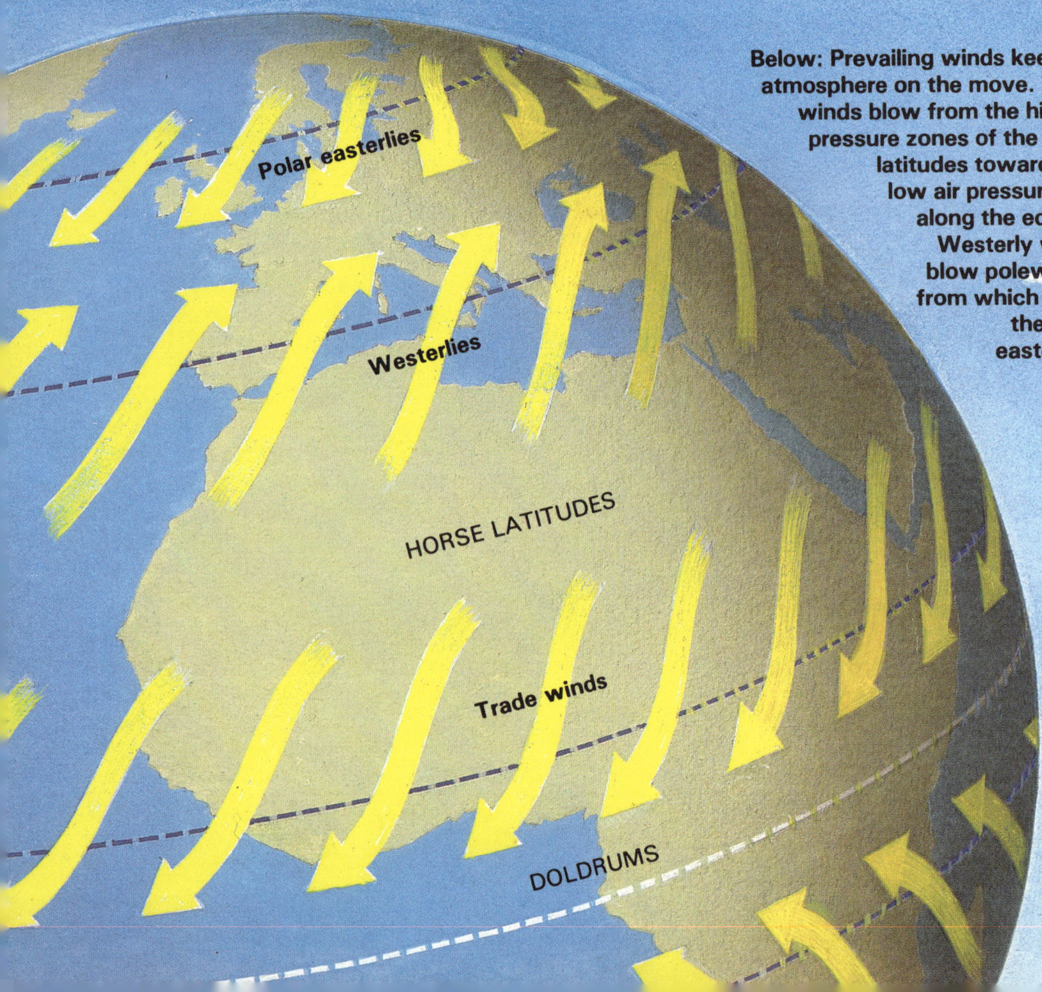

Below: Prevailing winds keep the atmosphere on the move. Trade winds blow from the high air pressure zones of the horse latitudes towards the low air pressure belt along the equator Westerly winds blow polewards, from which come the polar easterlies.

Polar easterlies

Westerlies

HORSE LATITUDES

Trade winds

DOLDRUMS

(1) Orographic rain occurs when winds blow over mountains. The rising air cools, clouds form and rain falls on the windward slopes. Beyond the mountain tops, the air descends and gets warmer, drying the land. This is a rain shadow region.

(2) Convectional rain occurs when the Sun heats the Earth's surface which, in turn, heats the air near the ground. The warm air rises in fast currents. Eventually, the rising air cools, clouds form and rain starts to fall.

(3) Cyclonic rain occurs in depressions (or cyclones) when warm air rises above blocks of cold air.

Cumulonimbus (thundercloud) may extend from 300 to 12,000 metres.

Stratus (a low cloud) is a grey layer cloud.

Storm and Tempest

About 45,000 thunderstorms occur every day around the world. They form when warm air rises rapidly, creating towering cumulonimbus clouds.

Some thunderstorms occur along cold fronts in the depressions that bring stormy weather to temperate regions. Others occur in tropical areas. Here, the Sun heats the surface in the morning and strong currents of air sweep water vapour upwards. Huge cumulonimbus clouds with anvil-shaped tops form and raindrops start to fall in the late afternoon. Following a storm, the sky clears in the early evening.

Less common, but more dangerous, storms are hurricanes, which occur north and south of the doldrums. Hurricanes have caused millions of dollars' worth of damage in the south-eastern USA. The USA is also hit by whirlwinds, or tornadoes. A tornado in 1925 killed 689 people in the south-central USA in three hours.

HURRICANES

Because of their size and high wind speeds, which reach 300 km/h, hurricanes are the most destructive storms. They form over the oceans a little way north and south of the equator. They are also called tropical cyclones, typhoons or willy-willies.

When these storms approach land, they cause floods. About 11 strike the coasts of North America every year. They are tracked by the Hurricane Warning Service at Miami, Florida. The meteorologists use satellite photographs and reports from ships and aircraft in order to discover in which direction and at what speed the hurricanes are moving.

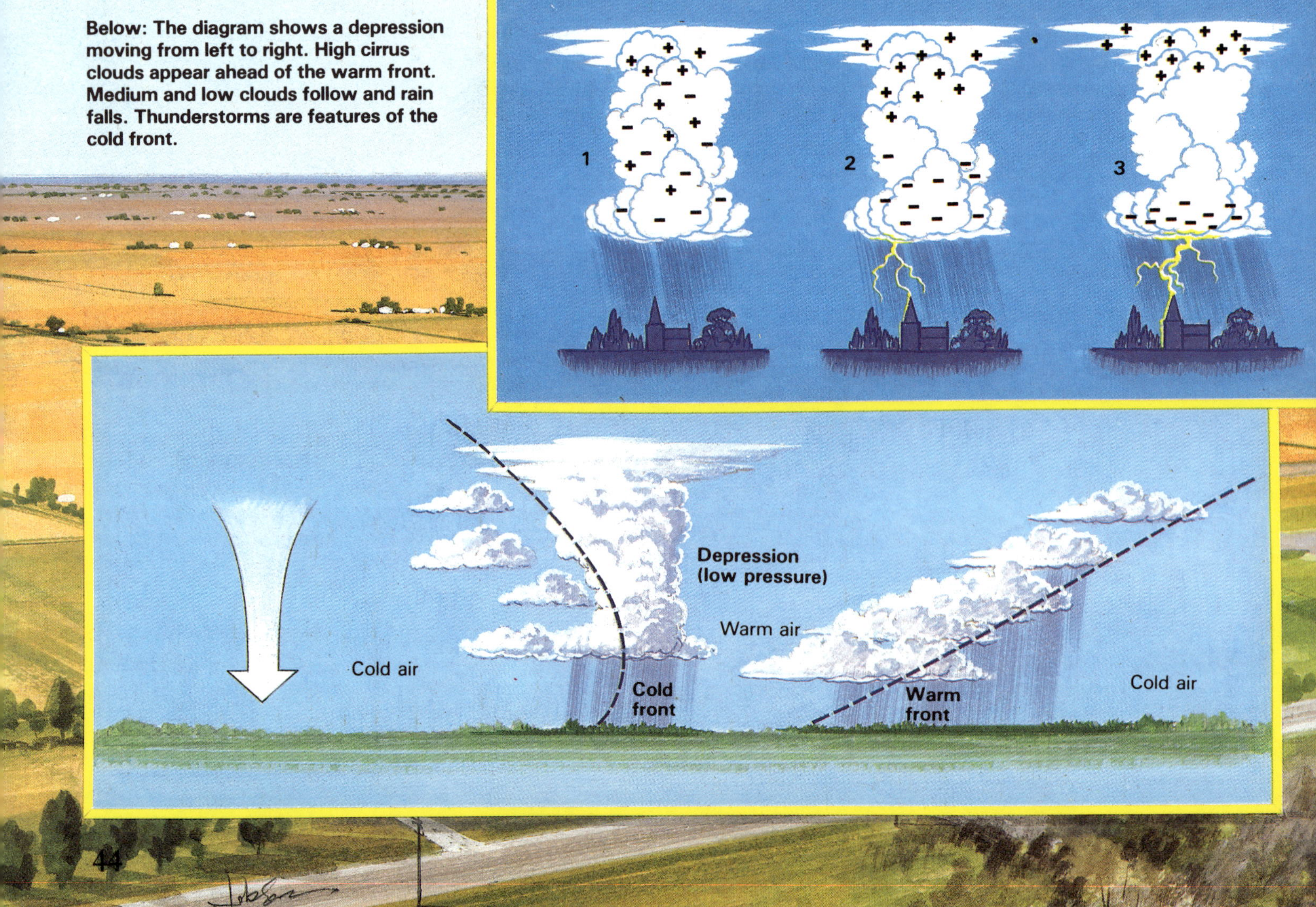

Below: The diagram shows a depression moving from left to right. High cirrus clouds appear ahead of the warm front. Medium and low clouds follow and rain falls. Thunderstorms are features of the cold front.

Right: Tornadoes are small but destructive storms. About 500 to 600 hit the mid-western USA every year. They form when a funnel-like column of air sinks down from a thundercloud. Warm air rises and swirls around this column. At ground level, tornadoes are only about 0.4 km across. But wind speeds may reach 650 km/h and people may be lifted into the air.

Left: Lightning occurs in cumulonimbus clouds, because positive electrical charges build up in the tops of clouds and negative charges at the bottom (1). When the charges have separated, the electricity is often discharged in a probe stroke (2) and a bright return flash (3). Lightning also leaps from the base of clouds to the positively charged ground. Thunder is caused by the intense heat along the channel followed by the lightning. We see lightning before we hear thunder, because light reaches us faster than sound.

Tomorrow's Weather

Ships' navigators and airline pilots depend for their safety on weather forecasts, while farmers need them so that they can protect their crops. Also millions of ordinary people plan tomorrow's activities only after they have checked the local weather forecast.

Weather Stations
Meteorologists at weather stations on land and at sea collect information about the weather every few hours. They use thermometers to measure temperatures, barometers to measure the air pressure and hygrometers to measure the humidity (moistness) of the air. They also record wind speeds and directions, rainfall amounts, hours of sunshine, cloud types and the visibility. Radiosondes send back readings of the temperature, pressure and humidity at various levels in the upper air (see the diagram on the facing page).

Weather satellites provide pictures of the cloud patterns on Earth, while radar networks show areas where rain or snow is falling. All the information obtained at weather stations is sent, in code, to weather forecasting centres.

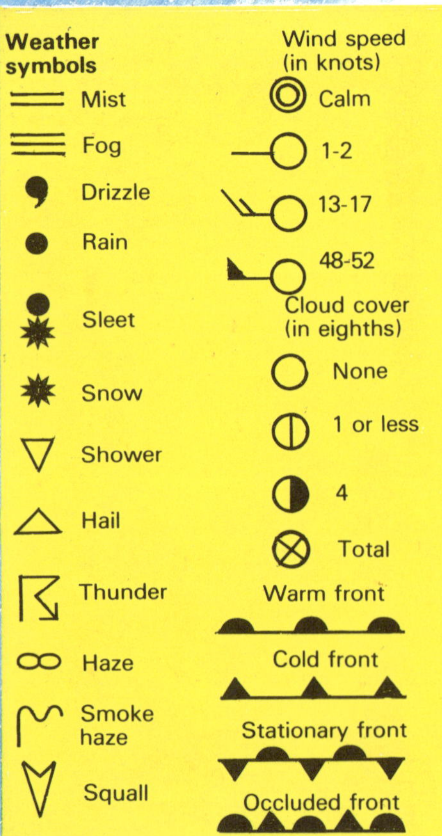

Preparing Weather Forecasts

At weather centres, the information from many weather stations is fed into a computer. The computer produces weather charts which show weather conditions at various levels of the atmosphere. These charts cover extremely large areas. Meteorologists study these charts and find out how the weather has been changing in recent hours. This gives them a good idea of how the weather will change over the next 12 to 24 hours. They summarize their ideas on *prognostic* (forecast) charts. Written forecasts for particular areas are then prepared from the charts. These are sent to newspapers and radio and television stations.

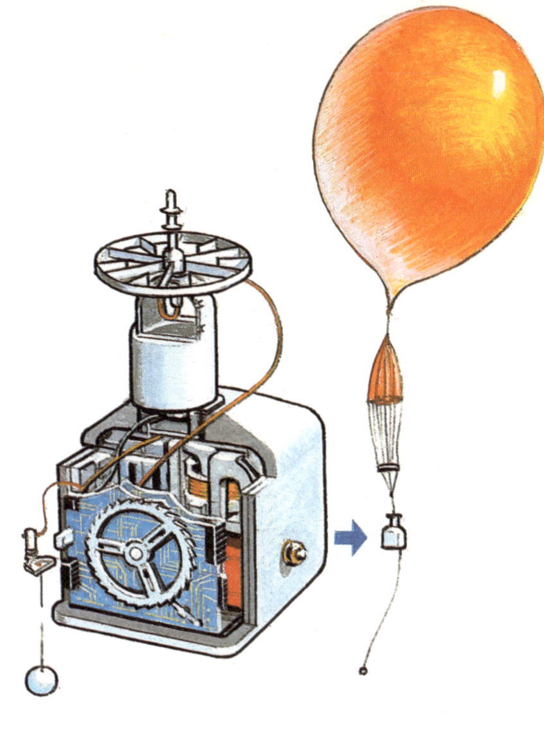

Opposite: Weather satellites circle the Earth taking regular photographs of the changing cloud patterns and collecting information about the upper air.

Below: Weather charts, like topographic maps, use many symbols which indicate weather conditions at various places. The numbered lines, resembling contours, are isobars. Isobars join places with the same air pressure. The fronts are zones of unsettled weather.

Right: Instruments used to measure weather conditions. Radiosondes (top) consist of balloons with automatic instruments and a radio transmitter attached to them. The transmitter sends back readings from the upper air. In mercury barometers (centre) the greater the 'weight' of air, the higher the mercury is pushed up the tube. The aneroid barometer (bottom) is a metal box, which expands and contracts as the air pressure changes. This makes a pointer move.

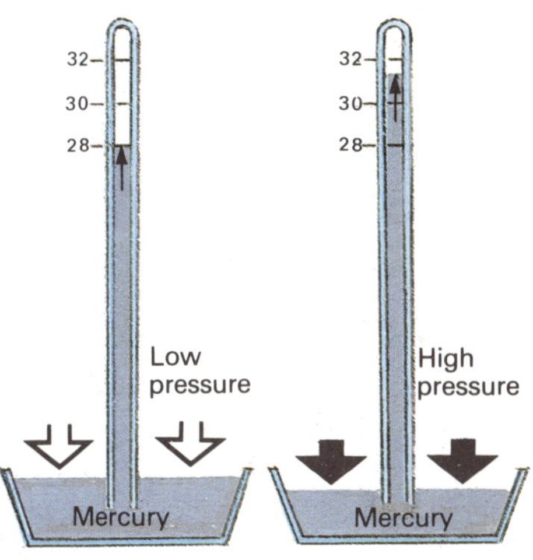

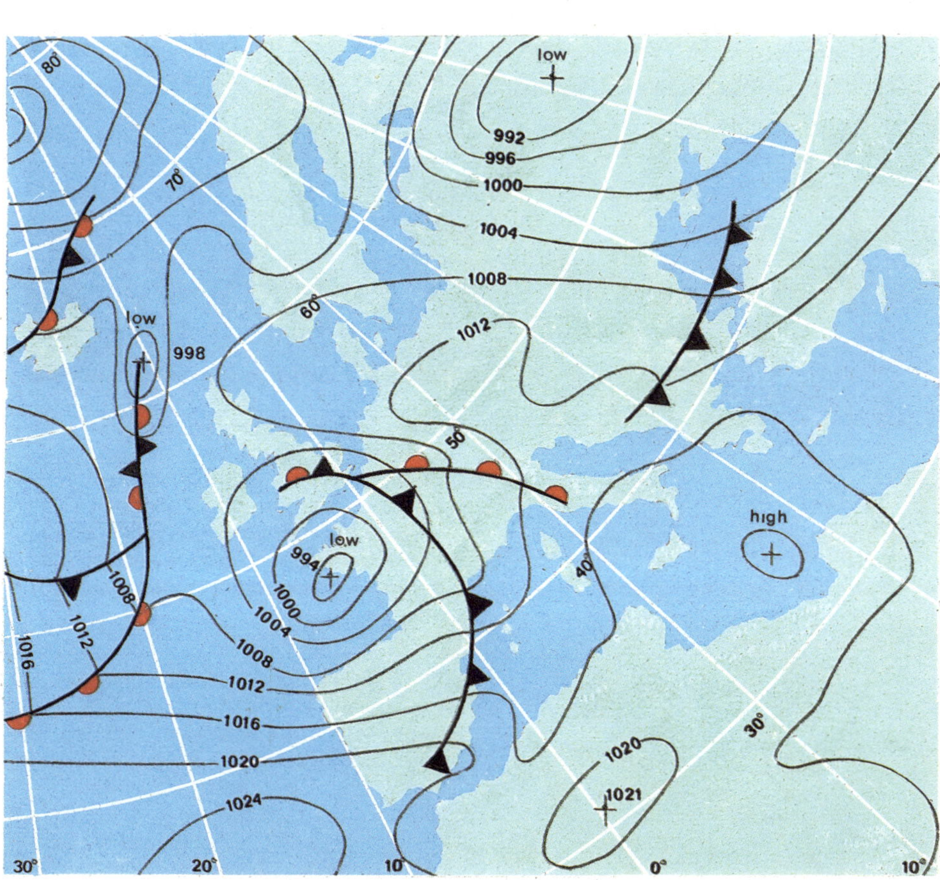

Climates of the World

The climate is the average, or usual, weather of a place. Climates vary between the poles and the equator.

Climatic Regions

There are six main climatic regions. *Polar climates* are regions where the average temperature in the warmest month is less than 10°C. This is the climate of the frozen wastes around the poles and also the tundra, where the snow melts in summer.

Cold (coniferous) *forest* climates occur in a zone that stretches across North America and Eurasia. The average temperature in the coldest month is less than -3°C. But in the warmest month, the average temperature is above 10°C.

Temperate climates have an average temperature in the coldest month of not less than −3°C, but not more than 18°C. This climate includes mixed forest, deciduous forest and Mediterranean regions.

In *dry climates*, the total average yearly rainfall is less than 250 mm. Deserts may be hot or cold.

Tropical rainy climates have average temperatures in every month that are higher than 18°C. Some places have rain throughout the year. Others have one or two marked dry seasons.

Mountain climates vary as one climbs upwards, because temperatures fall with height. Some mountains on the equator have tropical climates at the bottom and polar climates at their snow-capped tops.

Above: Dense rain forests flourish in tropical rainy climates, where high temperatures and abundant rainfall encourage plant growth. The thickest forests are in regions which have rain throughout the year. Less dense forests grow in monsoon regions which have a marked dry season.

Left: In hot deserts, the only places with water are oases. Many oases are springs or wells which get water from the rocks below. Palm trees grow around them and camels can get much-needed water.

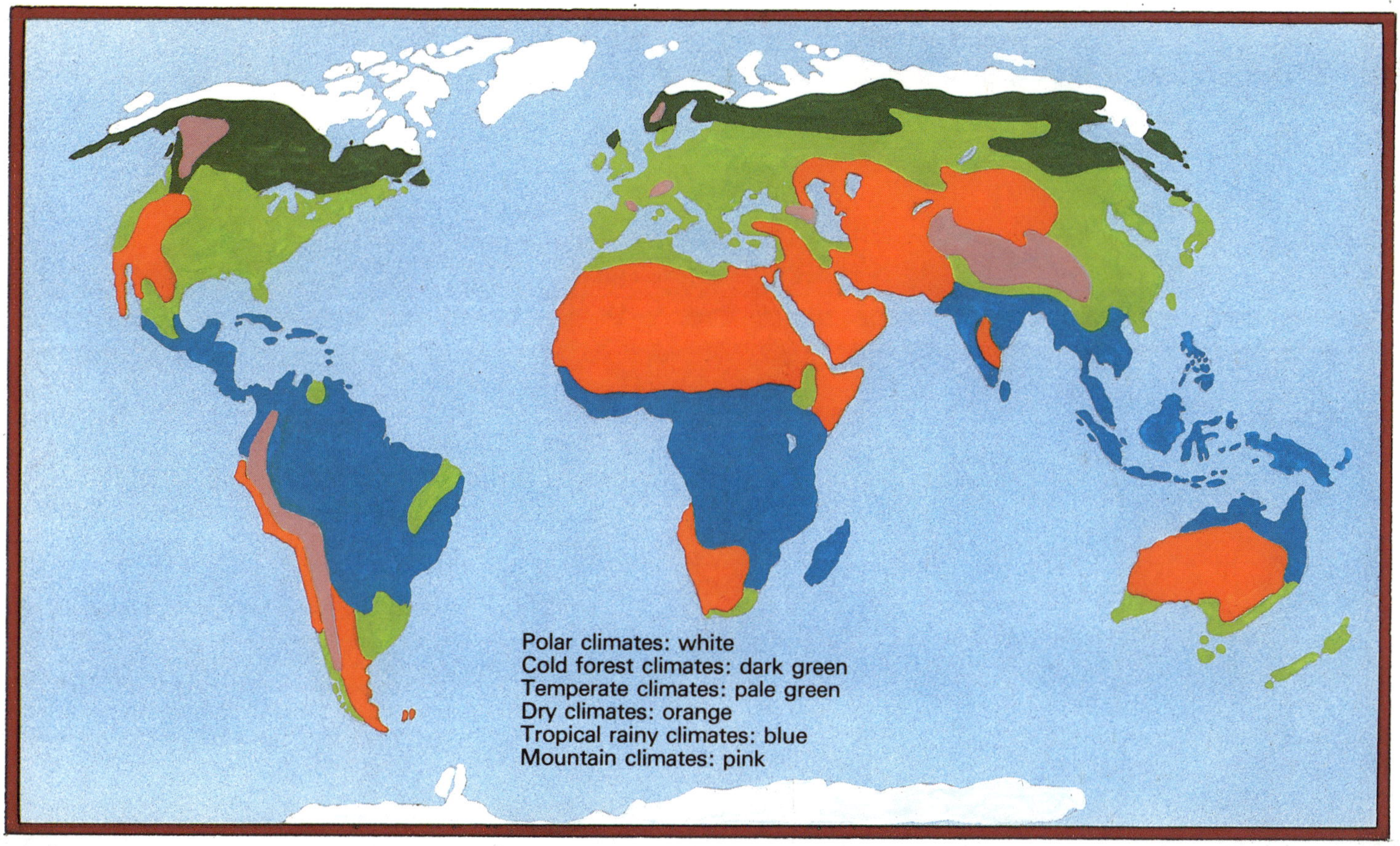

Polar climates: white
Cold forest climates: dark green
Temperate climates: pale green
Dry climates: orange
Tropical rainy climates: blue
Mountain climates: pink

Above: Vast coniferous forests, called taiga, grow in the northern hemisphere in the cold region between the temperate lands to the south and the tree-line, the northernmost limit of tree growth. Birds such as this capercaillie are quite common, though compared with other forests there are few plant and animal species.

Above: The temperate regions of the world were once covered by deciduous trees, which shed their leaves in winter. But most of the trees have now been cut down and replaced by farmland.

Top: The map shows the major climatic regions of the world.

Above: Around the poles, ice and snow blanket the land all the year round. But in the northern hemisphere, between the lands of permanent ice and the tree-line, is a zone called the tundra. This zone comes alive during the short, warm summer when the snow melts. Animal migrants such as musk-oxen and reindeer graze on the tundra. And the arctic fox's white coat turns red during the short summer months.

The Sea in Motion

The oceans cover about 71 per cent of the Earth's surface. Ocean water is always moving, even in the deepest trenches. We know this because fishes live there. If the water was still, the oxygen dissolved in the water would have been used up long ago.

Above: When a wave passes through water, the particles of water rotate in a circular motion, but they are not moved sideways. The wave length is the distance between the crests of two successive waves. Along coasts, there is not enough water to complete the wave and so the wave breaks.

Winds and Waves

Waves appear to move seawater. In fact, they make water particles rotate, but do not move them forwards. Most waves are caused by winds. Tsunamis are waves generated by earthquakes. These low but fast-moving waves often pass unnoticed in the open sea. But near land, they build up to great heights. A tsunami off Japan reached a height of 85 metres.

High Tide, Low Tide

Tides are caused by the gravitational pull of the Moon and, to a lesser extent, of the Sun. They occur twice every 24 hours and 50 minutes. This is the time taken by the Moon to complete one orbit of the Earth.

Ships caught at sea during a bad storm run the risk of capsizing. The highest waves in the open sea are caused by strong winds. The highest recorded wave measured 34 metres between the trough and the crest.

Rivers in the Sea

Sailors are interested in ocean currents, because they affect navigation. These currents, which are caused mainly by prevailing winds, only affect the top 350 metres. Other currents lower down often move in an opposite direction to those on the surface. Many deep-sea currents are caused by variations in the density of the water. These result from differences in salinity (saltness) and temperature. Salty, cold water is denser (heavier) than less salty, warm water.

The circulation of ocean water by currents has an important effect on climate. Warm currents convey heat to cool temperate and polar regions. Cold currents also modify the climate of tropical regions.

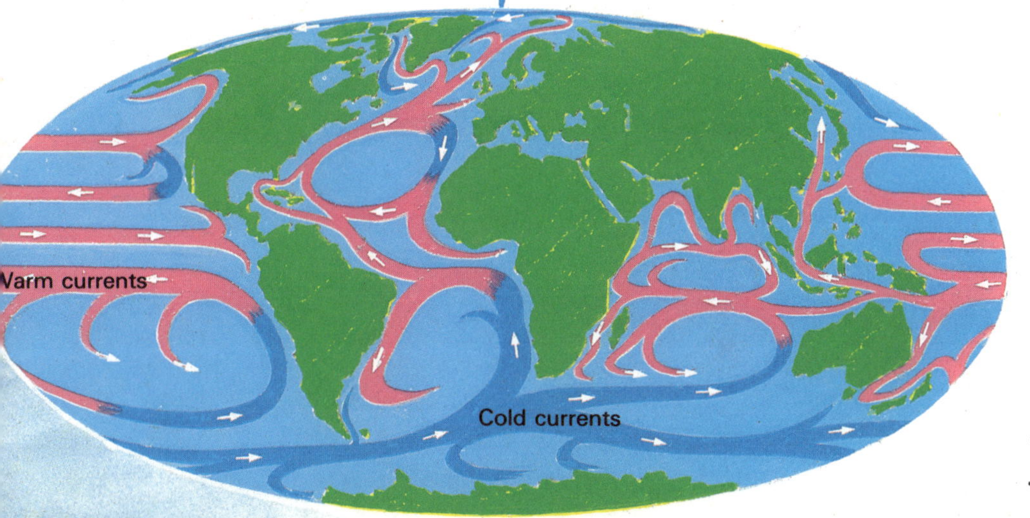

OCEAN CURRENTS

Ocean currents ensure that seawater is always on the move. The currents on the map (left) are caused mainly by winds. Ocean currents flow at 1-5 knots and so are important in navigation. Slower currents are called drifts. The slow northern extension of the fast Gulf Stream is the North Altantic Drift.

Other currents flow at lower levels. For example, warm currents flow towards the polar regions. There, denser (heavier) cold polar water sinks beneath the warm water and flows towards the equator.

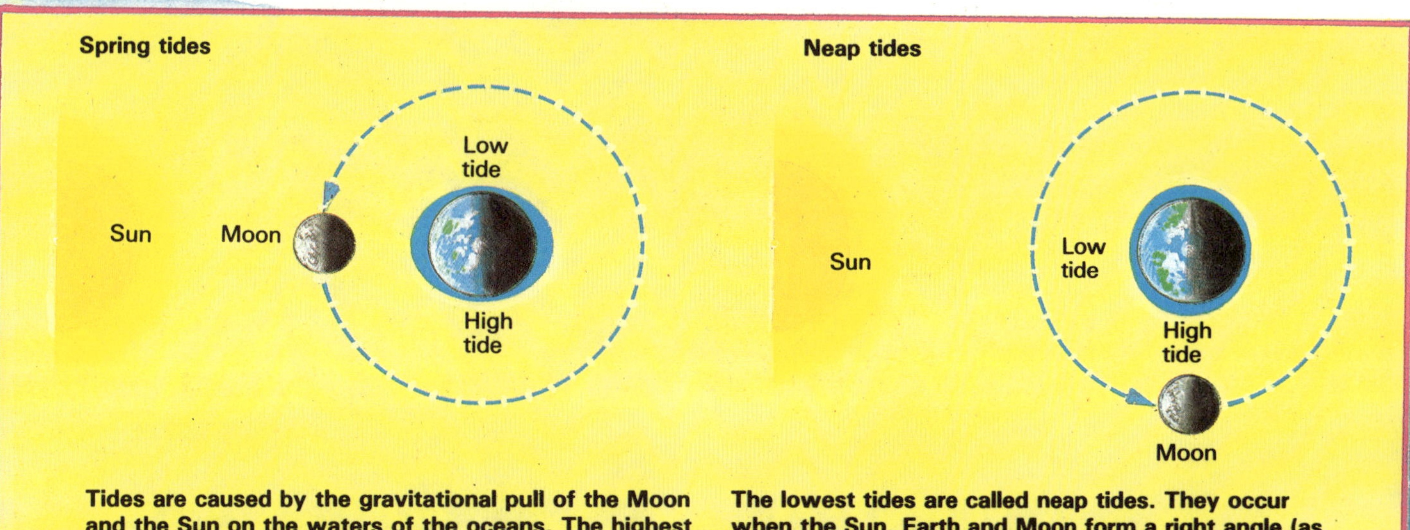

Tides are caused by the gravitational pull of the Moon and the Sun on the waters of the oceans. The highest tides are called spring tides. They occur when the Sun, Moon and Earth are in a straight line (above). The Moon's and the Sun's gravity are then combined.

The lowest tides are called neap tides. They occur when the Sun, Earth and Moon form a right angle (as shown above). The gravitational pull of the Moon is then opposed by the Sun's gravitational pull. Neap and spring tides each occur twice every month.

The Ocean Deeps

There are four oceans. The largest is the Pacific Ocean which covers about 165,724,000 km^2. This is about one third of the Earth's surface. The other oceans, in order of size, are the Atlantic, Indian and Arctic oceans.

Continental Shelves

Around land masses are gently sloping areas covered by shallow seas. These areas are called continental shelves. In places, such as western South America, the continental shelf is narrow. But off Land's End, England, the continental shelf extends 320 kilometres to the west. Continental shelves are flooded parts of the continents. They end at the steep continental slopes which plunge down to the abyss, the deep part of the ocean. The tops of the continental slopes are the true edges of the continents.

Left: If Mount Everest were placed in the deepest ocean trench, its peak would be about 2100 metres below sea-level. The diagram also shows the depths reached by various manned submersibles.

The Abyss

The abyss was once thought to be a mostly flat plain covered by oozes. But mapping has shown that it contains several striking features.

The ocean trenches are the deepest parts of the oceans. The Mariana Trench reaches a depth of 11,033 metres. The trenches are places where one plate is descending under another. As it descends, it melts (see pages 16-17). As a result, volcanic islands are found alongside the trenches. They get magma from the melting plates.

The ocean ridges are huge, long mountain ranges. Here, plates are moving apart and new crustal rock is being formed. Some volcanoes rise from the ocean ridges. Other volcanoes develop above isolated 'hot spots' in the Earth's mantle. Some volcanoes reach the surface as islands.

The largest ocean, the Pacific, is larger than all the continents combined. This view of the Pacific is called the water hemisphere.

Below: The diagram shows the main features of the oceans: the shallow continental shelves; the steep continental slopes; ocean trenches; volcanic mountains and islands; and long oceanic ridges.

Industry

Industry Around the World
In the last 200 years, the economies of many countries have changed, as farming and small-scale craft industries have become less important than mining and large-scale factory production. Such countries have been *industrialized.* The Industrial Revolution began in Britain in the late 18th century and Belgium, France, Germany and the USA soon followed. In the late 19th century, other countries, such as Canada, Japan, Russia and Sweden also began to industrialize.

The Pattern of Industry
The industrialized world now includes most of North America, Europe, the USSR, Japan, Australia and New Zealand. But most of Central and South America, Africa and Asia have not been industrialized, although some countries, such as Brazil and China, already have sizeable industries which are expected to expand rapidly in the near future. Many poor countries would like to industrialize, but they lack the money and skilled workers needed to found industries.

Light and Heavy Industry
Light industry produces a wide range of goods, which are generally smaller than those produced by heavy industry. For example, the many consumer products which we find in supermarkets, including clothes, foods and household goods, are produced by light industries. Light industries are now changing because of the introduction of computers and automation.

Heavy industry is associated with huge factories, which use bulky raw materials to produce heavy products. Examples include the iron and steel industry, the chemical industry and heavy engineering, such as shipbuilding. Heavy industries were once located on coal- or iron-fields, because this reduced the cost of transporting these heavy raw materials. But many industries which use oil have spread to other areas in recent years. This is because oil is easily transported through pipelines.

Some industries are neither light nor heavy. For example, car assembly and aerospace industries combine elements from both.

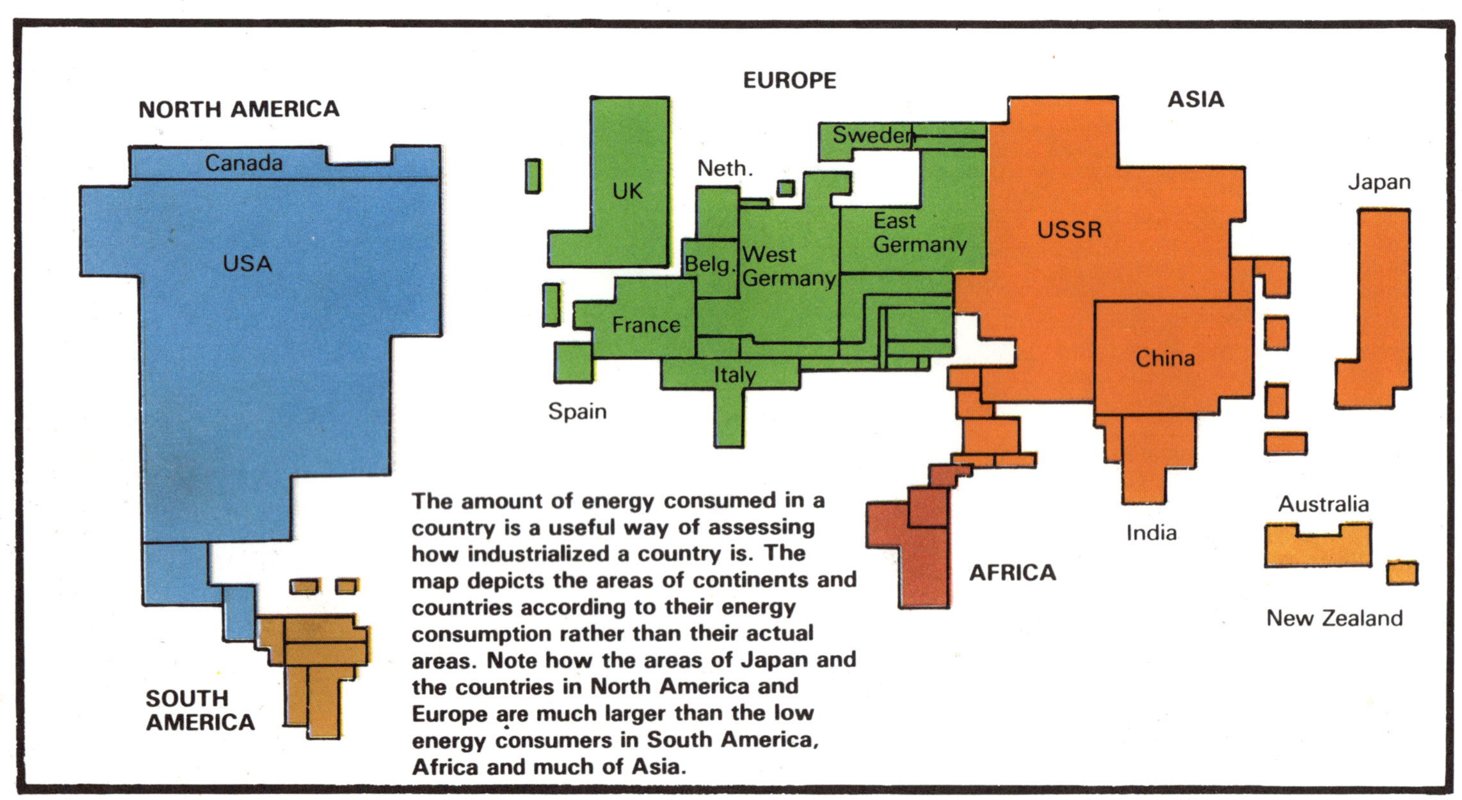

The amount of energy consumed in a country is a useful way of assessing how industrialized a country is. The map depicts the areas of continents and countries according to their energy consumption rather than their actual areas. Note how the areas of Japan and the countries in North America and Europe are much larger than the low energy consumers in South America, Africa and much of Asia.

Steel is the most important material used in shipbuilding, one of the world's leading heavy industries. In recent years, shipbuilders have made larger ships, including vast oil tankers, which can carry large amounts of bulk freight. Europe was once the main centre of shipbuilding. But by the early 1980s, Japan led the world, producing 48% of the world's merchant vessels, with North Korea accounting for another 9%. Following these two Asian countries were West Germany, Spain, Britain and Brazil.

Energy and Power

Manufacturing industry depends on a supply of cheap electrical energy. And we all take for granted that we can heat and light our homes at the turn of a switch. Energy is produced in several ways.

Fossil Fuels

Most of the world's energy is produced by oil, natural gas and coal. These fossil fuels are made of the remains of once-living plants and animals.

Oil and gas often collect, as shown in the diagram below, in upfolds of porous rocks, through which gases and liquids can flow. Above and below are impervious rocks which block the flow of gas and liquids. The gas and oil collect at the top of the upfold. Beneath the oil, the porous rock is often filled with water.

Coal is generally more expensive to mine and, by weight, it gives out less heat than oil and gas. But it is valuable in industry and coal production has remained roughly the same over the last 30 years.

Fossil fuels are being used up at a faster rate than they are being renewed naturally. As a result, they will eventually run out. Scientists are, therefore, looking for other ways of producing energy.

Petroleum is fairly easy to extract and to transport through pipelines. Below: Oil is often trapped in anticlines (upfolds) of porous rock layers.

ENERGY PRODUCTION

COAL Leading coal producers in 1981 were: USA (25.4% of world output); China (21.9%), the USSR (18.6%), Poland (5.9%), South Africa (4.8%) and the UK (4.6%).
OIL Leading producers in 1983 were: USSR (22.4%), USA (17.7%), Saudi Arabia (8.9%), Mexico (5.4%), Iran (4.5%) and the UK (4.1%).
NATURAL GAS Major producers in 1981 were the USA (29.9%), USSR (23.2%), Canada (3.9%), the Netherlands (3.8%), and the UK (2.1%).
HYDROELECTRICITY 99% of Norway's electricity supply comes from hydroelectric stations, 92% in Brazil and 70% in Canada.
NUCLEAR POWER stations supply 40% of France's electricity, 37% of Sweden's and 36% of Finland's.

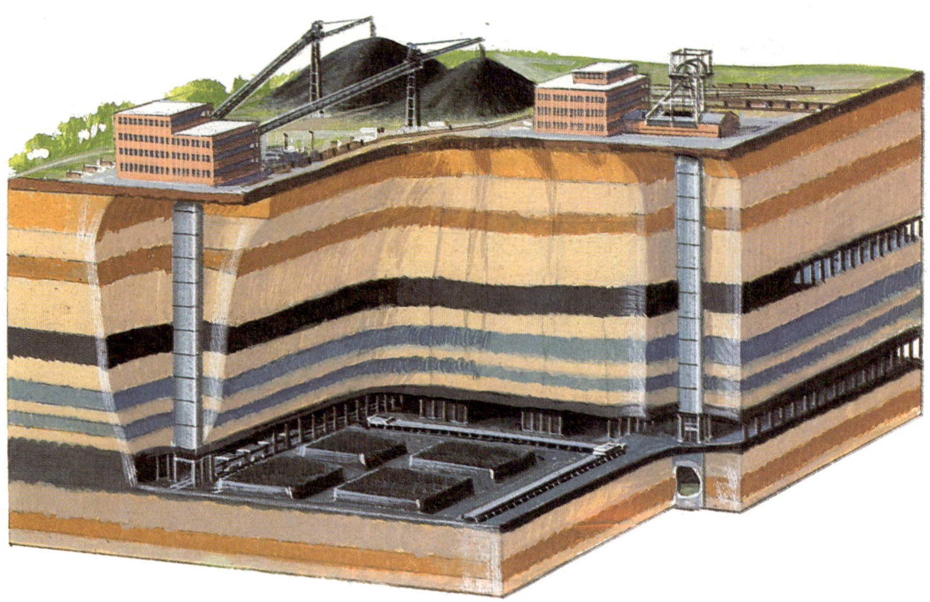

Above: The diagram shows an underground coal mine. Shafts are used to ventilate the mine and also to extract stale air. The coal is cut with modern machines. It is then transported to the upcast shaft where it is raised to the surface.

Other Sources of Energy

Some electrical energy comes from hydroelectric power stations. The cost of building dams and generating stations is high, but production costs are low and it does not cause pollution. Nuclear, or atomic, energy is also important, but some people are worried about the dangers involved in getting rid of nuclear wastes.

Other methods include improved windmills and solar power stations which use concentrated sunlight to heat water. In some areas, water from hot springs and geysers is used. Water can be heated by pumping it far into the ground. If this water was pumped back to the surface, it could be used to run generators.

Below: The chart shows the sources of world energy consumption. Oil is the chief fossil fuel, followed by coal and natural gas.

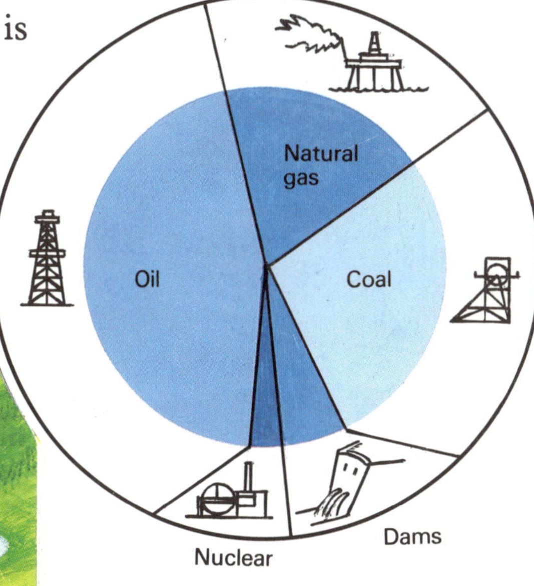

Left: In wet countries with plenty of steep slopes, such as Norway, rivers are dammed. The water in the man-made reservoirs is used to turn turbines which drive the generators that produce electric power for homes and factories.

Forestry

Wood is a valuable product. It is used in building, for furniture and in making paper. It also has many less obvious uses, as in the manufacture of such things as explosives, manmade fibres and medicines.

Forests cover about one-third of the world's surface. The *coniferous* (evergreen) *forests* are most widespread in the northern hemisphere. They contain cedars, firs, pines and spruces that are adapted to survive long, cold winters. These commercially valuable trees are also called *softwoods*, because most, though not all, species are easy to saw. The leading softwood producers are the USSR, the USA and Canada.

Temperate hardwood forests contain such deciduous trees as ash, beech, chestnut, elm, hickory, oak and willow,

In North America, northern Europe and the USSR, forestry is highly mechanized. Lumberjacks fell trees with powersaws and felling machines. Many of the trunks are transported from the logging camps to rivers, where they are floated downstream to a sawmill. Some heavy hardwoods will not float. They must be transported by road or rail.

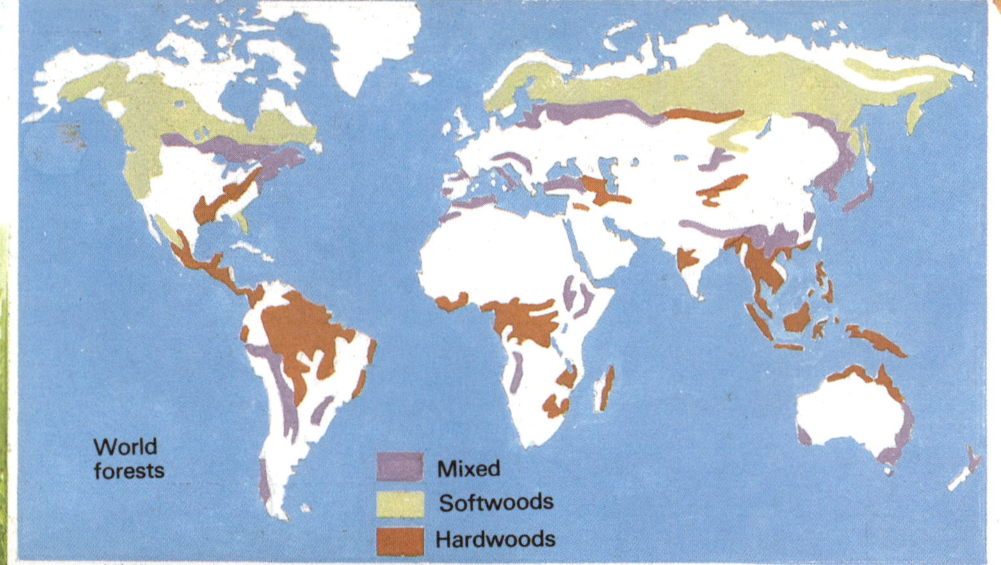

Above: The most valuable tropical hardwoods are usually scattered throughout the dense forests. This makes their extraction difficult. In southern Asia elephants are often used to drag the tree trunks through the forest to rivers or loading sites.

Left: The map shows that the world's main softwood forests are in the northern hemisphere — in North America, Scandinavia and the USSR. In some areas, these forests merge southwards into mixed forests and, eventually, deciduous (hardwood) forests. The largest hardwood forests, however, are in the tropics, especially the Amazon basin, central Africa and South-East Asia.

which shed their leaves in autumn. A third type of forest is the *mixed forest* zone between the coniferous and hardwood forests. The fourth type of forest, the tropical hardwood forest, contains such trees as ebony, mahogany, rosewood and teak.

Foresters in the northern coniferous forests carefully replace the trees they cut down with young saplings grown from seed in tree nurseries. However, in recent years, acid rain has been killing many trees. Acid rain is formed when raindrops dissolve harmful gases emitted from factories and power stations.

The huge tropical hardwood forests are being destroyed even faster. In the early 1980s, an area of tropical forest the size of Scotland was being cut down every year. If this continues, there will be no tropical forest left in 40 years.

Farming Round the World

Some countries are densely populated, but have only a small area of flat farmland. They build terraces, like a series of steps, down hillsides. The walls around the terraces stop rainwater running downwards washing away the soil.

The world's chief farming nations are China, the USSR, the USA and India. But their farming industries differ greatly. In the USSR and the USA, farmers use modern machinery and yields are high. In China and India, much of the work is done by hand and yields are lower.

There are two main types of farming. Arable farming is the growing of crops. Pastoral farming is the production of meat and other animal products.

Tropical Farming

Many farmers in the tropics are poor, producing only enough food for their families. This is subsistence farming. Some farmers move every few years, whenever the fertility of their farms is exhausted. Nomadic pastoralists wander around with their animals. These simple forms of farming contrast with tropical plantation agriculture, which uses scientific methods to produce such cash crops as cocoa, coffee and tea.

THE INVENTION OF FARMING

Farming was invented about 10,000 years ago, when people learned how to plant seeds. The earliest known farms were in south-western Asia, but farming began soon afterwards in many other parts of the world. In a short time, most people gave up the old hunting and gathering way of life and settled down to become farmers. The farmers founded the first villages and towns.

In the Nile valley in Egypt, in the Tigris and Euphrates valleys in what is now Iraq, and in the Indus valley of Pakistan, people learned how to irrigate the valleys by moving water from the rivers to their fields. From about 5000 years ago, these valleys became centres of brilliant early civilizations.

Left: In developed countries, farm machinery has largely replaced workers and only a small proportion of the people work on farms.

WORKING ON FARMS

The farming industry in developed countries is highly mechanized and so it employs few people. Examples, with the percentages of people employed on farms, are as follows:

USA	2%	Britian	2%
Belgium	3%	West Germany	4%
Canada	5%	Australia	6%

By contrast, the farming industry is the chief employer in developing countries. For example:

Chad	85%	Tanzania	83%
Ethiopia	80%	Afghanistan	79%
India	71%	China	69%

Farming in Temperate Lands

Farms near cities in temperate countries produce fresh food for city-dwellers. These farms are called market gardens (truck farms in the USA). This is a type of intensive farming. Intensive farming is important in densely populated countries. By contrast, ranching is a kind of extensive farming. Extensive farms are usually on land which is unsuitable for intensive crop growing. Another type of farming is called mixed farming. Mixed farms produce crops and animal products.

Below: In developing countries, ancient farming methods survive. Here, an Archimedes screw is used to extract water from the River Nile to irrigate farmland.

Working Together

In some countries, groups of farmers choose to work together through co-operatives. Collective farms in many Communist countries are similar except that people were forced to join them. On collectives, farmers work together and share the produce. They do not receive wages like the workers on the USSR's *sovkhozy* (government-owned farms).

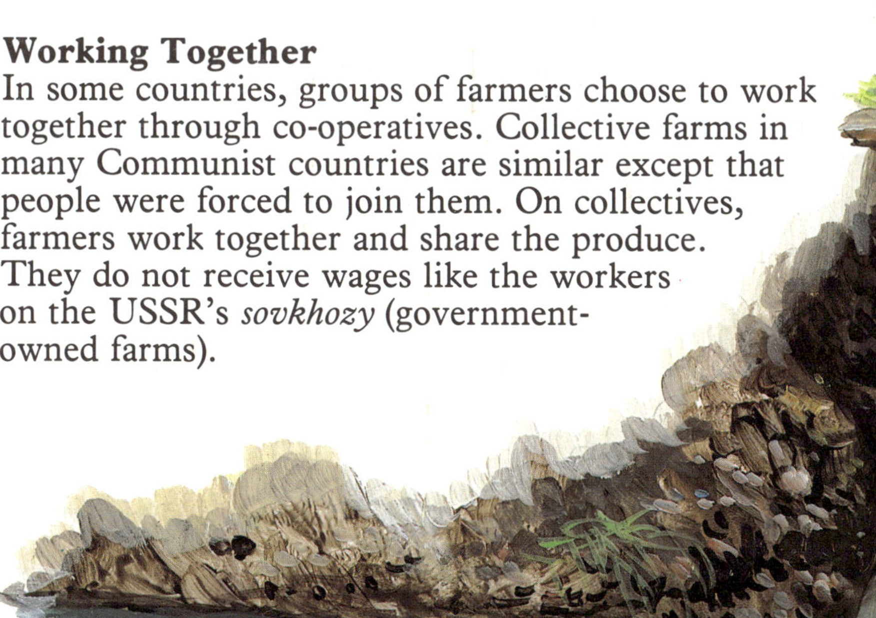

Harvest of the Sea

Fish is a valuable food. In some countries, including Japan and Norway, it makes up about one-tenth of people's diets. Freshwater fish form about one-tenth of the world's total catch of 75 million tonnes. The richest ocean fishing grounds are in the north-western Pacific Ocean and in the north-eastern Atlantic Ocean. More fish are caught in the shallow waters of the continental shelves than in the deep ocean waters.

Traditionally, fishermen were hunters, who were never sure of a good catch. Today, however, modern technology is aiding fishermen. For example, radar and sonic depth finders are used to locate shoals of fish.

The use of modern methods has led to overfishing in some areas. This has led to a search for new food products from the oceans. For example, krill, a shrimp-like creature, is found in great quantities in the waters around Antarctica. If ways can be found to package it attractively, it may become a food for people. It could also become a major animal food.

WHALING

Whaling is an ancient industry. The chief products are oil, meat for human and animal consumption, whale bones and ambergris, a waxy substance found in the intestines of some sperm whales, which is used to fix odours in expensive perfumes.

The chief whaling countries are Japan, the USSR, the Faroe Islands (Denmark) and Norway. About three-quarters of the catch is processed on large factory ships, which get their whales from small catcher boats equipped with harpoon guns.

Whaling has brought some whale species close to extinction. For example, the seas around Antarctica contained about 14,500 blue whales (the world's largest animal) in the 1930s. By 1968, there were only 600 left. Today, international treaties ban the hunting of many species.

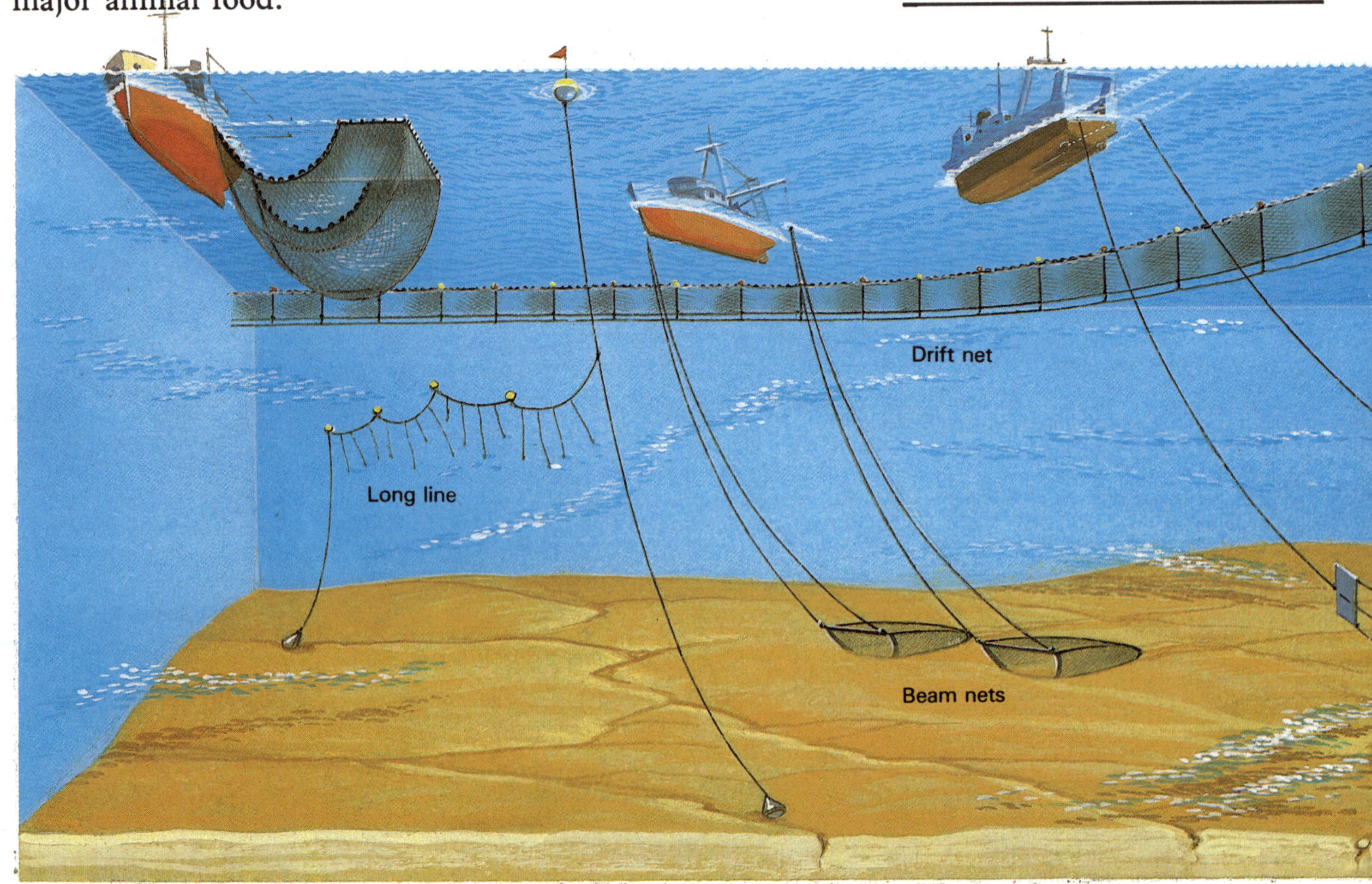

Fish Farming

Attempts are now being made to conserve fish and to develop fish farms. The breeding and raising of fish in tanks and ponds is called aquaculture. Carp have been raised in China for thousands of years, and oysters have been bred in Europe since Roman times.

Today, many species of freshwater fish, including carp, eels and trout are successfully raised. And young salmon are reared in fresh water and later moved to salt water. This mimics the conditions experienced by wild salmon which migrate from rivers to the oceans. The farming of saltwater fish is generally less economic, but overfishing in the oceans is making scientists study saltwater fish farming.

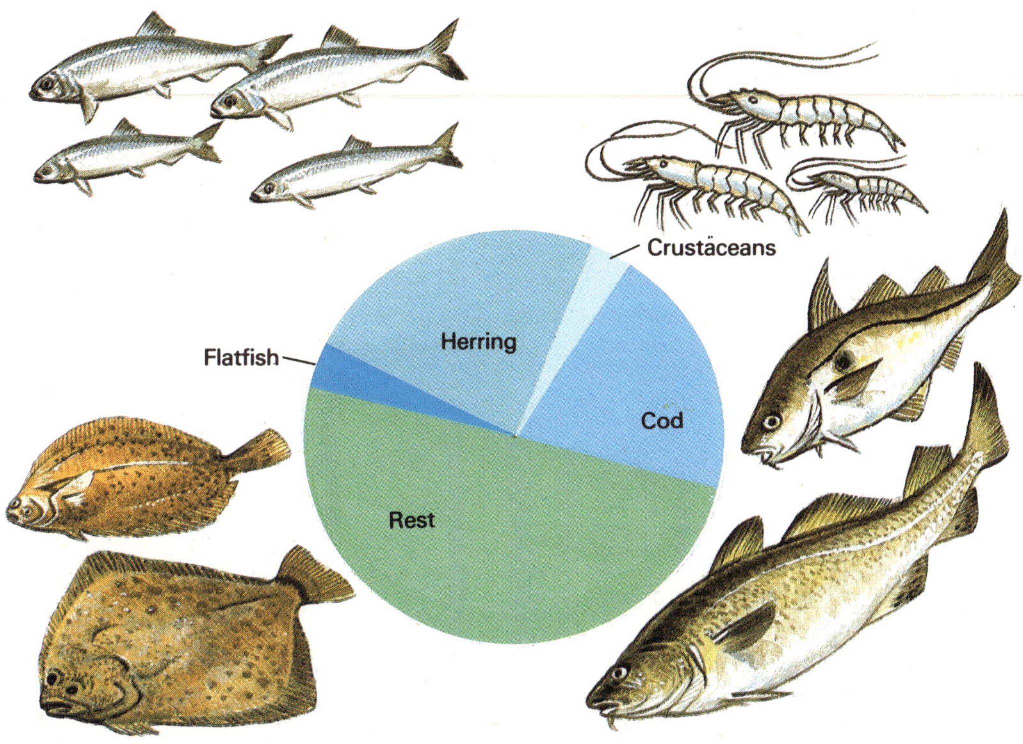

Above: The diagram shows the proportions of various fishes and crustaceans caught around the world. The chief fishing nation is Japan. It accounts for about one-seventh of the world's total catch.

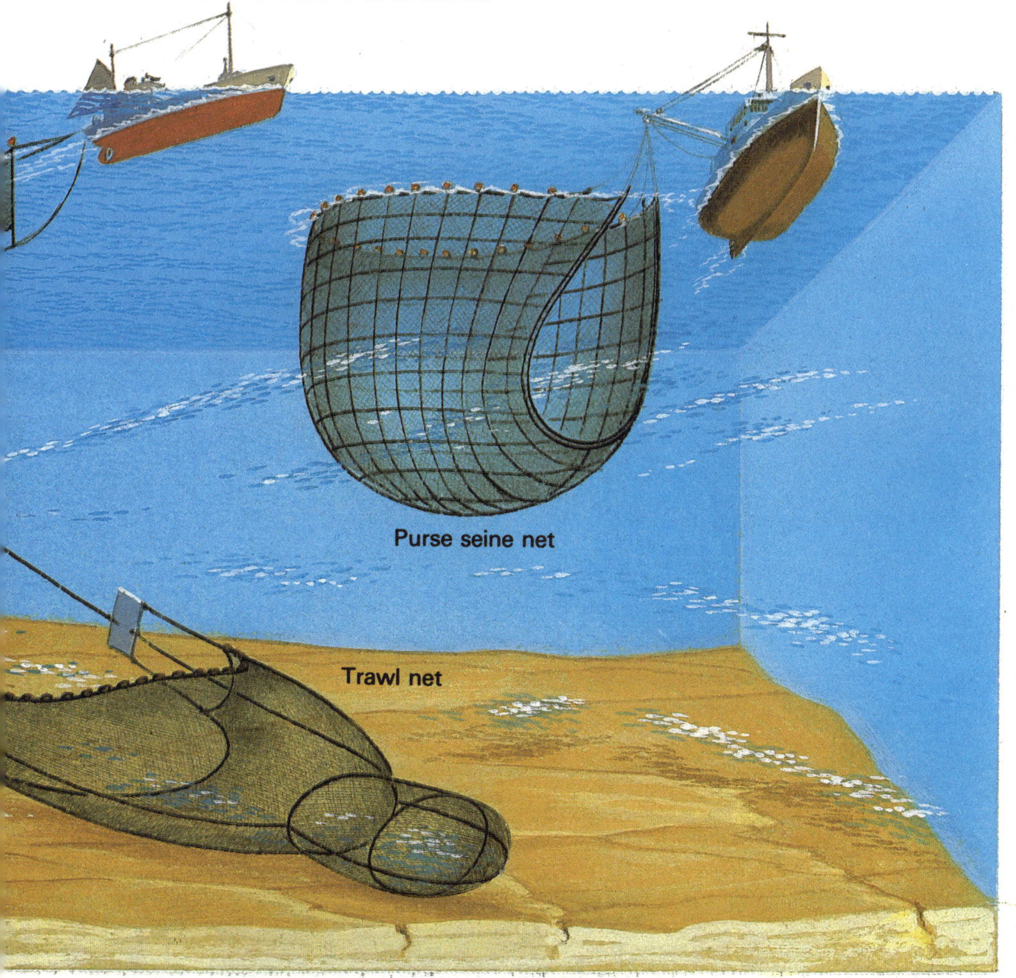

Left: The diagram shows various techniques used in the fishing industry. Long-lining involves putting out long, or ground, lines. Attached to them are short lines with baited hooks. This technique is used to catch tuna.

Drift or gill nets are held up by floats. The gills of fish which try to swim through the nets are caught in the mesh. Many herrings and mackerel are caught by drift nets.

Drag or trawl nets are large, bag-shaped nets which are dragged along the seabed at depths as great as 1000 metres. These nets are used to catch flatfish and other bottom-living fish and crustaceans.

Purse seine nets are used when shoals of such fishes as sardines and herrings are located on the ship's radar. The purse seine nets are then drawn around the shoal.

Pacific shrimp boats haul two beam nets across the sea floor. They catch prawns and shrimps. Many catcher boats now work with a mother factory ship. Instead of returning to port, they deliver their catch to a large factory ship. There the fish are rapidly processed and frozen.

Peoples of the World

People belong to the species *Homo sapiens* (intelligent man). They first appeared around 50,000 years ago. They displaced the closely related Neanderthal people, who died out around the end of the Ice Age.

People vary in appearance. Many of these differences are probably adaptations to the varied climatic conditions in which the people developed. The human family is divided into four main sub-groups: Caucasoids, Mongoloids, Negroids and Australoids.

Caucasoids include the mostly fair-skinned people of Europe and the many people of European origin in other continents. The Arabs of North Africa and most of the much darker skinned people of north-eastern Africa, south-western Asia and India are also Caucasoids.

Mongoloids, with the yellowish skin and straight, dark hair, include most of the people of eastern Asia, Eskimos and American Indians. Negroids include the Black people of Africa and Black Americans, the descendants of Black African slaves.

Australoids include Australian Aborigines, the Veddoids of southern India and the Ainu, the first inhabitants of Japan.

Below: Examples of members of the human family. Most Europeans, Arabs and most people in south-western Asia and India are Caucasoids. Australian Aborigines belong to the Australoid sub-group. The Negroid group includes Black Africans and Black Americans. The Mongoloid sub-group includes most people in eastern Asia and the American Indians. Members of the sub-groups have intermarried. For example, many Mexicans are mestizos, of mixed European and American Indian descent.

Above: The first North Americans came from Asia, perhaps 40,000 years ago, during the Ice Age. The sea level was then much lower than it is today and a land bridge connected northern Asia and North America. These Mongoloid people were the ancestors of the American Indians.

Ways of Life

The ways of life of people still vary greatly around the world. There are still a few people, including the Bushmen and pygmies of Africa, who live much like our ancestors before the invention of agriculture. They live by hunting animals and gathering seeds and roots. Other people are farmers, though many farmers in Africa, Asia and South America are poor. But more and more people are making their homes in cities and towns. The chief jobs in the developed western countries are in manufacturing and service industries.

Religions of the World

People differ in many ways. For example, religion divides many people. The world's main religions — Hinduism, Buddhism, Shintoism, Taoism, Confucianism, Christianity and Islam — all originated in Asia. The greatest number of people now belong to the various Christian churches. Of the more than 1000 million Christians, 73 per cent are Roman Catholics.

LANGUAGES

There are about 3000 languages and many more dialects. Many have large vocabularies and a written form. Others contain comparatively few words and have no written form.

Some languages are closely related to each other. French, Italian, Portuguese and Spanish all come from Latin, the language of ancient Rome. These languages form the Romance language group. This group belongs to a wider family of languages, called the Indo-European family. This is the world's largest family, followed by the Sino-Tibetan, which includes Chinese.

Some languages have spread around the world. The chief international language is English. French, German and Spanish are also spoken widely throughout the world.

Towns and Cities

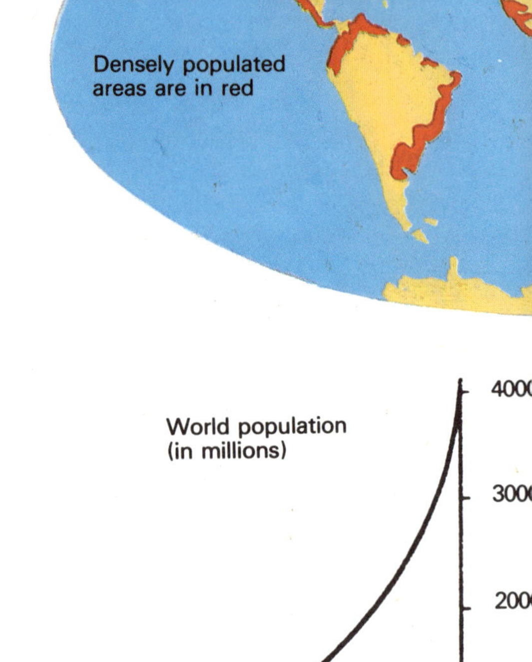

The world's population has steadily increased through human history and farmers have had to produce more and more food every year. In the late 1970s, the yearly rate of increase was 1.7 per cent, but there were signs that the rate was slowing. In some developed countries, populations were staying the same or even declining. But in many poor countries, the rates were still increasing. For example, Africa's population was increasing by 2.9 per cent a year, as compared with 0.4 per cent in Europe. Overall, the world's population is expected to continue growing until about AD 2100, when it will level out at around 10,200 million, as compared with 4800 million in 1985.

More and more people are living in cities and towns. For instance, 91 per cent of Britons live in urban areas. In poor countries, where most people are farmers, urban populations are much smaller. But even there, cities are growing quickly. Many do not have enough houses or jobs for their fast-increasing populations. Many people, therefore, are forced to live in unhealthy slums on the outskirts of cities.

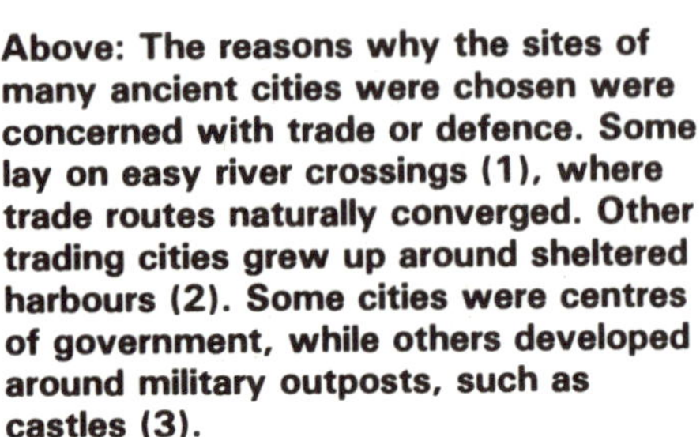

Above: The reasons why the sites of many ancient cities were chosen were concerned with trade or defence. Some lay on easy river crossings (1), where trade routes naturally converged. Other trading cities grew up around sheltered harbours (2). Some cities were centres of government, while others developed around military outposts, such as castles (3).

Below: Cities are growing throughout the world. For example, in Brazil, 45 out of every 100 people lived in urban areas in 1960, as compared with 69 in 1982. People are attracted by services and jobs which rural areas lack. But many cities have grown so rapidly that newcomers cannot find jobs. They live in shanty towns.

Above: The map shows that the world's population is unevenly distributed. Large areas near the poles, in mountains and in deserts are almost empty of people.

Left: The graph shows how the world's population has increased from AD 1000, when it stood at about 300 million, to the present day. It shows that the rate of population has been steadily accelerating. The world's population passed the 1000 million mark in the 19th century, 2000 million in the 1920s and 4000 million in the mid-1970s.

Rich and Poor

Our world is divided into the rich 'haves' and the poor 'have-nots'. In rich western countries, people have an average life expectancy at birth of more than 70 years. But in much of Africa and Asia people, on average, do not live much beyond 50 years.

The economies of most African and Asian countries are underdeveloped, or 'developing'. Most people are farmers and there is little manufacturing. Also, the countries' minerals are mostly exported to the rich countries. Many people have poor diets and many starve when the crops fail, after droughts or floods.

The rich, developed and industrialized countries give aid to developing countries. But this aid is often insufficient, especially because the populations of most developing nations are increasing rapidly.

Many poor countries want to set up industries, but this is expensive. Other countries are trying to develop agriculture. This wide gap between rich and poor nations, which in many cases is widening, is one of the most serious problems facing us all.

OUR DIVIDED WORLD

Developing countries include four main subgroups:

LOW INCOME ECONOMIES
These, the poorest countries, are found mainly in Africa and Asia. They include Chad, Ethiopia, India, Pakistan and Zaire.

MIDDLE INCOME OIL EXPORTERS
These are somewhat wealthier countries, largely because they export oil. They include Algeria, Mexico, Nigeria and Venezuela.

OTHER MIDDLE INCOME ECONOMIES
Some of these countries have begun to industrialize their economies. They include Argentina and Brazil.

HIGH INCOME OIL EXPORTERS
These include the oil-rich countries of the Arabian peninsula.

DEVELOPED COUNTRIES
The developed, industrialized world includes most of West Europe, the USA and Canada, Australia and New Zealand, and Japan. The East European countries and the USSR are regarded as a separate group.

Right: The map shows the world divided according to countries' per capita gross domestic products (the value of the goods and services created by each person in one year). This is a measure of a country's wealth.

Below: India is a poor country, with a per capita gross domestic product in 1982 of $210, as compared with $13,000 in the USA. Many city-dwellers in India are poor but the villagers are even poorer. The inset picture shows the contrast in the developed world where many people have money left over after they have paid for the essentials of life to spend on consumer products such as cars and even yachts.

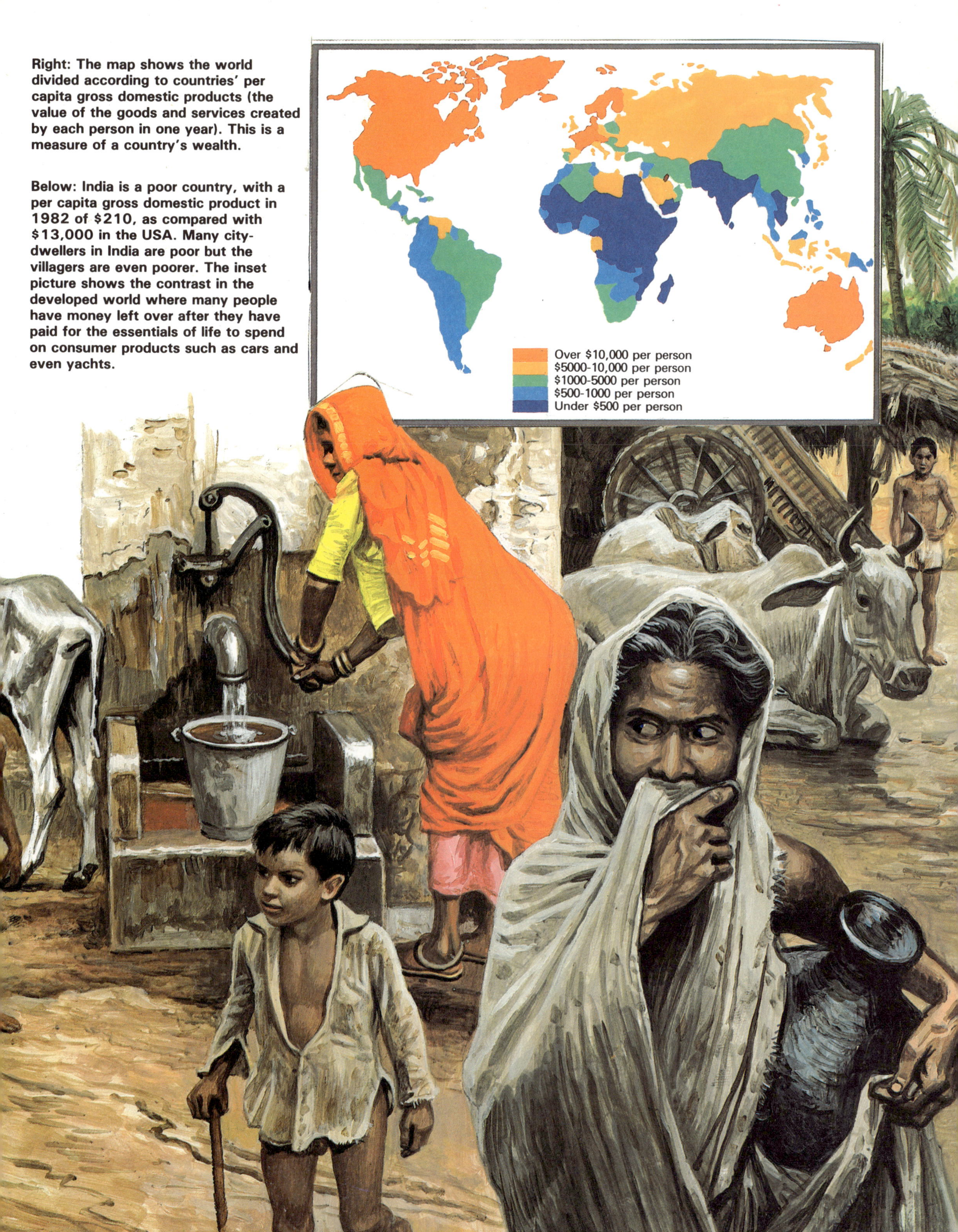

Transport and Trade

The richer countries have well organized transport systems. This is because the easy, rapid and cheap movement of goods is essential for their economies. By contrast, many poor countries lack good transport systems. This lack hampers their development.

In developed countries, railways became the chief form of land transport in the early days of the Industrial Revolution. But in recent times, road haulage has proved a cheaper and faster means of transport. Yet it is still easier to move bulky, heavy goods by rail or inland waterways, though oil, a fluid, is most easily moved by pipelines.

Oil is also transported by ocean-going tankers. In recent years, larger and larger ships have been built for carrying freight. Also, the use of large boxes, called containers, has speeded up the handling of goods at ports. Air transport is expensive, but it is suitable for light and costly goods.

The Trading Nations

World trade is concerned with the buying (or importing) and selling (or exporting) of raw materials, including food, manufactures and services. The leading trading nations, including the USA, West Germany, Japan, France and Britain, are all developed nations. The total value of the trade of developing nations is much smaller. They mostly export raw materials and import manufactured goods.

Trade helps to develop the economies of countries and raise people's living standards. To encourage trade, many countries work together through regional organizations, such as the European Economic Community (sometimes known as the Common Market). This organization was set up in 1958 by Belgium, France, West Germany, Italy, Luxembourg and the Netherlands. By the end of 1984 the original six countries had been joined by Denmark, the Republic of Ireland and the United Kingdom.

Left: Oil is one of the most important items in world trade. It is transported across land through long pipelines and across the oceans in huge oil tankers. The tankers deliver the oil to manufacturers who use it as a fuel, a lubricant and as a raw material in the chemical industry.

Right: The earliest form of transport was human labour, but domesticated animals proved much more efficient. Until about 150 years ago, beasts of burden were the chief means of moving goods. Camels are still important in desert regions. These sturdy animals can go several days without water.

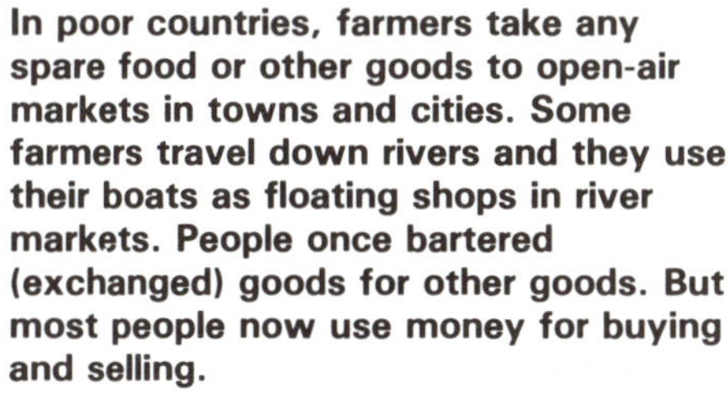

In poor countries, farmers take any spare food or other goods to open-air markets in towns and cities. Some farmers travel down rivers and they use their boats as floating shops in river markets. People once bartered (exchanged) goods for other goods. But most people now use money for buying and selling.

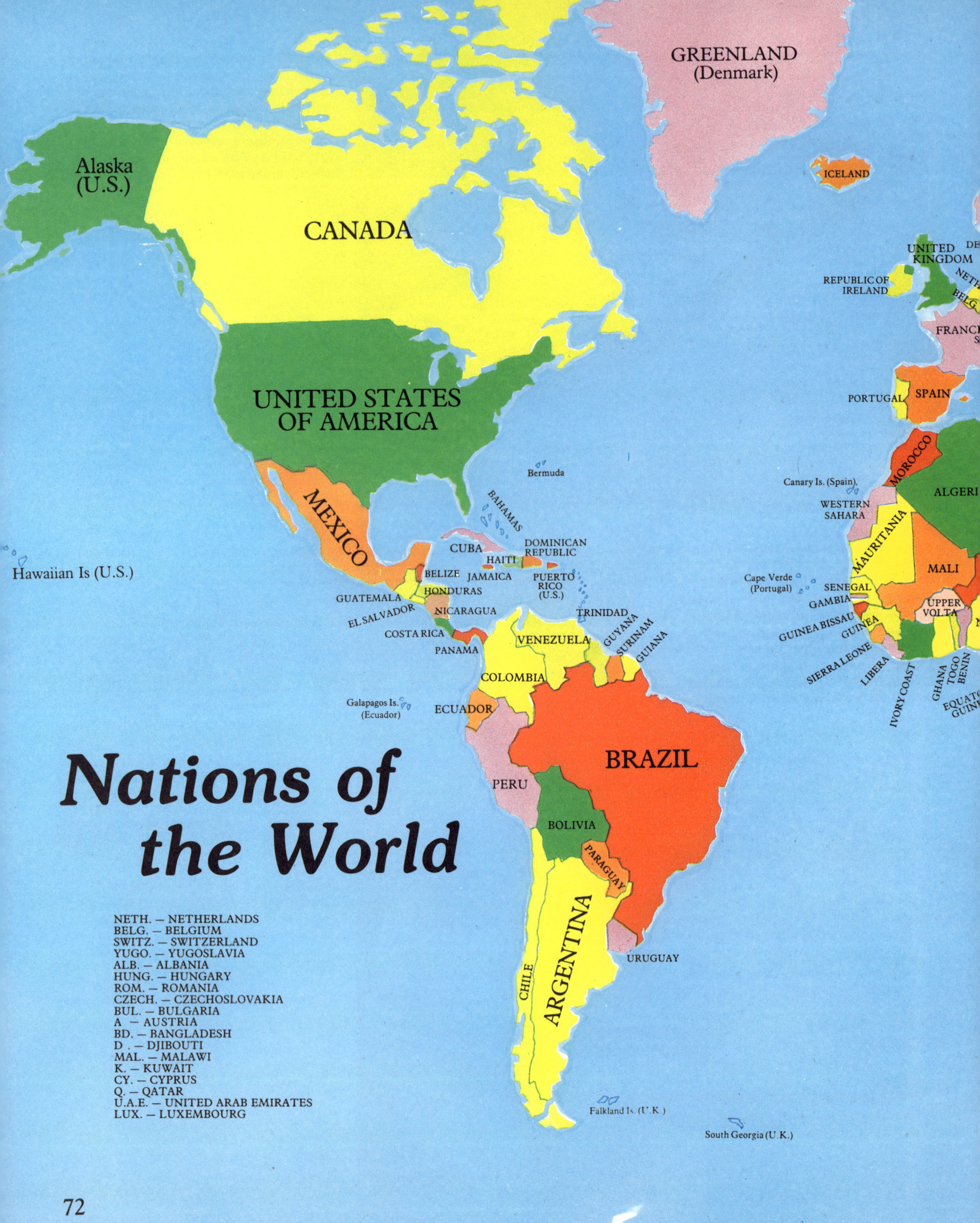
GREENLAND
(Denmark)
Alaska
(U.S.)
CANADA
ICELAND
UNITED
KINGDOM
REPUBLIC OF
IRELAND
UNITED STATES
OF AMERICA
PORTUGAL
SPAIN
MOROCCO
Bermuda
Canary Is. (Spain)
WESTERN
SAHARA
BAHAMAS
MEXICO
MAURITANIA
MALI
CUBA
DOMINICAN
REPUBLIC
HAITI
Hawaiian Is (U.S.)
BELIZE
JAMAICA
PUERTO
RICO
(U.S.)
Cape Verde
(Portugal)
SENEGAL
GAMBIA
UPPER
VOLTA
GUATEMALA
HONDURAS
EL SALVADOR
NICARAGUA
TRINIDAD
COSTA RICA
PANAMA
VENEZUELA
GUYANA
SURINAM
GUIANA
GUINEA BISSAU
GUINEA
SIERRA LEONE
LIBERIA
IVORY COAST
GHANA
TOGO
BENIN
COLOMBIA
Galapagos Is.
(Ecuador)
ECUADOR
BRAZIL
PERU
Nations of
the World
BOLIVIA
PARAGUAY
ARGENTINA
URUGUAY
CHILE
NETH. – NETHERLANDS
BELG. – BELGIUM
SWITZ. – SWITZERLAND
YUGO. – YUGOSLAVIA
ALB. – ALBANIA
HUNG. – HUNGARY
ROM. – ROMANIA
CZECH. – CZECHOSLOVAKIA
BUL. – BULGARIA
A – AUSTRIA
BD. – BANGLADESH
D . – DJIBOUTI
MAL. – MALAWI
K. – KUWAIT
CY. – CYPRUS
Q. – QATAR
U.A.E. – UNITED ARAB EMIRATES
LUX. – LUXEMBOURG
Falkland Is. (U.K.)
South Georgia (U.K.)

tsbergen
Jorway)
SWEDEN
FINLAND
UNION OF SOVIET SOCIALIST REPUBLICS
POLAND
CZECH.
HUNG.
ROM.
YUGO.
BUL.
ALB.
GREECE
TURKEY
CY.
SYRIA
LEBANON
ISRAEL
IRAQ
JORDAN
IRAN
K.
AFGHANISTAN
PAKISTAN
MONGOLIA
CHINA
NORTH KOREA
SOUTH KOREA
JAPAN
BHUTAN
NEPAL
BD.
INDIA
TAIWAN
LIBYA
EGYPT
Q.
U.A.E.
SAUDI ARABIA
OMAN
BURMA
LAOS
VIETNAM
THAILAND
KAMPUCHEA
PHILIPPINES
CHAD
SUDAN
YEMEN
SOUTHERN YEMEN
D.
ETHIOPIA
SOMALI REPUBLIC
CENTRAL AFRICAN EMPIRE
SRI LANKA
MALAYSIA
UGANDA
KENYA
CONGO
ZAÏRE
RWANDA
BURUNDI
TANZANIA
INDONESIA
PAPUA NEW GUINEA
Solomon Is.
ANGOLA
ZAMBIA
MAL.
MOÇAMBIQUE
MADAGASCAR
NAMIBIA
ZIMBABWE
BOTSWANA
Mauritius
New Caledonia (France)
AUSTRALIA
SWAZILAND
UTH AFRICA
REPUBLIC OF)
LESOTHO
NEW ZEALAND
ANTARCTICA

Glossary

Aborigine The original inhabitant of a country, such as the Australian Aborigines.
Alluvium Sand, silt and mud, which are carried and deposited by rivers.
Ammonites A large group of molluscs, the fossils of which are common in Mesozoic rocks. At the end of this era, they became extinct.
Anemometer An instrument used to measure wind speeds. Some also show wind directions.
Anticyclone A region of high air pressure, where air is descending. It is associated with stable weather conditons.
Aquifer A layer of rock through which water can percolate. Wells are sunk down to aquifers in order to bring water to the surface.
Atoll A coral island which is often circular or horseshoe-shaped. It often contains a lagoon.
Aurorae Lights, called the Aurora Borealis in the northern hemisphere and the Aurora Australis in the southern, that appear in the skies in polar regions. They occur when streams of charged particles from the Sun collide with particles in the ionosphere. They include streamers of light, and red and green lights lasting several hours.
Beaufort scale A scale from 0 to 12 for classifying wind speeds.
Biogeography The study of the distribution of plants and animals.
Caldera A crater in the top of a volcano. Some contain lakes.
Campos Tropical grassland in South America.
Canyon A steep-sided river valley.
Cash crop A crop grown for sale, not for use by the farmer.
Cave A hollow in the Earth's crust. Caves on coasts are worn out by wave action, while lava caves are found in hardened lava flows. The largest caves occur in limestone and dolomite. They are the result of chemical weathering.
Condensation A change of state, as when a gas or vapour turns into a liquid. Condensation occurs in cooling air when invisible water vapour is turned into visible water droplets (clouds).
Continent A large landmass, including adjacent islands. The world's seven continents are, in order of size, Asia, Africa, North America, South America, Antarctica, Europe and Oceania.
Coriolis effect The deflection of winds and ocean currents caused by the rotation of the Earth on its axis. Winds and currents are deflected to the right of the direction in which they are moving in the northern hemisphere and to the left in the southern hemisphere.
Cyclone A low air pressure system. It is sometimes used to mean the same as a depression.
Delta An area at the mouth of some rivers that has been built up by sediment brought there by the river.
Depression A low pressure air system which forms along the polar front where warm air brought by westerlies meets up with cold air in the polar easterlies. It is associated with unsettled weather.
Developing country A country which is either poor or, as in the case of wealthy oil exporters in south-western Asia, a country which is only partly industrialized.
Dinosaur A term meaning 'terrible lizard'. Dinosaurs were reptiles which lived in the Mesozoic era.
Ecology The study of living things and how they are related to each other and to the environments in which they are found.
Evaporation A change of state, as when a liquid becomes a gas or a vapour.
Frost Frozen moisture on the Earth's surface formed when water vapour condenses in air that is below 0°C.
Galaxy A system containing millions of stars, such as the Milky Way galaxy to which our Solar System belongs.
Gross domestic product or **GDP** The total value of all the goods and services produced in a country in a given period of time. The annual per capita GDP is the GDP for a particular year divided by the population in that year.
Gross national product or **GNP** The gross domestic product, plus income from investments and possessions owned abroad, less income earned at home that goes to foreigners.
Hail Pellets of ice that fall from clouds.
Hemisphere Half a sphere. The Earth is divided by the equator into the northern and southern hemispheres.
Industrialization A change in the economy of a country which occurs when mining and manufacturing become more important than farming. Countries going through this change are said to be undergoing an Industrial Revolution.
Insolation The energy which the Earth gets from the Sun.
International date line A boundary around longitude 180 degrees

East or West, where there is a time difference of 24 hours. This is because time is measured east and west of Greenwich Mean Time (GMT). Going westwards from Greenwich, 180° represents a loss of 12 hours. Going eastwards, 180° represents a gain of 12 hours. This gives a time difference of 24 hours, or one whole day.

Ionosphere A layer of the atmosphere, which starts at about 80 km above the surface, and ends at about 500 km, where the exosphere begins. The air here is extremely thin. Most gas particles are ionized (electrically charged) by cosmic or solar rays. Aurorae occur in the ionosphere (see Aurorae).

Jet stream A strong wind that blows around the Earth from west to east near the top of the troposphere and in the lower stratosphere. They occur in the middle latitudes. Airline pilots use them as tail winds but avoid flying into them.

Life expectancy The average length of people's lives. In 1982, the life expectancy at birth ranged from about 36 years in Afghanistan to 79 years in Switzerland.

Llanos Tropical grassland in South America.

Map projection A means of representing the curved surface of the Earth on a flat sheet of paper. Most projections are devised by mathematical means.

Monsoon A wind system in which the prevailing wind direction is reversed from one season to another.

Moraine The loose rock carried by glaciers and ice sheets. *Lateral* moraine is carried on the sides of glaciers. Rock frozen in the ice is called *englacial* moraine and rock frozen in the base is *subglacial* moraine. Fragments dragged along under the ice are called *ground* moraine. Moraine is dumped at the edge of the glacier or ice sheet to form various land features, such as ridges of *terminal moraine.*

Neanderthal Man A type of *Homo sapiens* which became extinct about 10,000 years ago.

Nomad A person who leads a wandering life, such as a hunter-gatherer or a livestock herder.

Oasis A place in a desert where there is water. Small oases occur around springs or wells. The Nile valley in north-eastern Africa is a large oasis.

Ozone A form of oxygen with three atoms in the molecule, rather than the usual two.

Pampas Temperate grassland in southern South America.

Parkland Grasslands in Australia.

Permafrost Permanently frozen subsoil in polar regions.

Prairie The grasslands of central North America.

Precipitation Any moisture caused by the condensation of water vapour in the air, including rain, snow, sleet, hail, frost and dew.

Pyroclasts Fragments of rock made of bits of magma which have been hurled out of volcanoes. They range in size from volcanic dust to large loaf-sized volcanic bombs.

Rainbow Arcs of coloured light which occur when the Sun's rays are reflected and refracted by raindrops in the air. The colours are red, orange, yellow, green, blue, indigo and violet.

Rain gauge An instrument used to measure precipitation. It consists of an open funnel leading into a collecting jar.

Savanna Tropical grassland, often with scattered trees.

Scarp A steep slope formed by movements of rocks along faults, or by the erosion of gently tilted resistant rocks.

Selvas The dense rain forests in the huge Amazon basin of South America.

Shifting cultivation A method of farming whereby people clear a patch of forest or other land and farm it until the soil loses its fertility. The people then move on to a new clearing. It is common in tropical regions.

Silt Fine rock grains carried by rivers. Silt is finer than sand, but coarser than mud.

Spring A flow of water from the rocks on to the surface. Many springs are the sources of rivers.

Steppe Grassland in south-east Europe and in the south-west USSR.

Synoptic chart A weather map that shows weather conditions over a large area at a particular time.

Transhumance The seasonal movement of livestock. In Switzerland, farmers keep their animals in the sheltered valleys in winter. In summer, they graze their animals on the lush mountain pastures.

Tropics The region between the Tropic of Cancer (latitude 23° 27′ North) and the Tropic of Capricorn (latitude 23° 27′ South).

Tundra The treeless region between the ice-covered polar regions and the coniferous forests (taiga).

Veld The high grasslands of South Africa.

Water cycle The process by which there is a constant interchange of water between the oceans and the continents.

Water table The level of ground water in the rocks beneath the Earth's surface.

Weather The day to day or hour to hour condition of the air.

Well A hole dug down to the water table so that water can be obtained.

Zoogeography The study of the distribution of animals, a branch of biogeography.

Geography Index